Fundamentals
Of Play
Directing

Fourth Edition

Fundamentals Of Play Directing

Alexander Dean
Lawrence Carra
Carnegie-Mellon University

Holt, Rinehart And Winston
New York • Chicago • San Francisco • Atlanta • Dallas
Montreal • Toronto • London • Sydney

Library of Congress Cataloging in Publication Data

Dean, Alexander, 1893–1939.
    Fundamentals of play directing.
    includes index.

1. Theatre—Production and direction.   I. Carra,
Lawrence, joint author.   II. Title.

PN2053.D4   1980   792'.0233   79–26236

ISBN 0–03–021551–X

0123   039   98765432

Chapter 12, Central Staging, Copyright © 1980, 1974, 1965;
Chapter 12, Central Staging, Chapter 15, Directing the Play,
including revisions and new material in all other chapters
copyright © 1980, 1974 by Lawrence Carra
Chapter 16, Directing Musical Comedy,
copyright © 1980 by Lawrence Carra

To the Memory of Henry F. Boettcher

Preface

This fourth edition of the *Fundamentals of Play Directing* continues to explore these fundamentals as they relate to the contemporary climate of theatre with the addition of new factual material, exercises, illustrations, and photographs. The basic purpose remains the same as in previous editions—to discuss and present disciplines that can give the beginning director a base of operation in any form of theatre without limiting his own creative contributions.

For teaching purposes these basic principles are applied first to proscenium-oriented stages. The chapter on Central Staging considers the special adaptations necessary to staging in-the-round. Adjustments to thrust stages and other forms of flexible staging fall readily between the demands of proscenium and central stages.

The chapter on Directing the Play discusses the elements to be considered in the whole experience of the play, procedures involved in directing, the process of evolving the ground plan, and steps in preparing the production script.

Also new to the fourth edition is the chapter detailing procedures in directing musical comedy.

The appeal of the book is also in its format—the step-by-step process of analysis that serves as a teaching method in class. The cross references are an important part of this format and should be referred to where noted for a full understanding of the subject under discussion.

Since no book for the beginner would fulfill its purpose unless the reader were acquainted with stage terminology, the Appendix includes a glossary in which terms and functions relating to the stage, the setting, and stage management are defined.

Appreciation is extended to the many who have graciously supplied production photographs and to my students and colleagues for their stimulation, advice, and criticism with a special acknowledgment to Professors Henry F. Boettcher, Wilson Lehr, and Frank McMullan who helped prepare the first edition of the *Fundamentals* when there was work still to be done on Professor Dean's manuscript at the time of his death.

This book on play directing evolved initially as an expansion of the first third of Alexander Dean's *Syllabus of a Course in Play Directing* and included the material covered in the first-year class in directing as he gave it at the Department of Drama, Yale University. To Professor Dean, play directing was not necessarily either a divine or a mysterious gift but an art in which, just as in other arts, certain principles could be both perceived and taught. Without belittling innate talent or claiming that an artist could be created where there was no inherent flair for the art, Dean believed that the knowledge and application of certain principles would avoid costly mistakes and eliminate economic and artistic waste.

L.C.
Pittsburgh, Pa.
January, 1980

Contents

Fundamentals Of Play Directing

1

Introduction

1

Drama as Art

Just as the writing of drama is an art, so, too, is its performance a work of art. Before we can have an understanding of the basics of dramatic performance, therefore, it is necessary to analyze the fundamental principles of art and apply them to theatre.

Art and Discipline

Art by definition means skill in performance, which may be acquired by experience, study, or observation. By general acceptance it means that the creator shapes a concept into a form arousing the emotions of the spectator. This shaping into a form, in its manner and means, has been in continuous flux from age to age and from culture to culture. Periodically, there have been violent reactions to the idea of discipline in art, bringing about movements like Nihilism and Dadaism, or closer to our times the rebellion of the sixties, when "do your own thing" was the cry for release from all rules and traditions. By their demise, these short-lived movements only have reaffirmed the truth that any individual's expression needs some form of discipline if it is to be something more than indulgent self-expression.

The Creation of a Work of Art

Concept

The creative artist must first form in his mind the image of an external object to which he attaches an impression, a thought, or any other product of memory or imagination. This product is the concept, the creation, the subject. It will have resulted from a deeply felt emotional experience in his own life—an experience not peculiar to himself, but universal and, in drama especially, common to a mass of people. The dramatist may conceive a human being or character; he may review an event or story; or he may have an idea or image. Whatever the concept, it must deal fundamentally with man in relation to greater forces, such as the social order or the laws of God.

Technique

Sheer imagination alone, however, is incapable of arousing emotional states in others. The artist, besides feeling his concept, must know his materials in order to reproduce it. The artist's emotion expressed in whatever material or means—clay, granite, paint, words, images, movement, or musical sound —will, without form, fail completely to stir the spectator or audience. The pure reproduction of the concept will not make the art product complete. If this were sufficient, all that the playwright need do would be to reproduce nature or a part of life literally, photographically, and minutely, or freely improvise on it. But to do so is not art. Literal reproduction or unfocused improvisation on the stage never succeeds in evoking emotional reactions of a profound sort. Theatre artists must shape or rearrange the parts into a whole, complete on its own terms. Art is not nature's creation—it is man's.

Of what does this rearrangement consist? Let us answer by giving it first a name. The rearrangement of the concept or nature is achieved through technique—known in drama as form, or structure. Each art has its own technique based upon fundamental principles. Time has developed them; trial and error have made them factual. At the beginning of any art there were few principles, if any; artists have added them by degrees and from experience.

We shall discuss those principles which are generally accepted as common to all arts: unity, coherence, emphasis and selectivity, proportion, rearrangement, and intensification.

Principles Common to All Arts

UNITY   Unity is one of the principles common to all arts—not the unity of time, place, and mood, as the French later declared, but of adherence to the subject. The earliest literature, like the *Iliad* and the *Odyssey,* as well as the earliest plays of all countries, lacked the quality of unity. In every art it was one of the first signs of technique to be acquired. The rambling, loose, and interrupted putting together of unassociated, irrelevant, and disconnected subjects through time shifted into the treatment of a single subject. This factor of unity in technique has a broader usage than at first seems possible. The "porter scene" in *Macbeth* is not irrelevant, because it is tied up in the technical writing of suspense which hinges on whether or not Macbeth will, in his murder of Duncan, be apprehended by Macduff who is knocking to enter.

Several plots in a play or several subjects do not violate unity if they eventually lead to a unified impression. The naturalistic style of writing practiced by Chekhov and Gorki, by O'Casey in *Juno and the Paycock,* by Rice in *Street Scene,* by Kingsley in *Detective Story,* and by Sheriff in *Journey's End,* does, in spite of the seemingly casual, adhere to a definite unity. This unity of impression, coming from the author's conviction and commitment to his subject, is often difficult to sense by the uninitiated, particularly in those plays classified under the all-encompassing title Theatre of the Absurd. Here again, the seeming contradictions and diversions in the writings of Beckett, Ionesco, Albee, Pinter, or Shepard have strongly unified roots. In any art the violation of unity tires and confuses the spectator.

COHERENCE Historically, coherence is closely related to unity. Each part of the whole should not only bear a relation to, but develop or evolve from, the previous part. Coherence demands logical and probable relationship of the parts; in a play this might be in the psychological relationships of the character to the action or in the motivation of character and action. Or coherence may rest in the contradiction of expected behavior so as to create a shock, as in the plays of Ionesco and Pinter.

In much of contemporary writing the making of the action becomes its own purpose. The work has another kind of coherence: each action lends to the totality of impression. Coherence, then, is achieved out of adherence either to the totality or to the causal relationships among actions.

EMPHASIS AND SELECTIVITY Emphasis is essential in all arts. The kernel, core, the heart and soul of every concept is expressed through the proper control of emphasis. In nature there is no emphasis; in man's expression of nature there must be. Through emphasis the artist is able to make the important parts of his creation stand out vividly from their background of lesser parts so that the spectator may recognize their importance more easily and clearly. Emphasis involves *selectivity;* in fact, one of the simplest ways to emphasize is to omit entirely certain elements of its nature. The parts omitted are no longer present to detract from the unity and coherence of the whole and by their very absence help to concentrate the spectator's attention more closely upon the important factor. Selectivity can also lead to greater beauty, since confusion and disorder, constantly existing in nature, may be discordant with our idea of a total esthetic effect.

PROPORTION Closely related to emphasis is proportion. Although emphasis demands certain omissions, it cannot call for the elimination of everything except the important part. In art, accordingly, other elements are included, but these elements are subordinated to the important parts. They take up less space or time. They may occur at the same time as the important part, but since they are in the background they are of less account or function.

REARRANGEMENT   The emphasis of the important part is conveyed not only by actual size in space or time but by rearrangement so that through its position the important part is readily recognized by the spectator. The placement of the important part becomes emphatic not only by the subordinate placement of the other parts but also by placing the subordinate parts in such a manner that they lead into and toward the important or dominant part. This consideration of rearrangement is fully discussed in the chapter on Composition.

INTENSIFICATION   Rearrangement further produces an intensifying effect. Dramatic or theatrical effect is a result of intensification; in fact the two terms are often used as synonyms. By technical devices of contrast, unexpectedness, movement, events, tone, or vibrancy in color, a reproduction becomes more effective, more compelling, more dynamic, and more climactic.

A simple example of how technique is applied to the actual reproduction of life and the need of it as far as the audience is concerned is illustrated in the following experience in actual production.

Some years ago Dean was directing a play whose locale was the corner of Forty-second Street and Broadway in New York. The weather was hot, the window was open and there was considerable dialogue in the play about the noise outside. For this outside noise effect, an actual recording of the noise at that corner was made. Those who forget their knowledge of the principles of art were delighted with the result of the record. At the first dress rehearsal the record was used without the knowledge of the actors or the audience. No one onstage or in the auditorium knew what the racket backstage was, and the rehearsal was stopped while inquiry was made. The actual reproduction of nature was not recognizable. It had no suggestion of street noises. It was a mad, discordant rumble signifying nothing. Every possible speed in the sound machine was tried, but nothing improved the effect. Finally a crew of eleven worked out the sounds of the dominant or emphatic elements. The sounds were selected, proportioned, and arranged in climactic order. They were timed, contrasted, and varied. In the end it was an orchestra that performed a technicalized arrangement of street noises.

Mood

A concept or idea when reproduced or given tangible form takes on the power to convey a certain amount of feeling to an observer. This same object rearranged in accordance with the principles of art is able to convey or suggest something more than the denoted object; it can convey the essence of itself which is an aggregation of its own attributes. This is the mood. For instance, one person may paint a picture of an open fire in which the observer can recognize the flames, the sticks of wood, and the coals. The real artist, on the other hand, will paint an open fire so that you may not see these things but instead feel warmth, coziness, security, and family affection. In this projection of an object's essence lies the power of art.

If in a painting of a battle scene the details are of horrible slaughter and attack, the spectator will receive a definite impression of what war is like. But if in his treatment of the scene the artist so arranges the spears, axes, helmets, and figures of the combatants that their lines and positions are opposite and in juxtaposition to one another, then a more intense feeling of war will be conveyed to the spectator. In fact we shall see later in our exercises under Composition that excitement, horror, dread, and anguish may be conveyed to the audience in the abstract by using only lines, masses, and the other principles of design. Even if the subject matter is abstracted from the picture, the sheer form will give rise to a mood quality that will stir the emotions of a spectator. In the same way, by structure alone, the staging of a play can convey excitement, fear, and pulsating life; or repose, introspection, and sadness; or brittleness, humor, and superficiality.

The Purpose of Technique

The purpose of technique in all the arts is the same, namely, to make the concept, or subject matter, clearer, more effective, more compelling, and more moving and to convey its mood to the spectator or listener by using the elements of art that will coordinate and express its inherent mood qualities.

The word *technique* is used in many different ways. Each art has its own definition of the term; but although the definitions vary in different arts, on analysis they are fundamentally similar. Furthermore, each art has its own minor technical points to master; these are usually the treatments of detailed rendering that time and experience have shown to be the most direct method of execution or the most effective manner of obtaining emphasis. Sometimes they regulate the control of visual considerations in respect to the audience or the control of timing, of articulation, or of the many other determinants that make for the best expression.

Technique is apt to change from age to age, so that in each art we find methods that have become obsolete or are used from a different point of view.

In playwriting, for instance, the structuring of plays has undergone a great change from motivation of cause and effect to dramatized metaphors and free associations without causal relationships. Foster's *Tom Paine* and the Open Theater's production of *The Serpent* offer good examples of the free form of playwriting growing out of an improvisational approach to rehearsals where the actor is an integral part of the creative process. The works of Durang, Shepard, and Stoppard stand quite in opposition to the tight structure of O'Neill, Miller, and Williams. Yet, in these plays, as in those of Beckett, Ionesco, and Pinter, technique supplies the essential discipline that makes the work an artistic statement.

Although technique changes from age to age, the principles of art evolved by technique remain fundamental truths; and even much of the technique of the past cannot be improved upon. This heritage of the ages, the fundamental principles of art, may also be valued as a great teacher of technique and execution.

Technique is often belittled, despised, and considered unnecessary by those who do not know its purpose or who wish to disassociate themselves from past disciplines. The truth remains that, though conventions may change, fundamental principles of art are operative in all forms of theatrical expression, whether it be environmental, participatory, ritual, open staging, theatre-in-the-round, or otherwise. In the hands of an expert, technique can do the work for him when his creativity is not functioning at its peak. In other words, an artist's creation may be inferior, yet the technique may be so brilliant that it is forced to do both its own work and that of creation. Any theatre season will include plays of mediocre, conventional, and spiritless subjects that by the sheer brilliance of their execution become refreshing, novel, and even convincingly dramatic. Conversely, many plays with noble and overwhelming topics are a mass of inarticulate and confused events.

Proportion in Concept and Technique

It is obvious, therefore, that the ideal creation is one in which there is perfect proportion of concept and technique. If we briefly survey for a moment the earliest English dramas up to Dryden, we shall see this struggle between creation and technique during the different periods of drama.

In the earliest mystery plays we find the art of dramatic writing to be a completely unhampered creative expression. It existed as a magnificent natural emotional outpouring of a soul feeling something that it wanted others to share. The authors of these plays had no predecessors to tell them how to write, so they relied merely on their feelings. The results had little unity, coherence, emphasis, selectivity, proportion, rearrangement, or intensification, though in their concept they were imbued with a sublime beauty.

Because the dramatic in the theatre is more compelling for an audience than the uneventful, the writers of dramas who followed these early writers added more technical elements; their incidents had a beginning and an end, and by degrees they developed a middle. Through the conscious desire for effect these later writers put more and more structure and form into their plays until finally their efforts resulted in a technically sound play.

With Marlowe we find a deeper context that brought his works toward becoming greater tragedies. His plays are interspersed with reflections on the themes or ideas of man in relation to other men, to life, and to God. Such plays demanded a more intricate form, a more exacting technique; but the spontaneity of divine inspiration was still present, although pure creation was diminishing as technique improved. Shakespeare, at his best, gave us the perfect proportion: creation and form. After Shakespeare, inspiration and imagination waned and gradually disappeared. Technical effects took their place. Critical analysis was carried to greater heights, until reason and theory destroyed imagination. In Dryden we reach the master of pure order and reason—and great drama disappears for many decades.

Such a cycle of concept and technique is observable in general literature as well as in drama. A preponderance of technique will destroy the greatness of spontaneous expression. But, and we repeat this emphatically, neither is of any great value without the other.

Art and the Teacher

Development of the Artist

Every art has had its geniuses who created masterpieces without the apparent aid of an instructor. Drama is no exception. This fact is frequently used as an argument that teachers are unnecessary—that if a person has the ability to create as an actor, a director, a designer, or a playwright, he will create. The great masters have done it in the past and will do it again in the future. This is true, but its corollary—that every gift will find its expression—is not true. Many of those most gifted have perished unknown, because they lacked a consciousness of form and a deductive mind that brings order and arrangement to the creative effort. This fact is usually overlooked.

Most people believe that mere feeling is necessary for expression, that an artistic genius is born fully matured and armed, like Pallas Athena from the head of Zeus. These mistaken beliefs arise from the fact that great artists are known for their greatest works and not for their early attempts and their later experiments and mistakes. Further ignorance exists about those creators, usually very good ones, who exercised their craft just before the artistic trend of their age culminated in a great master.

In the theatre, particularly, the predecessors of a great master have contributed highly to his success. And again, especially, in the theatre the various steps in the great master's development have been very apparent; whether it be Shakespeare, Racine, Calderón, Molière, or Ibsen, their study of their predecessors and their development in their own work show clearly the manner in which they taught themselves. Their native genius was such that they had not only the divine spark of creation, but also the purely deductive mind that pointed out to them the erroneous, as well as the successful, parts in their plays.

The theatre is fortunate in that it has an audience to tell it quickly and decisively whether or not the product is successful. Perhaps the most powerful method of learning is for a playwright to follow his own development through a study of his failures, as well as his successes. This self-instruction is distinctly noticeable in all the masters and is the complete proof of its merit. Sometimes the teaching is merely a consciousness on the part of the writer of his creation and of how it will affect an audience. Each great master in the theatre must have these two inherent qualities: the creative impulse and the consciousness of the way and manner of expression.

The creative impulse, imagination, and conception of idea are so nearly synonymous that they will be regarded as such in these pages. The manner of expression is generally spoken of as form, structure, or technique.

The genius, although an analysis of his work has constantly shown him to possess a consciousness of form, is likely to be the first to deny the fact, because conception and form are bound so closely together that he creates in form. Nature, moreover, does not produce the two different types of mind—the creative and the critical—simultaneously in one person. Numerous examples have proved that if a person has at the start of his career a good supply of both, the one that he works with most will destroy the other. In other words, if an artist possessed of both faculties works in the creative, his critical and deductive faculty diminishes in value. The converse of this is more frequent: The artist who uses his critical and technical faculties in the arts soon destroys his creative ability. This gives rise constantly to the accusation that the critic and the director, whose work calls for a fuller use of the deductive and conscious thought processes, are disappointed creative artists. This may be but is not necessarily true. The fact is that a person may be attracted to art at an early age when his knowledge of it and of himself in relation to it is little. He merely feels an emotional impulse toward the art and is drawn to work in some capacity in that field. Not until he has experimented with himself in the many phases of that art is he able to find in which particular aspect he excels. Many a playwright has found himself more proficient as an actor and vice versa. But in neither case should we accuse one or the other of being disappointed.

Following almost every period of great creation there has arisen a great deductor, or teacher. The most startling example is Aristotle. Greek drama started with natural simplicity and in a most spontaneous manner. Before there was any written history of this drama, beyond a purely religious rite, it developed a form of its own. The plays of Aeschylus (our earliest specimens of Greek drama) are magnificent combinations of creation and technique, showing a deliberate attempt on the author's part to utilize whatever of value had existed before his time and to develop the form with his own contributions. So marked are these changes of development within his own work that mere chance cannot account for them. Sophocles developed the form further than his predecessor, and in turn Euripides surpassed Sophocles at least in this one respect. These men have left us no explanation of what they were deliberately attempting; they merely executed their changing ideas of structure in their successive plays. It was left to Aristotle, a deductive thinker on many subjects, to write about the arts and to analyze the form, theory, and technique of his countrymen's plays.

Shakespeare, too, has left us no written record of his conscious study of dramatic technique, of what carried over to the audience and what did not, of what moved them and what did not, of wherein lay his mistakes and his success. Yet a careful examination of his predecessors and of his plays in chronological order is perhaps the greatest instruction that we can find in the fundamental technique of playwriting even for the present-day dramatist. This examination may be found in Professor George Pierce Baker's little-known *Development of Shakespeare as a Dramatist*.

Ibsen, on the other hand, in his *Drama Workshop* gives a full account of his struggle to master form. The comparison of the early *Doll's House* with the later and final version is a source of valuable knowledge in itself as well as a final proof of the consciousness of expression that this foremost creative genius possessed.

The following quotation from the letters of the composer Tchaikovsky furnishes an excellent example of a serious creator's attitude toward form:

Kamenka, July 7, 1878

Talking with you yesterday about the process of composing, I did not express myself clearly concerning the work that follows the first sketch. The phrase is especially important: What has been written with passion must now be looked upon critically, corrected, extended, and most important of all, condensed to fit the requirements of the form. One must sometimes go against the grain in this, be merciless, and destroy things that were written with love and inspiration. Although I cannot complain of poor inventive powers or imagination, I have always suffered from lack of skill in management of form. Only persistent labor has at last permitted me to achieve a form that in some degree corresponds to the content. In the past I was careless, I did not realize the extreme importance of this critical examination of the preliminary sketch. For this reason, the succeeding episodes were loosely held together and seams were visible. . . . I know also that I am very far from achieving the full maturity of my talent. But I see with joy that I am progressing slowly, and I ardently desire to take myself as far along this road to perfection as I can go. Therefore I was inaccurate yesterday when I said I wrote out my compositions unhesitatingly from the first sketches. It is more than a copy, it is a detailed critical examination of the first plan, corrected, rarely added to and very often cut.[1]

With men like Tchaikovsky and many others declaring the importance of form and struggling to achieve perfection in it, we still find beginners and even teachers in the arts who believe that the most or even the only important element in successful creation is the artist's conviction of the greatness of the conception, subject, or thought.

Creation and Form

The part that consciousness of form should play in the mind of the creator is open to endless dispute. It is true that the experienced and practiced worker in all arts creates in form—that is, in the process of imagination the concept appears directly to him in form—but he cannot do this until he has worked on and learned his technique so thoroughly that actual thought of it can be dismissed during the process of creation. The mental processes of concept and form become in reality only one. This, perhaps, is as responsible as any one factor for the frequent feeling that the distinguished worker pays little or not attention to form.

Samuel Beckett in his essay on Joyce's *Work in Progress* stated this view of the oneness in artistic creativity quite neatly: "The form, structure, and mood of an artistic statement can not be separated from its meaning, its conceptual content; simply because the work of art as a whole is its meaning, what is said in it is indissolubly linked with the manner in which it is said, and cannot be said in any other way."

Experience in dealing with the beginner for many years has forced the conclusion that the best process of blending these two elements into a fused whole is to learn each separately, to practice and use each separately, and to apply one to the other in separate stages. Time alone will blend the two parts into one mental process.

Art and Its Appreciation

Our previous use of the phrase "arousing the emotions of the spectator" makes it necessary at this point to qualify and explain this effect more fully and to digress for the moment into giving an account of those capable of judging a work of art.

[1] From *Beloved Friend*, the story of Tchaikovsky and Nadejda von Meck, by Catherine Drinker Bowen and Barbara von Meck. New York: Random House, Inc., 1937.

Although every real creation must arouse an emotional and intellectual response in the spectator, it does not follow that every creation that achieves this is a work of art; nor does it follow that every great creation must achieve this for everyone.

Training

The drama more than any other art suffers in these two respects from erroneous thinking on the part of the spectator. The most ignorant person does not hesitate to pass ultimate judgment on a play or its performance. Young and old alike condemn or praise with decisive and final words. The primary business of the drama is to arouse emotional states of one sort or another. The most critical of us can go to the theatre and laugh and applaud, even though the play and performance may be definitely mediocre. This sort of emotional pleasure is certainly not to be understood as being an acclamation of a work of art.

Appreciation of art is not, for most of us, a spontaneous reaction. Masterpieces of art make no impression on the untrained and unfamiliar eye or ear. It follows, then, that not only the individual but a great mass of individuals as well must be trained to appreciate any single work of art. Hundreds of people view the "Sistine Madonna" at Dresden daily. Hung in its own room—ideally lighted—the majority of visitors look in and pass by; some remain to buy a post card; but only a few sit before it reverently for an hour and absorb its beauty. Is it art's fault that more do not appreciate? Yet how many people believe it so: "It doesn't move me. So off with its head!" Who is it that should be moved by a work of art and what must he have in order to judge its worth? We shall see presently. Let us recall in passing the number of artists who never received the acclaim during their lifetime that should have been theirs but who received posthumous recognition in later years when the public had matured sufficiently to appreciate their works.

Sensitivity

The first requisite for the appreciation of an art work by the spectator is an inclination within himself toward that art. There must be an affinity between art and its appraiser. If a man is tone deaf, he can never appreciate music; if he is color blind, he can never love painting; if he does not like the theatre, he does not like the theatre. There are, however, many degrees of this sort of insensitivity, and these extreme conditions are not necessary for an indifference to an art or to art in general. But, without exception, the man who in his maturity is to be a specialist in the field of art must have a marked degree of sensitivity and harmony in his natural make-up.

Association and Familiarity

We often hear that the appreciation of art is an acquired taste. The saying is only partially true. You do have to have contact with an art, the closest contact, before your power of consuming it to the fullest is reached. Frequency of contact and association is a necessity—not that one needs to know anything about the art or should study it at this early stage but that one should experience repeatedly for many years the pure emotional reaction to the art as a spectator.

Nothing is so distressing as the neglect of this requirement in young people anxious to succeed in the theatre. All over this country there are aspirants in acting, with long tales of woe about their earnest desire, who have not attended any productions of the theatre to which they are applying. The inferior plays that are submitted in the contests throughout the country show that what the author needs is to go to the theatre, not once but again and again.

With the ever-expanding growth of university, regional, and professional theatres throughout the nation, every effort must be made to attend the theatre often, for continuous association with an art is as important as an inherent predilection for it. The earlier in life this association begins the better it is for one's future development.

One of the reasons the professional theatre failed on the road in the recent past can be attributed to this fact: New Yorkers from a long and intensive familiarity with the theatre had been educated to appreciate the advances being made in writing and production, but those communities who had not had the opportunity of frequent association with the theatre were not prepared to accept the deeper concepts in writing and the new forms of expression. Lately, however, the impact of innovations in film-making along with some of television's better dramatic fare, and the flow of drama graduates, schooled in the new forms, to many communities, encouraged in part by the economic strangulation of the Broadway theatre itself, are factors that have stimulated a resurgence of professional resident companies throughout the country where the newest advances in theatre arts are finding fertile territory.

The reason why frequency of attendance increases the demand for better plays is quite easy to understand. If a person goes to the theatre two or three times a year, he does not become saturated with the drama: he does not become tired of timeworn ideas and stereotyped theatricalities. There may be nothing wrong with the plays; but let a person go to conventional theatrical performances sixteen to twenty times a year for ten years, and we find that he becomes anticipatory of the material and aware of the form. For him the play will become a dead and unexciting product, and he will soon be demanding something richer and truer, something more vital and more fundamental. What he demands is given him, and he supports it. This demand, arising from frequency of association, produces gradual changes in the drama and is one of the most fundamental causes of its development and ever-changing structure which is evident in the continuing experimentations in dramatic form.

Furthermore, experimentation in the creation of any art demands a greater knowledge on the part of the artist than creation along conventional lines. Until the creator has mastered the accepted form, he cannot express his ideas in an unusual manner. Experimentation without a thorough knowledge of the past usually amounts to a mere repetition of mistakes that have been made a thousand times before. The greatest innovators in the drama as well as in other arts, before they became the revolutionary figures as which they are famed, first became distinguished in the accepted form. They first mastered thoroughly the fundamentals of their art. A complete study of Shakespeare, Molière, Ibsen, Shaw, and O'Neill in their different stages of development furnishes sufficient proof of this fact. Experimentation by the unschooled against traditional forms, despite momentary bursts of energy, always seems to expend itself through lack of substance as it did in the sixties and early seventies, when the rebellion against discipline attracted the amateurs, the uninitiated, and the pseudo-idealists.

The critic, then, as well as those others who would judge a work of art, must possess a thorough knowledge of innumerable plays and the performance methods of the past, because in addition to having a keenly appreciative nature the critic must be able to judge intellectually the value and originality of the subject matter as well as the originality and suitability of the form that expresses the subject. The knowledge of this relationship has already been mentioned as a necessity for the creator. The critic or real student of an art is required to be even more aware of this inherent relationship and the quality of execution.

The director, too, must understand the merits of each of these factors and must be able to analyze them in order to handle them in the finished product.

The Creative and the Interpretative Artist

There are two kinds of artists: the creative and the interpretative. The composer, the sculptor, the painter, the writer of literature—as also the actor, dancer, musician and director *when creating the subject matter*—are all creative artists. They conceive a subject and through the medium of their respective materials and instruments give form to the concept. With most arts the work stands complete when the creative artist has finished. Music, dance, and drama, however, often require other artists to give the created product its complete fruition and expression. These artists—conductors, musicians, directors, actors, dancers, and other workers in the theatre—normally do not produce their artistic expression out of the void but interpret what is already created. In some respects their powers as interpreters must be greater than those of the creator. The demands on their native and trained abilities are more exacting, particularly as regards the technical requirements. Interpretative artists must know their own technique as well as the creator's. Their imagination is different but must be no less vivid. They must sense emotionally and intellectually the creator's emotional and intellectual expression. Frequently they must drive their imagination beyond his—sensing the creator's imagination and adding to it.

They are, nevertheless, interpretative because they must bring to life for an audience the particular product given them and not some other that might be their own or one that the original reminds them of. Just because he is romantically minded and has a natural flair for picturization the director must not direct *The Dark Lady of the Sonnets* as if it were written by Shakespeare; he must direct it as written by Shaw—as an artificial, arbitrary, verbal battle. In the theatre the playwright alone is a creative artist; the director, the actor, and the designer are interpreters, unless they have assumed the role of playwright. In searching for relevance or radical departure or a way to assert their egos, some directors will continue to take over the role of creator and use the classics as vehicles for their own personal conceptions, replacing the writer's imagination with their own. This practice is neither right nor wrong as long as we recognize it. Exciting productions like Peter Brook's circus-like *A Midsummer Night's Dream* have come out of this "usurpation of text." On the negative side, a "new revelation of the text" may end up with artiness, excessive staging, or gimmicks.

The Director—Interpretative and Creative Artist

More than at any other time in theatrical history, new approaches to theatrical expression have placed the director in roles other than that of interpretative artist, not that he has been completely denied creative opportunities in this capacity before. In the experimental groups in any of the larger theatre centers the director may function as co-creator with the actors who are conceiving their own subject matter out of improvisational explorations; he may also act as both philosophical and spiritual guide to the group. Fundamentally, these experimental groups see the actor not as an *instrument* for the playwright, but as an *object,* subject only to himself. As Grotowski says: "To play a part does not mean to identify with the character. The actor neither lives his part nor portrays it from the outside. He uses the character as a means to grapple with his own self." This search of the actor and director for self-discovery is no different from that of artists in other fields. The painter Jackson Pollock states it concisely: "Painting is self-discovery . . . you paint what you are . . . it is the act."

The search for self-realization and drive for self-expression are natural impulses of any honest artist and certainly should be encouraged and given the proper climate to flourish in, if artistic expression is to be ever-expanding. At the same time, the artist, in this case the student director, must build his resources, out of which he creates. He must also realize the responsibilities involved in his role as interpretative artist where his work as director is to convey to the audience every segment and quality of a play in its fullest dramatic value and, relative to this form of theatre, make sure that his actors not only play their characters but convey the concept and take advantage of the heightened effect made possible by technical control.

Versatility in Directing

As interpretative artists, many directors, year in and year out, direct every play in the same manner with identical technique, forcing their own personality and mark on every part. As plays vary in their inherent nature and manner, these directors change the costumes and scenery (seldom the furniture arrangement) but continue to stamp the products with their own individual styles. No matter what particular and individualistic qualities the plays possess, the direction for them all remains basically smiliar, and little quality, beyond that of the director's, comes across to the audience.

Professional New York directors are not above this severe criticism. Much has been written about versatility in acting; little about versatility in directing. As a matter of fact, although type casting is frowned upon, type setting of directors is an acknowledged and accepted fact. If a producer has a mammoth spectacle, he hires one director; if he has a humorous fast-moving farce, he obtains another. A serious introspective realistic drama must have a third, improvisational theatre a fourth. Each professional director is catalogued according to type, and he works only within the confines of his typed field. It is not uncommon for such a director actually to boast about his own individual treatment that he brings to plays. If the producer is his own director, we can follow the trail of the rubber stamp with perfect ease.

The reason for this lack of versatility and adaptability in directors is that most of them have a preponderance of either auditory or visual imagination. Only a few have or acquire both types of approach. The innate tendency of these directors toward one or the other of these elements in stage directing leads them to emphasize their particular bias. For those who only hear the characters speaking, interpretation becomes their main interest; their directing becomes "a living of every character in every scene." Those who are visually minded "see" the actors in an effective composition. The stage picture may be constantly formalized with the result that a static, heavy, and classic quality will predominate even though the play is light or realistic. Others have a vivid visualization or picturizing trend, often with continual physicalization of text or superimposition of violently picturized actions. Constant and rapid movement constitutes another director's "feeling" for any play, even though it may have been written by Chekhov. "I imagine each play as a series of ocean waves," says a certain director, "some scenes billowing with might and strength, and others quiet but seething." Forced changes of tempo will make the most sincere and honest character play into a claptrap piece of theatre.

Knowledge of Fundamentals as the Basis of Directing

All these methods are purely instinctive for the director and will result in hit-or-miss productions. Years of experience along the line of the instinctive directing will seldom develop a director who can reproduce a play's inherent quality or one who has variety in his directing ability.

Let us compare the study of the wide field of play directing to the study of medicine. Of a four-year course in medical school, the first three years are devoted to the learning of many facts—sometimes related, sometimes not. The last year is given over to diagnosis which considers a certain given condition in the patient. Because of the nature of the condition the facts of medicine may become modified, restricted, or even contradicted. But before the young doctor can learn to diagnose a case, he must first learn the medical facts concerning the normal ordinary condition of a person, even though in actual diagnosis under different existing conditions he may radically deviate from what he has learned.

So it is with play directing: It is the contradiction of the normal that makes the exposition of technique difficult. Many statements that one is forced to write, when read literally, may or may not be true. Their truthfulness depends on the given condition. In writing, however, it is impossible to stop frequently and explain all the exceptions and restrictions that accompany the diagnosis of a particular case. Nor is it the purpose of this present text to explore the many experimentations in theatrical expression. Its major purpose is to discuss and present disciplines that can give the beginning director a base for operation in any form of theatre without limiting his own creative contributions. The following pages, therefore, are concerned with facts that we shall call absolute, that is, true under normal conditions and under a given point of reference of a realistic play performed on a proscenium stage. They are true, then, with all other factors being equal—true if the intellectual concept, the mood, the style, the kind of play, or the physical stage does not restrict, control, or change them. When the facts are known, then comes the time to learn the exceptions and restrictions and how they affect the absolute; then comes the time to learn how to diagnose a play, to learn to a far greater depth and length what we have merely touched upon in this chapter.

The director's task, therefore, as interpretative artist, is to study the projection of the qualities of a play. This does not deny the director his function as creative artist to whatever degree his talents or his concept permits. But before the technique and the method of conveying these intangible and evasive factors can be learned, the rudimentary technique of play directing must be mastered.

2
The Director's Function

In the first year of his teaching Dean received a postcard from a school-teacher in a small town in Montana. She was to direct the junior class play, but, being—probably—a specialist in mathematics, she was in a complete quandary as to how to go about directing a play. The card, written in a very fine hand, was covered with endless questions. If merely the first question after the "Dear Sir" had been answered, 500,000 words would have been none too many. The definition of the duties and required knowledge of a play director would have been made clear. The sentence was simple: "Dear Sir, what do you do with your actors when you get them on the stage?"

The complete ignorance of most people about the function of a director is not, perhaps, surprising, since, unlike the playwright, designer, and actor, his contribution remains intangible and not easily perceptible. Even in music, the presence of the director's counterpart—the conductor of an orchestra—is seen and felt, but not so the play director.

This ignorance is not so startling to one as the incompetence that one feels in explaining to the layman just what a director has to do. The task is a baffling one and is usually given up as hopeless. After one of Dean's early and lengthy explanations, his listener remarked, "Oh, I see, you tell them when to come in and when to sit down." And Dean, with honor, found himself replying: "And when to go out. Yes, that's it."

The History of Directing

In the entire history of dramatic production we find the director's nearest counterpart in the *choregus,* or trainer of the chorus, in the Greek drama. His work consisted not only in teaching the techniques of dancing to the individual dancers and in perfecting the synchronization of movement but also in interpreting the subject matter of the strophe and antistrophe in terms of positions, movement, and rhythm. To the verses of battle he had to convey the mood and feeling of battle; to the poems of woe he had to contrive a pattern for his dancers that would arouse in 10,000 people a feeling of grief, even though this audience did not hear every word of the chant that the chorus delivered when dancing. The *choregus* had to fit the interpretative movement to the spoken word so that the word, besides being reinforced and clarified, might connote a definite mood quality for the spectator. As we understand the term today, the *choregus* was a play director. What was done for the principal speaking actors is uncertain. Except for pure speech coaching, probably very little was done. Certain conventions developed with time, and these were familiar to actor and audience: Royalty entered by the center large basileus gate and remained in that emphatic position; the less important personages used the rear side entrances and held their distances from the leading actors; the mutes came in by the side openings and for the most part remained beside them. With only three or four speakers at a time on stage, the problem of ensemble playing did not exist. The sightlines and acoustics, furthermore, did not allow much freedom in positions, nor did the buskin and mask allow much opportunity for movement. Usually, performances by the principals were static declamations and recitatives.

The French classical school with revolutionary originality developed from a soliloquy underneath a chandelier to a conversation on two benches. Their direction consisted mostly in speech training, since the power of performance lay in reading the speeches as if they were operatic arias.

Although Goethe and many others urged the use of greater realism in dramatic performances, Goethe also had rules for his actors that contradict our modern conception of realism. For example, they were fined if they took their eyes off the balcony. In time, however, realism was stressed more and more, and gradually instead of two benches we find radical innovations —a bench or sofa on one side of the stage and a table with three chairs on the other. This radical setup has continued for centuries; even today set arrangements remain basically the same, although designers sometime cleverly disguise the setup. Furniture arrangement, as we shall learn later, is in part a stylistic consideration in projecting the values of the play and the director's concept.

When Gordon Craig conceived dramatic productions as a unity and looked upon scenery, lighting, and costume not as separate entities but as correlated and related parts of a whole, a revolution in the accepted standards of theatrical production took place. The art of the theatre became a reality.

There had been, of course, forerunners of the movement. In 1874 the Duke of Saxe-Meiningen presented in Berlin a company that for the first time stressed the "ensemble" method of playing. He devised a system in which a single directing mind brought scenery, costume, stage lighting, and actor into artistic unity. Berlin received these players with wholehearted enthusiasm, as did the audiences in other European cities where they played. Antoine and his Théâtre Libre in Paris felt their influence. Stanislavsky, when he founded his Moscow Art Theatre, borrowed directly from the Saxe-Meiningen group and also welcomed into his theatre Craig and his revolutionary ideas. Other leaders appeared. Adolphe Appia set down in printed analysis the principles of the new method in staging plays, and Max Reinhardt was soon to begin his bold experiments in staging.

Although many of Craig's actual practices were necessarily discarded and others were extreme and impractical, and although he himself was unable to apply his own ideas to practical usage, his concept became the basis for others in this country to develop and utilize. Simply expressed, this was the concept: scenery should be created as a unit which followed the principles of art and interpreted the style and mood of the play. The design, however, was not intended as a reproduction of the actual in painted perspective but a work possessing the qualities of selectivity, proportion, rearrangement, intensity, and emphasis—all of which would convey the inherent qualities of the play. Not only the scenery but the lighting and costumes as well were designed with the same principles, so that each, besides being an artistic unit in itself, bore an artistic relationship to the other.

Productions continued to attain a high artistic standard, but in staging the actors were still arranged in formalized positions, a carry-over from the past. They were not expressing the qualities of the play no matter how ably they acted their roles. The visual aspect of the actor conveyed none of the qualities of the play; sometimes the formalized and artificial arrangement and movement actually contradicted or fought against the qualities of the drama that they were meant to interpret. The need for direction of the actors to contribute to the total artistic expression of the production became apparent.

Actors on a bare stage without the help of scenery, lighting, or costumes should convey the very style and mood qualities that the other factors of production contribute. The director like the scene designer then becomes an artist. His materials for staging are actors in place of paint and canvas. He must shape and form his group using principles of art and coordinate conception with form.

Directing the Actor and the Group

For a further understanding of the principles of staging let us use the dance as an example. A solo performance of a spring dance is an individual expression of the feeling of spring. A good dancer is able with movement and posture to convey to an audience the connotation of spring. If, however, we work out the dance pattern for eight dancers, training them minutely, and then place these eight on a stage in a double row of four; and if now we let each dancer give individual feeling to the routine, the inherent qualities of spring will not come across the footlights. The eight dancers will convey the feeling of spring less ably than the solo. The mood and emotions of the eight placed in arbitrary form, even though each dancer is expressing "spring" to the utmost, have little tonal connotation to the audience, because we are dealing no longer with the problem of the individual but with that of the group.

No group in which each individual member is expressing an emotion or idea can convey that emotion or idea to an audience. Individual expression of this kind is what the old-fashioned stage manager or stage director worked for; what the actors did, or where they went so long as they did not cover one another and took a position subordinate to that of the star, did not concern him. To such a director each individual actor was a soloist who expressed his own part. A cast of eight, grouped arbitrarily on the stage, with each expressing his own characterization perfectly, was a directed play. This manner of directing fails to give any tonal connotation as far as an audience is concerned. Today, only when the relationships and visualization, movement and rhythm, of the group convey the emotional qualities of a play do we consider the play completely directed.

Our contemporary ballets are not dances of individual expression, but of group relationship and movement. In comparing the performance of a classic ballet such as *Les Sylphides* with that of a recently created ballet, one sees the difference between the old form of dancing and the new. One also sees the difference between the old-fashioned play directing and the new. The performance of the classic as originally choreographed is a disassociated series of solos, *pas de deux*, trios, and choruses; that of the contemporary is a semipantomime of violent and contrasting activity coordinated by rhythm and connotative business—all controlled by the principles of composition.

The foregoing paragraphs show clearly the essential difference between coaching and directing. In coaching we are concerned with the individual; in directing we are concerned with the group.

The well-staged ballet contains in the group entity not only the artistic expression of the choreographer but also perfection of conception and technique, of feeling and thought in the individual. The choreographer has spent his imagination, knowledge, and energies on each individual as much as he has on the effects of the group. And so does the play director.

The relationship of the director to the individual, as well as his relationship to the group, must be emphasized strongly. The play director must also train, coach, and labor on the speech, voice, expression, body movement, and character portrayal of each actor. Nothing discussed hereafter under the Five Fundamentals of Directing is to be understood as meaning a neglect of the individual actor or of auditory coaching and text interpretation of a play, which are inherent parts of the dramatic performance—all are requisites of a good director. This book is called not *Play Directing* but the *Fundamentals of Play Directing*. This does not mean, however, that because these five elements deal solely with the visual aspect of a production we must look upon the auditory considerations in play production as unimportant. The play director, moreover, who hopes to succeed professionally must also know dramatic construction and playwriting as well as the coaching of speech and acting and the methods of group expression. But again, although dramatic technique is touched upon but lightly in this volume, it does not follow that it is unimportant. Nor does it follow that character and emotional reality, body expression, and study of the role, which are treated briefly in this volume, are any the less important.

By play directing, therefore, we mean the presentation of a play on the stage for an audience interpreted both in terms of dramatic action and dramatic sound and in terms of the emotional and intellectual concepts of an author's script. These should be projected through the creative contributions of director, actors, and designers, although our present primary concern is with the director.

The Five Fundamentals of Directing

In the following chapters we deal briefly with the sound, or auditory, portion of interpretation and then proceed to concentrate in detail on the action or visual aspects. Furthermore, we do not deal with the intellectual and emotional concepts, *but merely with those elements that furnish the means of conveying these qualities.* We shall refer to *these means* as the five fundamentals of directing. They are composition, movement, picturization, rhythm, and pantomimic dramatization. These constitute a five-note scale of play directing. These in different combinations and degrees of emphasis are the means by which a director may express the emotional and intellectual qualities of a play—again reminding you that the present emphasis on five fundamentals is not meant to diminish the importance of acting requirements in the total expression of the play.

The director must use parts of each fundamental element in every play that he produces. Although every play according to its nature and the characterstics to be emphasized uses a varying degree and combination of the fundamental elements, every directed play must contain some use of all of them.

The five elements together with their principles are drawn from the different elements of painting, dancing, and music. Play directing is a combination of the elements of these arts and not an entirely separate art. Frequently the principles taken from one of these arts are slightly modified to meet the demands of the stage. This especially is true with the elements of painting, since, in directing, the third dimension becomes an additional factor to be considered.

The five fundamental elements will be first analyzed and discussed in reference to the acting areas within the convention of the proscenium stage. The application of the five fundamentals to central staging and other forms of theatrical presentation will be discussed in a separate chapter.

The Actor

3
The Demand for Technique

At first consideration it might seem that there would be little need for a section on the various phases of acting; there are a number of excellent texts for the development and training of actors. However, not included in these specialized books are many things that a director expects a beginning actor to know, even though the actor is thoroughly drilled in voice and body expression. The following pages are devoted to material on elementary stage technique for the actor and on acting as it concerns the individual actor, material that the director as coach must know and that should serve as common terminology between director and actor. The beginning actor will find this material of extreme importance. However, our intention is not to develop an actor by thorough instruction in this sort of knowledge but merely to assist a promising actor in obtaining and holding a position in an acting company.

The acting profession today is crowded—perhaps too crowded. Competition in obtaining a part, even a small one, is keen. A professional director is impatient with raw material because he has more important things to do than teach a beginner the fundamentals of stage technique no matter how gifted he is. He gives directions and expects them to be followed. He is occupied with the playing of a scene as a whole; and when directions in movement and coordination are bungled by the player of a small part because he cannot understand them, the director is justified in his impatience.

The existence of a large group of more experienced actors does away with the necessity of putting up with the inexperienced.

The professional all-year-round stock company which was originally the training school for many distinguished actors now exists in only a few places. Schools of the theater and of acting are hence an importance source from which the professional theatre, be it for Broadway or the growing regional resident groups, may draw young actors. Besides these there are the summer companies to which the amateur from school or college goes for professional experience. These summer groups, for the most part, have taken the place of the old stock companies.

Directors of summer theatres are so overrun with requests from beginners that they do not have to bother with the would-be actor who has not had sufficient experience. The applicant must have learned from his own study or from his previous work in amateur companies—college or community—or in dramatic schools all that is expected of him—stage deportment, which includes promptness at rehearsals, coming with a pencil for notes, readiness for all entrance cues, ability to take "direction" by understanding the director's vocabulary and approach, how to study and approach his part and his characterization, how to adjust himself to the company and to the manner of playing.

Summer theatres usually devote one week to producing a play. This is altogether too short a period for the director to stop the rehearsals to teach while he is directing. Fundamentals must be mastered before joining a company so that the director may work on characterization, on the timing of the play, and on the hundred other matters that absorb his mind and energy.

According to existing conditions then, the beginner today must be more than a beginner; he must have had some experience even to begin. This experience is in essence derived from exhaustive reading and studying with teachers.

Knowledge of any art is gained through a process of deduction from what has already been created successfully: it is the constantly repeated form and manner known as technique. Time has shown that there is a "best way" of executing an idea; major exceptions and variations of the original accepted manner of executing the idea do exist, but these are variations of what is ordinarily done. Technique in any art is teachable, and it is universally agreed that a beginner will do best to learn those elements which have been long accepted before he experiments with a new technique and manner of expressing his idea, whether it is an idea in a play or in a characterization.

Mere instruction in an art cannot make an artist out of a person who has no inherent quality or natural tendency or feeling for the art. Instruction, however, in any art and particularly in the art of the theatre is experience condensed in ordered form. Without question, practical experience is the best teacher, but that oft-repeated saying does not mean that each actor must spend ten years of his life in the trial-and-error approach to acting—that he must by a long-drawn-out experience teach himself. Teachers of acting and books on the art have gathered and arranged the experience of many years so that a beginner can benefit by this experience in two years instead of ten. Good instruction, whether in personal contact or within the covers of a book, is practical experience in condensed form. This section on acting is not a theoretical or idealized treatment of what acting is; nor does it cover in detailed analysis the development of body and voice for expressive response. But in it is contained not only the terminology that the director has in common with the actor but also the fundamentals that a director expects an actor to have mastered.

Since, therefore, we make no pretense of developing a person into an actor, there is no need to discuss the moot question of whether acting can or cannot be taught. We take for granted that the beginner has unusual and excellent natural talent for acting. Without this talent and this experience it will be extremely difficult for anyone, no matter how gifted, to succeed in obtaining even a chance to show his ability. Although the authors sincerely believe that this information is of extreme importance to the actor of talent, they are the first to admit that, unfortunate as it may be, an actor could know and be able to execute all that follows hereafter and still be a very bad actor. That is the mystery and often the tragedy of any art.

4
Basic Technique for The Actor

The director must have an absolute knowledge of the elementary stage technique for the beginning actor. He will find that in directing amateurs much of his rehearsal time will be spent in teaching them these technical principles.

The beginner, interested in acting and endowed with emotional feeling for a character, often rushes into acting without consideration for the articulate playing of the part. He relies on the inspiration of the moment and, not having technical control, defeats his purpose by disregarding important fundamental technicalities. These technical considerations involve (1) the relation of the actor to the parts of the stage, (2) his relation to the audience, (3) his relation to other actors, and (4) the visible and smoothly executed way of handling himself in relation to certain properties and business. These points in themselves may seem of negligible importance. They are, however, of infinite value in conveying a precise and clear creation to an audience. They are the coordinating positions and "timed" movements which will arise in practically every play and in the playing of all characters.

Without the knowledge and execution of these "do's" and "don't's" the actor will fail to consider the audience, will upset the other actors, and will confuse the group ensemble. His playing will be rough and untimed, and a jerkiness will enter into his work and spoil the flow of his scenes. If he is at all sensitive, he will feel immediately the crudeness and awkwardness of his execution of the simple ordinary actions. He must, accordingly, master this coldly calculated technique which is comparable to the five-finger piano exercises that enable the pianist to play without technical consideration when he is performing a long run in a concerto. This technique is the foundation through which talent is expressed and without which talent is impotent. Each point should be learned so thoroughly that it becomes a part of the actor's physical coordination and motor responses. He should have little or no consciousness of them but should execute them as a natural body expression. They should be practiced with all seriousness and so mastered that they may subconsciously underlie all further effort.

The moment that a point is violated, the resulting awkwardness and the breaking of the timing should be felt by the actor. He should immediately sense this; but should he fail to do so, the director can quickly, by technical explanation, correct his manner of execution. The terminology should, therefore, be known so that he may understand the director's instruction.

The student is reminded that for teaching purposes these basic principles are applied only to proscenium-oriented stages. The chapter on Central Staging considers the special adaptations necessary to staging in-the-round. Adjustments to thrust stages and other forms of flexible staging fall readily between the demands of proscenium and central stages.

Stage Positions

Right and Left Stage

All stage directions of right and left are given from the stage's right and left as the actor faces the auditorium. This means that the director working from the auditorium must reverse his idea of left and right. The full direction should be "cross to stage right," but this is usually shortened to "cross right." "Go to the right" means "stage right" though not necessarily the actor's right, for he may be turned with his back toward the audience. In such a position of back to the audience, stage right is then the actor's left; and in any directions given to him, "look or go to the right" must be taken as meaning stage right.

Downstage

This is a term used for that part of the stage nearest to the footlights and the audience.

Upstage

Upstage is near the back of the set away from the footlights. This terminology is the result of the historical convention of the stage having a floor that sloped from the rear down to the footlights. Because of this the audience could easily see people in the rear, and the star, who usually kept upstage of the other actors, would have, consequently, a higher position and be more readily seen by the audience than the supporting cast.

Above

This term is used virtually as a synonym for "upstage of," as when an actor crosses upstage or behind (from the point of view of an audience) another actor or a piece of furniture, property, and so on.

Below

This is used when an actor crosses downstage of or in front of another actor or a piece of furniture.

Stage Areas

Since the actor must know how to distinguish by name one part of the stage from another, it has been found expedient to divide the stage into six so-called *areas:* down left (DL) and up left (UL); down center (DC) and up center (UC); down right (DR) and up right (UR). In addition, stage positions may be designated right (R), right center (RC), center (C), left center (LC), and left (L). These positions are between the areas. All these areas are named from the actor's point of view.

Exercise in Stage Positions

An actor on the stage with a table RC and a chair LC may be given the following directions: Begin DL, cross above chair to UC, cross to DC, R, below table to C, DR, RC above table, UL above chair and to DL, below table to R, DC, upstage of the table, DR, UL, UC, downstage of chair, above table to R, and DC.

Body Positions

For many years actors faced the audience on important lines or speeches. Comedy was also "pointed" in this manner. The old technique was to direct speeches to the first rows of the balcony. Today, the actor is no longer restricted by this arbitrary convention. It is not necessary to act directly to an audience; although the face may be of great benefit in conveying the intellectual and emotional expression of a part of the play, the body is able to express just as much as the face if it is handled correctly. So, too, can the voice. A well-projected speech can be conveyed to the audience even if the actor has his back to it. In realistic playing a good actor never looks directly at the audience—his position onstage must bear relationship to the characters onstage as well as to the audience. He keeps within his picture-frame stage. Sometimes, when an actor is giving voice to lofty thoughts and ideas or

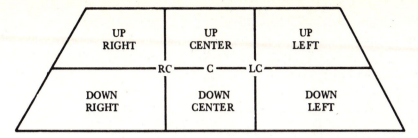

FIGURE 1 *Division of stage into areas and designated positions*

reflecting inwardly, he may naturally look away from the person to whom he is talking. Under these conditions, the actor may open up toward the audience. It is needless to say that no actor should ever look closely at people in the front rows of the theatre to recognize friends.

We shall first consider the body positions of the actor in relation to the audience. These are important not only for receiving directions but also for adjusting an actor to the style of the production. Without elaborating on style at this time, we shall merely state that some plays require and some directors rightfully insist that actors play with varying body positions. Style may demand that the actor play with the body full front to the audience; or with the body slightly turned away; or, so turned that even the backs are frequently toward the audience. It must be constantly remembered that the turn of the body and not the turn of the head is what determines the style or manner of a performance, as it concerns the body positioning of the actors. When the director says "turn in and blend more," it does not mean keeping the body full front and turning the head in but rather just what the words mean literally: "Turn the body from full front away from the audience and toward the other actors onstage."

The Body in Relation to the Audience

1. A *full-front* position is one in which the body and head directly face the audience.
2. A *quarter* position is approximately forty-five degrees away from the audience, or the turn from full front toward the audience halfway to profile.
3. A *profile* position is a ninety-degree turn so that the side of the body is toward the audience.
4. A *three-quarter* position is at a point halfway from profile to full back.
5. A *full-back* position is with the back directly to the audience.

Whether these positions are to the right or the left does not enter into our present consideration.

Terminology of Body Positions

In order to obtain the blended, or pictorial, effect he desires, a director often wishes a change in the body position of his actor. The following terminology will be used by the director to relate an actor's position to other actors and to the picture, or composition:

1. To *open up* is to turn more of the body around toward the audience or, for example, to change from a profile to a quarter or full-front position.

2. To *turn in,* or *close in,* is to turn away from the audience and toward the center of the stage, resulting in giving more profile or back to the audience.

3. To *turn out* is to turn more of the body to the audience and more away from center, so that more of the face and body are toward the side of the stage. On *turning out,* an actor *opens up.*

4. To move *two feet downstage* is to move perpendicularly toward the footlights a distance of two steps, being careful to maintain the body position.

5. To move *two feet up* is to move perpendicularly away from the footlights a distance of two steps, again being careful to maintain the body position.

6. To move *forward three feet* is to walk, in the direction in which one is facing, a distance of three steps.

7. To move *one foot back* is to step back from the exact position in which one is standing a distance of one step.

8. *Blend in* is a general direction entailing minor changes of body position so as to obtain better relationship to other actors.

Exercise in Body Positions

Bare stage with actor LC, full front, taking the following positions: Turn profile L, two feet upstage, one step forward, turn three-quarter to R, full back, three-quarter to L, two feet downstage, full front, blend into R, profile, turn out, turn in, two feet downstage, two feet forward, one-quarter position to L, profile to L, upstage three feet, full back, one-quarter to R, turn out.

Exercise in Body Positions and Stage Positions

Bare stage except for table RC and chair LC: Actor start C, then full front, turn out to L; cross to L below chair, three-quarter position to L; cross above chair to UC, one-quarter position to R, two feet upstage; cross below table to DR, DL, blend in, two steps forward, two steps downstage, cross up to R of chair, full back, two steps to R, two steps down; cross below table to DR, above table to

UC, below chair to L, profile position to R, full front, turn in, turn out; cross to DC, three-quarter to L, two feet upstage, one step back.

Positions in Relation to Other Actors

The standing position of two people who are playing a scene may be such that they *share a scene,* that they are in profile, or that one may *give the scene* to the other.

1. When a scene is shared, each person is presenting three-fourths of his face and body to the audience or is in a one-quarter body position.

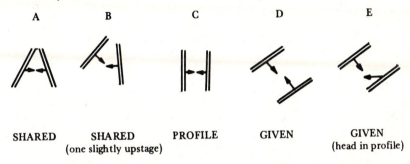

A	B	C	D	E
SHARED	SHARED	PROFILE	GIVEN	GIVEN
	(one slightly upstage)			(head in profile)

FIGURE 2 *Positions of two actors in relation to each other*

2. In a scene played in profile, the actors face each other directly, and the audience sees the face and body of each in profile.

3. When one actor gives the scene to the other, he must turn to a three-quarter body position to face the other actor, who is upstage of him.

The most frequent position is to share a scene (*A* on chart). An actor should take this position immediately when the scene is between two characters, unless the nature of the scene is one that requires a profile or a given position. Great care should be taken to see that both actors are directly opposite each other and that neither is slightly upstage of the other. There is nothing more common with the beginner than to take a position slightly above the other actor. This is a breach of elementary stage etiquette, and it shows either bad manners or ignorance. Getting upstage of another actor, unless definitely indicated, will cause immediate complaint from one who knows his technique. To go directly and literally opposite the other actor should be a movement that requires no thought.

When there is a *slight* backing off or "giving" in a scene, this movement should be made back on the very same parallel line and *not* slightly upstage. Moving slightly upstage is known as *working upstage.* A first-class actor simply does not work upstage of another, except where the director orders it for a particular effect or interpretation.

When the speeches of both people are very important and the reactions of each are equally so, another treatment of the shared position can be used. The positions of both actors are more easily opened up to the audience for a big scene by having both face one-quarter turn in the same direction and having one actor slightly upstage of the other (*B* on chart). This relationship, demanded by the content of the scene, is apt to connote secrecy, introspection, confession, denunciation, and certain heightened emotional states.

The *direct-profile* position is similiar to the shared except that it is more intense and is used in scenes of an intense, exciting, and climactic nature (*C* on chart). Often it will be the culmination of a scene that starts shared. Cross-questioning, accusing, or denouncing scenes use the direct-profile position.

The given position (*D* on chart) is used on occasions when the main interest of a scene obviously rests in one person and when his speeches are long and narrative and the "giver" merely has an occasional remark or question. The dialogue of a scene very easily determines from its import and meaning whether it should be a shared or a given scene. The only exception to these positions is in the case of certain stars who insist that virtually everybody give them the scene. Their excuse is that it is important for the audience to see their reactions; but in most cases they will take the scene whether their reaction is important or not. The beginning actor on joining a company should watch carefully the general stage conduct of the cast toward the leading actors. If the beginner finds himself unable to share his scene with a leading player, he can hold himself in a given position and turn his head profile (see *E* on chart). This same treatment is used when, for certain reasons, the placement of actor *A* is necessarily upstage of actor *B*; for a short time, *B*'s lines become very important to the play, and they must be delivered to actor *A* upstage. This treatment is frequently and easily used when there is a wide distance between them. With actor *A* on stage up right and actor *B* down left, the head of *B* can very easily be kept profile and only the eyes directed upstage toward *A*.

This is a definite steal, but it is successfully used because the audience cannot detect the angle between the horizontal line along which *B*'s head is directed and the line that his head would make were it turned directly upstage to *A* (see *F*, Figure 3). *B* accordingly will seem to the audience to be speaking directly to *A* upstage, and yet being in profile his voice will be more clearly audible and his expression more readily seen.

4. When three or more people are on the stage, the scene may be given first to one and then to another by means of the body positions of each. The actor to whom the scene is given takes the scene by turning more nearly full front to the audience, and those giving it to him turn toward him and

FIGURE 3 *Given position with head in profile*

slightly more away from the audience. By shifting this focus, first one and then another will take the scene.

5. The instruction *focus* directs the actor to turn both body and face directly toward another actor or object, usually upstage.

6. *Dress stage*—when one actor, *A*, crosses in front of the other, *B*, it is necessary for *B* to cross to approximately the point that the moving actor *A* has left (Figure 4a). When there is a group of three in a triangle form *A, B, C*, and *C* crosses right, in front of, or below, the group, the actor *B* at the apex of the triangle crosses down from the apex to approximately the point that the moving actor *C* has left (Figure 4b). This is called "dressing stage" and involves the principle of balance in the stage picture. Furthermore, by "coming down," *B* gets into a position to share the remainder of the scene with *A*. The experienced actor does this without being told.

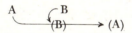

FIGURE 4a *Dressing stage (B moves as A crosses in front of him)*

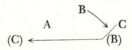

FIGURE 4b *Dressing stage (B moves as C crosses in front of him)*

7. The term *steal* is used with various meanings. Stealing is very frequently a derogatory accusation and refers to an actor's taking the attention or focus of the audience when, considering the value of the scene, he should not have it. If *A* has an important speech and *B* waves a handkerchief or a fan or moves conspicuously for any purpose whatsoever, this is stealing. It was done frequently by the old stars who likewise always kept the forward position on the stage. Disturbing movement such as this, when the focus of attention is elsewhere, is bad etiquette, and considerate actors avoid it. Actually, when a scene is staged with definite focus on the speaking actor,

the audience's attention is so drawn to the speaking actor that their eyes and ears remain with him. The other actors contributing to the focus should be aware of this and not feel that they are doing "nothing." It is doing "something" that distracts and takes attention from where it should be. Beginners sometimes do know, but more often do not know, when they are stealing. Sometimes pure ignorance of what distracting business and movement can do to a scene and an overenthusiasm and desire "to act" will lead them to keep up a perpetual commotion, thereby upsetting the focus on the actor to whom the scene belongs. Actors who are not speaking the emphatic lines of the scene should, of course, act and react, but they should express their emotions in an inconspicuous manner. Never, under any circumstances, should they do any distracting piece of business—like fixing a dress—or making any noise such as jangling a bracelet. A beginner should never steal deliberately. He should constantly watch his "feeling" for a characterization and see that it is not conspicuous when the immediate part of the scene belongs to somebody else.

To steal, however, is often used legitimately as a stage direction. It has already been referred to in discussing body and head positions in Figure 3. It is often used by the director when arranging the position and pictures of a group—when, for instance, he wants an actor to get into a certain position in an inconspicuous manner he could have him move slightly toward the desired position as a reaction to the subject matter of the speaking actor, and thereby not divert attention from the actor who has the important lines.

If *A* is upstage left in a group and the focused attention of the audience is on the right stage, and the director then wants to have *A* downstage for a later speech, *A* can steal down left in this unobtrusive manner and be there at the proper time without the audience being conscious of his movement. *To work* is a synonym for steal in this sense. For instance, you work downstage during the scene. Other terms for this kind of movement are *ease down* or *up, drop down,* or *cheat out.*

To steal is also used legitimately when an actor varies from the actual, or lifelike, position so that he may become more articulate and clear to the audience. For instance, a person on a throne in real life is always approached from directly in front. When, on the stage, a throne is placed upstage with *A* on it, and *B* is required to approach it, the realistic position for *B* is directly in front of it with his back to the audience. But a very important scene between *A* and *B* follows. *B* cannot play it with his back to the audience. His first approach, therefore, will be to kneel, not directly in front of *A* but slightly to one side; and then, as he rises, he will definitely swing upstage so that he opens up and can play opposite in profile or with his body slightly downstage but with his head in profile. This stealing will necessarily arise in many instances besides those in which a throne position is involved.

To steal, or "to fake," is also used to mean to pretend. If a prolonged bit of realistic business which is not necessarily important is taking too much time, an actor fakes it, cutting short its duration by eliminating some of the detail or taking less time than it would actually. Eating and drinking in general are faked on the stage. Frequently unlocking a window or door, tying or binding a person, using handcuffs, and packing or unpacking bags are not carried out in minute detail.

8. To *cover* is to get downstage of another actor or important object and thereby block him or it from the audience's view. Usually it is bad to cover, and the responsibility for not covering is with the downstage, not the upstage, actor. However, the upstage actor is expected to be quick to aid in uncovering; and if he can move his position slightly, thereby saving the downstage actor from an awkward move, he should do so. It is surprising how quickly professional actors will hesitate to carry out directions that necessitate covering another actor. Few beginners have any awareness of it and so should quickly learn to sense such a situation.

There are times, however, when covering must be done if certain business or properties are being faked. An actor faking the playing of a piano can well have another actor cover the keyboard. Turning the body slightly upstage aids in covering the use of a dagger or a gun. In lighting a lamp when there is a necessary coordination between the action of the actor lighting it and the action at the switchboard, the actor should cover the lamp and definitely block off the audience's view of the actual business. This is also true of switching on or off lights from a side switch. An actor, furthermore, besides covering the switch, must always keep his hand on the switch until the lights onstage have changed. The same principle should be followed in faking the turning on and off of sound equipment and television when the actual controls are offstage.

Exercise in Stage Position of One Actor in Relation to Another

CAST: *A* and *B*.
> SET: *Double door UC, table RC, chair LC, lamp on table, light switch to left of center door.*
>
> At start *A* is DR, *B* is L. *A* talks to *B*; *A* crosses to C, shares scene; *B* gives scene to *A*; *A* crosses to below table; *A* turns one-half to R; *B* crosses to *A* and shares scene; both face one-quarter right; *A* crosses to LC, *B* dresses stage; *B* crosses to R; *A* and *B* focus on center door; *A* crosses DC; *B* crosses DC; *A* and *B* share scene; *A* and *B* in profile scene; *A* takes scene; *B* goes to UR; *A* dresses stage; *B* crosses to UL, *A* dresses stage; *B* turns off light switch L of door C; *A* crosses to center of table RC and turns off lamp.

Standing Position

Actors should stand still on the stage except when they have definite move-ment to execute. Too many inexperienced actors are apt to shift from one foot to the other constantly and to make nervous and jerky bodily move-ments. Poise is extremely important. Beginners should watch this most care-fully and train themselves to stand in repose even when expressing the more violent emotions. Furthermore, they should stand with their weight on the balls of their feet. This enables them, whether they are talking or listening in a scene, to seem alert and attentive. When the weight comes on the heels, the body is apt to slouch, and the character seems inattentive and inactive.

Sitting Positions

The attention of the audience must not be broken by an actor's turning to look for his seat. In most cases he should approach the seat beforehand and feel for it with the back of the leg. If he tries to take a step toward the chair, his action of sitting will be poorly timed. Of course this looking for the seat when it is the natural expression of a character is not only legitimate but should be pointed up as a character action.

1. When a woman is sitting, one foot should be extended slightly in front of the other—one foot partly under the seat or both in front. With a man, both feet should be planted on the floor in the same plane. Girls should not cross their knees onstage unless it is particularly in character; and men should not conspicuously, if at all, pull up their trousers before they sit down.

2. In rising and sitting it is very easy to slip into one's own personal manner, and special care should be taken by the actor to keep in character. Oftentimes ingenious business that reveals character traits can be thought up and inserted.

3. Many chairs onstage face profile or upstage. It is always advisable when sitting in such a chair to open up by sitting in a profile or one-quarter position. One should not sit far back in an overstuffed chair when it is down right or down left.

4. This opening up is particularly necessary when a character must sit downstage and talk to a person upstage, as is already shown in Figure 3. In such cases it is inadvisable on important speeches to turn constantly to the upstage person. The head may be turned occasionally toward the general direction of the upstage character, or the body shifted slightly downstage while he is talking. This opening up, together with tilting the head up, pre-vents the head from being tipped in such a manner that the top of the head is toward the audience, thereby covering much of the actor's face.

5. When two people are sitting on a sofa and the sofa is on a slant, the actor sitting at the upstage end of the sofa should sit on the front edge, and the actor sitting downstage should sit far back in the seat. The actor having the most lines in the scene should sit upstage.

Rising

In getting up from a chair an actor should have one foot in front of the other; he should lean forward and put his weight on the front foot; he should push up with the back foot, lift himself up, and put forward the rear foot for the first step. Here, again, characterization will change this procedure, as old people will often get up with strained difficulty.

Turns, Gestures, and Kneeling

1. Turns are ordinarily made so that the actor faces the audience as he turns. Exceptions to this rule occur when the turn toward the audience is obviously awkward and unnatural, because the body is already turned more than halfway around the complete turn. In this case the body turns toward the new position through the shortest distance. For example, if an actor is turned a three-quarter position upstage and he is turning for an exit behind him, he does not turn to profile and complete the semicircle turn but rather turns upstage directly. This gives the back pictorial value in delivering a line over his shoulder. This movement is called *turning in*.

2. In gesturing and holding or passing objects onstage, care should be taken that the actor does not cover himself in the process. He should gesture or hand something to another actor with the upstage hand whenever it is possible—as it almost always is. Special care should be taken if an arm is raised, as the downstage arm will cover the head. Often the natural movement would be to use the right arm; yet if it is the downstage arm, the left arm should be used.

3. It is also better to kneel on the downstage knee, because that opens the actor up to the audience. Incorrect handling of these problems may mean the loss of important lines or facial expressions.

Exercise in Turns, Gestures, and Sitting

CAST: *A* and *B*.

SET: *Table with lamp RC, sofa at LC, double door UC with light switch to L, window DL, chair DR, chair DL, door R.*

A and *B* at C; share scene; profile; *A* crosses to window DL; turns and speaks. *B* crosses to sofa LC; *A* speaks to *B*; *B* crosses to *A*; *B* hands *A* a letter; *A* crosses DR; *B* crosses to DR and kneels; *A* crosses to window and addresses mob outside, during which he gestures profusely. *B* crosses UC; takes three-quarter position to R; turns to *A*; *B* turns on electric lights at L of C door; *A* crosses to *B* up L. *A* crosses to sofa and sits at upper end; *B* crosses below sofa and sits at lower end; *A* rises, crosses DR; *A* speaks to *B*; *A* sits chair DR; *B* rises; *A* speaks to *B*; *B* sits on sofa; *A* rises; *B* crosses to window DL. *A* and *B* focus on lamp; *B* crosses above sofa to table and puts out lamp. *A* turns three-quarter right; *B* goes to window DL and addresses mob with many gestures, turns, crosses to DC. *A* turns; *A* sits DR chair; hands *B* a letter. *B* turns and exits UC door.

Approaches

Two general types of approaches must be recognized: the direct and the curved.

Direct

When an actor approaches another in the same line parallel to the footlights, he makes the simple direct approach—defined as a straight-line advance to a person or thing.

Curved

In the exercises so far, the approaches have probably been direct. This has invariably left the crossing actor in an awkward position, and in order to share a scene he has had to take a jerky upstage or downstage step to arrive directly opposite the other actor. This movement is bad and can be avoided by a slightly curved approach.

CURVED APPROACH WITH ONE ACTOR APPROACHING ANOTHER   When an actor must approach another actor who is in an upstage or downstage area, he is forced to make a curved approach. This approach digresses from a

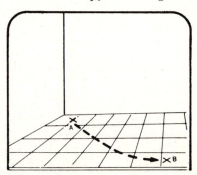

FIGURE 5   Curved approach to downstage

straight line and reaches the object after an unnoticeable curve maneuvered in order to get opposite the other actor instead of above or below him. If the actor to be approached is downstage, the curve is a downstage curve. (See Figure 5). If he is upstage, the curve is an upstage one (Figure 6).

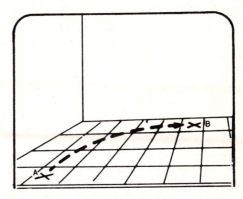

FIGURE 6   Curved approach to upstage

If the actor needs to be on the other side of *B*, a large curve crossing below *B* will put him in the right place. (See Figure 7.) This is particularly usable when the approach is to an inanimate object such as a window or door.

Obviously the curved approach is invaluable in many cases for keeping the actor open to the audience, for sharing the scene with another actor, for softening a cross, and in getting the greatest effect from a costume.

CURVED APPROACH WITH TWO ACTORS APPROACHING THE SAME OBJECT Approaches and crosses become more intricate when two people are involved. Problems arise when two or more people approach an upstage window from down right and down left. If the object to be viewed outside the window is to the right, the actor on the right must make the curve, and vice versa

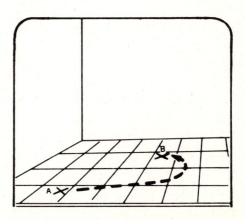

**FIGURE 7
Curved approach
crossing below
object**

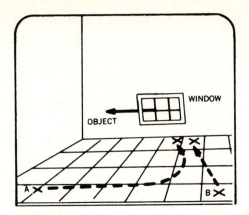

FIGURE 8 *Two actors approaching same object*

(Figure 8). The approaches must be timed so that the person who is to stand next to the window arrives first.

In any approach the actor should always take a position directly opposite the other person—the shared position—unless told to take an upstage or downstage position by the director.

It is generally agreed that objects outside a window will be placed as follows: if the window is on either of the side walls, the object or event offstage is usually placed downstage; if the window is on the rear wall to right or left, the object outside is toward center. If the window is center, the director must settle which way the focus is to be. All these offstage placements are settled in this way so that, in looking out, the actor will keep himself opened up. The actors should accentuate their positions by opening up more than they would in reality. Most windows are higher than the street, and consequently the gaze is directed down, except, of course, when the actor looks at objects of nature such as trees and mountains.

Crossing

1. An actor must take the shortest and most direct line in crossing to a person, an object, or an exit. He cannot circle about furniture or other people if that circling takes him out of the natural direct line of crossing. If it is desirable for an actor to cross above furniture and the direct line would ordinarily take him below it, he must work upstage with a motivation or a steal before it becomes time for him to cross, thus making the direct line of crossing above the furniture. This does not retract what has been said about the curved approach which is a technical movement and will not be noticed by the audience.

2. Except for servants and certain action demands on character, actors pass

in front of each other, because when an actor passes behind another he loses his hold momentarily on the attention of the audience. An actor should cross in front of (below) other actors only when the cross is made on one of his own speeches that allows it or when there is a break in another actor's speech.

3. When two actors cross the stage talking, the upstage actor should walk about one step in advance of the downstage actor and turn slightly toward the downstage actor, thereby opening up to the audience. The actor with the more important lines should be upstage.

4. For *cross* in scripts the signs X or Xs are used; frequently, the words *go* or *come*.

Exercises in Approaches

1. Repeat the exercises on pages 41 and 43, putting in straight and curved approaches where they should be used.

2. SET: Armchair DR, window DR, table and lamp RC, arch UC, sofa LC, door DL, armchair DL.

CAST: *A* and *B*.

At start *A* and *B* are DC; *A* Xs to chair DR; *B* goes to table RC; *A* sits DR; *A* and *B* look at accident out of window DR; *A* and *B* rush up to arch and look R; *B* Xs to sofa LC; *A* goes to R; *B* sits upper end of sofa; *A* Xs to *B*; *A* and *B* walk to door DL; *A* and *B* walk to window DR. (*A* is doing most of the talking.) *B* Xs to left of table RC; *A* Xs to R of table LC; *A* hands *B* a letter; *B* drops letter on table, Xs and sits on sofa; *A* Xs to him and takes scene; *B* rises, shares scene with *A*, and then Xs DRC; *A* runs to him giving scene; *B* Xs to R of table for letter.

Position of Doors and Windows

Doors and windows are designated as follows: Those on the right stage wall are down right and up right; those on the left stage wall are down left and up left; those on the rear wall are up right center, up center, and up left center. Care should be taken to recognize at once the difference between up left and up left center, as up left is in the side wall and up left center is in the back or rear wall.

In old scripts you will find these doors referred to as R-1, R-2, R-3 and L-1, L-2, L-3. On both sides the 1 is the opening in the flat nearest the downstage, or proscenium; and 3 is the opening farthest upstage. Even in modern scripts these designations are frequently used to indicate entrances in exterior sets—they are the openings between the wings.

Entering and Exiting

Opening and Closing Doors

Except in designated instances, an actor should close the door after entering. Practically all stage doors swing offstage, with the exception of outside doors which should swing onstage. Doors in the side walls are hinged on the upstage side. In entering by a side-wall door, take hold of the knob with the upstage hand, and open the door; enter; take hold of the knob with the downstage hand, and close the door. This technique keeps the actor opened up to the audience during his entrance. In entering at a door in the rear wall, if the hinges are on the right, the opening should be done with the right hand; and, after entering, the closing should be done with the same hand. If the hinges are on the left, both opening and closing should be done with the left hand.

When exiting, the actor should open a door on the side wall with the upstage hand, exit, and close it with the downstage hand. Doors in the rear wall are opened under conditions established by the approach; as always, the upstage hand should open it unless the exit requires the actor's back to the audience.

Cues for Entering and Speaking

The cue for speaking cannot be taken as the cue for entering. The entrance cut must precede the speech cue by the amount of time necessary for the actor to come onstage and hear his speech cue. This statement is, however, modified according to the place where the speech is to be delivered. If it is supposed to be heard from offstage, one cue may be taken; if delivered at the door, the entrance cue precedes the speech by a very short space of time. Ordinarily, a character on entering the stage should speak at the point of entrance and not wait to walk to center stage.

Servants should not announce until they are in place. A butler's cues are therefore extremely difficult. For entering, the cue should be early enough to allow him to enter and get in place before speaking on his line cue. If he has been rung for, however, he speaks on entrance.

Entering in Character

It is always essential to start getting into character before an entrance. "Step into the character's shoes" at least five or six steps before the entrance, being certain to open and close the door in character.

The relation of the character to the room is often woefully disregarded, to the detriment of all reality in the stage picture. An actor should not think that he is entering a stage but that he is a definite character entering a certain place; and his relation to the place should be immediately shown. By his action or reaction to the set upon entrance, the owner of a room should establish himself as such.

A servant should enter a room in a manner that clearly distinguishes him from a salesman. A friend of the family, the son of the house, a formal guest, a prospective buyer, a burglar, and so on indefinitely—although each may enter by the same door during the course of the play—each one must have his distinctive way of entering. It is this kind of enrichment through pantomime that establishes character and makes a play live and breathe.

Several Characters Entering

When a number of people enter together from a side entrance, the speaker, with few exceptions, should enter first. He then can pick up the cue more quickly; and furthermore, in addressing the actor following, he can "open up" to the audience. When the entrance is in the rear, the speaker often comes second and addresses the first to enter. There are times, however, when he enters first, such as when his remarks are either general or delivered to someone onstage. A servant announcing the arrival of a guest would enter first, placing himself in a position that clears the entrance.

The Exit

The technique of leaving the stage differs little from that of entering. Character must be maintained. The character, if important, should stay open by making a curved approach to the exit.

When two people exit, the speaking character leaves last, either addressing the person in front of him or delivering his words back to a character onstage.

It is often effective to deliver a final speech before exiting just as the door is reached; or a speech may be broken, the first part delivered in the room and the rest at the door as the actor turns. This depends on the situation, but in general it is bad to have a long cross on an exit hold up the dialogue. This is permissible, however, when the exit is very much a part of the dramatic action of the play.

Examples of an exit involving two people with dialogue:

A and *B* are down right talking. *A* is right of *B*. They are to exit together. *A* is to have the last line of the scene. *B* gives his last line and turns to exit. He crosses and opens door. *A* delivers his last line while he crosses. *A* exits through the open door, and *B* follows.

This may also be handled so as to emphasize or point the last line to greater advantage. The same situation exists; only this time *B*, after his next-to-the-last speech, crosses and opens the door. *A* follows and gives his next-to-the-last speech. As *A* reaches *B*, *B* gives his last speech; *A* crosses *B*, stands in the door, turns to face *B*, and delivers his last speech.

If the door is in the side wall, the exit is simple. When the exit is in the rear, it is more difficult: If the actors are downstage right or down left, the main speaker on the exit should start upstage first. If the speaker is nearer the center, it is simpler if he keeps ahead, talking over his shoulder to those behind, thereby opening up. If the speaker on the exit should happen to be near the side wall, he must of necessity cross in front of *B*, turn back to talk to *B*, and keep ahead of him on the way upstage. The curved approach is necessary in either case.

If *A* and *B* are sharing the scene, center, and an exit is made upstage, they both turn in and walk upstage. If the lines are divided, they keep abreast of one another but turn their heads in profile. If *A* has more to say or is more important than *B* in exiting, *A* keeps slightly ahead of *B* and turns to look at him.

Entering and Exiting through Curtains

When a person enters through curtains and is compelled not to disclose the backstage, as in going out through the act curtains to make an announcement or exiting through curtains that if opened will disclose another set, he must keep the two halves of the curtains so that they overlap and one is downstage and the other upstage of him as he passes through on a nearly horizontal line. For the entrance, as the actor steps through, with the downstage hand he pulls the downstage half slightly in the direction in which he is going and with the upstage hand pulls the rear behind him. (See Figure 9.)

When he turns to exit through these curtains, he strikes the upstage curtain with his upstage hand before he is ready to leave; when he turns, he will be able to see the break in the curtains by the streak of light showing

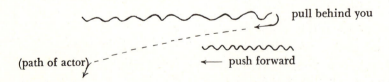

FIGURE 9 *Entering through curtains (reverse action for exit)*

between them where he has struck them apart. He then slips his upstage hand ahead of him to grasp the upstage half of the curtain and hold it ahead of him as he passes through again on the horizontal line. With his downstage hand he pulls the downstage half behind him, keeping the lap as great as possible during his exit just as during his entrance. (See Figure 9.)

When the backstage may be shown, the actor takes the two halves of the curtains with his two hands, parts them, and steps through in a vertical line. His exit may be accomplished in a similar manner.

Entering from Right or Left

Whenever a character enters or exits through an open door or arch upstage, care should be taken to find out whether he comes in from the right or the left stage. As the space between the rear wall of the set and the backing is supposed to be a hall or room, the direction from which he comes in or goes out is important. And, again, if he is exiting, he will have his back to the audience so that "off left" will mean to turn to his right—remembering that stage directions of left and right are given from the actor's point of view as he *faces* the audience.

Position after Calling through a Door

When an actor has to go to a door to call an offstage character, he usually steps back three or four steps after calling and waits for the person to enter. This leaves sufficient space to keep the actors from being too close to one another during the ensuing scene. It is, however, technically obvious and arbitrary. If possible, it is better to find a motivation for this opening up. The actor who has called can cross away from the door to some position in the room. If this is undesirable, the caller can approach the side door from above and, after calling, step up slightly and allow the person entering to pass well on to the stage before turning and seeing the caller who comes down and shares the scene with him.

Entering and Exiting at Rehearsals

At rehearsals when there are no doors with which to practice, the actor should roughly time his cue for entering. When he has entered, he should stamp his foot fairly loudly so as to let the other actors know that he has entered. This is a convention of rehearsals and is a definite aid to the actors and director. Frequently an actor will give the same loud stamp on his exit through the imaginary door to acquaint the actors remaining with the fact that he has departed from the set.

Exercises in Entering and Exiting

1. SET: *Window DR, UC arch with drawn curtains, door DL, chair DR, table RC, sofa LC, chair DL.*

   (*a*) Each student enters and exits, opening and closing door DL.

   (*b*) Each student enters and exits through curtains UC, being careful not to disclose backing to arch.

   (*c*) *A* sitting DR, *B* standing by *A*. They exit off DL—*A* does most of talking.

   (*d*) *A* and *B* on sofa (*A* right of *B*). They exit UC to R. *B* does most of talking.

   (*e*) *A* and *B* on sofa (*A* right of *B*). They exit DL. *A* does most of talking.

   (*f*) *A* sitting DR, *B* standing by *A*. They exit DL, *B* does talking.

   (*g*) *A* looks out window DR; *B* enters UC from R, Xs to window DR, and looks out. *B* Xs to sofa; *A* and *B* hold scene; *B* sits on sofa; *A* Xs to R of table; *A* and *B* look off UC to R; speaking, *A* and *B* exit UC to L; *A* and *B* enter UC from L, *A* speaking; *A* and *B* X to DL and exit DL; *A* and *B* enter from DL, *B* talking; X to UC; *A* and *B* hold scene at C; *A* and *B* exit UC to R, sharing scene.

2. Character enters. Problem: each student in character enters separately, closes door, reacts to room, and sits.

   SET: Any room. A real door UC.

   CAST: The lady of the house.
   Woman friend.
   Burglar.
   Friend of a friend with a letter of introduction.
   The husband who owns the house.
   The daughter's friend.
   Salesman.
   The blackmailer.
   The maid.

Listening

Too much cannot be said about the value of listening and the development of the art of listening on the stage. If a character drops out of the scene the moment he stops speaking, the illusion of reality is immediately broken. This is bound to happen unless, firmly grasping the role, the actor reacts characteristically to every person and line in the play, as a character following the thoughts of the others. Reactions should be made when the actor is one of a group, but, as already noted, they should be made more softly than when he is the focus of attention or the emphatic figure.

When the actor is in the midst of a scene and the other person is speaking, the silent actor should

1. Listen. Then, even before the speaking actor has finished his speech, he should
2. React to the idea of the speaking actor, then
3. Think of his idea in reply,
4. Take his breath, and
5. Speak on cue.

Asides and Soliloquies

The aside is a short speech delivered at a time when other characters are on the stage. It usually expresses audibly what the character is thinking or what he knows that the other characters do not know and what the playwright wants the audience, but not the other characters, to hear. As a convention of the theatre the aside or soliloquy is thought of as belonging to plays of an early vintage, though contemporary writers use the form to serve their own special dramatic purpose.

If the director, producing a play of a period when the aside was an accepted convention, wishes to tone down the asides when it is impossible to cut them out entirely, the actor should read them not directly to the audience but turned slightly away from the other actors onstage; he should also read the asides in a lower speaking tone accompanied by some appropriate business and pantomime. Emphasis should not be on the lines but on the pantomime and expression that accompany them. The other actors should be concerned with minor and inconspicuous business or movement.

In classic dramas asides are an integral and legitimate part of the play. Furthermore, they are most important in establishing the style and manner of the historical production. They should be spoken directly to, but not necessarily at, the audience. While the aside is being delivered, the characters on the stage who are not speaking may hold their positions, or "freeze." If the production is a burlesque an actor may glance at the front row of the audience and cup his hands at his mouth to prevent the other characters on the stage from hearing what he has to say. Such procedure may prove effective and comic.

The soliloquy is a long speech delivered when the actor is alone on the stage. The contents may be direct exposition, planning, plotting, explanation of situation, or, in the highest form, thoughts and mental predicament. In classical dramas the soliloquy may be spoken directly to the audience with the actor coming down to the edge of the stage to deliver it, or it may be blended into the scene if the purpose is to tone it down. As with the aside, appropriate business and pantomime can be introduced. The treatment will depend upon what the director has chosen to use for the style or manner of production.

In a modern-dress version of *Hamlet* Basil Sydney in delivering the famous "To be or not to be" never once directed it to the audience but lighted a cigarette, stood upstage looking off through a French window, came slowly downstage with pacing and thoughtful movement to a backless bench near the footlights, and then lay down flat on his back and continued to smoke; while in John Gielgud's modern-dress "final run through" concept of staging, Richard Burton kept the same soliloquy along more traditional lines, delivering it within his sphere of concentration without business elaboration.

Opening Up and Covering

If the preceding technique of movement and positions has been analyzed carefully, one will discover that it is planned primarily and basically so that the audience will see the actor. All the actor's technique is arrived at in order to keep the character in correct relationship to the other actors and, at the same time, to include the audience so that it may see what is taking place as well as the facial and body expressions that convey the mental and emotional states of the character.

We have already practiced covering, or masking, such things as the switching of lights. This action is covered deliberately so as to conceal a mechanical process which might not be coordinated. The majority of the business in a play, however, should not be covered but deliberately opened up for the audience.

Business, or *bus.*, in acting is movement connected with the handling of property or a definite pantomimic action. It may be executed while the actor is speaking or while there is a distinct pause in the flow of dialogue. Some business is faked and covered. Frequently it is accomplished with no marked attention given to it, but more often it is done with great emphasis so that the audience is distinctly aware of it.

At rehearsals all business is worked out carefully along with positions and movement. At the first meetings it is usual for the actor to read aloud, but in a lower tone than his lines, the business written in his script. In stock where he learns his business just as he does his lines, he is apt to read all directions carefully. The actor should always do the business in pantomime at rehearsals, taking care to imagine each individual step of the procedure in the use of a property. He should fit his action as best he can to the actual timing of handling the real property at final rehearsals and performances. This careful timing of the use of a property at the early rehearsals will save the actors and director much valuable time at the technical and dress rehearsals. With proper consideration and imagination the execution of business can be gauged correctly. Along with the timing problem the execution of business in relation to the audience should be planned. Is it to be covered or open, held down or emphasized?

When the business includes movement over a part or all of the stage, an actor will do well to come early and plan and time his actions to the actual space. Any long and involved business requires this special rehearsing.

Cases of Deliberate Covering

EATING AND DRINKING   Actors do not like to eat property food or to drink quantities of cool tea or other substitutes. Not only is it unpleasant to consume such stuff night after night, but, owing to the convention of not speaking when the mouth is full of food, carrying on a conversation in an eating and drinking scene becomes extremely difficult.

All phases of this business are faked. When there is eating to be done, the actor spends time cutting or breaking the food, which is usually soft and easy to swallow. Eggs in one form or another are used for all sorts of food. Actually, very tiny morsels are put into the mouth. The actor eats each bite with jaw movements suitable to a larger mouthful. This is pure pantomime, but it must be convincing if it is to convey the effect. Very little is served, so with a few small mouthfuls and a great deal of cutting up, the actor actually leaves on the plate most of what has been served. If he is sitting with his back to the audience on the downstage side of the table, he of course eats nothing but fakes the whole process of putting food into his mouth, cutting it up, and reaching for articles.

Whenever possible, receptables are used that are not transparent. Often the liquid is faked so that only water is used or else nothing at all. Whether there is something or nothing in it, the actor tips the cup or mug as if he were drinking but allows none or very little of the substance to enter his mouth. He then must be sure to swallow or to pantomime swallowing so that the cords of the throat may be seen to move while the cup is raised to the lips.

If the liquid is in a transparent glass and can be seen by the audience, the process is a combination of the two preceding elements of eating and drinking technique. The glass should seldom, if ever, be full. If it ever happens that a beginner is to pour out a liquid and give it to a more experienced actor to drink, he should be told never to fill the glass. Three-quarters or a bit over half full is sufficient. Then the actor drinks just a little, pretends to drink more, and finally ends up leaving a goodly portion. There are, of course, exceptions where the lines point to the fact that the liquid is all gone or the actor has to drain a glass, but in these cases very little is in the glass to begin with.

Often it is sufficient for the actor to keep his hand around the glass to cover just how little liquid is actually in it. Another method is to invert a small tumbler (usually plastic) inside the transparent glass. If the liquid is being faked and the actor is supposed to drink a long draught, care should be taken to allow him sufficient time. All too often an actor drains a mug too quickly and discloses the faking.

It is important for an actor to eat and drink convincingly on the stage. If the drink is supposed to be a strong one (liquor should always be faked), the actor must be certain to pantomime according to the character's natural reaction. This consists in making faces of varying intensity and, sometimes, coughing. Even a habitual drinker has a definite facial reaction.

Handling Violent Scenes

Shooting, Stabbing, and Suicide

In these situations a great deal of masking and covering is necessarily employed. In killing a character by shooting, the killer must keep at a distance from the one killed. This will lessen the danger of fire or injuries from the wads in the blank cartridge. The killer should, except in extreme cases, be below the one to be shot, so that there is no shooting at or toward the audience. The actor shooting should aim the pistol slightly downstage of the about-to-be victim; the audience will not be aware of this steal. If the actor to be shot at is downstage of the shooter and on one side of the stage so that he is near the side wall, the shooter can aim slightly upstage of him. The aim should never be toward the audience. If it has to be and the killer must be upstage, he should then be covered by another actor or be directly above and covered by the one to be killed. Then the killer can shoot down on to the stage floor just above the downstage actor, and the steal will not be seen by the audience.

If the killing is to be done with a dagger, as in many Shakespearean plays, again the actual stabbing must be covered. The director may want the scene to be done in one of many ways, but in any case the actors should be able to realize the problem and help him. If the director has the killer upstage of the other actor, the stabbing may be done in the back of the other, thereby covering the action. If the thrust is to be in the front of the victim, then the one being stabbed may turn and cover the blow himself.

If the killer is downstage, he himself must cover the thrust by covering the victim.

The stabbing must be started with great force and a violent motion and lessened in speed as the knife approaches the body. As soon as the dagger is covered, the thrust is directed away from the person. A dagger goes into a body more easily than it is withdrawn—consequently, much forceful effort must be used in pretending to withdraw the weapon. Nothing will disclose the faking more obviously than quickly and easily withdrawing the knife.

When the weapon is not a knife or dagger but a sword, as in a duel, the same covering treatment is employed, and the actor passes the sword between the upstage arm and the body. Often the sword's point should show behind the body. The apparent force when it is withdrawn must again be pantomimed.

The weapon used in any of these last cases must be disposed of immediately in order to keep the audience from seeing the lack of blood on the instrument. It may be thrown on the floor toward a far corner of the stage. It may be wiped off at once on something that can be disposed of and kept out of sight, or it may be returned immediately to the scabbard. But it must be kept out of sight.

The actor stabbed should *not* fall immediately. He staggers a moment. He will help the illusion by grasping the part of the body shot or stabbed and by showing a definite reaction of agony as he sways and partially sinks. After this reaction it is good business and more convincing if the actor breaks his fall by first falling against a piece of furniture and supports himself by it as he sinks to the floor. Only the last part of the action is a complete fall. In falling the knees are the difficult part to protect. Once the knees have touched the floor, the fall on the hip and down is easy.

If the fall is from the full standing position, the actor must be sure that the feet stay down on the floor and do not bounce up.

He should plan to have his head more downstage than his feet, as these are apt to give a humorous aspect to a corpse.

If an actor has to help carry a body offstage, he should see that the head of the victim is higher than the feet. In most cases he should be on the downstage side of the body, as the prone figure is apt to be ludicrous, and covering it is a valuable aid in maintaining the mood of the scene. In carrying a body offstage the head should go out first.

In suicide the actor must himself cover the method from the audience. Usually he uses a knife, because it is the more easily masked. He begins partly open to the audience; as he thrusts the knife toward himself with great feigned strength and effort, he turns upstage. He must not let the knife fall, but he must keep it in his hand as he falls. His falling is the same as before, staggering until he gets one knee down and then falling on his hips.

In turning a gun on oneself the action should also be feigned. The shot should be directed, parallel to the body, at the floor. There have been instances when the gun has been kept in the pocket, which again means that the shot is made directly in front and parallel to the body or that the shot has been fired behind. It is also possible to turn the back to the audience and shoot directly at the floor.

A gun that goes off during a scuffle is fired in the following manner: The actors get into a clinch with their bodies and downstage arms, leaving an open space on the upstage side. When in the firm grip of the other, one shoots at the floor. The actor who does not shoot is the one who struggles violently while the shooter cocks the gun and fires.

Guns are nearly always fired onstage and not off, as many people think. A property man offstage has a cartridge ready; and if the onstage gun fails to go off the first time, the offstage gun will be fired. An actor should have this arrangement with the stage manager or property man. It should be settled how many attempts the actor should make; usually only one is made before the prop gun is fired.

Slaps, Fistfights, and Pushing

Handling of slaps need not necessarily be faked. Many actors prefer to be slapped to help the reality of the scene. However, care must be taken that the slap be held partially in check and directed at the lower flesh of the cheek with the hand slightly cupped and fingers closed. It is important to avoid hitting over the ear which can prove harmful to the recipient. Also, to create the sense of a strong impact yet soften the slap itself, the recipient should follow through by turning his cheek away at the moment of contact. This same technique of "follow through" away from the direction of the slap is employed in fist fights where contact is faked by covering as the recipient turns upstage at the moment when contact should be made and by receiving the blow on his upstage hand which has been raised as if for protection. In both instances, some actors, as the recipient, prefer to make the sound of the slap or blow by slapping or hitting their own hands covered from the audience on the turn upstage. Violent scenes of this nature should be worked out in step by step progression and executed in slow motion until each action is secure and timed. In any violent action, including pushing, it is the recipient and not the attacker who controls the reaction. In other words, in pushing the other actor, the attacker feigns violent contact while the recipient responds physically under his own controlled momentum, whether it be against an object or a fall to the ground.

Handling Certain Emotional Scenes

Embracing and Kissing

A kiss is often covered and faked for reasons of not smudging make-up, perspiring, or other technical factors. If the embrace is to be performed while both actors are standing, the correct position is arrived at by first taking what amounts to a natural dancing position. The right hand of the boy is placed under the left arm of the girl and around her back toward her right shoulder. Instead of taking the girl's right hand, the left hand of the boy either goes around the girl's waist or high on her upper arm or on her right shoulder blade. The girl then puts her right hand on the boy's left shoulder, on the lapel of his coat, or around his neck, or she may smooth his hair. Her left arm is around his right shoulder. The boy should place his downstage foot below the girl's downstage foot and very close to it. He then puts his weight on it so that his general body position is leaning slightly forward. This covering will result in the audience's seeing the two in close contact, but as a matter of fact only the downstage sides of the actors are in close contact, and there will be considerable space between them on the upstage side.

In kissing, the girl, whether standing or sitting, should tilt her head upstage, and the boy his head downstage. This is to be done whether the kiss is actual or covered and faked.

The covered kiss is executed by the boy's turning the girl's head slightly upstage and bringing his own directly below hers. His head will cover and mask the process, as his face will be directly upstage and his shoulders and the back of his head toward the audience. From the waist down he will be in profile.

When the head is in this position he can either not kiss at all or can put his lips on her cheek or chin, or he can put his face to the side and back of her neck.

If the couple is sitting on a sofa and the man is downstage, the covering is as simple. If he is upstage, the procedure is similar except that the girl will do the covering.

Sobbing

When an actor sobs on his arm, on another actor's shoulder, in the embrace of another actor, or into a pillow, care should be taken to see that the mouth is not covered—that there is space open in front of it. The forehead and not the face should be laid on the arm, and this will allow the mouth to be protected and the words audible. When an actor cries in the lap of another actor, the upstage side of the face must be in the lap with the front facing out toward the audience.

Handling Properties

Character Properties and Business

Character properties and business are used mostly to convey characterization to an audience rather than to clarify the story or idea of the play. Much will be said later about their choice, their variety in use, and their relation to line and timing of the play. For the present we are concerned solely with their relation to the audience.

Character properties consist of fans, shawls, sewing, flowers, books, canes, brief cases, cigarettes, pipes, glasses, papers, and the like. They have been selected by the actor for an enrichment of his characterization. Their use as a general rule is unemphatic as far as the audience is concerned. Occasionally they may be used for a "laugh point," and they are sometimes tied up with the plot; but these are exceptions, and when they occur, the properties would be considered emphatic plot props or business.

Whether covered or open, the use of character properties should not be overdone. In using them an actor must be careful not to steal. Distraction and confusion of interest can result from their playing an important part on the stage. Waving a fan will cause great visible damage, rustling a newspaper will disturb auditory focus. Lighting a pipe or a cigarette or slowly pouring wine will hold up the delivery of lines when the scene should be progressing rapidly. A beginner should watch these interruptions of focus and timing. He should be certain that they are kept down to their proportion of value to the scene as a whole. They are to be definitely blended. If the entire audience does not see or is not impressed with them, there is no injury to the play.

It is best for an actor to use character properties on his own lines and speeches.

Emphatic Properties and Business

Properties and business in themselves are often vitally important to the progress of the play's action. Great care must be taken to plant and open up such properties and business to the audience.

HANDLING THE TELEPHONE   The actor should handle the telephone with due consideration for the audience. He should be above or to the side of the object on which the telephone is placed. The mouthpiece is held slightly below the mouth. The actor begins with his body either definitely profile or in a three-quarter position. If the conversation is short and only fairly important, he does not change his position; if it is long and important, the actor turns full front by slow degrees.

While on the subject of the telephone, we shall discuss a second important consideration of telephone scenes, one that is much abused, namely, listening to replies. They should be planned carefully—the pause, for example, indicating the time that the actor is supposedly listening should be slightly shorter than the actual would be though the actor must mentally fill in what is being said in order for him to create true listening and reaction.

Exercise in Telephone Conversation

From **The House of Blue Leaves** by John Guare.
Copyright © 1971
Reprinted by permission of Viking Penguin, Inc.

Write out the speeches of the person on the other end of the telephone.

ARTIE: (*After dialing*) Operator, I want to call in Bel Air, Los Angeles—

BUNNY: (*Standing next to him*) You got the number?

ARTIE: Tattooed, baby. Tattooed. Your heart and his telephone number right on my chest like a sailor. Not you, operator. I want and fast I want in Los Angeles in Bel Air GR 2-4129 and I will not dial it because I want to speak personally to my good friend and genius, Mr. Billy Einhorn . . . E–I–N–don't yon know how to spell it? The name of only Hollywood's leading director my friend and you better not give this number to any of your friends and call him up and bother him asking for screen tests . . . my number is RA 1-2276 . . . and don't go giving that number away and I want a good connection . . . hang on, Bunny— (*She takes his extended hand*)—you can hear the beepbeepbeeps—we're traveling across the country—hang on! Ring. It's ringing. Ring.

BUNNY: (*His palm and her palm form one praying hand*) Oh God, please—

ARTIE: (*Pulling away from her*) Ring. It's up. Hello? Billy? Yes, operator, get off—that's Billy. Will you get off—(*to* BUNNY) I should've called station-to-station. He picked it right up and everything. Billy! This is Ramon Navarro! . . . No, Billy, it's Artie Shaughnessy. Artie. No, New York! Did I wake you up! Can you hear me! Billy, hello! I got to tell you something . . . I know you can fix up a tour of the studios and that'd be great . . . and you can get us hotel reservations . . . that's just fine . . . But, Billy, I'm thinking I got to get away . . . not just a vacation—but make a change, get a break, if you know what I'm getting at . . . Bananas is fine . . . She's right here.

PLANTING AN OBJECT   We have seen how the use of the dagger or gun must be covered, but in their *planting* they need not only be shown to the audience but shown in such a way that the attention of everybody in the audience will be held by them. Usually early in the scene the author will call attention to them in the lines of the play, and by this pointing the suspense values will be increased. The actor must, however, do his share of pointing. The lines tell us of an unusual Indian knife which is now used as a paper cutter. The actor must pick up this sharp and threatening object and examine it in such a way that the audience will see just how full of potential danger it is. The property must be opened up so that it registers with all.

Here is a story of a jewel robbery. Pearls or a necklace or rubies are to play an important part in what is to follow. Not burlesquing the action, the actor planting them should hold up the property, run his hand over it, and even admire it. It must be opened up and focused. The object becomes more important for the moment than does the actor. Innumerable examples might be cited, but the same principle of pointing up important story objects in emphatic business or pantomime is essential.

An actor may be called to light a lamp, turn on a switch for the side lights, close a window, pull down the shade, put another log on the fire, close a door, get a book and sit. These can be actions of no particular consequence to the story. They are just business; but if they are followed by a plot action such as the actor taking a paper from his pocket and putting it in the fire, this last bit becomes important to emphasize. The actor will open up and point up the paper as he takes it from his pocket before he throws it into the fire. As a matter of fact he can plant it earlier by taking the paper out of his pocket and returning it before he does any of the other business. Through proper handling he will gain suspense from the action that can hold through the sequence of business. If the first planting is pointed sufficiently, he need not point it so strongly immediately before he puts the paper in the fire.

Whenever an actor has definite business or pantomime to handle alone on stage and visual cueing is not possible, he should make a slight noise with the last part of his business so that it may serve as a cue for a speech offstage or for an entrance. This may be an accidental rattling of fire tongs or some business such as putting down a glass heavily, a slight cough, hitting a chair, or sitting down heavily.

The following is an exercise in which every move and each use of a property is of vital importance to the audience. Each action must be opened up and yet be blended into a natural relationship of the characters to the locale.

Exercise in Emphatic Business

From *Dial "M" for Murder* by Frederick Knott. Copyright 1953 by Frederick Knott. Reprinted by permission of Random House, Inc. Act II, Scene 1.

ACTION: Tony has set the trap for the murder of his wife, Margot, by an accomplice. The strategy is to leave her alone at home and to use his going out with Max as an alibi.

SETTING: *The living room of the Wendices' flat in London. At R are French windows with heavy full-length curtains. Fireplace at L. UL is a door leading to the bedroom, at the back is a small hall. R of hall is the entrance to the kitchen. Back center of the hall is the entrance door to the apartment.*

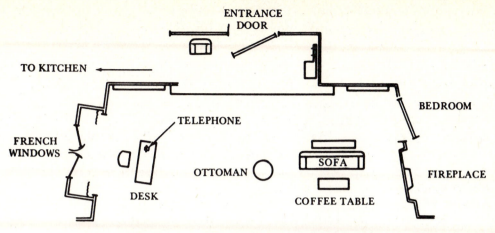

FIGURE 10 *Ground plan of* **Dial M for Murder**

EMPHATIC PROPERTIES: The latchkey and scissors are very important in the development of the plot.

TONY: [*To* MARGOT *as he moves to hall.*] By the way, darling, did I lend you my latchkey? I can't find it anywhere.

MARGOT: [*Getting up.*] I may have them both in my handbag. I'll just look. [MARGOT *exits to bedroom.* MAX *goes to hall to get his overcoat.* TONY *goes to French windows. He unlocks and opens a window and peers outside.*]

TONY: Raining pretty hard. I think I could lend you an old raincoat, if that's any good.

MAX: [*Taking down overcoat from rack.*] This will do. It isn't far, is it?

TONY: No—just around the corner. [TONY *glances around at* MAX *to see if he is looking but he is putting on his overcoat and has his back to* TONY. TONY *deliberately opens the door of the French windows a few inches, draws the curtains across the windows.* MARGOT *enters from the bedroom carrying a handbag. She opens it and takes out a zip purse. Out of this she takes a latchkey.*]

MARGOT: I've only got one here. Are you sure yours isn't in your overcoat?

TONY: Yes, I've looked there. Could you lend me yours?

MARGOT: [*Holding key in hand.*] Well, that's a bit awkward.

TONY: [*Turning to* MARGOT.] Why?

MARGOT: I may want to go out. [*Pause.*]

TONY: Tonight?

MARGOT: Yes. I thought I might go to a movie or something.

TONY: But—aren't you going to listen to the radio—"Saturday Night Theater"?

MARGOT: No, it's a thriller. I don't like thrillers when I'm alone.

TONY: [*Casually.*] I see. [*He goes and picks up raincoat on hall chair.*]

MARGOT: In any case I'll be back before you so I can let you it.

TONY: [*Putting on raincoat.*] We won't be back till after midnight. You may be asleep by them. [*He crosses to desk, taking gloves from raincoat pocket to put them on.*]

MAX: [*To* MARGOT.] You can always leave your key under the proverbial mat. [TONY *drops his key out of one of his gloves onto desk.*]

TONY: [*Picking it up.*] All right, chaps. Had it here in my glove all the time. [*Puts key back in raincoat pocket.*]

MARGOT: That settles that. [*She returns her key to her zip purse. She puts purse back in handbag, closes it and leaves it on oblong table behind sofa. NOTE: The back of the sofa must not obscure handbag from view.*]

TONY: What movie are you going to?

MARGOT: *The Classic,* I expect.

TONY: Will you get in? Saturday night.

MARGOT: I can always try. Now, don't make me stay in. You know how I hate doing nothing.

TONY: Nothing? But there're hundreds of things you can do. Have you written to Peggy about last week end? And what about these clippings? It's an ideal opportunity.

MARGOT: Well, I like that! You two go gallivanting while I have to stay in and do those boring clippings. [TONY *suddenly goes sullen.*]

TONY: Oh, very well then, we won't go. [*He moves L. above couch removing raincoat.*]

MARGOT: [*Astonished.*] What do you mean?

TONY: Well, it's quite obvious you don't want us to go out tonight—so we won't. We'll stay here with you. What shall we do—play cards? [*Puts raincoat on hall chair.*]

MARGOT: Now, Tony darling . . . [*She rises and goes to front of coffee table.*]

TONY: [*Going to phone.*] I'd better phone the Grendon and tell them we're not coming.

MARGOT: Tony, please. Don't let's be childish about this. I'll do your old press clippings.

TONY: [*Still sulking.*] You don't have to if you don't want to.

MARGOT: But I *do* want to. [MARGOT *picks up newspapers, press clippings and album from coffee table.*] Have we any paste?

TONY: There's some in the desk, I think.

MARGOT: Good. [*Takes album, newspapers and clippings to desk.*] And some scissors. In the mending basket. [TONY *goes to mending basket. He opens it, looks underneath a pair of* MARGOT's *stockings and takes out a long pair of scissors.* MARGOT, *taking out empty paste tube from desk drawer.*] Oh, look . . . the paste tube is empty. [*Exasperated.*] It would be. [TONY *stares at the empty paste tube which* MARGOT *is holding.*] Never mind. Mrs. Lucas is bound to have some.

TONY: Who's she?

MARGOT: She lives just across the road. I'll drop around later. [TONY *can't hide his annoyance.* MARGOT *reaches for scissors.*] Thank you, darling. [TONY *passes her scissors.*]

MAX: Why not make some? All you need is some flour and starch.

TONY: [*Pleased.*] Good idea. Do you know how to do it, Max?

MAX: [*Moving R. to kitchen.*] In two shakes. [MAX *exits to kitchen.*]

TONY: Good old Max! [*To* MARGOT.] I'm sorry, darling. Was I very unreasonable?

MARGOT: [*Moving to* TONY.] No, I don't mind. I tell you what . . . I'll paste these in tonight and you put up that extra shelf in the kitchen . . . as you promised.

TONY: First thing tomorrow. Promise. [*He kisses her.*]

MAX: [*Calling from kitchen.*] Where's the starch?

MARGOT: I'll show you. [MARGOT *exits to kitchen. We can hear them talking through the open door.* TONY *looks at oblong table behind sofa. He glances quickly toward kitchen and then picks up* MARGOT's *handbag and opens it. He takes out purse, zips it open and takes out key and puts it on table. He then zips the purse shut, returns it to handbag and closes bag, leaving it in exactly the same position as before. He picks up key and goes and opens hall door, leaving it wide open. He then looks along passage and to the landing above, then he lifts the stair carpet and places the key underneath. As he does this* MARGOT *gives a little peal of laughter from the kitchen.* TONY *turns backs, a little startled, as he strolls back into the room.* MARGOT *enters from the kitchen with a cup and spoon.* MAX *follows her. As she is entering:*] It looks like vichysoisse without the chives.

MAX: If it starts to get thick, add a little water—and keep stirring. [MARGOT *puts down cup on desk and starts to arrange the newspapers and clippings.* TONY *and* MAX *stand in hall.*]

TONY: Keep the fire in for us, darling. [*He gets raincoat from hall chair.*]

MARGOT: I will.

TONY: Oh, and it's just possible old man Burgess will phone tonight. If he does, tell him I'm at the Grendon. It may be rather important.

MARGOT: What's the number?

TONY: It's in the book.

MARGOT: All right. Well, look after each other.

MAX: We will. Good night, Margot.

MARGOT: 'Night, Max. [*To* TONY.] You'll run Max home in the car afterwards, won't you, darling?

TONY: Of course. We'll drop in here first for a nightcap. Sure you won't be up?

MARGOT: I shall be fast asleep. And I don't want to be disturbed.

TONY: Then we'll be as quiet as mice. [TONY *kisses* MARGOT.] Good night, darling.

MARGOT: Good night.

TONY: Come on, Max. [*They exit through hall door, closing it.* MARGOT *switches on lamp, turns on radio. Then she turns off chandelier and bracket. She turns to her work at desk. She looks resigned to it. She unfolds a piece of newspaper, picks up scissors, starts cutting. Music swells to:*]

Curtain

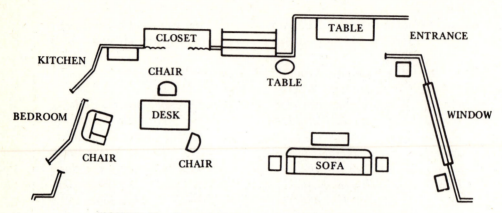

FIGURE 11 *Ground plan for exercise in stage technique*

Exercise in Elementary Stage Technique

Using Figure 11 ground plan, two students plan and rehearse a three-minute pantomime employing all the basic techniques outlined in this chapter. A telephone is on the desk. Use essential hand properties.

5
Body, Voice, and Role

With this understanding of the actor's technique of handling himself in relation to the audience and to the other actors, we now begin a wholly new attack: the actor in relation to himself—his body, his voice, his role—free from any stage technique.

The purpose of this material is to furnish the director with the tools by which he may work with the actors toward the proper results, not through imitation or coercion but through explanation and imaginative suggestion. Though the emphasis is on technical training and techniques, the director and actor must continually keep in mind that the actor creates not by technique or line memorization, but by imagination. However, in order for the imagination to be effective, the use of the voice and body, the projection of emotions, and the insight into text interpretation must be trained and developed. It is through actions, gestures, voice, and speech that an actor awakens associations in the audience—consciously or subconsciously.

In discussing body and voice only the most salient principles will be touched upon. Those chosen are the ones that are most likely to arise during rehearsals. As we mentioned earlier, the exercises that this chapter reccomends are meant not to train and develop an actor but to keep the beginner practicing as the singer would practice musical scales between public appearances. The exercises first should be practiced under proper guidance to make sure that beginners approach them correctly. The director should remind the beginning actor that training exercises and sessions evaluating one's voice, taped or live, for articulation, resonance, pitch, emphasis, and so on, belong in the practice room and not on stage when performing. These exercises will also furnish a step-by-step outline on which the teacher can elaborate with his own lectures and demonstrations. These sections have been handled at such great lengths by whole volumes that to proceed with more detail would be to repeat what has been already ably accomplished.

Principles of Direction for the Actor

For the actor working with a director who leaves it to him to feel the movement and business, it is necessary to learn certain principles of directing. The material in this book, written from a director's point of view, thus becomes invaluable information for his use. Many an actor has admitted that this is the very thing he does—supply his own movement and business —when he is left alone by the director. Such an actor viewing the scene like a director adds treatment upon treatment, and enriches and develops his character in the course of rehearsals. The actual director out front may believe the part is being played solely as the natural expression of the actor grasping the characterization. The fact is that the experienced actor does know a great deal about directing, especially the purely technical side. If he is unable to grasp more, it is solely because of the difficulty in contributing part of the whole and grasping the whole at the same time. In instances when the director is also the actor, a stand-in often is used for technical reasons.

Whether the actor is working with a director who believes that directing a play consists solely in letting each actor act to his heart's content, and the actor accordingly has to direct himself, or with one who believes in contributing to the play and its expression by his ability to dramatize the inherent characteristics, mood, and meaning—the actor who understands the simple fundamental principles and theories of directing will achieve an infinitely better coordination between himself and the director. If, after the director has asked him to make an arbitrary movement without explaining technical, business, or character motivations, the actor anticipates the reason for such a movement, unquestionably this actor is bound to be in closer accord with the director. Many times, after a piece of direction, a good actor will grasp the reason for the direction even before the director has a chance to give the first few words of explanation. This is the type of actor with whom a director most enjoys working. Every beginning actor should try to grasp direction quickly, and the way to achieve that faculty is to understand some of the simple elements of directing.

Subjective and Objective Acting

Objective Creation of Character

There was a time when the way to express the different emotions was catalogued. The face and voice took on stereotyped expressions and tones which were learned by imitating a teacher or coach. Actors handed such traditions on to actors, and teachers handed them on through books for generations. The neophyte studied emotional expressions before a mirror with emphasis on nonverbal actions—he would watch himself imitate the manners, the gestures, and the movements of a character. He studied the character from the outside and even listened to himself playing the role.

This approach to the reproduction of a character became known as the objective method. In it the actor is outside himself, looking at himself as an object of speculation and analysis. The external approach to creating convincing emotions has had many advocates, with Delsarte as one of its principle exponents and teachers. The approach is directly opposite to the subjective method. The following exercises offer two simple demonstrations of the objective approach:

1. Extend your arms upward as if in prayer. Give yourself fully to the moment, concentrating on the action. Extend your arms more intently as you think, and then utter to yourself, "Please, please!" Ultimately, the true feeling of pleading will result.

2. Clench your fists tightly, and with unrelieved intensity and concentration, pound the table with your fists. Continue pounding as you first think and then utter, "No, no, no!" Depending on your imagination, the resultant emotion may be self-condemnation, disbelief, desperation, or angry negation.

This consciousness of manner of body and quality of voice presents a psychological obstacle for many actors. To get within the character and to convey to the audience that sense of reality, of depth, and even of sensitivity essential in honest characterization requires for them a more subjective approach. The objective method of creating character has produced great actors who sounded the depth of human nature, but it is considered detrimental by many practitioners in the contemporary climate of theatre. For this reason the exercises to follow will be based on the subjective approach to character. However, we should not dismiss completely the objective creation of character. It has gained strong support from advocates of the Artaudian Theatre, where the authenticity of the actor's personal feelings (subjective creation) is replaced by the discipline of shaping feelings into projected communicative language.

Basis of Subjective Creation of Character

The subjective method of re-creating a character from life consists first in getting the body and voice in a thoroughly relaxed condition. Neither body nor voice must feel restricted or be inhibited, awkward, tense, or stiff. The actor should not be mentally conscious of either. When these external obstacles have been eliminated and the full freedom of the body and voice from muscular strain has been achieved, the mind is then in a condition to create an image. This image, however, is not to be of a physical event but instead must be a stirring up of former emotional states that the actor has experienced or imagined. This internal feeling will grow slowly until it expresses itself through the body, taking form in body mimicry, expression, and gesture. The voice, too, as the mouth shapes the words, will bring out the inner emotional feeling in a concrete expression. With this external manifestation of an inner feeling we have the basis for the subjective creation of characterization and emotional states. The energy from inner feeling will work on the deeply ingrained lines of memory, and as a result of this a natural spontaneous reading will pour out through the actor's vocal equipment. This attack, remember, is only the beginning; there is much more to be done to carry the inner feeling and imagery to full expression.

Subjective Creation and Stage Technique

Before proceeding further with the subjective method of creation, let us pause to consider and understand the relation of pure creative imagery to the abundance of technical considerations that we have minutely detailed in the preceding chapter. For the moment let us disregard the voice and concentrate solely on movements of the body.

Let us suppose that emotional energy seeking expression through the body gives the body an impulse to move, to run hastily toward a door and rush out of the room. It is easy for us to understand how such an outward expression could occur in violent action. Performed in the actor's own sitting room, this outward expression would present no particular problem; it would be the natural emotional outlet. But now let us transfer the sitting room to the stage. Let us suppose that the actor is to run the width of the room and exit out of a door down right or, better still, to run across the room and exit out of a door upstage center that has to be opened and closed. When to this movement must be added very important lines for the full outward expression of an emotional state, the problem becomes much more complicated. The actor must make a curved approach so as to arrive upstage in an open position; he must open and close the door, and so on. Clearly, the problem becomes one of letting the inner re-creation of an emotional state give expression to an outward movement that, controlled under stage conditions, must be made with technical consideration, restriction, or modification. It is largely for this reason that the need for mastering stage technique becomes paramount. These technicalities must become so much a part of the unconscious motor reactions that, when an impulse from emotion comes, the body will naturally and without thought or consciousness react in technical form.

Let us consider another simple adjustment of inner impulse to technical control. We have already mentioned that when an actor sobs on his arm he must leave the space in front of the mouth open so that the audience can hear what is said. The natural physical movement of this action is to throw the arm on the table with the head face down on it.

Demonstration

Have the actor do the natural physical movement of sobbing on his arm several times. His arm will probably come across his eyes, covering his nose and most of his mouth. The table will be in front of whatever part of the mouth is not covered by the arm.

This movement will be completely without technical control and unsuited to any consideration of a group of people interested in what he is saying. Now have the actor perform this movement with technical control so that the space in front of the mouth remains open.

Demonstration

Have the actor arbitrarily and with no emotional feeling put his arm on the edge of the table. Have him throw his head down so that the forehead and not the nose rests on the arm. Have him do this several times until he performs the action without any thought of his motor physical reaction.

The movement is now under mechanical control and takes into consideration the group of listeners. Moreover, this second way of performing the movement is neither false nor insincere. If possible, the actor, having mastered the technical form, may now awaken his emotional impulse and without thought of technique, stage, or audience express his inner emotional state. This simple demonstration tells the complete story of the relationship of emotional expression to technical control. This is why the actor must study and master technique first so as to ingrain it into his system as a part of his natural body reaction. Following this technical mastery he may work freely on the development of inner emotional states and their outward expression.

So far we have dealt only with the body and have not touched upon the voice in relation to this theory. We shall come to it later. For the time being we shall consider the necessary physical conditions of getting the body ready for the outward expression of the emotional creation.

Bodily Responsiveness

Before the body or voice is able to express subjectively the concepts of the character and its emotional state, it must be freed from muscular strain and tightness which restrict, inhibit, and fetter the person not only on the stage but in everyday life. Mental self-consciousness can often be broken down by physical exertion. The more the actor is mentally tied up the greater the physical action required to achieve flexibility and mobility of action.

The exercises in Appendix B are only a few of many that a director will find invaluable for actors as practice work in relaxing the body. Those given are sufficient for the usual requirements that a director expects of an actor, since they cover not only the separate parts of the body but the whole of the body itself. The conscious actor should never cease to practice these exercises for the continued maintenance of a relaxed and responsive condition of body and voice.

Vocal Responsiveness

In the study of elementary stage technique for the actor we have seen that it must be learned so thoroughly that the actor's movements onstage may be accomplished with little or no thought. Then we have seen how the body must be made to relax so that it is in a free and unrestricted condition to express the creative concept of character and emotion. Now we come to a study of the voice for its use onstage.

In real life ordinary speech is for the most part monotonous, unemotional, and weak. Words are usually poorly enunciated and often made irrelevant. Little regard is given to color, variety, emphasis, or unity of vocal melody. Few people with the exception of speech connoisseurs notice these deficiencies in everyday life. But put the naturally distorted yet passable voice onstage, and many of the defects immediately become apparent to the layman. The magnifying qualities of the stage on voice are the same as on movement; getting up out of a chair in real life is generally done in an awkward, clumsy way, but onstage this bit of business must be done inconspicuously with ease and grace.

Hence, the voice must be handled so that it will be pleasing, flexible, colorful, strong, varied, and impressive. Words and sentences must be spoken in a clear, articulate, and harmonious manner. Phrasing with use of emphasis must be liquid and expressive. Developing the voice is a matter of technique; the vocal organ, like the body, must be trained so that its qualities will not only arrest the attention of an audience but convey with ease the thoughts, the imagery, and the inner emotions that call for expression.

As with the body, the voice must be trained so that the actor will use it correctly without self-consciousness. The actor who is consciously aware of his voice restricts it from being the free organ and faithful conveyor that it must be to express the inner emotions and ideas. Continual work through exercises is essential to prepare the voice for technical proficiency and to make it relaxed, receptive, and flexible. Only when this is done will the director have actors with voices prepared to respond to and convey the subtleties of inner feeling.

Again as in body training, with the many excellent texts written on voice and voice training, it is not our intention to enter into a treatise on the subject. The director, however, will find that the exercises in Appendix B cover the requisites for a well-trained voice that he should expect to find or to develop in his actors.

Breathing

Most faults of the speaking voice are due to poor or incorrect breathing. People who breathe incorrectly are not able to get enough air into the lungs. They have little control or the wrong control in letting this air out as they speak. They spend too much breath on the first part of a sentence and have only a little or a forced breath left to complete the important part of the sentence. If they do attempt to hold sufficient breath, they tighten the vocal cords and become tense in the throat so that they hinder rather than help speech. Once a person has achieved correct breathing, many of the other voice difficulties will take care of themselves. Accordingly, we shall discuss first what constitutes correct breathing and, second, what exercises will help develop it.

Proper breathing demands the correct use of the diaphragm, lungs, and intercostal muscles. Most people breathe with only the upper part of the lungs instead of using the diaphragm and the full lung capacity. The diaphragm is a muscle that forms the floor of the chest cavity. Upon its control through the correct use of the abdominal muscles depends the control of the voice. In inhalation the diaphragm straightens out, allowing the lungs to expand and fill with air. In exhalation the reverse takes place. We exhale as we speak. To control the breath in speaking is therefore a matter of controlling the contraction of the diaphragm so that breath is forced out of the chest cavity in a smooth, steady stream. The exercises in Appendix B help the actor strengthen the diaphragm and train him to use this part of the body properly in speaking.

Voice Quality

The correction of a second common fault of the inexperienced actor lies in the development of good voice quality. Too many beginning actors have harsh, high-pitched, nasal, and generally unpleasant voices. A student who is taking his acting work seriously will try to develop a pleasing and appealing voice. There is no better way of gaining the immediate attention of an audience than through the beautiful sound of a musical voice. This has become particularly apparent in watching and listening to television, the movies, and sound recordings; the greater appeal to the audience of one actor over another rests not only on how he looks but more and more on how he sounds, on the appreciation of the beauty of his voice. Furthermore, this growing awareness of voice quality is producing a stricter critical interest in these qualities among viewers and listeners.

Before working directly on voice quality, it is necessary to perform certain exercises to get the throat in a thoroughly relaxed condition. Relaxation is as fundamental for the voice as it is for the body. (See Appendix B for exercises.)

Resonance

After the throat is thoroughly relaxed and open, we should begin to work for the first element of voice quality—resonance. By resonance is meant the element that gives overtone, vibrancy, and brilliance to tone. Resonance brings out the most appealing quality of the voice; it is the element most responsible for stimulating emotional contact with an audience. Accordingly, we should work to develop this quality of resonance in the speaking voice. Experiments have shown that the chest, the back and upper part of the roof of the mouth, the nose, and that part of forehead just above the nose will act very much as a sounding board in a piano. If you strike a note on a keyboard and listen to it acutely, you will hear the aftertone or overtone of the note resounding. This is the beauty of the tone. Our task is to utilize these sounding boards.

Without entering into the actual physiological structure that accounts for quality, we shall explain one practical and psychological way to obtain resonant tone.

Say the word "one" as you probably would naturally, with the sound coming through the mouth without striking the sounding board. Then with a conscious effort throw the sound against the back part of the roof of the mouth, being particular to hold the *n* sound. You will notice its resounding quality. Alternate the two ways of saying "one"—first without this resonance and then with—until you are perfectly certain that you understand what the quality of resonance is and how it is gained. Notice how as you increase the intensity of the *n* sound the passages of the nose tend to quiver. The emphasis on *m* or *n* sounds is excellent for improved nasal resonance. (See Appendix B for other exercises.)

Pitch

The second element in voice quality is pitch. We all know that in the several musical scales there are a great number of notes. The human voice encompasses many more speaking tones in its range than can be charted musically, since it is able to sound the many gradations between the notes of the musical scales. The actor's pitch is his tone place on the musical scale; his range is the distance between and number of different pitches on the musical scale that he is capable of using. This variation in pitch is generally known as intonation, or inflection, of the voice.

We must consequently develop a flexible range of pitch and learn which notes we should use in the various demands of acting. It is generally agreed that the tones of the middle register are the most pleasing for the natural voice on the stage, leaving higher and lower tones, or pitches, for expressing the different emotional states. Normally, the higher pitches are for exasperation, terror, fear, hysteria, nervousness, and other phases of nervous emotion, the lower pitches for the deeper states of emotion, such as love, grief, deep sincerity or religious expression. Accordingly, it is very necessary for the actor who must be able to convey a great variety of emotional states to have a wide range of pitch. (See Appendix B for exercises.)

Enunciation

The next main common faults of the inexperienced actor are poor enunciation and pronunciation. In everyday life poor diction is a frequent and generally accepted fault, but onstage it becomes a serious failing. The audience cannot understand the actor with poor enunciation. The magnifying power of the stage makes the natural faults of both pronunciation and enunciation stand out clearly and obviously.

Good diction depends upon the clear and correct sounding of the vowels and diphthongs (pronunciation) and the distinct articulation of the consonants (enunciation), especially those at the beginning and end of a word.

Since the voice depends a great deal on vowels for its beauty, expression, and carrying power, particular attention should be given to the pitch, emphasis, and duration of vowels. Too long a hold on vowels will make the voice monotonous and drawling. If the vowels are slurred, the speech will not be clear. Vowels, therefore, should be pronounced smoothly and easily.

In everyday speech, the final consonants are apt to be neglected and slurred; and whereas one may not be caught slighting them in ordinary speech, when an actor is onstage his neglect of these final letters is apparent even to an undiscriminating audience. The final *ed, t, th, ing, d, f,* and *v* are the letters most likely to be slurred. *Wh* at the beginning of a word is apt to have the *h* eliminated in careless speech. *D, k,* and *g* are difficult almost anywhere in a speech and need special attention; and the letter *r* presents a problem all its own. Standard stage diction requires that this consonant remain unpronounced and unsounded except when preceding or between vowel sounds.

Great care has to be taken not to make the words of a speech sound like the words in a column of a spelling book. They must not have equal emphasis or stress. The meaning of lines must never suffer because of over-distinctness. Lines may be spoken with the greatest clarity and still have the inflection, variety, and proper stress to carry the full meaning of each line. The chief reason that overcarefully enunciated sentences become so artificial is not because of enunciation but because of the emphasis, or stress, on each word; the lack of phrasing in the sentence; and the lack of properly proportioned stress to bring out the important word, usually the final ones in a dramatic sentence.

Faulty enunciation results from incorrect or careless lip and tongue movement and from a tight jaw, mostly due to laziness in the use of lips and jaw. Faulty enunciation can also result from tension. (See Appendix B for exercises.)

Projection

Projection, or carrying power, is the ability to convey the spoken words a distance. As children, when we make ourselves heard by a playmate farther up the hill, we yell. Now, yelling is opening the mouth wide, retracting the tongue, tightening the throat muscles, and forcing the tones. It results in what is called a diffuse, or undirected, nonfocused tone. This is nearly always accompanied by a high and shrill pitch. Obviously, when we are acting before an audience, we cannot yell. Not only is it unpleasant, but it is also unintelligible.

In order to be heard when playing in a large auditorium, an actor is presented with a problem. He cannot yell. He cannot take a high pitch with the ordinary voice. (Unfortunately, he often does both.) What he should do is to *project.*

Esthetically, proper projection is an energizing process that brings theatrical life to an actor. Technically, projection involves support of tone both by diaphragm and by voice placement. For good tone support the actor must have excellent breath control, for only with the ability to take deep breaths correctly and to let the breath out with great conservation can he project successfully. He should practice humming and other resonance exercises. The actor whose tone is well placed and well supported is sure of reaching his audience. A third factor in the process is careful enunciation. The actor's lips and tongue must be trained to execute his speeches with freedom, flexibility, and force.

We shall see shortly the need for the actor to express with the voice different emotional states; but first we must stress the point that only through projection is he able to convey emotions to the audience. He cannot express emotional states by shouting.

When projection has been developed so that it becomes a natural part of both stage and ordinary speech, the audience will be able to hear and understand what is said, whether the actor faces the audience or the rear of the stage. Projection cannot have too much practice. (See Appendix B for exercises.)

Emotional Responsiveness

Sincerity, depth, and conviction of feeling as expressed through the voice are conveyed to an audience only when that feeling comes from an internal energy in the body. Otherwise the emotional expression of the voice sounds hollow, false, and forced. This type of dramatic reading is frequently heard and easily detected over the radio. The romantic, heroic tones in many a broadcast of the romantic operetta, as well as the portrayal of character parts and emotional states in "dramatic sketches," are empty, insincere, and unconvincing—often they are embarrassing. This is because the readers are acting from the neck up. There is no body feeling, no inner creation. Certain conventionalized tones and mannerisms of voice are arbitrarily used. It is voice for voice's sake, tone for tone's sake. There is an objectivity in voice use that warrants comparison with the study of body expression before a mirror. The voice stands without support, and the emotional expression exists disassociated from body.

Many people have a capacity for strong emotional feeling but are neither able to express this with the body because of physical inhibition nor with the voice because of vocal inhibition. We have seen that when an actor feels emotions but is unable to express or project them, the best correction for the situation is exercises for body relaxation. The same holds true for the voice; exercises for vocal relaxation will develop the ability to express emotions through the voice. The throat and vocal cords need to be in such a physical condition that the voice will express the entire gamut of emotions. For visual and auditory expression, both body and voice must have freedom, elasticity, and a sense of natural rhythm.

This ability to express emotion through the body and voice is called responsiveness. It consists of getting the body into a relaxed condition and then feeling emotion and allowing it to pass through the relaxed and passively receptive vocal cords. It is absolutely essential for the expression of real emotion in the voice that the inner body receive the emotion first, then the external body, and finally the voice. This procedure for preparing the voice to express the emotions of the internally created image is closely similar to that of preparing the body.

In executing the exercises in Appendix B it should be constantly borne in mind that the body must first be in a relaxed condition. It is probably wisest to review many of the body-relaxation exercises before doing each of the exercises in emotional responsiveness, although the student may find that as he becomes more proficient and experienced he can get the body into the proper receptive condition by mere conscious relaxation without actual body exercises. Emotional responsiveness to these exercises is dependent, of course, on the degree of your concentration and extent of your imagination.

Variety in Speech

If the exercises have been done correctly and the student stops to recall how his voice sounded, he will notice that he has utilized a large and contrasting range in his vocal expression. This brings us to the element of variety in stage speech.

Variety is one of the primary factors to consider in the theatre. Just as it is important in all phases of production and directing, it is equally so in the use of the voice by each member in the cast.

One of the greatest faults in the speech of real life and with the voice of the inexperienced actor is monotony. Words are spoken in one continuous straight line of pitch and emphasis, the same degree of loudness or softness, the same pattern of melody. Imagine a violinist just playing one note on the middle register.

Monotony is due primarily to the lack of emotional feeling on the actor's part. Perhaps the greatest aid in gaining variety is the approach through responsiveness. Later we have an analysis of the technical considerations, but far more important than these are the contrasts that are arrived at through the minute shadings of the emotional states inherent in dramatic speeches. When each sentence in a speech is given the correct expression, variety is bound to result. This is variety of emphasis. Another element, which we have already touched on, may at first seem a different point, but basically it ties up with responsiveness in its contribution to variety. That is pitch. When the student actor has succeeded in training his emotional feelings and when he has learned to express them through a relaxed body and voice, he will of his own accord arrive at different pitches for the different emotional states.

In addition to variety of emphasis and pitch, we have:
1. Variety of tempo of speech in delivering lines.
2. Volume or intensity of projection.
3. Tone: quality of voice including resonance and placement.

Body and Voice in Subjective Acting

Now that we have worked to get the voice in a neutral, relaxed, and responsive condition, let us work on an exercise in subjective acting whereby we may achieve true emotional expression in body and voice. The exercise should not be studied or thought out. The actors should not have an opportunity to read it until they are onstage. This is how the exercise should be performed: two actors read through onstage in the relaxed and responsive state for which we have been working. By repeatedly reading and acting it out on the stage, without a single instruction from the director-teacher as to positions, gestures, reactions of body, variety, build, or emotional expression with the voice or body movement, they should see how highly developed they can become in these respects, merely through repetition of the scene.

In doing this scene, as in all scenes onstage, the actor should make full use of his imagination; he should concentrate on the actor playing opposite him so that, unmindful of the audience around, he will focus on the scene rather than expend his energy elsewhere. There should be a strong sense of communication between the two actors in order that the action of one will find reaction in the other. This last comes not only from listening to what the other actor has to say but from observing his manner of saying it as well.

Host *A* is approached by guest *B*

A. How do you do?
B. How—What are you looking at?
A. How do you do?
B. Are you looking that way at me?
A. I'm really very glad to see you.
B. I know you are looking at my nose.
A. Won't you sit down over here?
B. Don't look at my nose.
A. This seat is very comfortable.

B. I hate you when you look at my nose.

A. Come.

B. I hate all the world. They look at my nose. It drives me mad.

A. You are my husband's sister. I am very fond of you.

B. No, you're not. You are laughing at my nose. You're not fond . . . and I hate you. Good-by.

Theatre games, designed to develop communication and spontaneity, are basically an extension of this exercise in improvisation. They encourage the actor to make immediate and motivated responses through close observation of his fellow actor's feelings, movements, changes in attitudes, and circumstances.

The Study of the Role

Assimilation and Visualization

You have seen by the preceding exercise how, if your body and voice are in a relaxed and responsive condition, by reading a part over and over again a definite feeling for the character seeps into your whole nature. You have seen how, in responsiveness, you have let an emotional feeling work into your system and have found for this feeling its natural expression in body and voice.

Assimilation of a part is very similar to this except that, instead of having merely one emotional feeling to contain, we now have, for the first time, a whole series of traits and emotions that constitute the character. Assimilation is the response to a character as you read the lines in the play over and over. You accomplish this along similar lines as your exercises in responsiveness. If you feel and think the lines, then your assimilation will give vent to expression in the body and voice. One needs to read and reread his part. Furthermore, he needs to give vent to this character in body and in vocal expression. In learning his part, the actor needs to yield himself to it through business, movement, and the character's natural expression in language, even though they may be irrelevant to the immediate action of the play. These applications help the actor to assimilate the feeling of the part.

As soon as you have assimilated a part that you are to play, you should work with imagination to visualize that character as a person—what his face looks like, what sort of hair he has, how he holds his shoulders, how he walks, how he sits. You can go even further and imagine the sort of things he eats for breakfast, for dinner; you should know what he considers a good time, how he spends his spare time, how he makes his living, what kind of people he knows and comes in contact with, what he thinks about them and about life in general. Does he know what is going on in the world or just in his town or merely in his own neighborhood? Often it is possible to think of somebody within your own experience who is like the character. Often you will see him in public places. The main point is either to draw the complete figure vividly from your recollections or to search about you for people that look, think, and act like that man. Along with this process of visualization you should consider the reasons for all the characteristics that you find in this character. Why does he walk as he does? What is there in his experience that makes him think, look, and act as he does? How did he choose his means of livelihood? Did he choose it, or was he forced into it? The answers will aid the actor in understanding his character thoroughly.

Demonstration

1. In assimilation (subjective approach):
   (*a*) A blind man walking along the street with no help.
   (*b*) A movie star getting off a plane.
   (*c*) A lame man running to catch a bus.
   (*d*) An old man putting a log on a fire.
   (*e*) A child in the zoo or at a circus.
2. In visualization:
   (*a*) Select a character from a play with which you are familiar. Do not imitate or pantomime him, but describe him fully, and tell much about him that is not told in the play according to the enumeration given under Visualization.
3. In assimilation and visualization:
   (*a*) Show the reactions of a character at the following ages to the dropping and breaking of a glass of water: seven, fourteen, seventeen, twenty-one, thirty, forty, seventy.
   (*b*) Have the girls in the class be introduced to a boy, and show their reactions at the ages of twelve, seventeen, thirty, sixty, and eighty; repeat, with the boy introduced to a girl.
   (*c*) Show the expression and reactions of a character, which you should first describe fully, in a trial when he has been convicted. Then show him when he has been freed.
   (*d*) Take a character from a play, and act out his reactions to a situation in the play. Then take the same character, and confront him with a situation that is not in the play.
   (*e*) Take the exercises under emotional responsiveness, and do them at different ages of your choosing.

Observation

Let us now consider a problem in characterization where part of building the character must come from observation rather than visualization; from this we shall learn how we make the study of physical traits a part of the subjective characterization. Certain traits are characteristic of age, old or otherwise; others are characteristic of nationalities such as Italian, Scotch, Irish, and French. All these have physical and vocal mannerisms that are outside the possible visualization (or normal response) of anybody who has not been closely associated with these types or observed them closely. The actor who is to play such a character part must find a similar person in real life and carefully watch his physical and vocal actions. After observation, he must imitate from an external point of view the body and vocal mannerisms.

In order to adjust this observation to the subjective method, it is absolutely necessary for the body and vocal observations to be practiced until they become part of the unconscious physical expression and coordination of the character. Then, and only then, when the body posture and the vocal idiosyncrasies have been mastered so that the actor need have no conscious consideration of them, will it be possible to approach such a part from the subjective point of view. Only then is the actor ready to forget the observational study and revert to his subjective expression of the visualization of the character. He is ready to throw himself into the emotional and mood states of the character and continue with his vivid expression of them. He has adjusted himself so that his bodily and vocal responses to a subjective interpretation will include the idiosyncrasies and mannerisms of the character.

Pantomimes from Observation

1. A successful businessman.
2. A lady traveler in a hotel lobby.
3. A conservative preacher.
4. The entrance, ordering, eating, paying, leaving, and so on of a person you have seen at a lunch counter.
5. Examples a–e under Demonstrations in assimilation.

The Technical Study of a Part

SUGGESTIONS FOR MEMORIZING   A good way to memorize a part is to take it scene by scene, a scene for purposes of this study constituting the period from a time at which the character enters until the time he leaves. The actor should analyze accurately the definite points of thought development and know what facts he is bringing out to the audience and to what point he arrives in the development of the play.

Secondly, he should read the complete scene aloud three or four times, other people's speeches as well as his own, being certain that he knows the continuity of the scene. Next, he should read his own speeches over many times. Then he should take the cue of each of his speeches and say over the cue and the speech as one continuous unit. He should continue this last process until his lines are learned. The way to have someone hear his lines is to have that person read him the cues that come before his speeches and check him on his lines. An equally good way is to write the cues in succession on cards and then read the cues to himself, saying the speeches that follow, being careful not to add a "well," a "but," an "oh," or an "uh," to the beginning of each speech.

EMPHASIS IN THE SENTENCE   The important words of a dramatic sentence, it should be recalled, come at the end, and the important parts of a well-written speech are its closing phrases. Accordingly, this is the time for an actor to practice his breath control and apply it to his speeches. He will then have sufficient breath to last during the entire sentence so that he can lift the final words of the sentence with greater clarity and volume.

He should, furthermore, determine what words earlier in each sentence need to be stressed in order that the entire sentence may be clear. Usually the important words are one or two at the beginning, the verb, and the final words. Let us take for example:

1. "You mean <u>you</u> want to <u>discuss</u> it <u>without</u> me <u>here</u>?" The underlined words are sufficient to convey the idea to the audience.

2. "I should even go further and say that <u>any</u> man who is <u>loved</u> by her is an extremely <u>lucky</u> fellow."

INTERRUPTED SENTENCE   Whenever a line in a play is incomplete in its statement of thought, it is known as an interrupted sentence. The actor needs to handle this with great care in two respects. First, he must always continue in his own mind the thought of the interrupted sentence and supply one or two of his own words, so that there is a moment when both characters are speaking—the person interrupted and the person interrupting. The second point which is extremely important is that the interrupted sentence must be built up, in pitch, tone, volume, or some other way that will make it stronger at the end than at the beginning. The usual tendency is to reverse this process.

THINKING OUT LOUD   In thinking out loud, as when enumerating a list of things, the working of the character's mind must be made apparent during the thought pause; illustrative movement used; and the situation made as real, vital, and interesting as possible.

SEEING OR HEARING SOMETHING FOR THE FIRST TIME   On seeing or hearing something for the first time, the character must take care to express the quality of unexpectedness and surprise. He must not anticipate the unexpected sound or sight but must "build" the movement or speech preceding the break and stop suddenly. At the moment the actor sees or hears the thing he must not be too quick in locating it. Then comes the bodily reaction to it. and after that the speech. In seeing something unexpectedly, like a letter on a table or a jewel on the floor, the actor in passing usually crosses slightly beyond the object and then steps back or turns to pick it up. This is true to real life. The mind and body are usually so intent on an objective that there is momentum enough to continue after the sight of an interrupting object registers in the mind. The body is stopped only after it has passed the interrupting object. When a noise is heard, the movement of the head accompanies the hearing; the eye then moves in the direction of the sound; the head and body turn toward it; and finally the character may walk in that direction to investigate.

LAUGHING, CRYING, OR OTHER EMOTIONAL OUTBURSTS   When laughing, crying, or other emotional outbursts are accompanied by lines, the purely technical principle to keep in mind is that of separating the laughing or crying from the lines so that the line values are preserved. The outbursts should be executed between the lines and on lines that are obviously not important. The order should be line, line, sob, line, sob, line, sob, sob.

CALLING A PERSON WHO IS NOT ONSTAGE   In calling a person who is not onstage an actor (as he enters) must not sweep the stage with his eyes and then call a person who is obviously not there, but his call must be the culmination of a preceding speech or movement. Often he can call before he gets onstage and stop abruptly in repeating the call as soon as he gets there and sees that the person is not present.

CHARACTER PROPS   The actor must choose his character props with deliberation and plan minutely his use of them. Too often the consideration of hand props is neglected, and seldom are any used that are not specifically called for by the script. They are often helpful in establishing character and in playing certain scenes. A man may use a cane, an umbrella, a brief case, glasses, or gloves to good advantage in enriching his characterization. A woman may use jewelry, sewing, a scarf, as well as many other period articles such as handkerchiefs, a parasol, a fan, a lorgnette. The choice of these is determined by the characterization, but the use has to be determined by the actor. First, he must have variety in handling them. He must not use them all the time. He had best not use any one for more than one act. Each one of these has many uses. Take the cane, for instance: The actor may lean on it to one side or behind him; he may merely hold it in his hand; he may point with it, slam it, or hold it behind him; he may hold an end in each of his hands, in front of him or behind him; or he may go through the process of laying it down on a table with his hat and picking it up. There are still other uses. A prop should be used for enrichment of character and should never become a hindrance. Such props can frequently be used for pointing comedy or for emphasis on plot or idea lines.

Variety

We have seen that if the actor has his body and vocal responsiveness well developed, a great deal of variety will naturally result. He needs, however, to study his speeches further to see whether or not his natural responsiveness has taken care of all the necessary variety. Whether the speech is short or long, variety in delivery must be considered. Even if the speech is so short that it contains only two words such as "Stop, stop!" we have to get variety in the reading of those two words. They cannot be said in exactly the same way. (Incidentally, this applies to any repetition, especially when it is in succession.) If one enlarges this "Stop, stop!" to "Where am I to go? Oh, where am I to go?" we have again to consider the problem of variety. In both these cases the first one may be louder and stronger than the second, or the second may be louder and stronger than the first.

When a speech is a long one, we can begin the first sentence low and the second one a little bit higher, and so on until we come to the last sentence in our highest pitch, fullest tone, and greatest volume. Or we may begin a speech with the first sentence pitched high and then drop the second and begin to build. If the speech will allow for it in its content, we can begin high, drop it, build, drop it, and then go even higher. In any speech of emotion there must be this element of variety in the delivery of the different lines, developed out of indications in the text.

The method of attaining variety selected for a speech must correspond to the inherent build of the speech itself. This contrast is easier in emotional passages. In narrational ones it is much more difficult but none the less imperative. Often the actor in narration and description after exhausting the possibilities in the text may have to superimpose variety upon the different sentences in order to make them contrasting and varied. Whenever there is a series of words, phrases, or clauses, the variety should usually include a build; that is, each should be greater than the one before in tone, volume, or intensity.

Exercise in Variety

In the following excerpt from Molière's *The Affected Young Ladies* experiment with the suggestions above for variety in delivery, particularly with the words italicized.

MADELON: I should imagine it must be great pleasure to see one's name in print.

MASCARILLE: Undoubtedly. By the way, let me repeat some extempore verses I made yesterday at the house of a friend of mine, a duchess, whom I went to see. You must know that I'm devilishly clever at impromptus.

CATHOS: An impromptu is rightfully the touchstone of genius.

MASCARILLE: Listen, then.

MADELON: We are all ears.

MASCARILLE: *Oh! oh!* I was not on my guard.
While thinking not of harm, I you regard.
Your cunning eye my heart does steal away.
Stop thief! Stop thief! Stop thief!
    Stop thief, I say.

CATHOS: Ah heavens! It is gallant to the last degree.

MASCARILLE: All I do has a gracious air about it. There is nothing of the pedant about my writings.

MADELON: They are hundreds and hundreds of miles from that.

MASCARILLE: Did you note the beginning? *Oh! oh!* There is something extraordinary in that *oh! oh!* Like a man coming to a sudden conclusion—*Oh! Oh!* Surprise is well portrayed, is it not?

MADELON: Yes, I think that *oh! oh!* admirable.

MASCARILLE: *Oh,* it's not much, really.

CATHOS: *Oh!* What do you say? These are words that are beyond value.

MADELON: Unquestionably. And I would rather have written that *oh! oh!* than an epic poem.

MASCARILLE: *Oh,* my goodness, you have good taste.

MADELON: Well, yes, perhaps it's not altogether bad.

MASCARILLE: But do you not also admire, *I was not on my guard? I was not on my guard*: I was not aware of it, quite a natural way of speaking, if I say so: *I was not on my guard. While thinking not of harm*: while innocently, without forethought, like a poor sheep, *I you regard!* . . . that is to say, I amuse myself by considering you, observing you, contemplating you. *Your cunning* eye—what do you think of this word *cunning*? Is it not well chosen?

CATHOS: Absolutely perfect.

MASCARILLE: *Cunning,* stealthily: as if it were a cat just going to catch a mouse: *cunning.*

MADELON: Nothing to surpass it.

MASCARILLE: *My heart does steal away*: carries it off from me, ravishes me of it. *Stop thief! Stop thief! Stop thief! Stop thief!* Would you not imagine it to be a man shouting and running to catch a robber? *Stop thief! Stop thief! Stop thief! Stop thief!*

MADELON: It must be admitted that it has a witty and gallant turn.

Intellectual Understanding

Now that the actor has mastered the ability to visualize his character and to express that visualization with technical control, he must next give his attention to the intellectual understanding of the play and of his part:

1. He should first gain a perfect understanding of the idea of the play, including its type and style.

2. He should understand the director's concept of the play.

3. He should know the story thoroughly and its different complications.

4. He should determine the purpose of the main characters and their contribution to the play.

5. He should determine the purpose of his own character to the story and idea, relating his role to the demands of the play and not to his own personal feelings about it.

6. He should discover any descriptions of himself in his own or other characters' speeches, including any physical characteristics mentioned.

7. He should know his character's background—cultural, social, psychological, and moral—to the degree required by the type and style of play.

8. He should realize in detail the given circumstances of the situation in which he is involved and his character's attitudes and feelings toward these circumstances.

9. He should determine the purpose and thought of each of his lines. Also he should read over carefully the lines of the other characters in each scene he is in and plot his character's reaction throughout.

10. He should determine his character's objective, which means analyzing the purpose that his part plays in every scene in which he appears and knowing his line of action; then he should understand the purpose of every action he performs in relation to his character's overall objective in the play.

11. He should analyze the language of the play for its denotative, connotative, and vocal values both for phrasing and to develop imageries.

12. He should recall his visualization of his character in physical terms, determining his makeup, costume, posture, manners, and what properties he should have in playing the part and adjust this visualization to the given circumstances determined by the text.

13. He should plan any business or pantomime that is expressive of his

character and determine which of the given circumstances in any of the situations would be appropriate for the business or pantomime.

14. Through full use of his imagination he should think out what his character is doing when he is not in the scene of action, that is, offstage.

15. He should understand why the character enters each time he does and what is on his mind when he enters.

16. He should understand thoroughly why he leaves the stage.

17. If he does not have a great deal to do in a scene, he should be perfectly conscious of what is going on and his character's reaction to these actions so that he may listen better.

18. He should decide on the lines that need to be emphasized for the audience to understand the situation.

19. He should determine his comedy lines.

20. He should understand his thought phrases and plan his breathing places accordingly.

21. He should notice the intensity of the other players in the later rehearsals after lines and business are learned and see that his own is similar to others.

22. For plays outside his experience, like those of Shakespeare, he should state the thought of the line in his own words (paraphrase) to understand its meaning fully.

23. In brief, through these and other considerations that enter into the preparation, creation, and performance of a role, the actor, as an interpretative artist, should strive to raise himself to the demands of a role rather than bring the role down to the actor's limitations—physical, ethical, or otherwise.

Conservation and Build

In studying a part, the actor should consider the problem of conservation and build.

By conservation we mean the holding back of certain phases of character until later in the play. A great failing of the less experienced actor is his attempt in the first scene to reveal too many phases of the character, whereas a more experienced one will disclose one or two new characteristics with each scene in the play, thereby slowly revealing his character in the progression of the play.

By building, we mean the increased enrichment of the characterization as the play progresses, so that in the last scenes we have still to discover new traits. One of the best ways to approach this is by planning in the early study of the play what traits of the character will be disclosed in each scene of the play. An excellent way to do this is to make a list of the qualities of the character after you have read the entire play twice, and then divide them among the different scenes, according to the demands of the circumstances of each scene.

An actor should also look out for the conservation and building of emotional intensity of a role during the play as a whole. Even if the part demands great emotional expression at the beginning, it should be held down; or, if it cannot be, the first scenes should be played with great intensity. After the drop the actor can begin a gradual build. In this case care should be taken that the first scenes do not exceed the emotional intensity of the later scenes of the play.

Not only are conservation and build of the emotional qualities necessary for the composite play, but they should be closely watched in each individual scene so that there is an increase within each scene. Such a consideration of the emotional conservation and build is necessary for the general emotional effect on the audience; and also it furnishes variety and constantly renewed interest, avoids monotony, and allows an actor to reach the audience, first by a natural emotional contact, and then to lead it into the same emotional states that he himself reaches. If he begins in a high emotional strain, the audience will not be in a condition to receive the emotion, and the actor will fail to attain emotional contact with it. As a result the audience will never be moved to the heights to which the actor is moved. If, on the other hand, the actor begins in an emotional state approaching that of the audience, the emotional contact will be made, and his audience will live his emotions with him.

So far we have seen how, in addition to mental and emotional interpretation, acting consists of a relaxed and responsive body and voice expressing the visualization of a character and have observed the technical considerations involved in the selectivity and control necessary when this visualization is put onstage.

Sustaining a Role

In our exercises we have worked for visualization in character, in several different movements, in several different ages, and in several different actions and reactions to situations. Thus we have grasped the character, his age, and a large number of his reactions. Now we need to see how these various parts are to be related and tied together into a whole. This tying together is called *sustaining a role*. It is the filling in, between the high moments of action and reaction and detailed business, with an equal amount of emotional intensity and with continuous body and vocal expression, so that complete continuity results through the entire course of the play from the actor's presentation; it is the development of a complete character in a unit of action.

Demonstrations in Sustaining a Role

1. A cafeteria. Have different characters, one at a time, select a luncheon. From the pantomime show the audience what food it is they are selecting and picking up. See that the characterization is sustained between the choices.

2. First obtain your visualization of a seven-year-old child. Think out his movements and natural manner, then the way in which he would act and react in the following pantomime. Do it again as a fourteen-year-old and at seventeen, twenty-one, thirty, sixty, and seventy. The scene is a dining room. The character is alone in the house. Notice how the whole pantomime changes as the character and age change.

(*a*) He enters the room and wonders where everybody is.

(*b*) He is at first surprised and then does not mind it.

(*c*) He hears that it is raining, goes to the window, raises the shade, and *sees* that it is raining. Whether or not he pulls down the shade is left to the actor to determine. He then busies himself with setting the table. Be sure that this is done according to the character of the person.

(*d*) After the table is set, he goes to sit down; where and how are determined by characterization.

(*e*) He does something to amuse himself. What?

(*f*) He hears a terrific noise offstage. Reaction?

(*g*) The character finds for himself a solution of the noise and turns to a new kind of activity. What?

(*h*) The noise is repeated. Reaction? He ends by going to the door and locking it. The storm outside definitely increases.

(*i*) He turns a third time to a different activity. What?

(*j*) Almost immediately the noise is repeated again. Reaction?

(*k*) There is a pounding on the door of the room. Reaction?

(*l*) A voice tells the character that it is the return of a member of the family. Reaction?

Pantomime for Sustaining a Role

A play does not consist of the sustained continuity of a single person but rather of several people each carrying out his own continuity. With great regard and consideration for the problems that evolve when more than one person is on the stage, work out in pantomime the following exercise; be sure to include many of the principles of the actor's stage technique as well as of directing, especially the establishment of time and place, emphasis, picturization—all done with a proper degree of variety.

THE CAST: (*a*) A mother, about sixty years old. She has had a hard life with a great deal of physical labor, many disappointments. She is cheery and pleasant through it all.

(*b*) A boy about twenty, very vigorous, alert, and strong, has had little education and a hard life and has been going with a gang of crooks, although because of his mother's careful bringing up he still has a fine, tender side to his nature.

(*c*) A young sister, about seventeen. She has had little schooling and has had to work hard to help support her home.

(*d*) Three plain-clothes policemen, alert and quick to grasp a situation.

The scene: A living room in a tenement: after midnight. The stage is empty.

The action: (*a*) The boy enters in a manner that shows the following: He does not want to meet anyone in that room. He is not certain whether his mother and sister are up or have gone to bed. After entering, he looks for a place to hide a bundle of clothes. Where he is to hide the bundle is left to the actor's imagination. He is still stealthy. For one thing, he looks out of the window to see if anybody has followed him and then pulls down the shade and lights a lamp. He then takes a bag from a closet and packs it for going away. He takes material from the dresser and from the closet. In doing this, he should choose very carefully what articles he would pack and show clearly what they are.

(*b*) While he is in the midst of this packing, his mother enters. She has just wakened and heard him. He pretends to be doing nothing. They talk about casual matters. Finally she sees his bag half packed. He tells her that he is going away on a business trip that night. He wishes to be left alone. He asks her to go. They embrace, he knowing that it is probably good-by forever, and she thinking it a good-bye for a short time. She leaves.

(*c*) He continues to pack, more hurriedly this time.

(*d*) The door opens, and his sister enters. He finishes his packing, answering her questions. He then sits down and starts to write. She asks him further questions. He is distracted between the letter writing and the questions. He asks her to go. She does not want to. Finally she goes.

(*e*) He finishes his letter which is a farewell one to his mother, puts out the light, goes to the window, looks out, crosses the room to the door, opens it—and three plain-clothes policemen enter. His reaction. Their reaction. One covers him with a gun; two others search him and the room. They find the bundle that he had brought in at the beginning. He tries to escape; a chair is upset; they seize him. The mother's voice is heard calling offstage. Their reaction. The son motions the men that if they will not tell, he will go with them.

(*f*) The sister bursts in. The mother follows. Reaction. The policemen act as the son's friends, and the boy introduces them as such. They shake hands, not as policemen but as friends, with the mother and sister. They start to go. The boy crosses and takes his bag, returns to the door. His mother runs to him, embraces him once more; his sister does the same.

(*g*) The policemen and the boy exit. Be sure to visualize the exit so that, although the policemen are acting as friends, they show in their positions and relationship to the boy that they are arresting him.

3

The Five Fundamentals of Play Directing

6

The Director's Media

The materials with which the director works to express the play are two: the actor and the stage. As with the other arts, there are certain important facts that the director must know about the characteristics of his materials.

It is important to remind the student of directing about the remarks made in the introduction: this study deals with the fundamentals of play directing that furnish the means of conveying the intellectual and emotional qualities of the play, and the present emphasis on these five fundamentals is not meant to diminish the importance of acting requirements in the total expression of the play. The student should also remember that these studies, though referring only to the proscenium stage, form the foundation for adapting the fundamentals to central, thrust, and other forms of flexible staging.

The Actor

Body positions

The actor onstage has a changing tonal quality, since while staying in any one area his body may change its relation to an audience. By relation to an audience we mean the numerous positions that the actor may take, from facing the audience directly to turning his full back on it.

This tonal quality we shall designate in various degrees of strength and weakness. These words, strength and weakness, we use not only in describing the position of the body to the audience but also in regard to the various positions on stage and later in relation to various movements. A clear under-standing is necessary at the outset. Strength and weakness are not synonyms for goodness and badness. There is no approval or disapproval, commendation or aspersion in the application of these terms. Strong positions may be bad, and weak positions good. This terminology is merely descriptive of the relation of body positions to the audience.

In considering the strength and weakness of the body onstage, it must be constantly borne in mind that we are concerned with the tonal value of the body position alone in its relationship to the audience. All the other factors, such as place onstage, level or height of person, color of costume, or lighting, must be eliminated from consideration in the demonstration of these points on body positions. These are all modifying factors, and, as we shall see later, they will build up a weak body position or soften a strong one.

There are five designations in the relation of body position to audience:

1. Full-front position is very strong.

2. One-quarter turned-away position is still strong but less so than the full front.

3. The profile, or one-half turned, position is less strong.

4. The three-quarter turned-away position is weak—the only really weak position.

5. The full-back position is as strong as profile but, other things being equal, not so strong as a one-quarter turn.

The reason for the proportionate strength and weakness of these body positions is that the greatest emotional contact with the audience comes from the full-front body and face, and this emotional contact diminishes as the position of the body gradually breaks its close contact with the audience.

Demonstration

1. One person will show the relative strength of the standing figure in its several body positions in relation to the audience.

2. Test the comparative strength and weakness when the figure turns to stage right or stage left.

3. Test the comparative strength and weakness of one figure in relation to a second figure onstage by change of body position.

The Stage

Areas

The stage is divided into three definite parts by two equidistant imaginary lines running from downstage to upstage and perpendicular to the foot-

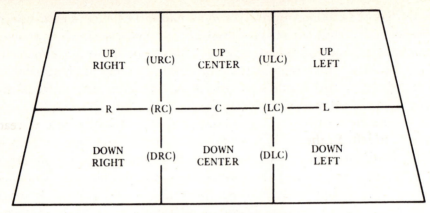

FIGURE 12 *Stage areas*

lights. These parts are designated as right, or R, center, or C; and left, or L. R and L are from the actor's vantage and not from the audience's or director's point of view. The director must learn to use these terms glibly when speaking to the actors.

Considering the strength of these three parts of the stage, we find that C is the strongest, that R is strong, and that L borders on the weak.

If halfway between upstage and downstage we draw a line parallel to the curtain line across these three parts, we shall divide the stage into six major areas, each having a designated name (see Figure 12). The subdivisions in parenthesis are often used to designate more exacting area placement. An acting area for comfortable playing requires a minimum space of approximately six feet in diameter. This minimal spatial requirement should be considered in the director's ground plan. Larger stages, of course, can afford larger acting areas.

Demonstration

Note the relative strength of each area by having an actor stand full front in each area of the stage successively.

All other factors being equal, the relative strengths of the areas should be in this order: DC (strongest), UC, DR, DL, UR, UL. Both UR and UL are too weak to be used for important scenes unless they have other factors of composition to strengthen them.

For the moment let us consider the peculiar phenomenon that we have noticed from the demonstration—the fact that right stage is stronger than left stage. Why this should be so is an unsettled fact in the psychology of esthetics. Years of tests in the classroom have shown it to be a fact but have given no satisfactory reason. The obvious reason is that we are naturally inclined to look from left to right in reading and that we carry this inclination into all phases of observation. In looking at a painting the first glance is in the left direction; and in the theatre, as the curtain rises at the beginning of an act, the audience can be seen to look to their left first in taking in the immediate impression of the stage setting.

The Chinese theatre roughly substantiates this theory. Orientals read from right to left. In the technique of their stage, the important position is on the right as you look at the stage or, in other words, on stage left. Here are placed the chairs not only for the important actors and the more important members of a family but also for the higher social positions of court life. If a scene is between the hero and the villain, their highly technicalized stage convention demands that the hero sit on the right side of a table as you view it and the villain on the left. We have no such set conventions, but the fact remains that with us the left side of the stage, from the audience's point of view, is more dominating.

That stage right is a strong area has long been known in the theatre, though its esthetic use as a strong tonal area is a development that came along with the director's rise in the theatre. Heretofore actors recognized that in a scene between two or three people the actor standing on the spectator's left has an advantage. Aware of this superior position, the stars always preferred this area.

Planes

The stage is divided into an indefinite series of imaginary lines parallel to the footlights. These imaginary lines, or planes, are as long as the scenery opening and as wide as the actor standing in the plane. All other factors being equal—that is, the position of the body and the level and distance from left to right being the same—the figure downstage, or near the front edge of the stage, is stronger than the figure upstage, or near the rear wall. The degree of strength of the actor lessens proportionately as the figure withdraws upstage.

Demonstration

Have a person take a certain spot downstage in a full-front body position and retreat slowly backward, or upstage, on the many lines perpendicular to the curtain line.

This would seem a contradiction to the often-told stories of the star who likes to stand upstage and the minor character who strives to get upstage of the other minor characters when the star is not present. This apparent inconsistency comes from the fact that when two people are onstage, and figure *A* is on an upstage plane to figure *B*, the downstage figure must turn and face the upstage figure *A*. In this case the strength that *A* derives by forcing *B* to face or turn up to him allows *A* the stronger and more opened-up body position, while in turn it forces *B* into a weaker and more closed-in body position (we discuss this factor under Emphasis and Focus). This difference in body positions is what makes up for the weakness of an upstage plane.

Demonstration

Place *A* and *B* on stage C. Have *B* downstage of *A* but facing upstage to *A* who is on an upstage plane. Now change the facing positions so that *A* faces stage left one-quarter position, while *B* faces stage right one-quarter position. If they are in the same C area, with all things such as color of costume and lighting being equal, *B* should become much stronger.

The actor must consider planes in his approaches to other actors in a different plane. These are the cases where the curved approach is used—the approach that brings him in the same plane with the person to whom he has moved. In any kind of approach a figure must come to the other and remain in the same plane, unless the director specifies otherwise. The actor, furthermore, should be conscious of the technique that he is required to use when speaking to an actor in a plane upstage of him. In such a case the downstage actor turns only his head slightly upstage and talks in a profile position with occasional glances upstage.

Levels

By levels is meant the height of an actor above the stage floor. A few of the different levels in their relative proportion of strength, beginning with the weakest, are: lying on the floor; sitting on the floor; sitting in a chair; sitting on the chair's arm; standing; standing on one step, two steps, three, and so on, until he reaches the height of a stairway or high platform. Ordinarily, the higher the level of the figure the stronger his position.

The exceptions to this rule are the cases where the level of the actor in relation to the stage floor is in sharp contrast to that of the other actors onstage. The attention of the observers is attracted by anything that is out of the norm. An example of this is an actor prone on the ground or sitting when the remainder of the group is standing.

Demonstration

1. Show the relative strength of different levels.
2. Seven people on the stage in the same plane. They all stand, then all sit, and then all take different positions of sitting and standing.
3. One figure on the floor, six sitting.
4. One figure sitting, six standing.

To test the strength and weakness of body positions, areas, and levels in relation to one another.

1. Two actors in the same plane compare the relative strength of different body positions with one standing and the other using different levels. For example, is the person standing profile of equal strength to a person sitting full front?
2. Do the same between the different body positions and areas. For example, does a three-quarter position DC have the same strength as a full-front position UR?

With this understanding of the inherent quality in the positions of the actor and the areas, planes, and levels of the stage, we are ready to consider composition, the first fundamental element of play directing.

7
Composition

Composition is the structure, form, or design of the group. It is not, however, the meaning of the picture. Composition is capable of expressing the feeling, quality, and mood of the subject through color, line, mass, and form. It does not tell the story. It is the technique; it is not the conception.

Composition is the rational arrangement of people in a stage group through the use of emphasis, stability, sequence, and balance, to achieve an instinctively satisfying clarity and beauty.

Since composition can not be avoided in the placement of set pieces, furniture, objects, and people on the stage space, both director and designer should create effective compositions that serve the demands of the situation, rather than haphazard arrangements that prove distractive, contradictory, or intrusive.

Emphasis

The first factor of composition for us to take up is emphasis. As every art product must have its emphatic element, so every stage group must have its emphatic figure or figures. The director's first problem resolves itself into that of selecting the figure upon whom the eyes of the audience should rest immediately. This is determined by the importance of the character in the scene being played and by the importance and length of the lines being spoken. Naturally, in any written scene, the important speakers should readily be seen as well as heard. The composition should emphasize this figure so that audibility of voice is reinforced by visibility.

An amusing example of the lack of emphasis in staging is illustrated by the remark of an estimable person who was asked about the quality of production of a newly established summer-theatre company. "Oh," she said, "they did excellent work, and we enjoyed them ever so much. But there was one very peculiar thing about them—you never knew who was speaking. You could hear them, but your eyes were always trying to find out who it was that was speaking."

The director must always make the question of who is speaking clearly answerable by his stage group no matter how realistic or naturalistic he wishes his style to be. There is no excuse for not having an emphasis— an emphasis that must necessarily change from figure to figure as the scene progresses. He may even have to emphasize several figures at the same time. He must also use a wide variety of methods in emphasizing his characters and not resort continuously to the same method, as this creates monotony and is technically unimaginative. The director, accordingly, must utilize every means of composition at his command to obtain proper emphasis on the speaking or key person and relative emphasis on other people in the group in proportion to their importance to the emphasized person.

Then, again, the director may have a large number of people, even a crowd, onstage. How is he to save the important characters from being swallowed up by those around them? In a scene in which a character has been unimportant up to a certain moment, how does the director make this character become important, or *take stage?* All these demands require a knowledge of how to obtain emphasis without regard to other production considerations such as color of costumes and lighting.

Methods of Obtaining Emphasis

The simplest methods are the uses of the strong body positions, areas, planes, and levels. We have discussed these four factors under the Media of the Director, and we have seen how each one in itself contains a definite value described as varying degrees of strength that contribute to the first factor of composition—emphasis. Emphasis may also be obtained through contrast. If actual demonstrations are made, what is meant by each type of emphasis mentioned below will be apparent.

Through Body Position (see Plates 1, 10, and 11.)

The strong body position is one of the simplest methods of obtaining emphasis. In a group of people onstage standing in various body positions the one with full-front body position will receive the emphasis. In realistic productions, however, the strong body position is seldom practical to use alone: the positions of the actors need to bear relation to one another. Ac-

PLATE 1 **The River Niger by Joseph A. Walker**
Emphasis: *Full-front body position at C. Secondary emphasis on figure on floor through visual line and contrast in level. Notice contrasting horizontal line of sofa to accentuate emphasis on figure at C.*

Illinois State University Theatre. *Director:* Carl Morrison. *Designer:* Earl Stronger. *Costumes:* Marian Zielinski.

tually, the relationship of body positions to other actors and audience is a staging consideration dependent on the type and style of play.

Through Area (see Plates 1 and 17.)

The strong area position is used often in emphasis. If a group of people is spread over the stage without much form, the actor in the center area will take on emphasis, other things, such as body positions, being equal. However, if other factors giving emphasis enter into the stage picture, then the emphasis from strong area position is only relatively true.

Through Plane (see Plates 2, 9, and 10.)

With other factors, such as body positions, equal, the downstage plane is the strongest. A figure in this position will receive emphasis. In the use of planes for emphasis, however, many other factors such as focus enter into consideration, as we shall learn later on. For this reason the strong plane can seldom be used alone.

PLATE 2 The Time of Your Life *by William Saroyan*
Emphasis: *Downstage plane, space, visual line.* **Variety:** *Counterfocus at UL and DR.* **Balance:** *Asymmetrical.*

Carnegie-Mellon University Theatre. *Director:* Henry Boettcher. *Designer:* Albert Heschong. *Photographer:* Daniel P. Franks.

Through Level (see Plate 3.)

Levels present a much used method. The attention of the observer is attracted by whatever is higher than the regular line of vision. If a group onstage is sitting, and the important person stands or sits on an arm of a chair or even sits in a chair with a higher seat, he will be emphasized.

A scene in which a person is allowed by the content to stand on a chair is one where level is used for emphasis. The feminine star of the past liked the advantage of height for her first appearance and often maneuvered to make a sweep down a flight of stairs, only to remain standing a step or two from the bottom.

Through Contrast (see Plates 12 and 13.)

We find that a new factor now comes up for evaluation. An actor in a position that is in sharp contrast to the positions of the other actors will receive emphasis, even though this position is considered weak in itself. This method of obtaining emphasis is known as emphasis through contrast, or counteremphasis. It occurs frequently and in many different forms.

Listed below are examples of the use of contrast in each of the four factors studied so far.

1. Body position: If all the members of a group take the strong one-quarter body position and one takes the weaker three-quarter, or full-back, position, by sharp contrast alone the weaker position becomes emphatic.

2. Area: If all the members of a group take full-front body positions in the DC area, and one takes the full-front body position in the UL area, by sharp contrast the weak area position becomes emphatic.

PLATE 3 The Shewing Up of Blanco Posnet *by George Bernard Shaw*
Emphasis: *Level, visual focus, and apex of vertical triangle.* Balance:
Asymmetrical, gained from figures at LC and L.

California State University, San Jose. *Director:* Hal J. Todd. *Designer:* Donald Beaman.
Costumes: Nancy Johnson. *Lighting:* Weldon Durham. *Photographer:* James Lioi.

3. Plane: The example under 2 also serves as an example of emphasis through contrast for plane. Down-center area is a downstage plane; up-left area is an upstage plane.

4. Level: The actor prone on the ground or sitting when the remainder of the group is standing will receive emphasis by sharp contrast.

Demonstrations in Emphasis

1. Have a group of six onstage stand facing front in a straight row. No one will receive emphasis.

2. Have each of the six take a different body position so as to see the different values of the body and to see which takes the emphasis.

3. Have each of the six take a full-front position in a different area. Emphasis from area strength.

4. Have each of the six take different levels. Body position must be the same.

5. Have the six figures all stand, all sit, all take different positions of standing, sitting, and kneeling. Analyze the relative degree of emphasis for each of the six figures.

6. Have five figures take a one-quarter position and one take a full back (contrast of body position).

7. Have five stand full front and one sit; then have that one figure kneel (contrast of level).

PLATE 4   **A Midsummer Night's Dream** *by William Shakespeare*
Variety: *Body positions, areas, planes, and levels. New concepts and schemes of production in staging historical plays.*

Williams College, Adams Memorial Theatre. *Director:* Jean-Bernard Bucky. *Designers:* Richard W. Jeter and Calvin Tsao. *Photographer:* Clyde Herlitz.

Variety in Emphasis

Since proper use of composition enriches the stage picture, it is important at this point, before taking up the other factors of emphasis, to consider one of the most important contributors to this quality of composition—variety.

Although variety is applicable for use in all the elements of composition—emphasis, stability, sequence, and balance—it is especially useful in obtaining emphasis through body positions, areas, planes, levels, and contrast, as well as in obtaining emphasis through three factors that are yet to be discussed—space, repetition, and focus. Monotony is a state to be avoided in most phases of life; in art it is absolutely taboo, except when uniformity is used to gain a special effect or to achieve some purpose such as a specific style. Except for the unusual play, variety is a most important consideration in all aspects of direction, one of which is its use in the details of composition.

Considering variety only in the four factors of body position, area, plane, and level, we find that there are endless opportunities for its application.

Variety in Body Positions (see Plates 4 and 15.)

With the possibility of eight different body positions, one can easily imagine the monotony of having most figures on the stage hold only one (for instance, full front) during the course of the entire play. Variety in body position is obtained (*a*) by having one figure use many or all of the possible body positions during the course of the play, (*b*) by having as many different body positions as possible used in any one scene by the different figures.

Variety in Stage Areas (see Plates 2 and 5.)

An area may be one-sixth of the stage, or it may be one-tenth. Actually in production an area is not so much a proportionate part of the stage as it is a unit of furniture or furniture grouping. For example: a large armchair, although it might be near another piece of furniture, is often considered an acting or playing area. This is especially true if the armchair stands beside a fireplace or has a footstool in front of it. Instead of having a figure just sit in such a chair, twelve to sixteen different positions may be found in relation to it. They contribute the factor of variety within that area. This is known as *breaking up within the area.*

Exercise: Variety within the Area

Work out several different positions for each of the following:

1. One person in one chair.
2. One person on the floor.
3. One person on floor, another in chair.
4. One person on a flight of stairs.
5. Two people in one area. No furniture.
6. SET: One armchair. CAST: Two people. Problem: One in chair and one around chair.
7. SET: A sofa. CAST: Two people.
8. SET: A table and two chairs. CAST: Two people.
9. SET: A fireplace and one chair. CAST: Two people.

Another elemental way of obtaining variety is to use different areas for successive scenes and to vary the use of one area with two or all areas in successive scenes. This is known as *between-area playing*, or *breaking up*. In using this form of variety one should always consider the number of scenes already played in a given area, as well as whether a scene is to be played within one area or between several areas. The term *scene*, as used in this connection, designates the action between new entrances and new exits.

Exercise: Variety between Areas

1. Play the following scenes for greatest variety in the use of acting areas.
Scene 1: Two people playing DR, using one area.
Scene 2: Three people playing DR and UC, using two areas.
Scene 3: Four people playing DL, using one area.
Scene 4: Five people playing DC, DRC, and UL, using three areas.
2. Have seven pieces of furniture on the stage grouped according to playing areas. Place seven people on the stage, and work out the largest number of positions that they can take, considering the problem of variety between areas.
3. The maximum number of positions between areas.
   (a) SET: Nothing. CAST: Two people.
   (b) Same with five people.
   (c) SET: Three benches. CAST: Three people. Use three playing areas.

There have been several plays in which one character for physical reasons has not been able to move out of a chair or sofa. This becomes a difficult problem for the handling of variety. In directing such scenes, the amount of variety in body positions, areas, planes, and levels that the other figure or figures may use can be appreciated: different standing positions around the sitter, different positions of leaning, sitting, and so forth. The stationary figure may use a large variety of sitting and reclining positions.

PLATE 5 **The Mousetrap** *by Agatha Christie*
Variety in Stage Areas: Several acting areas achieved by the different units in the furniture arrangement and the breakup in levels (raised upstage floor and stairway).
Purdue University Summer Theatre. *Director:* Dale E. Miller. *Designer:* I. Van Phillips. *Costumes:* Marsha Wiest. *Photographer:* Natalie Leimkuhler.

The full scene consists of one figure breaking up within the area, while the other figure will make use of the principle of breaking up between areas.

Exercise: Variety within the Area and between Areas

1. SET: One armchair. CAST: Two people. Problem: Maximum number of positions, first within the area and then between areas.

2. SET: One bench with back. CAST: Two people. Problem: Between areas and within the area. Maximum number of positions with both moving at different times.

3. SET: Three benches with backs, in three front areas. CAST: Three people. Problem: Maximum number of positions.

Up to now we have dealt only with the positive, or active, aspects of variety. There is another aspect, however, that comes from the arrangement of furniture and the conservation of areas. In a play of one setting, two considerations are necessary in regard to variety. The first of these is the arrangement whereby as many units of furniture as possible are obtained. (For possible arrangements of furniture to obtain playing areas see Plate 5.) Each of these units really constitutes an acting area. Occasions arise when as many as eleven different acting units may be obtained. The second consideration concerns the conservation of areas when the same arrangement of furniture must be used for the entire play. In such cases there is need to refrain from using all the acting areas in each of the acts. Conservation for the final act comes about by not using some of the acting areas for important scenes in the early part of the play, thereby saving these areas for important scenes in the final act.

Variety in Planes (see Plates 4 and 11.)

Since the stage has three dimensions, it is important that stage groupings take the third dimension of depth into consideration and make use of more than one plane in composing the stage picture. Objects, views, and groups in life are three dimensional; a stage grouping that has this quality will become more lifelike than a group of people staged in a single plane.

In normal conversational groups in life one seldom sees a straight line-up of people; onstage such a line-up, even though it may curve slightly, appears to be in one plane. Even though this form is suitable and satisfactory for musical comedy patter and jokes, the use of one plane causes the figures to fall into a straight line, and the stage picture is consequently monotonous, flat, hard, and unnatural. In more advanced problems of directing when style is considered, flat compositions will be found usable for formalized staging. For the present we are discussing the realistic style of directing, and in shaping the positions of our actors in terms of composition we should realize the contributing values of many planes.

The straight line, then, whether it is parallel or diagonal to the footlights, gives an objectional and obtrusive quality to composition. Lines, therefore, should be carefully avoided by the director in realistic styles. Left to their own devises actors readily form straight lines, and the director is forever having to take such a form out of his composition. There are two ways to eliminate it: (a) by forming irregular groups out of the figures in a line; (b) by using a variety of planes so as to have some figures in a lower plane, or downstage, and others in an upper plane, or upstage. Aside from the sheer breaking up of the line, the whole composition becomes more interesting when many planes are utilized.

This variety in body positions and planes produces a greatly enriched treatment of the line; moreover, the three-dimensional quality obtainable in the stage composition adds a depth, a richness, and a lifelike quality to the form. This treatment is especially important in ensemble scenes and in scenes between two people. Just as we have seen the need for varying the placement of scenes in different areas, we should now value the effectiveness and need for varying planes.

Demonstration

1. Place eight figures in a row in a downstage plane, all facing front.
   (a) Have #2 back up halfway to rear wall.
   (b) #3 halfway to #2.
   (c) #4 halfway to #3.
   (d) #5 clear to rear wall.
   (e) #6 forward one step.
   (f) #7 and #8 halfway to rear wall.
2. Have each take different body positions.
3. Have each take different levels.

Variety in Levels (see Plates 7, 14, and 21.)

The vast importance of levels lies in their unlimited possibilities of varying the stage composition. When the large number of possible levels in an ordinary living-room set—stools, chairs, sitting positions on arms of sofas and chairs, sitting positions on a table, standing positions, floor, stairways and steps leading into the room—are considered, one can easily picture the extent of variety obtainable. When variety in level is considered in relation to and combined with variety in body positions, areas, and planes, the possibilities are almost endless.

These four factors alone would prevent the director from repeating the same composition in a one-set play. Yet each one of the factors of composition that is to be discussed from here on contributes further variations to the total composition.

Other Methods of Obtaining Emphasis

Through Space (see Plates 2, 6, and 10.)

To the emphasis from the strength of body position, area, plane, and level and its contrasts, we now add another powerful factor of emphasis—space.

Space around a figure gives it emphasis. Emphasis may be obtained by creating greater space around one figure as compared with that around the other figures or by separating a figure from a group by means of space.

Space is frequently and widely used. It is the easiest method and, accordingly, can be much overdone. Many stars use it constantly and monotonously. There have been absurd treatments of intimate scenes merely because the star would not allow the subordinate characters to come near her. The most flagrant case was in a death scene where neither mother, father, husband, nor nurse was allowed to come near the star in her death agony but had to keep a respectful distance, that is, respectful to the star. In this scene the emphasis should rightly have gone to the star, not because she was the star but because her action was the emphatic action of the scene. The family could have been close, even touching the star, and other means of emphasis could have been used, had the actress and director known their business.

PLATE 6 **Black Elk Speaks** *by Christopher Sergel*
Emphasis: *Figure at R through space primarily, reinforced by visual line.* **Mood:** *Compact mass of group adds solemnity and severity to the scene.*
Folger Theatre Group. *Director:* Jonathan Alper. *Designer:* John Kasarda.
Costumes: Karen M. Hummel. *Photographer:* Jeb.

Demonstration

1. Have seven people onstage take full-front positions in a straight row. All take even spacing, except one at either end.
2. Try the breaking of the even spacing with each one consecutively.
3. Keeping in the same plane, vary the groupings in spacing.

Through Repetition (see Plate 7.)

Whenever a figure is repeated by another figure at a short space behind it, the front figure is emphasized. As the number of the rear figures is increased, the emphasis is increased. Thus, an actor is more emphatic when supported by two attendants than by one; a king with a court in attendance is more

PLATE 7 The Merchant of Venice *by William Shakespeare*
Emphasis: *Apex of triangle reinforced through repetition of vertical lines of figures, visual line.* **Variety:** *Levels.* **Mood:** *Formal and austere through vertical lines and compact mass.*

Oakland University, Meadow Brook Theatre. *Director:* Terence Kilburn.
Designer: Peter Hicks. *Photographer:* Richard Hunt.

emphatic than a rebel leader with two followers. In the cases where the attendants or followers increase to any large number, space becomes a contributing factor of emphasis.

Not only do other actors serve as a repeat-motif in emphasis, but furniture will also act in this capacity. An actor standing by or sitting in a high-backed chair is emphasized by the mere repetition of the perpendicular line from the chair. A door frame also serves the same purpose.

Besides the repetitive line we have the contrasting factor of the horizontal line to obtain emphasis. The horizontal line of a table, a sofa back, or even a couch emphasizes a figure not by repetition of line but by contrast of line. (See Plate 1.) If a person is playing a scene lying on a couch, space, as we have seen, is not the method of emphasis. Three or four figures standing above and kneeling below the couch will emphasize the horizontal figure, so long as they keep a predominantly perpendicular line themselves.

Demonstration

1. Have seven people onstage take full-front positions in a straight row. Place a high-back chair beside and partly behind one. Place a table in front of one. Again emphasize a figure other than the center figure so that it is a clear example of the emphasis from the furniture and not from the area.

2. Place a figure RC and another LC, one-quarter body position on the same plane. Place a third figure to the L of the LC figure and slightly behind it. The LC figure should be emphasized.

3. Same as before but this time with a table in front of the RC figure. These two groups should now be equally emphasized. Have the RC figure sit in a regular chair to R of the table. The RC figure should lose in emphasis and become slightly weaker. Try the RC figure sitting in a high-back chair. The two groups should be of equal value in emphasis.

Exercise in Emphasis without the Use of Focus

Experiment with a group of seven figures in practicing emphasis using body position, area, level, space, and repetition, with the added possibilities from the contrasting factors. In this case the same plane must be constantly used; otherwise the element of focus will enter into the composition.

Through Focus: Direct, Counter-, and Indirect

DIRECT FOCUS In the demonstrations and exercises so far used, a warning has constantly been given to keep all figures in the same plane. Consequently the emphatic value of the different areas has necessarily been neglected. This avoidance of the use of different planes has been done consciously; for if one figure were placed downstage or upstage of another figure (always remembering not to cover), a direct diagonal line would be formed between the two figures. This line has an emphasizing quality. It illustrates the use of *direct focus*. (See Plates 8 and 17.)

To give a figure *direct focus* is to emphasize it by use of *actual line*—either by one line created by a figure downstage of the one to be emphasized or by two lines created when a third figure is also downstage of the emphatic figure. In the first instance we find that when two, three, or more figures are in a diagonal line on the stage the figure on the upstage end, whether it be up left or up right, receives focus and therefore is the emphatic figure (see Figures 13 and 14). This use of focus is an exception to our earlier statement that the downstage plane is more emphatic than the upstage one.

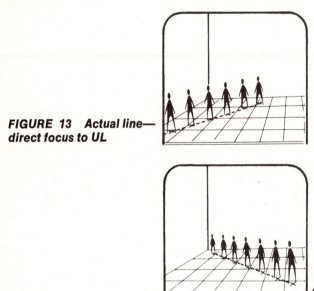

FIGURE 13   Actual line—direct focus to UL

FIGURE 14   Actual line—direct focus to UR

In the second instance both lines converge to form the apex of a triangle in which the apex is the emphatic placement. Basically both instances are the result of the *actual line* focusing or terminating at the desired place or person. Actual line does not mean a solid line but the placement in the line of a series of figures in such a manner that the sweep of the line of the spectator's vision is from one person to another until the eye comes to the focal person.

Demonstration

1. Form a diagonal line with five figures facing full front with equal spacing between them.
2. Form a regular triangle with five figures facing full front with equal spacing between them. The actual line is further reinforced by the direction and

feeling of movement from the body as it is turned toward the focused figure.

3. The same as before, but this time with the bodies turned toward the apex figure. The actual line is frequently reinforced by the tops of the heads of the actors in a gradual sweep either up or down toward the focused object; or it may be reinforced by figures on a planned series of levels.

4. The actual line may also be strengthened by the use of arms or legs pointing in the direction of the focus.

5. In realistic drama actual line through use of parts of the the body is too extreme a method. But even in realism an occasional pointed hand or crossed knee will serve the same purpose.

In addition to actual line for obtaining *direct focus* we have the *visual line*. A person standing on the street looking constantly at an object will attract others to do likewise. The same principle holds true onstage. Up to now we have constantly referred to the body position, and that has meant a literal position of the body and not just a turn of the head. Now, regardless of body position, we find that a group of actors looking at one point will cause the audience to follow their lines of vision to the same point. This is one of the simplest methods of gaining focus and must be done with great conservation. When done at all, it should be used with a great amount of counterfocus; this we shall discuss later. The use of actual line and visual line gains a very strong direct focus and should be subtly used in realistic directing; otherwise it becomes hard, formal, and monotonous. (See Plates 2, 3, and 10.)

Demonstration

If two lines of figures lead in direct focus to an emphatic person, and their bodies and faces are directly focused on the apex, we have a case of actual and visual line focus. If the figures turn their backs to the focused figure and look in the opposite direction, the apex figure is emphasized merely by actual and not by visual line. If seven figures are scattered around the stage so as to avoid any obvious triangle, and the bodies all take different positions but with the heads all facing the emphatic figure, we have a clear example of the part that visual line plays in emphasizing a figure.

Visual line is especially effective when the focused object is offstage or when it is a very small object onstage or when it is deliberately covered as in the case of a physical fight, a mutilated body, a killing, or a corpse.

Demonstration

1. Place five figures scattered at random but not covering one another from the sight of the audience. All face DR; then all look UL and offstage.

2. Place two figures *A* and *B* downstage center on their knees with backs to the audience; they focus down on floor of stage. Place a third figure *C* at up right with body turned toward offstage but focusing on spot above *A* and *B*. Place a figure *D* down left focusing on same spot. Place a figure *E* at center focusing down and a figure *F* at UL in a full-back position.

The basic treatment of two figures focusing on a third, the apex, is often considered as the only form of emphasis; this we have found to be untrue, as we have already discussed several methods of obtaining emphasis. To these methods already mentioned we have, in addition to the diagonal line and the triangle, the semicircular formation. Theoretically, it can be argued that the semicircle has a far different connotation; except to an acute observer it appears as a different and varying form of the triangle. The focused figure can stand either in front and in the middle of the semi-circular form or in the form itself with a very slight added assistance from a small space, a slightly higher level, or a more advantageous body position.

Even with reinforcement from one of these methods, it is actually the circular form that does the emphasizing; the actual line itself will achieve the focusing, but visual line will add to its strength. (See Plate 11.)

Demonstration

1. Place seven figures in a large semicircle, each facing front.
2. Have center figures take a step forward. Have one on side step forward.

DIRECT FOCUS AND THE TRIANGLE   The triangle, resulting from the converging of two lines, actual or visual, has the person to be emphasized placed at the apex. The triangle is easy to form in directing. Its use is bound to be frequent, even though the obvious triangular form is extremely monotonous, hard, and formal in the realistic play.

Overemphasis is as great a fault as underemphasis or no emphasis at all. For every play directed in which the audience is unable to discover who is speaking, there are hundreds that use a hard overfocused form time and time again in the course of the same play. This allows for no beauty, no subtlety, no variety, no tone or mood. In order to see what to avoid here-after, it is advisable to give a demonstration in which every imaginable factor of emphasis will be piled on one person.

Demonstration

1. Place a figure UC, standing on a stool in a full-front body position. Place three figures leading downstage on a diagonal on stage R and three figures

doing the same on stage L. Have a distance of four feet between the apex figure and the first figure on each side. Leave a distance of two feet between each two figures on the sides. Have each side figure take a three-quarter body position and face the apex figure. Place two figures behind the apex figure, one on each side but standing on the stage floor.

2. Analyze each factor of emphasis in this composition.

To avoid overuse of the obvious triangular form, means must be studied whereby the triangular focus may still perform its service of emphasis but without being obvious and formal to an audience. We have several ways of disguising its hard form and of obtaining variation in its use. Each of the following variations are to be demonstrated.

1. The size of the triangle may be varied, not only in different successive scenes but in the same scene.

2. The form of the triangle may be varied. The angle at the apex may be of different degrees or the legs of the triangle may be of different lengths. Isosceles triangles should be avoided.

3. The placement of the triangle onstage may be varied by using differ-

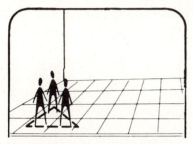

FIGURE 15 *Small triangle at stage right*

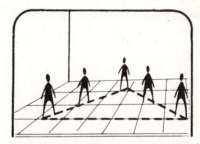

FIGURE 16 *Triangle with wide angle at apex*

ent areas. The right and left sides of the stage being softer in tonal values than the center, the placement of the triangle in these areas gives an entirely different quality.

4. Its placement may be varied by changing the relation of its base to the footlights. Furthermore, the apex may vary its position in relation to the legs; it may be up- or downstage. Usually the apex is upstage and the legs downstage, but often the context of the scene allows the apex to be down and the legs up or the apex to be to one side of the stage.

5. The lines of the legs of the triangle when more than three figures are used may be made irregular; the several figures making up the legs may break up slightly the straight-line formation leading to the apex.

6. The space between the figures forming the legs may vary; the figures in the leg of the triangle may be closer to the apex figure than to the figure at the base of the triangle, or vice versa.

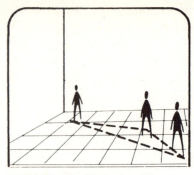

FIGURE 17   Triangle with use of levels

FIGURE 18   Triangle with apex at side of stage

7. The levels of the tops of the heads of the figures may be of different heights. This is done by having some figures sit, while others kneel, stand on steps, and so on. Even though the actual triangular form may be quite

PLATE 8   Tartuffe *by Molière*
Direct Focus: *Downstage position of apex of triangle. Figure on steps breaks obviousness of triangle.*

University of California, Riverside. *Director:* Richard Risso. *Designer:* Gerry Hariton. *Costumes:* Nancy Wilkinson. *Photographer:* Tom Neff.

regular, different levels resulting from different positions will disguise the basic form.

8. Figures added to the basic form, thereby creating a double triangle, are of tremendous aid in keeping the triangle from becoming obvious, especially when the added figures are unimportant so that they may be placed upstage of the emphatic, or apex, figure. From this upstage position the added figures form an actual line down to the apex; and even though

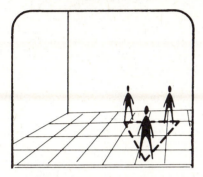

FIGURE 19 *Triangle with apex in downstage position*

they may not be seen from all parts of the house, they contribute a richness and depth to the composition. (See Plates 3, 7, and 8.)

COUNTERFOCUS AND INDIRECT FOCUS   Direct focus, besides the use of the actual and visual line and the triangular form, may be strengthened by the use of *counterfocus.* (See Plates 2, 9, 15, and 17.)

This works on the same principle of contrasting factors that we have seen demonstrated by the contrasting level and by the contrasting horizontal line in repetition. Not only does counterfocus serve as a strengthening element, but it also adds variety to the stage picture.

Demonstration

Place a figure at C; have a second figure stand below and to the R, focusing on the first figure. We have direct visual focus. Now have the second figure turn to the R in a three-quarter body position. The focal emphasis of the first figure is now just as strong if not stronger than before.

If two lines of several figures lead in direct focus to an emphatic person with the faces and bodies facing this person, we have, as we have seen, a case of an overemphatic actual and visual focus. This composition may still retain sufficient focus if a small proportion of the group—two or three—face and look in a direction other than that of the emphatic figure. Those who counter by focusing their attention on a figure near them and that figure in turn focuses on the emphatic figure are giving *indirect focus.* (See Plate 10.)

PLATE 9 **A Streetcar Named Desire** *by Tennessee Williams*
Emphasis: *Direct—space, visual line, and downstage plane. Counterfocus from figure seated at table.* **Balance:** *Asymmetrical.*

Sam Houston State University Theatre. *Director:* Maureen V. McIntyre. *Designer:* I. Jay South. *Costumes:* Robert N. Locke. *Photographer:* David Ravelle.

Demonstration

Using the ground plan on page 66, place seven figures as follows: *X* at foot of stairs UC, *A* standing below chair DR, *B* seated in chair above desk, *C* seated in chair below desk, *D* seated on sofa, *E* standing at LC, *F* at window. Last six begin with actual and visual focus on *X* at UC. *A* faces directly off-stage DR in a profile position; *B* focuses on *A*; *C* focuses on *X*. On the left, *D* turns and focuses on *B*; *E* focuses on *X*. *F* focuses on *E*.

The focused strength of *X* is not injured because the contrasting, or counter, body positions of *A* and *B* and *D* and *F* strengthen not only *X* but *C* and *E* as well, who in turn strengthen *X*.

Counterfocus, then, is created by the contrast from the actual line of the body positions and by the contrast from visual line as in indirect focus. It is always difficult to separate the emphasis that comes from actual line from that which comes from visual line, as they both appear in most cases of counterfocus.

Demonstration

Continuing with the area positions of our previous demonstration: *A* focuses on *B*; *B* on *C*; *C* on *D*; and *D* on *X*. If their bodies are in several contrasting positions but their heads are focusing, we find that *X* is finally greatly emphasized by the eye, which wanders from one to the other before reaching the emphatic *X*.

To summarize—we have learned the purpose and methods of emphasizing the important figure in our stage composition. We may obtain emphasis by the proper use of (1) body positions, (2) areas, (3) planes, (4) levels, (5) space, (6) repetition, and (7) focus. We may vary our use of focus in the common triangular form by change of size, form, position of apex, or placement of the triangle or by a variation in the spacing, in the straight-line formation, or in the levels of the figures making up the triangle or finally by the addition of figures to the basic form or by the use of counterfocus. Furthermore we have learned how to obtain emphasis through the use of contrasts in body positions, areas, planes, and levels, and how counterfocus can strengthen emphasis.

The following exercises are given as a summary of emphasis up to this point.

Exercises in Bringing Emphasis to the Important Figure

1. Work out the different ways of varying the triangle, and devise forms additional to those described. Use seven figures.
2. Spread seven figures over the stage in any way that has no form or emphasis. Rearrange them so that there will be an emphatic one. Vary the emphasis.
3. Place a figure DR, using six other figures to emphasize it. Do this for each area of the stage. Be sure to use a great variety in your method of emphasis.

Kinds of Emphasis

So far we have discussed bringing emphasis to one person. More often in a play, however, we need to emphasize more than one. In some scenes or climaxes of a scene it is sufficient to emphasize one person, but on the other hand most scenes require the emphasis on two people. Occasionally we have ensemble scenes that require emphasis to shift among several people. There are four kinds of emphasis:

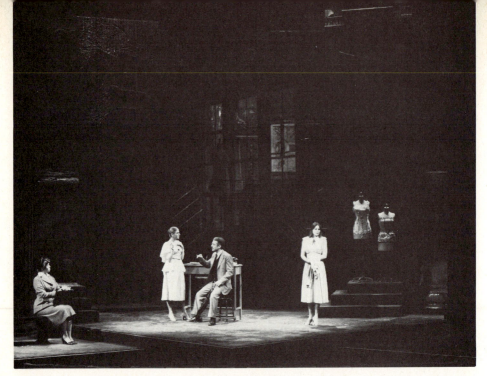

PLATE 10 **Faith, Hope, and Charity** *by Odon Von Horvath*
Emphasis: *Space, visual line, downstage plane, and full-front body position.*
Balance: *Esthetic.* **Variety:** *Indirect focus given by seated figure at table.*

Carnegie-Mellon University Theatre. *Director:* Walter Eysselinck. *Designer:* William Matthews. *Costumes:* William Brewer. *Photographer:* William Nelson.

1. Direct   3. Secondary
2. Duoemphasis   4. Diversified

Direct Emphasis (see Plates 8, 10, and 17.)

Figures onstage are so arranged that attention goes directly, easily, and quickly to the one important figure. It is accomplished by one or more of the means of gaining emphasis already discussed.

Duoemphasis (see Plates 11, 12, and 13.)

Figures are so arranged that the attention goes to two of equal importance in a scene. It is used when the essence of a scene in the script is carried by both people, or in an "equally divided scene."

Demonstration

The simplest form of an equally divided scene is when two people, each taking a one-quarter or profile position at center stage, face each other.

To enrich this, place (*a*) a table between them; (*b*) a high-back chair on stage L of table, and have one sit (here the chair and table strengthen the weaker level so that the two figures are of equal importance); (*c*) two figures adding repetition to the stage-right figure, and three figures in a semicircular formation around the stage-left figure (once again we have emphasized the two figures so as to make them of equal importance).

In (*b*) and (*c*) we have shown the great problem in duoemphasis—the finding of different methods of emphasis. Analyze the factors of emphasis that are used for each.

Whenever two figures of equal importance are in a scene of a realistic play, the methods of emphasis should be different for each figure. The same method of emphasis leads to symmetry; however, it is usable in plays of a particular style quality. In realistic plays, as in a scene of extreme opposition where figure *A* is antagonistic to figure *B*, variety in the methods of emphasis adds to the reality. The additional figures used to emphasize *A* are usually his supporters in the scene; that is, they are on his side and of the same mind and opinion. This is likewise true of those emphasizing *B*.

PLATE 11 **The Robber Bridegroom** *by Alfred Uhry and Robert Waldman* Duoemphasis: *Seated figure at R through actual and visual lines and full-front body position; figure standing at L of table primarily through position at center of semicircle.* Stability: *Figures DR and DL.* Variety: *Areas, planes, and levels in body positions.* Balance: *Asymmetrical.*

Western Illinois University Theatre. *Director:* Jared A. Brown. *Designer:* David E. Patrick. *Costumes:* Joy Butler Mrkviaka. *Photographer:* Creative Studios.

PLATE 12 The Little Foxes *by Lillian Hellman*
Direct Emphasis with Secondary: *Figure DR receives secondary through counter-focus, contrast in level, and downstage plane.* **Note: outstretched arm of emphatic figure at C brings momentary emphasis to figure at L—a duoemphasis.**

Indiana Repertory Theatre. *Director:* John Going. *Designer:* Richard Ferguson-Wagstaffe. *Costumes:* Joan Thiel. Photographer: Joe McGuire.

Frequently there are likely to be one or more people onstage who are not tied up with either of the two emphatic groups, who are neutral in their opinion. In the case mentioned above of opposition between *A* and *B* the placement of these neutral figures, especially if there are several, is usually center upstage of *A* or *B* and midway between them. They are in "no man's land," as it were. They can serve as a shifting focus, sometimes looking toward *A* and sometimes toward *B*. Care must be taken that they do not change their focus in unison. If, however, there are only a few people in this scene and *A* and *B* have only one or two supporters, then neutral *C* may be placed down right or down left, provided there is room for sufficient space between *A* and *B*. The problem of the placement of the neutral figure belongs not so much to composition as to picturization which we come to later. Composition, however, involves the placement of figures in their technical tie-up, and it is on this ground that we discuss the problem here.

Besides the neutral figure, we often have a figure who has been neglected by the author. A character who has been important in the play up to a particular scene when the author completely disregards him, except possibly for a line or two, is called a "suspended figure." Such a character is a sign of poor writing technique, but it occurs frequently, even in good plays.

The suspended figure, neglected by the author, must not be ignored by the director. The natural impulse is to leave such figures at one side of the stage out of the picture; this is definitely wrong. An important character who is onstage but who has, for the major part of the scene, little or nothing to say must be placed in the picture and related to the two emphatic figures who are carrying the scene. Even if the center between the two emphatic figures is not the correct placement for this figure as far as the picturization of the emotional relationships is concerned, he still must have an important placement in the compositional arrangement. Suspended figures may have a definite placement in the scene from the point of view of emotional relationship or picturization; but if they do not and are neutral emotionally, then the up-center position is always a possibility.

Secondary Emphasis (see Plates 1, 12, 13, and 21.)

At first, the use of secondary emphasis may seem very similar to duo-emphasis. There is no desire to split hairs over terminology, but the place-

PLATE 13 *Volpone by Ben Jonson*
Duoemphasis with Secondary: *Figure C through area and body position; figures horizontal and kneeling through contrast in body positions and level, visual line. Figures on balcony receive secondary emphasis through level and actual line.* **Balance:** *Symmetrical.*

Carnegie-Mellon University Theatre. *Director:* Lawrence Carra. *Designer:* Steven Graham. *Costumes:* Arnold Levine. *Photographer:* William Nelson.

ment and emphasis of a secondary figure are definitely different; more often than not it is neglected altogether. A secondary emphatic figure may be in a group that has only one major emphasis, or it may occur where there are two, three, or even four other emphatic figures.

The clearest way of explaining fully the secondary focal point is by means of the well-known story of Solomon. Two women appear before him claiming motherhood of a babe. He listens to both and then commands that the infant be cut in half and that one-half be given to each woman. The impostor agrees, but the real mother cries out to give the whole infant alive to the other woman.

In staging this scene we have three emphatic figures: the king-judge, the mother, and the other woman. The infant is of course important even though it has no lines; it is a clear illustration of secondary emphasis. The king and the women must have distinct and evenly delineated emphasis, the

PLATE 14   **The Seagull** *by Anton Chekhov*
Diversified Emphasis: *Attention carries from one figure to the other, or attention can be brought easily to any figure through actual and visual lines and a slight shift in body position.* **Variety:** *All factors.* **Mood:** *Diffused form, preponderance of horizontal lines, regular spacing, and variable body positions express a sense of isolation, somberness, and melancholy.*

Carnegie-Mellon University Theatre. *Director:* Lawrence Carra. *Designer:* Richard W. Kerry. *Photographer:* William Nelson.

king perhaps slightly more than the women. The infant, however, must be placed in a position where the actual lines from the placement of the three emphatic figures will convene, where all three may focus by look as well as by line from the hand when referring to it. The infant never takes the emphasis of itself.

Frequently, but not always, the secondary emphasis goes to the character about whom the scene is played. The person may or may not have occasional lines. Often, too, a character who is saying little or nothing but whose reactions to the situation are of great importance receives secondary emphasis. It may also go to a character who is surveying a scene, not having at the time much to say, but who will later become a major part of it. This frequently happens to a principal who momentarily does not have much to contribute but who later in the scene takes full leadership or control. The figure then goes from a secondary to a duo- or even a single emphatic position. This change from a secondary to a primary emphatic position, brought about by a character's walking into the new composition at the psychological moment, is much stronger for gaining emphasis than in the case of one who remains in an emphatic position when he is at the time not important.

Inanimate objects such as a ring, a mortgage, a piece of furniture, or even a body or corpse frequently come into this category.

Diversified Emphasis (see Plate 14.)

This is the most difficult form of composition, but one that is frequently called for in an ensemble scene in many plays that includes five, six, or more of the principals. Ensemble scenes may be of the sort described under Duo-emphasis; although any number may be present, the greatest amount of the dialogue and thought of the scene is carried by two characters.

On the other hand an ensemble scene may be the discussion by a family in which several characters are important, if not every minute, at least at repeated and frequent intervals. These figures must then be placed in a composition whereby the attention of the audience may go from one character to another—to a third, to the first, to the fourth, to the fifth, to the second, the sixth, and so on. All are alternately important and all should immediately be able to take the focus of the composition with a slight change of body position and without movement from one part of the stage to another. Many plays, especially comedy of manners and ideas, have scenes of this nature.

Demonstration

SET: Living room. CAST: Seven people.

The first consideration in creating a composition of diversified emphasis is to spread the figures roughly over the stage on the different pieces of furniture. Break the monotony of even spacing by having two sit on one sofa, another on the end of a desk, and so on. Be sure to avoid straight lines but use many planes and areas. Have each actor take a different body position. In a composition such as this no one person is emphasized. Great care must be taken that focus from actual and visual lines does not stop at any one figure but carries from one to another and that even the seventh carries focus back to an earlier figure. The group should be so arranged that the eye, left to roam without the aid of sound, should go from one figure to another. Here, again, we have an opportunity to use many different methods of emphasis—one might say every method. Those serving as counterfocus may even move to the extent of taking a direct focus while delivering their lines and then after finishing return to their original positions.

Give a number to each person. Then as that person's number is called he should turn his body or head to open up and recite four or five letters of the alphabet. The next number should continue with the next letters of the alphabet. Call them in various orders:

(a) 2, 3, 7, 5, 1, 4, 6.

(b) 1, 5, 3, 7, 6, 2, 4.

(c) 1, 6, 1, 3, 1, 4, 1, 2, 1, 5, 1, 7.

After using all three of these tests, choose one, and rehearse it so that the members of the group know from whom they take their cue. Now repeat it without calling the numbers.

In (c) you will notice that 1 is definitely more important than the other numbers. Readjust the composition so that, although all are equally important, 1 is definitely more emphasized than the others.

Special Problems in Emphasis

Offstage Emphasis

We have seen minor instances of offstage emphasis in the emphasis given to an entrance of a particular character when somebody looks through a window or door and says that so-and-so is coming. This is a simple but clear case of bringing focus to what is offstage. More important instances occur frequently in plays: the description of any action offstage, such as an accident, a gathering of a mob, an army marching off to war, all these are part of the emphasis in stage composition.

A specific case is the description of the race in Act III of Synge's *The Playboy of the Western World*. Actually the narrator or narrators describing the event to someone onstage for the benefit of the audience would seem to be the emphatic point; but in these cases the window, or rather what is outside the window, becomes the focal point; the audience must be able to visualize clearly the action or scene outside. The window or door, accordingly, through which the action is seen should be the main apex of the form that the stage group shapes for this scene.

The best placement of the door or window for such a scene is on the side wall either right or left. This allows the figure or figures describing what they see to remain opened up. Occasionally, the fabric of the play makes it necessary for certain reasons that the window be placed in the rear upstage wall of the set. The problem here of including the audience in the description becomes more difficult. In both these placements it is necessary to motivate one or more characters to remain on the side of the stage opposite the opening so that the narrator may have a motivation to open up completely, as he must when talking to these characters; in this way he includes the audience. This becomes extremely important when the opening is in the rear wall. In this instance the narrator must see offstage action either to the right or to the left so as to remain on the diagonal. The character listening must be motivated to remain on the opposite side of the stage from the one where the action occurs.

Whether the opening is in the center or rear, the listening figure on the opposite side forms a line that contributes to the focusing of the offstage action. Usually with only two figures onstage this line is a straight diagonal form which, as you will remember, brings the emphasis to the upstage end—in this case offstage.

In addition to offstage action, we have a large group of dramas where the environment plays such an important part in the events of the characters' lives and actions that it practically becomes a character in the drama—a character, however, that never appears. The destructive sea, the oppressive mountains, the deadening plains, the sun-scorched wheat fields, the turbulent slums, the deserted and lonely prairie, the bigoted neighbors, the cherry orchard—these all have played an important role in one drama or another. These cannot be physically brought onstage; nearly always they are fully described by the characters early in the play. A crude method of emphasizing this offstage character is to have a large window in the rear wall through which the audience may see it in silhouette, painted canvas, or projections. This method is far from effective. Actually it is far better to have the opening in the side wall where the audience may not see the effects and to have an actor build the description so vividly that the audience imagines the terror and oppression or the beauty of the natural elements by the power of the words. Given a design where the actor describing and the offstage thing described are the emphatic parts, the atmospheric environment may be so vividly impressed on an audience that for the duration of the play they feel about nature and value it in the way that was intended by the author. Such a scene must be emphasized from among the many scenes of a play, and this can be achieved through the form of the composition, which is one of the greatest aids to the visualization of this offstage character.

Since this problem of scenery and scenic description has arisen, let us comment upon it. The power of the descriptive word is far greater than any stage reproduction of nature in impressing the mind and stimulating the imagination of the audience. For instance, Shakespeare's description of Cleopatra's barge creates a far more magnificent object than any stage designer, builder, and painter could produce. But this, as you will immediately reply, is a classical play. That is true, and, what is more, it was written at a time when a theatrical production had little or no scenery, when the playwright had to design and light his production by the use of words. As soon as painted settings and electric lights did this work for the playwright, he promptly left these values to be conveyed by the director, omitting so-called description from his script. When today we give full technical productions to plays that were written either during a period when the playwright put these values into his work or by contemporary playwrights who choose to make use of the word, two unfortunate results follow: (1) The verbal description belittles the attempt of the designer and technician, and the audience realizes the shortcomings of the attempt to reproduce nature; (2) the descriptive speeches cause the play to drag. Since the eye is quicker than the ear to catch the idea, the audience catchs the idea from the scenery no matter how poor or good it may be; the words seem and are superfluous. The scene drags because the audience has absorbed the idea immediately upon seeing, and yet the dialogue continues on and on. Furthermore, when the eye has been filled, it is impossible for an audience to concentrate on its own imagination.

This understanding allows us to determine from the play whether or not the reproduction is to be in the setting or is to be left to the imagination. If the author has not put the environment into the script, then the director must; but if he has, it is best to omit as much of what is described in the text as is possible. This holds true whether the play is classic or modern.

Emphasis on the Important Entering Character

This is planting the important character (not the actor) by *building an entrance*. It is very important but should not be overdone during any one production. The methods given below build a strong entrance. (Great care should be taken that a character does not enter without the audience's seeing him, unless, of course, it is expressly explained in the script that he is not seen. This is not to be confused with an entrance that the other people onstage should not notice. In this case the entrance must be very carefully emphasized for the audience.) Not only do the following methods employ visual emphasis, but some command the attention by sound and a pause before entrance:

1. One person comes down a flight of stairs and then pauses for a line at foot of stairs. This entrance employs both level and space.

2. A group comes down a flight of stairs with the emphatic figure using space between him and the group.

3. A minor character enters through a door, stops, focuses on door, and principal enters.

4. A minor character (servant) opens double doors, takes position, and principal enters.

5. A group of people are not focusing on an entrance; a figure enters, stops short, and the group focuses.

6. An important character entering as one of the group enters last. The others should enter one right after the other at regular short intervals, take their positions, pause while the last gets to his position, and the principal enters. The pause before the emphatic entrance should be twice as long as the regular and rhythmic entrances of the minor characters.

7. A knock on the door, a pause, an entrance.

8. The character speaks offstage and enters.

9. The use of noise offstage: sounding of automobile horn, others speaking, loud orders, mumblings of mob, formal announcements as for a queen, and so forth.

10. The character offstage is seen passing by a rear window; pause; entrance by a door on the side.

11. A character onstage hears someone coming, speaks to a third character, and focuses.

12. A character onstage hears something, stops short, goes to look out of door, returns, goes to a mirror to primp, and focuses on entrance.

13. Loud talking onstage builds up to a height and suddenly stops short as emphatic figure enters; pause before the next speech. In this case focusing need be done by one or two figures only.

14. A pause (term—*holding for an entrance*) either in movement or in dialogue.

15. Topping in voice and amount of movement by entering figure.

Exercises

1. Have each group demonstrate five of the foregoing methods.

2. Prepare an emphatic entrance, not on the list, when other people onstage do not see the entrance.

Of course any unusual entrance is of itself emphatic. The simplest is an entrance through a window. Others include sliding down a banister, falling immediately after entrance, entering through a trap door or a hidden panel, entering backward and then turning. This last is frequently used, especially if the person has lines to speak to someone offstage. In "dream plays" a very effective entrance is made when a character appears apparently out of nowhere by coming through an unseen slit between the flats on the side wall. Similarly, when a character who has been hiding behind curtains or furniture since the beginning of the act suddenly appears either on an empty stage or in a full scene his presence has the unexpected, or surprise, element that emphasizes.

The methods of building or emphasizing an entrance or exit are endless, but all utilize in some manner the principles of composition. Often two or three methods are used to emphasize a single entrance, but this is usually too obvious and artificial. Several years ago in New York, two stars of great reputation were required by the play to enter together. For stars of such magnitude to enter together was out of the question, so their build-up was of even greater magnitude. The script reads

BUTLER: Mrs. B! Mr. A! [*Mrs. B. comes in followed by Mr. A, and the butler exits.*]

In performance the entrance was executed in this manner:

1. *A* and *B* were heard quarreling offstage. (The voices were easily recognizable.)
2. *C* onstage rushed to the window and looked in their direction, announcing to *D* who was coming. He then returned to a position that did not obstruct the view of two large windows to the audience.
3. *B* passed by window talking back to *A* and then turned forward. *A* strolled slowly along. Both passed out of sight.
4. Pause while they were out of sight.
5. *B* made her entrance through a door on the upstage right side wall (much applause). She then took her position onstage left.
6. *A* entered just as *B*'s applause was beginning to die down (greater applause).

There was hardly another device that could have been squeezed into this. The execution may seem endlessly long; actually it was beautifully timed. *A* was the star of slightly greater prestige and so took the choice of entering second. As we have seen, the last entrance is stronger. Moreover, *B* warmed up the audience and by starting the applause prepared it to go one better on *A*'s entrance.

The same principle is apparent in the arrangement of curtain calls

PLATE 15 The Wedding *by Anton Chekhov*
A Table Scene with A Large Group: *Note variety in body positions and placement of chairs, emphasis on bride, and counterfocus from figures at R.*

Long Wharf Theatre. *Director:* Morris Carnovsky. *Designer:* Marjorie Kellogg. *Photographer:* William L. Smith.

where the minor characters come out first and warm the audience for the appearance of the stars.

Such built-up entrances are seldom seen today, as their obviousness is apparent even to the rare theatregoer. A director, however, should plant the important character just as the playwright does. Furthermore, after the important character has entered, he should "take stage"; that is, he should hold the focus of attention for a reasonable time so that he may be clearly introduced as a character both visually and orally.

Emphasis in a Table Scene (see Plates 15 and 16.)

Of all scenes that involve great maneuvering of the figures so as to protect the important characters, none is more difficult than a dinner scene. These do not occur frequently but frequently enough to require careful study. In the former days of staging the handling of these scenes was easy, because theatrical convention allowed us the privilege of seating everybody on the upstage side of a table, thereby keeping all characters open to the audience. Contemporary realism demands otherwise, except in scenes of formal banquets or dinners of royalty which we shall discuss later.

In today's realism, if more than three people sit at a table, some must sit downstage of the table with their backs to the audience. This is unfortunate, as the figure downstage is not only in a difficult position but covers the figure on the upstage side of the table as well. How to avoid this becomes our immediate problem.

The best shape for a table is round. This allows a small steal in placement of individuals. Instead of seating the people perpendicular and parallel to the audience, they may sit near to each other; instead of sitting north, south, east, and west, which would be the perpendicular and parallel result, they should sit northeast, southeast, southwest, and northwest as illustrated below. In this latter arrangement more of the faces are seen. NW and NE may steal slightly nearer to each other, and SW and SE may also not only work slightly upstage but take profile positions.

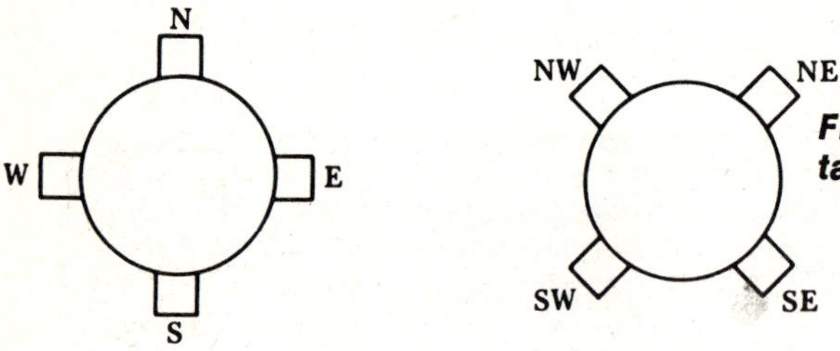

FIGURE 20   Seating at a round table

If there are to be more than four at the table and a long rectangular one is necessary to allow these open positions, this can easily be achieved by placing the table on a slant. This necessitates the ground plan of the set to be triangular in form, for the long side of a table in the center of the room should be parallel to the side walls of the room. Furniture should be placed in relation to the set. With the diagonal line given by a rectangular table, the positions are opened up. We find the emphatic position to be the upstage end with third emphatic place on the upstage side nearest this; the second and fourth in order of emphasis are on the downstage end; and the fifth and sixth, on the downstage side. The reason for this ordering is that those on the upstage side are somewhat injured in emphasis by the people on the downstage side. Those on the lower end can easily open up and even move slightly away from the table, stealing to a profile position. If it is impossible to slant the table, and its position is parallel to the footlights, these same positions still hold good in their emphatic rank. If people are sitting on the downstage side, the ends are still the most important positions; but if there is nobody downstage, then the upstage side becomes the most emphatic.

When it is necessary for six or more to sit at the table as in O'Neill's *Ah, Wilderness,* there are certain ways to counteract the many disadvantages.

a. For the upstage side: It is possible to use higher seats or to place pillows in the chairs. This steal on level will not be noticed and is particularly good for actors who are not tall enough. If possible, the taller actors should be placed on the upstage side. Moreover, if the context of the scene allows it, the actors should stand on their important lines. For instance, if there is a quarrel shortly after the scene has started, the motivation for the actors' standing is their anger. Or if the dinner is at all formal or even a minor celebration, toasts could be made standing.

b. For the downstage side: When possible, the shorter actors should be placed here. More important than this is finding a motivation for one who would sit here not to join the group immediately. If it is a family, the

PLATE 16   J.B. by Archibald MacLeish
A Table Scene: *Note use of lower stools for the downstage side.*
Alfred de Liagre, Jr. Production. *Director:* Elia Kazan. *Designer:* Boris Aronson.
Photographer: Freidman-Abeles.

children may be late to dinner, especially if they have no lines at the beginning. Or those downstage may finish earlier and rise. If they can do neither of these, the characters may be the sort that would lean over when eating; youngsters particularly may do this. If those downstage have a conversation, it is easy to motivate their sitting sideways and open up in profile when speaking. Or possibly the people downstage could get up and pass the food.

c. For the end positions: The people at the ends may very easily open up in their chairs. Or they may easily find motivation, particularly if they have finished the meal, to move their chairs slightly backward, arriving at a more informal position.

Of these various possibilities, one would seldom, if ever, use all in any one play. One or two devices are possible, however, in almost every situation.

Unless the class of society depicted dictates otherwise, regular table etiquette should be carefully observed at any dinner scene: the food should be served on the left side of each character; the finished plates should be picked up on the right side of each; the hostess should be served first, to name a few of the many points of good manners. Great care has to be taken at rehearsals to time the serving so that a waiter will avoid passing in front of a character at the table who is speaking. At banquets and royal meals, furthermore, there should be many waiters. One for every two people is none too many to effect a change of plates quickly and in unison.

The seating of royalty or the seating of people and speakers at a banquet is very simple. In these cases the table should be parallel to the audience, for no one is supposed to be on the downstage side, although the ends are used. The most emphatic position is the center place on the upstage side, but this does not always go to the emphatic person, since here the problem of rank enters into consideration. The king or toastmaster occupying center place may be only a minor character in the scene. The lower side, however, being clear of obstruction, allows the emphatic figures to sit on different sides of center so as to make these positions the emphatic ones. The two or three characters who are most important should not be placed next to each other but should have space between them to allow opened-up positions for them during speeches. Except for this consideration, the placement of the people, beginning at center and running to the ends, should be in diminishing rank and importance.

A buffet meal is much easier to stage than an ordinary dinner scene. It is wise, therefore, to make use of it in a play whenever possible. A few of the people may draw up to a table, but most of them should be scattered over the room. As each must serve himself, usually at the side or rear of the set, care must be taken to avoid crosses in front of a character who is speaking.

Emphasis in a Crowd Scene

Although it is impossible to discuss here the many problems of large-scale or mob productions, frequently in a simple play the director is confronted with scenes in which a figure must address a group several of whose members have important lines that must be emphasized. We have witnessed scenes in which such a problem has beaten the director. He has had the emphatic figure face the audience while the figures whom he was supposed to be addressing stood at his side or behind him. We have seen such an arrangement even when the emphatic figure was supposed to be stirring the group to bloody revolution. We have seen the emphatic figure swamped by the surrounding mob so that only a few members of the audience were able to see him and then only intermittently. We have also seen groupings in which all members of the mob who had speeches were so completely covered that the mob leaders were neither seen nor heard.

As a matter of fact, the problem of emphasizing the important speakers in a crowd is quite simple. The easiest method, of course, is to use a level. The principal speaker should be placed on a higher level upstage center, and a motivation should be found for so doing. This higher level may be his standing position as he talks to his followers who are sitting on the ground or on various objects about the scene. Or it may be the step of a flight of stairs or a building; it may be a chair, a soapbox, a curbstone, a tree stump, a chair, a table, or whatever other possible positions the setting may motivate. But level he must have. With the level to give him advantage, no matter how far upstage, he may dominate and control the scene.

With the speaker on a higher level, the majority of the crowd should be to the left and right of him, with a thinner grouping in front. When possible the groups in front should be made up of children, shorter people, or figures who through exhaustion or some other motivation would sit on the ground. But even if none of these is possible and full-grown figures must be in front, at least the higher level will make him head and shoulders above the rest and thus give him an advantage that is often sufficient. The placement of groups to the left and right of the speaker allows him an excuse to cover the full extent of the stage in addressing first one side and then the other.

There are almost always in such a scene several people in the crowd who need to be emphasized. Their placement needs even more careful consideration. The best places for these are down right and down left—positions that are quite strong. These positions allow the figures to open up at least to a three-quarter position when addressing a person upstage and even allow them to steal to a profile position quite frequently. Furthermore, when addressing a figure next to them, they can open up fully to the audience.

Members of the group whose important contribution is comments among themselves should be placed downstage center. As they talk together, often they can motivate turning away from the speaker and opening up to the audience. If, however, they must address the main speaker often, the best positions are on the two sides of the stage. As the worst positions are those up center nearest the speaker, only those members should be placed there who have occasional speaking or shouting of short lines.

Where the architectural background allows levels lower than the main emphatic position, these are excellent for secondary emphasis. When no levels are possible, the emphatic figure should be placed stage left or stage right facing the group who stand opposite him on a slight diagonal going downstage. The member of the crowd to be emphasized should be opposite the speaker and a little in front of the crowd; the second is downstage; and the third is halfway between the first and the second. The third is also often down center.

Now that we are dealing with crowds, two other considerations, not necessarily concerned with emphasis in crowds, should be taken up. First, when a larger crowd than can be handled or put onstage expediently is required, the crowd should straggle offstage but within vision of part of the audience. This conveys the impression that the crowd continues to an indefinite distance offstage. Secondly, a crowd should not be grouped too closely together but far enough apart to allow complete freedom of bodily movement. This spacing of the crowd also serves to give the impression of a larger crowd than is actually onstage. (See the section on sequence, below, for space relationships in crowd scenes.)

These general principles of emphasis in a crowd scene apply not only to actual crowds of large numbers but also to smaller groups.

When Emphatic Figures Are Related to Parts of the Setting

IN A THRONE-ROOM SCENE. Although this problem does not occur so frequently as to make its staging a major consideration, it does arise, particularly in several of Shakespeare's plays, and needs to be understood. It occurs not only in throne-room scenes but also in any meeting or gathering of people with a chairman or speaker of importance. In many ways the problem is very similar to that of emphasis in a crowd scene.

The place for a throne, according to most directors and scene designers, is along the upstage wall. The opportunities for setting off to full view this position is correct; the king should have all the emphatic elements to build him up—center area, level, space, and repetition, as well as a spotlight and a brilliant costume. This position, however, is so emphatic that it is impossible to build anybody else in the scene sufficiently to approach him in strength. All characters that address him are forced to speak with their backs to the audience. At most, a three-quarter body position is possible from the side. For this reason this placement should be used only when the content of the scene definitely warrants such an emphatic position.

In many plays, however, the characters subordinate in rank are far more important and emphatic as far as the scene in the play is concerned. In these cases the king has to be sacrificed and the throne placed along the right or left wall. There can be a slight steal by bringing the throne out a foot from the wall, and the level itself can be lowered—this change brings the actual position of the throne right or left center. At such a position both the king and the other important figures may receive equal emphasis. A figure may also easily steal upstage of the king to deliver an important speech. Approaches, moreover, are simpler to handle, and the king remains sufficiently emphatic for his rank and for his character in the play.

The throne can also be placed on a diagonal so that its position is actually up right or up left. In this case the whole ground plan of the throne room has to be designed on the diagonal. Such a setting allows the king to be in a one-quarter position and allows the important figures approaching him to be upstage of the king, taking either a one-quarter or a full-front position.

As we mentioned earlier, these placements come into consideration at any meeting or gathering of people with a chairman or speaker of importance. The speakers, for instance, in the meeting scene of *The Enemy of the People* are the sole emphatic figures, and their placement should be upstage center with their listeners sitting or standing with their backs to the theatre audience. More frequently, however, some speaker from the floor has a great deal to say in answer to the chairman. In such a situation the meeting should be staged profile to theatre audience or on the diagonal.

IN A COURTROOM SCENE   In staging a scene in a courtroom we have in many ways the same problem as in a throne room. In these scenes, however, we have a greater restriction in so far as the arrangement of the various portions of the setting are determined for us by the actual layout of a real courtroom.

The layout of a real courtroom, seen from the back of the room, takes in the following factors:

1. Judge's bench on a high level along center of wall opposite the spectators.
2. Witness stand on lower platform with chair and railing around it, close by at left of judge's bench.

3. Door to judge's and lawyers' rooms at right of judge's bench.

4. Jury box with two rows of seats along the left wall.

5. Door leading to jury rooms on left wall above jury box.

6. Clerk's table directly below the judge's bench.

7. Tables for lawyers and principal witnesses in front and slightly to the right and left of judge's bench.

8. Window along the right wall.

A railing usually separates the spectators' benches from the actual courtroom area. Either of the two doors may lead to the detention rooms.

In reproducing a courtroom onstage, we must make certain modifications of the aforementioned arrangement in order to arrive at the correct position for the emphatic factor of the play. This may be a witness, the jury, the spectators, and so forth.

The best procedure in arriving at this modification is to draw a ground plan of the real courtroom and then determine the emphatic element in the play. Consider this element as placed along the rear, or upstage, wall; draw a line across the plan (taking out the fourth wall) on either the straight or the diagonal. This, then, becomes the floor plan for your setting. It must be constantly remembered that, as in the throne room, the right and left walls are excellent places for emphatic positions.

The layout of the courtroom onstage puts the judge's bench up center against the rear wall. In this case the necessary changes from the actual demand that the spectators' benches along with the tables of the lawyers and the principal witnesses be placed onstage right in the same relation to each other. This clears the space in front of the bench and places the lawyers in an emphatic position at right. We also steal on the witness stand by bringing its position slightly forward so as to be on a downstage plane to that of the judge. This allows space on each side of the witness stand so that the lawyers may approach the witness in profile position. In the regular layout the witnesses are constantly the important people and are emphatic above every other factor in the act.

There are plays in which the jury is the emphatic factor. In this case, they should take the emphatic position along the upstage wall. This would mean that the judge would be downstage right with the witness stand up right and the lawyers' tables left. The wall opposite the judge would be vacant, and the spectators eliminated. There have been plays where the spectators were important and the jury eliminated.

Owing to the fact that the actors' positions are bound to be tied up with the set, this method of determining a ground plan is an excellent approach in many other types of settings besides the courtroom.

Stability (see Plates 11, 17, and 19.)

Stability is the factor of composition that pulls or ties down the picture to the stage. It confines and defines the space. It is the factor that satisfies the innate sense in the human being for coordination of ourselves and all that we see with the force of gravity. Pictures without stability seem to fly

FIGURE 21   Composition without stabilizing factors

off into space and for this reason are displeasing. This is easily demonstrated by placing a group of seven people all upstage; no matter how much this group is broken up, there will remain a peculiar dissatisfying feeling as one looks at it.

After the important figure or figures are emphasized, the next step in composition is to add stability. In scenes with two or three figures in which only one or two areas are used (no more than two), stability will always enter into the arrangement without any conscious consideration from the director. This is because such area playing becomes a focal unit, and the audience eliminates the rest of the stage from consideration. But the moment all or nearly all the areas are used and the visual aspect includes practically the full stage, then the factor of stability becomes an important conscious consideration.

Stability is arrived at by using the weight of a figure or figures at the down right or down left areas, or both. Sometimes a group standing or sitting, or in a mob scene, squatting or lying on the ground at down center, can be used as the stabilizing factor to tie down a group that is largely up center.

When the number in the entire scene is large, as in a mob scene, we find that the stabilizing weight must become greater than in a scene with six or seven people where usually one person on one side of the stage is sufficient or, at the most, two people either one on each side or both on one

FIGURE 22 Composition with stabilizing factors

side. The stabilizing element necessary to tie down the stage picture varies in proportion to the number in the entire picture. The more weight there is upstage the more weight is needed for stability. If a large crowd is used upstage and on a high level, several figures are needed in both downstage areas.

A diagonally straight or broken line of figures placed anywhere on the stage has an inherent value of stability. The line can begin center and run up left or up right; in either case stability is included. The diagonal line also includes emphasis: Whatever figure is on the upstage end becomes emphasized, since the eye has a tendency to run to the end of a line before it stops. The diagonal line, thus, adds both stability and emphasis.

This also holds true for a triangular form where the apex is stage left or right, and the legs of the triangle are one short and one long. In this instance the long leg together with the short make what amounts to a broken diagonal line.

Sequence (see Plates 14, 17, and 21.)

In focus, line has been used to tie the different figures together into a whole stage unit. Line has made each figure a part of the stage composition. Frequently, however, we have instances in which the exigencies of placement do not permit three or more figures or groups of figures to be tied together by line. So much space is necessary between the figures or groups of figures that they seem to bear no relation to one another but instead appear like several unrelated figures or groups. Large family scenes; tea, dance, or cocktail scenes; or many exterior scenes, in which the people as far as meaning is concerned have no relationship, present this problem. Considered purely from the point of view of meaning, these figures or groups are quite independent units, but from a compositional point of view they must be

PLATE 17   Pillars of Society *by Henrik Ibsen*
Sequence: Full-stage composition tied together by rhythmic spacing; also notice use of sequence in treatment of crowd. Emphasis: Full-front body position, C area, actual and visual lines. Variety: Areas, planes, and levels with counter-focus at table. Stability: Chair DR, figures DL. Balance: Esthetic.

Carnegie-Mellon University Theatre. *Director:* Lawrence Carra. *Designer:* Romain Johnston. *Photographer:* Regis Cejrowski.

brought together into a single one. These disintegrated parts which cannot be united by line may be tied together by space.

Sequence is the tying together of units on a stage by space. This established space must have a regular recurrence or a repetition of a proportion of that space. Sequence, speaking more broadly, therefore, is space relationship. In effect it is a regularly recurring accent. It is rhythm in composition, rhythm of distances between figures or groups of figures onstage.

Demonstration

1. Take the space between two figures *A* and *B* as a unit; the space from *B* to *C* should be multiples or divisions of that unit. Place *C* at a distance equal to twice the space between *A* and *B*. In this last example, the figure *C*, since he has the greatest space between him and the others, is isolated and, therefore, becomes emphasized.

2. Place three figures equidistant from one another; *A* on stage R, *B* at C, and

C on stage L. Add two figures to each basic figure. Have the groups bear no relationship to one another; that is, figures of one group must not focus on other groups but must keep the focus of attention within their own groups. These three groups of figures will appear as separate units which are in no way tied up into a whole unit composition. (See Figure 23.) This is the sort of composition that a director does not want, as it distracts the audience. To correct this, divide the distance between *A* and *C* into thirds; place group *B* one-third of the distance between *A* and *C*, so that the space sequence becomes the unit between *A* and *B* and twice the space unit from *B* to *C*. *A* is now onstage R; *B* onstage RC; and *C* on stage L (see Figure 24).

By this use of sequence, group *C*, although it is off by itself L, will be tied up into the compositional unit.

3. Try space relationship with three figures tied up to one. Establish a good distance between *A* and *B*; repeat this distance between *B* and *C*; but double the distance between *C* and *D*. Repeat this with halving the distance between *D* and *C*. Discuss your findings.

Rhythmic spacing is not confined in its use to straight lines. It may be used (1) in a triangular formation, (2) in a semicircular formation, (3) in a diagonal line, (4) or in an irregular formation by the placement of each figures in a different plane.

Demonstration

Place four figures in each one of the aforementioned formations. Cover the entire stage, and use rhythmic spacing or sequence in each case.

Figures in sequence may be on different levels as long as the spaces between them are in space relationship. It makes little difference if *A* and *B* are sitting and *C* is standing. Of course, if *C* is standing, the contrast in levels will increase *C*'s emphasis, as well as increase the space around him if *C* is standing at a point that is twice the distance between *A* and *B*.

In crowd scenes, figure *A*, raised high above the massed group with a space that jumps from the crowd to him, will not be tied in to the picture as well as if two or more additional figures were spaced so as to show sequence from the crowd to him. (See Figures 25 and 26.)

To give a scattered effect or an illusion of a mass of people, space should be used in arithmetical progression.

Demonstration

1. Place *B* a certain distance from *A*; place *C* twice that amount from *B*; *D* three times that amount from *C*; *E* four times that amount from *D*; and *F* five

FIGURE 23 Three groups as separate units

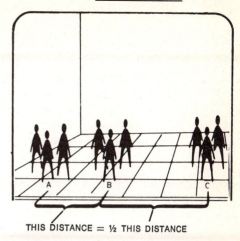

THIS DISTANCE = ½ THIS DISTANCE

FIGURE 24 Sequence in composition—
the distance from A to B equals
half that from B to C.

FIGURE 25 Figure on level not tied into picture

THESE FIGURES ADDED TO SUPPLY SEQUENCE

FIGURE 26 Added figures aid
solitary figure and form sequence

times that amount from *E*. Place each figure in a different plane. The figures should not focus on one another, but each should busy himself with a different activity. Place each figure in a different level and body position.

2. Instead of using only single figures, to *A*, *C*, and *F* add one more figure. We now have both groups and single figures. Add another figure to every unit except *D*. Now we have units of one, two, and three figures. Each figure in each group should bear no relationship to any other group but his own. Give each group a focus with use of variety so that each group differs from the other.

Sequence is most important as a means of tying the composition together when it is broad, spread out, and covering the entire stage. Diversified focus nearly always requires the use of sequence. Even in scenes that require a figure to be away from others of a group, there is a limitation of distance at which the figure may be away from the group; beyond this point the figures will be ignored by the audience.

Balance

There is a human tendency when looking at unevenly balanced scales to push up the overloaded side. The longer one watches it the more irritated one becomes at the unevenness. This is true in painting or photography as well; if one side of a picture is overloaded, the observer immediately senses it and in time starts lifting his shoulder in an unconscious reflex action as a compensating gesture. More often than not, viewing an unbalanced scene is distinctly unpleasant.

When one part of the stage composition is equalized in weight with the other, the composition is said to have balance. This is an important factor in giving a pleasurable and satisfying effect to the composition.

When Question of Balance Arises

Balance is utilized in full-stage or at least in four-area composition and in all compositions of two or more figures that employ both halves of the stage. In speaking of full-stage or four-area composition we mean those compositions in which the figures are in two groups that are made up of one or more figures with an area or more between them. We need not consider balance in small-unit compositions in which the group of figures is placed in one or two adjoining areas. Here, as with stability, balance comes of itself, since the spectator dismisses the remaining areas from consideration. Theoretically, in this instance the factor of balance should undoubtedly be taken into account, but in actual practice the director need not consider it, for he arrives at balance, as at stability, from the consideration of other factors such as emphasis. As in small-unit compositions, we need not consider balance in compositions that employ only one-half the stage.

Balance in Setting, Furniture, Costume, and Lighting

Before going further into the problem of balance we must first consider its relationship to setting, furniture, lighting, and costumes. The setting and furniture should be balanced in themselves so that the balance of the actors will not be affected. The entire background of the actor should neutralize itself in balance. This is important; for if the setting should have a strongly focalized point, it would continually counteract the focal point in the director's composition, or else the director must be forever taking the set focus into consideration in balancing his own composition. The same holds true for costumes and area lighting. Since the different hues, brilliancies, and saturations of color have varying weights, the costuming and highlighting must have their own relationships in weights for the principal and minor characters. As this relationship in the well-produced play will correspond to the director's evaluation of the emphatic and unemphatic characters, the question of costume and lighting balance need not enter into the consideration of balance in the director's stage composition.

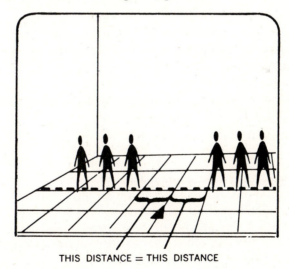

THIS DISTANCE = THIS DISTANCE

FIGURE 27 Symmetrical balance—two groups equidistance from a center

Physical Balance

Balance is weight against weight, so the stage must be thought of as a large balance scale with the fulcrum at any point on an imaginary line running perpendicular to the footlights and dividing the stage into two halves, right and left. This imaginary center line, running from downstage to upstage, is as long as the depth of the setting. Furthermore, the arms of this scale with fulcrum as axis can pivot to assume any angle to the footlights. Physical balance, then, is definitely the balancing of this scale in order to obtain equilibrium between the two halves of the stage.

SYMMETRICAL BALANCE   The simplest way to obtain balance is by having an exactly equal grouping on both sides of and equidistant from the imaginary center line. This is known as *symmetrical balance*. (See Plate 13 and Figure 27.)

Demonstration in Symmetrical Balance

NOTE: In doing all demonstrations under symmetrical and asymmetrical balance great care should be taken that all figures are of the same weight—that the strength from body positions, areas, planes, and levels is the same for all figures; that focus does not enter into consideration. As an attempt to eliminate strength from the factors of emphasis, it is best to do all exercises with the body of the figures standing and facing full front. Even with such precaution it is difficult to eliminate strength gained from area and actual line.

1. Place one figure three feet to the right of the center line of the stage; place a second figure three feet to the left on the same plane.

2. Place three figures in a close grouping at the same positions on each side. (See Figure 27.)

3. Now imagine the fulcrum as turning on its axis so that the line of the arms of scale is a diagonal. On this diagonal place one figure four feet to one side of the axis; place a second figure on the other side at the same distance.

4. Do the third demonstration, using five figures for each side.

5. Turn the line of the arms of the scale at any angle, and place two groups of two figures each in symmetrical positions. Then add a third group at the axis; move this up- and downstage on this center line.

NOTE: The group on the axis will not change the weight of either side. In the balance of a stage composition those figures on the center line do not add any weight to either side; therefore they can be disregarded in considering the balance.

6. Experiment with symmetrical balance using different numbers of figures at different distances from the axis, at different turnings of the arm of the scale at the axis, and with the fulcrum moving up and down the center line.

Although symmetrical balance with its many variations allows for a large variety of positions, it leads to a certain monotonous and obviously mechanical grouping onstage. Its form being set and geometric, it is not conducive to a realistic treatment of the stage composition. It is, however, extremely effective for conventionalized and formalized styles. Alternated with asymmetrical balance it is suitable for modern farces and high comedies. There was a period in directing when physical balance was extensively used, as in the Greek, the Restoration, and the nineteenth century Romantic drama.

ASYMMETRICAL BALANCE The second form of physical balance is *asymmetrical balance*. If a figure is placed a certain distance from the side wall of the stage, it will balance another figure placed on the opposite side of the center line at the same distance from the fulcrum.

In this form of asymmetrical balance, the eye of the audience unconsciously but quickly divides the stage into two halves with the figures in the same relation to each half. These halves balance as two separate units.

Demonstration in Asymmetrical Balance

1. Place a figure DR two feet from the right wall; place a second figure two feet to L of the center line on the same plane.
2. Place three figures in a close grouping at the same positions on each side (see Figure 28). Compare this with the illustration under symmetrical balance.
3. Pivot on its axis the line made by the arms of the scale to any angle.
4. Vary the distances from the wall and fulcrum.

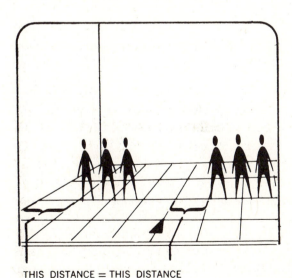

THIS DISTANCE = THIS DISTANCE

FIGURE 28 *Asymmetrical balance—distance left to the wall equals distance left to the center*

A form of asymmetrical balance used more frequently than any other form of physical balance is that of unequal numbers of figures. It is best explained by an example:

When figure A must balance figures B and C, A will balance if he takes one ordinary step away from the position where A would be if he were balancing B alone. When A must balance B, C, and D, he must take another step away, as illustrated in Figure 29.

However, in balancing B, C, D, and E he need take only a half step more away, as illustrated in Figure 30.

In other words the weight of four or five figures in a group does not change materially with the addition of more figures. Because of this a point can be found at which A does not need to retreat farther away in order to balance any additions to the group. When levels are included in the increase of weight, the problem remains practically the same. One step up on a level adds as much to the balance as a step away from the fulcrum. If the group opposing A continues to increase after A has stepped away twice or three times A need mount only a step at a time for every two or three additions to the crowd until, as in the example above, he does not need to mount higher. (See Plates 2, 3, 9, 11, and 19.)

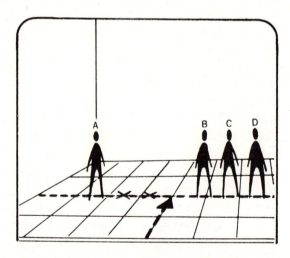

FIGURE 29 Asymmetrical balance—position of figure A balances B, C, and D

Esthetic Balance

If realism is to be taken into consideration in stage grouping, physical balance alone cannot solve the problem of balance. It is necessary to turn to the art of painting and apply to the stage the painter's principles known as esthetic, or occult, balance.

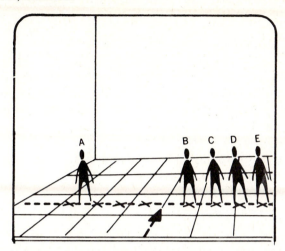

FIGURE 30 *Asymmetrical balance—position of figure* A *balances* B, C, D, *and* E

Esthetic balance, though it may seem difficult and involved compared to physical balance, is actually the most common and frequently used kind of balance. (See Plates 10 and 17.)

In doing the demonstrations of physical balance we have noticed how difficult it is to eliminate the weight on certain figures derived from the contributing factors of emphasis; frequently it has been arrived at by angling the line of the arms of the scale on a diagonal whereby the figures downstage have thrown emphasis on those upstage. In this single example we have one of the main points of esthetic balance. Downstage is a stronger area than upstage, yet the nearly full-front body position of the upstage figure is stronger than the three-quarter body position of the figure downstage. Not only is the strength of the body position counteracting the weakness of the upstage area, but the line focus as well from the downstage figure to the upstage figure contributes esthetic weight to the upstage figure. These two contributing factors of full-front body position and focus, therefore, make the upstage figure far stronger and heavier than the downstage figure, not in actual weight, but through the contributing forces of built-up emphasis.

Since in obtaining esthetic balance the director deals with the comparative weight, or strength, of the emphatic figures, we should review here the values of the factors of body position, area, plane, level, space, repetition, and focus, so that we may obtain a balance between the figures by various means. We shall find that esthetic balance is virtually a balancing of equal emphases.

Demonstration

1. Balance the weights of two figures, using merely body position, area, and plane. Try to eliminate focus from entering into the placements.

(*a*) Place one figure UR and one DL. Find the body position of each that will equalize the strength of each figure.

(*b*) Does a one-quarter position DC balance a full-front position UR?

(*c*) Use a profile body position for one figure and a three-quarter position for the second. Find out in what areas these body positions will balance each other.

2. Balance the weights of two figures using body position, area, plane, and level.

(*a*) One figure sitting and one standing. Use only one area. Does the figure standing profile balance the figure sitting full front?

(*b*) The same using area.

(*c*) One figure on a throne balancing one figure before the throne.

(*d*) One figure DR on the floor. Find the area in body position to balance the weight of this.

So far these demonstrations have balanced figures merely by the strengths or weights gained from body position, area, plane, and level. The emphases from space, repetition, and focus, which offer far more complicated problems, require much more experimentation.

Demonstration

Using as many figures as are necessary, balance:

1. A figure emphasized by a circle of figures with one at the apex of a triangle.

2. A figure on a level with one using repetition.

3. The important figure in a sequence of four with a single figure with space.

4. A figure sitting, built up by any furniture, with one built up by repetition.

5. A figure built up with focus with another built up with a different focus. Try at least three different methods of this.

6. One figure lying on the floor, surrounded by a semicircle of five focusing on it, with a group of your own composition.

7. One figure on a throne UC with another in any position and with any emphasis that you desire.

It is evident from these demonstrations that all figures who are contributing to the strength of an emphatic figure are not considered in the balance so long as the emphatic figures are equally balanced.

So far we have used one focal point balancing another. Now let us consider one focal point balancing two.

Demonstration

1. Place two figures in profile; opposite these find the body position and plane of one that will balance the two figures.
2. Have five figures in a group balance one figure. Here you will notice that

   (*a*) The one figure will be upstage of the group. This gives him a stronger body position while the figures in the group are forced into weaker body positions.

   (*b*) The group acts as a focus.

   (*c*) The one figure is reinforced by space.

   (*d*) The weight of the mass of figures is not the total weight of the individual figures in the group. The aggregate weight of a mass of figures increases only slightly with additional figures as we have previously mentioned.

   To test this add three more figures to the group; the one balancing figure will require only a little more weight.
3. Have two figures balance five. Use all forms of emphasis and variety.
4. Place a figure at a piano with three figures about him. Arrange them so that they balance eight figures sitting.

   In this case the figure at the piano is strengthened by the piano, and the three figures will have to be weakened as much as the eight sitting figures will have to be strengthened. This process is often used, that is, the weakening of an overemphatic figure when it has to balance a figure or a group of figures that are necessarily limited in how much they can be strengthened.
6. Have four figures sit more or less around a table at center stage; place a single figure of great importance away from them in such a manner that he will balance the four figures at the table.

The weight of the mass as demonstrated above is our first introduction to mass as a factor in composition. Mass is a very important determinant in composition. For the time being, however, we shall consider it as a part of balance.

Mass, as defined in the dictionary, is an assemblage of things that collectively make one quantity. In directing, the "things" are figures. A mass, therefore, becomes a quantity of figures considered as a unit.

Mass may have a focal point of its own; usually it has few or no characteristics. But whether it has detail (composition within itself) or no detail, mass does have a definite weight which must be considered in balance. We have dealt with undetailed mass in one or two demonstrations above. We have seen how the esthetic weight of the mass does not amount to the total of its parts; in other words, seven people in a mass do not have an esthetic weight of seven times the individual. In both physical and esthetic balance, after a mass of three figures is reached, the added weight lessens with each added figure until, when a mass of about seven figures is reached, the weight does not increase materially.

With detail in the mass, however, its weight increases. By detail we mean a small composition within itself: as a small space around one figure who has a few lines and who must be protected from being swallowed up by the group; or a great deal of whispering among the figures of the group; or the action of an unimportant figure who has been killed or has fallen to a low level from exhaustion; or the variety of positions in the group scattered on several levels. The value to the director of knowing these varying weights is to aid him immediately in increasing the weight of the opposite unit that is to balance the mass.

Balancing mass against mass is simple, but balancing mass against individuals requires great dexterity and experience.

As we have seen, there is weight to space; furthermore, there is weight to an expansive distance. For instance, if a figure stands on the part of the terrace that has the sea or the mountains beyond as background, that figure has greater emphasis and weight than a figure on the other side of the stage backed by the house. The latter figure would need a build-up strength if he were to balance the one surrounded by an expansive distance. In a case such as this great care has to be taken with the lighting in the distance and behind the figure. Bright lights behind a figure make it impossible to see the person.

The fact that strength is obtained by adding an expansive distance also holds for a figure standing in front of a large window or door. And distance is helpful here in strengthening the figure so that greater strength is needed to balance it. The frame of a window or door acts as a repeating or contrasting line to the figure, thereby adding more weight or strength.

In summary, esthetic balance is the achievement of equilibrium in the stage composition of the strength or weight of the emphatic unit or units. All unemphatic units bear relation and contribute to the weight of the emphatic unit or units.

The weight of the emphatic unit is the degree of strength created by any of the factors of emphasis—body position, area, plane, level, space, repetition, and focus.

Any unit may be balanced in any part of the stage, provided its emphasis is equalized in strength in its relation to another emphatic element or provided the single emphatic element is equalized in value with the unemphatic elements related and contributing to it.

Effect of Composition on Audience Emotions
(see Plates 6, 7, 14, 18, 19, 20, and 21.)

It is a well-known fact that the human being is moved emotionally by shapes. In nature we experience emotion when looking intently at a mountain or when looking at a broad, flat plain. A tall tree may stimulate in us as powerful an emotional state as the huge flat expanse of the sea extending to the limitless horizon line. Living in a small house at the bottom of a valley or at the foot of a mountain gives the occupant a feeling of being shut in. The close surrounding mountains stir us to different emotions: Some may feel cozy and warm; others may feel oppressed, shut in, and stifled. But no matter whether the reaction to the closed-in surroundings is pleasant or unpleasant, it acts as a stimulus to the emotions.

So strong is this effect on the human being that, whether he is conscious or unconscious of it, when viewing a piece of art he feels a kindred association with what he feels when watching excessive shapes in nature. The great perpendicular slabs that form the skyscrapers of New York City, the single shaft of the Washington monument, or the sweeping curve of the great arch in St. Louis, all arouse in man an emotional reaction. Huge masses like the pyramids in Egypt or the Coliseum in Rome affect us differently from the lofty tree or the inspiring tower. The perpendicular line sends us heavenward; the horizontal makes us want to relax. The weight of a large mass may impress us even to terror. The large open courts of the colleges at Oxford affect us very differently from the cramped catacombs in Sicily.

Shapes, then, are made up of line, mass, and form. The emotional feeling aroused in the spectator by the arrangement of line, mass, and form is known as *mood*. We are not considering, at this time, all the aspects of mood in a dramatic production, but merely mood resulting from composition. Staging that makes its impact on the audience primarily through use of composition for mood is one tool of experimental directors who are using the Greek and Shakespearean classics as vehicles for their own concepts. From this restricted point of view, though frowned upon by traditionalists, they are presenting provocative and innovative theatre.

Though every element in nature or in architecture includes these three factors of shape, usually only one of them has greater emphasis and, therefore, a dominating effect. It is from the dominating effect of the kind of line, the kind of mass, or the kind of form that we receive our emotional feeling, or mood. This is true for all spatial art; painting, particularly, adds the factor of color.

Color plays a vitally important part in the study of composition in painting, yet in this study of play direction it is omitted completely. In painting, color affects the principles of emphasis, stability, and mood. Its omission here is due to the fact that in actual stage production it is furnished by the costumes, lighting, and scenery and not by the director as such in his directing. The director may design his costumes; but if so, he does it not as the director but as the designer of costumes. If he does not design them, he is cognizant of what they will be and has approved them. In either case there is a system of color determination and arrangement that distinguishes the important figures and that expresses the mood of the play. The color blends and emphasizes. The costume designer's scheme will not conflict with the director's scheme for handling his figures; rather, the two schemes will coordinate and support each other.

Even when an unimportant character, dressed in a neutral or unemphatic color, becomes important for a short scene, the director by any of the means for obtaining compositional emphasis will make that character emphatic—emphatic beyond the power of color in the other figures to detract from him. No matter how vibrant or brilliant the hues of a costume are, this color may be subordinated to a less emphatic color by its placement in the composition. If there is still a slight consciousness on the part of the audience of the important character during a scene that at the moment belongs to an unimportant figure, that is not necessarily bad, for it keeps the former in the total picture; after all, the important character should seldom be forgotten entirely.

Just as the art of painting has taught us much about what to do with our actors when on stage, it now has much to teach us about the effect that line, mass, and form of our composed picture have upon the audience as they watch it. Many people in looking at a painting rendered more or less realistically merely observe the subject; a few may appreciate the beauty of composition; but only a very few go deeper to appreciate the treatment of line, mass, and form and its success in conveying a mood to the spectator —a mood, as we shall see later under Picturization, that is identical with the subject matter. A further appreciation of the effect of composition on mood can be found in the study of cubism and abstract expressionism where the treatment of line, mass, and form is more immediate and direct.

The best way to discover the mood produced by line, mass, and form in the more realistic paintings is to subtract the parts of each object that make it a recognizable thing and to reduce these to their basic line, mass, and form. For instance, place a thin piece of paper over Plates 6, 7, 14, 18, 19, 20, and 21 and draw straight lines for the dominant lines, masses, and forms of the figures. Be certain to trace the outer frame of the entire picture itself, so that the abstract shapes will be in relation to a definite space. On viewing this abstract arrangement of shapes the spectator can now detect

PLATE 18 The Pretenders by Henrik Ibsen
Mood: Solemnity and spiritual quality of occasion reinforced through vertical lines, triangularity in position of figures, and rising diagonals of beams.

The Guthrie Theater. *Director:* Alvin Epstein. *Designer:* David Lloyd Gropman.
Costumes: Dunya Ramicova. *Photographer:* Boyd Hagen.

the factors of line, mass, and form and from them feel an emotional quality which immediately creates a flow of imagery in the spectator's mind, an imagery that rises out of or is qualified by the emotional quality. The emotional quality may be one of joy, of pity, of great terrorizing impressiveness, of sorrow and oppression, of loneliness, of peace or turmoil, and the imagery expressed will be in terms of such qualities or mood. This process of stimulus, mood, and imagery is a sudden one; the spectator gets it immediately or not at all. Almost all physical places and scenes in life, and even the qualities of writing, have a dominant feeling; this mood may be expressed to the spectator by the abstract shapes arrived at from the amount, kind, and dominance of line, mass, and form.

So far we have analyzed and deduced the emotional quality or feeling that comes from a picture. Now let us analyze further the feeling or mood that comes from the different kinds of predominating lines, masses, and forms.

Dominant quality is stressed because, though every picture will contain some line, mass, and form, only one of these factors will be utilized by the composer more than the other two. Each factor, moreover, will have a variety of treatment; in a composition in which line is dominant there will be some horizontal and some vertical lines, but one or the other of these will be predominant. A composition in which mass is the dominant factor will have some concentrated mass and some scattered mass, but one will be used more frequently than the other.

Line (see Plates 7, 18, and 20.)

Dominant lines in a stage composition are arrived at from the position of the bodies of the figures. Reclining positions, many sitting positions, a general evenness in the heights of the tops of the heads—these are some of the ways in which a director may obtain the predominant horizontal line. A great number of standing figures, use of levels, very tall people or headgears —all these stress the perpendicular line.

A dominance of *horizontal lines* creates a restful, an oppressive, a calm, a distant, a languid, or a reposeful feeling in the spectator. Horizontal lines express stability, heaviness, monotony, relaxation, and other similar qualities.

Perpendicular lines express height, grandeur, dignity, regal or forceful impressiveness, frigidity, spiritual or ethereal qualities, or soaring aspirations.

Diagonal lines are seldom used, but on the rare occasions when they are they express a sense of movement or an unreal, an artificial, a vital, an arresting, a bizarre quality, or quaintness.

Straight lines express strength, sternness, formality, severity, simplicity, regularity.

Curved lines express naturalness, intimacy, quiescence, freedom, gracefulness, flexibility, warmth.

Broken lines express informality, disorderliness, humbleness, anxiety, quaintness, independence.

Obviously these types are not all distinct and separate. Perpendicular lines may be straight or curved; horizontal lines may be straight or broken; but when the director achieves these combinations, he obtains different and mixed values. Broken perpendicular lines give a feeling of violence; broken horizontal lines, a casual feeling.

Or consider the contrast created by the use of broken horizontal lines and straight horizontal lines in the same composition. The former give the feeling of oppressiveness, languidness, and coziness, whereas straight horizontal lines give the feeling of sternness and strength. Such a composition could be a scene at the beginning of *The Lower Depths* or the final scene of *Beyond the Horizon* where the characters have disintegrated under the destroying forces of the environment.

Let us reverse this process so that we begin with an actual situation in a play and from there decide its feelings or mood and from these feelings arrive at the dominating lines that will express these qualities. It is the living room of a New England farmhouse after supper. The family consists of a grandmother, a father, a mother, an older son who has worked all day, a son in school, and a younger daughter. Such a scene calls up in us the reactions of repose, warmth, intimacy, informality, casualness, and independence. The lines that will express these qualities are horizontal, curved, and broken.

For the purpose of showing the sort of mixed feelings that arise in situations in a play, let us suppose that a neighbor enters into this farmhouse scene and suddenly begins a vigorous fight with the elder son. In the midst of the qualities achieved in the beginning we now need conflict, or a vigorous and contrasting value. The perpendicular lines of the two figures, strengthened by the diagonal body attack of one and the raised arm (level) of the other, will supply the contrasting value. At this time we must not consider the handling of this situation in terms of picturization. We are merely interested in the treatment of lines in composition to express the desired mood effect.

Mass (see Plates 6, 19, and 20.)

Mass is a group of figures as opposed to a single individual. Its weight is an important consideration in balance; the impression of mass on an audience is an important consideration in mood effect.

Is the effect of a scene on the director light, dainty, delicate, charming,

PLATE 19 **Six Characters in Search of an Author** *by Luigi Pirandello*
Mood: *Line, dominant verticals; mass at RC, compact; form, diffused. Dominance of vertical lines, heavy compact mass at RC, and diffused form project a feeling of isolation and expectancy.* Stability: *Figures DL.* Balance: *Asymmetrical.*
Williams College, Adams Memorial Theatre. *Director:* Jean-Bernard Bucky. *Designer:* Richard W. Jeter. *Photographer:* Clyde Herlitz.

and gentle; or is it heavy, ponderous, severe, austere, and massive? Does the scene show power and strength, or weakness and indecision? Is it full and rich? All in all, mass is the degree of lightness and heaviness conveyed by the number of people involved and how they are grouped: compactly, dispersed, individually spaced, or in small groups. Large masses can give a feeling of power, strength, menace; small, compact masses of solidarity and resolution; diffused masses of weakness and indecision.

If large numbers of people inherently produce one effect and small numbers produce another, it might seem that the director's use of weight to affect mood is limited by the number of people the author includes in a scene. This, however, is not wholly true. The director may handle a group of seven or eight figures so as to give a heavy mass feeling as in the graveyard scene in *Our Town,* when the mourners with umbrellas open gather together for the ritual of burial. In working on a new script he may persuade the author to include more people in a certain scene; and in crowd scenes the director himself determines the number of figures in the crowd, the number of attendants to a regal or military personage, and the number of listeners and figures for atmosphere. For a light effect the director naturally employs fewer figures.

Let us study a specific example: A man is going to perform public prayers in a public place to invoke rain which the community needs badly. The number of townspeople that turn up to join in the prayer is at the director's discretion. The stage can be crammed to capacity, or it can be sparsely filled. The application of this approach would guide the director to examine the feeling of the scene and to determine from that the number of figures required. If it were a seriously religious scene in a tragic play, the stage would be filled to overflowing. If it were a light, fantastic comedy, the number of figures would be much less with greater space between them.

If the scene does not call for a crowd of people but for only seven to eleven figures, the decision of the director rests upon whether these few are to be divided into masses of two, three, and four figures or whether they are to be treated individually. Can you imagine the difference between three masses of figures and nine figures treated individually? Can you react emotionally to the mood effect of the two treatments? If so, then you have mastered the ability to decide on the treatment of mass in a stage composition.

The mere statement of the scene and the nature of the play should immediately stimulate an impression in the practical director concerning the use that he is to make of mass in the composition. Each scene has an inherent weight, to be conveyed by mass, that projects a specific value or mood effect to the audience.

Form (see Plates 14, 19, 20, and 21.)

Form is significant in expressing the mood effect of the subject through compositional arrangement. To be sure, it seldom needs consideration in two-character or even three-character scenes, but the moment the scene becomes ensemble in effect, then form is one of the first factors to be determined.

Form may be symmetrical or irregular, shallow or deep, compact or diffused.

Each one of these arrangements of form creates a totally different mood effect; the director should give special attention to the expression of a scene in terms of form. Variety in staging a play is obtained by a great variety in form during the course of the action. So expressive is form that, as the

PLATE 20 **Pericles by William Shakespeare**
Mood: *Dominance of diagonal line, heavy mass, and compact form project mood of supplication. Visual dynamics of composition are accentuated through contrasting line of kneeling figure in open body position.*
Carnegie-Mellon University Theatre. *Director:* Lawrence Carra.
Designer: Robert McBroom. *Photographer:* William Nelson.

subject of the play progresses in its various manifestations, so will the form.

As with line, let us analyze the mood effects of the different arrangements of form:

a. Symmetrical, regular, or repeated form expresses formality, artificiality, coldness, quaintness, rigidity.

b. Irregular form expresses a casual, impersonal, natural, informal, or free quality.

c. Shallow (single-plane) form expresses quaintness, artificiality, shallowness, excitement, alertness.

d. Deep (multiplane) form expresses warmth, richness, mellowness, sincerity, naturalness.

e. Compact form expresses warmth, force, power, menace.

f. Diffused form expresses indifference, coldness, turmoil, disarray, individualism, isolation.

The possible combinations of form, as well as the combinations of line with form, give mixed emotional effects. An irregular compact form is entirely different in effect from an irregular scattered form. What is the effect? What is effect derived from a symmetrical deep form in contrast to that derived from an irregular shallow form? What is the effect from a scattered form with perpendicular lines in contrast to that from a scattered form with predominant horizontal lines?

Although the sensing of the emotional effect obtained from form or line-and-form arrangements may be difficult at the start, the director will eventually visualize scene after scene in a play that he is reading in such terms, rather than in terms of technical composition or in terms of minute picturization of the subject matter. He will learn first to feel certain qualities in his scene and then will strive to convey these feelings to an audience in a general manner of composition; the arrangements of details will follow afterward.

This treatment of the composition, derived from the emotional effect of shapes on an audience, is one of the most marked ways in which a director demonstrates his real artistry—his real interpretative power. It amounts to developing an ability to visualize the qualities of a scene in a play and to reproduce these qualities onstage. A play similar to Pinter's *The Homecoming,* for example, requires highly delineated compositional treatment to strengthen and project its basic mood. The director must determine the correct lines, masses, and forms. For example, the intensity of emotions indicated in Figure 33 on page 181 when contained by the characters as composed in stark rigidity in Figure 31 can achieve the strong tensions between characters so characteristic of a Pinter play. It is extraordinary how the untrained mind of the beginning director will be quite inventive in this creative process. In a short while he will conjure up the desired mood effect of the scene that he has read. In doing this he should be as free as possible from the confining stage directions and details of the text.

Often, it is possible to imagine the mood effects by the mere mention of a scene from a play. It is within our control to project these moods primarily through character or through the many degrees of abstraction where the strength of line, mass, and form takes dominance over individual character.

Physicalizing emotions through gesture and body control and group formations as practiced by many contemporary theatre and dance ensembles has created a theatre where the effect of composition on audience emotions becomes the direct means to stimulation rather than a control where text speaks through character, reinforced though it may be by the various compositional controls analyzed above.

The opportunity for emotional release through group participation can prove most stimulating theatre and can be used creatively. All too often, however, in instances where the intention is to project the inherent values of the play, the inexperienced director will superimpose physical actions on a scene with the actor or group running a gamut of gestures, distortions, gymnastics, group entanglements, and so on with little or no relationship of these to the circumstances or moods implicit in the text. This is not to say that the feeling or mood of a scene cannot be transposed into a metaphor and that metaphor staged into meaningful compositions of line, mass, and form. (See page 214 on staging a scene from *Othello* as a metaphor.)

To test our powers in this respect, let us first describe the mood effect that we receive from the following scenes and then explain how we are to convey this feeling to an audience by means of line, mass, and form. Great care must be taken not to picturize or to visualize these scenes photographically but merely to describe the feeling and execution.

Demonstration

1. A large cocktail party in the tastefully decorated New York studio of a concert pianist.
2. A confrontation between a revolutionary group and an authority—as students; as factory workers; as housewives.
3. A family at home in their sun parlor on a Sunday morning.
4. Explorers on the moon.
5. The head of state receiving an ambassador.
6. Tourists visiting a notorious cafe at midnight.
7. Inhabitants of a large slum house in the courtyard on a Sunday afternoon.
8. A conspiracy of five men in a cellar.
9. A disco on Saturday night.

Exercises in Composition

NOTE: Try to keep storytelling pictures from creeping into the composition. Use at least six people in each composition.

1. One composition with one emphatic figure from each person in the group.
2. From entire group one composition of each of the following:

   for emphasis— (a) composition with duoemphasis
   (b) composition with secondary or offstage emphasis
   (c) composition with diversified emphasis

   for moods— (d) composition with mood of grief
   (e) composition with mood of joy
   (f) composition with mood of loneliness
   (g) composition with mood of turmoil
   (h) composition with mood of oppression
   (i) composition with mood of peace

3. Each member of group analyze in writing the mood of a scene from a play of his own choosing. Stage the scene, conveying the mood by means of line, mass, and form. Have the class members describe their reactions to the scene.

8
Picturization

After the technique of procuring articulate and pleasing arrangements has been mastered and a mood value obtained with our compositions, we are ready to inject meaning into the stage picture. Already in doing the demonstrations and exercises under composition, we have found it difficult to prevent meaning, or a storytelling quality, from entering the work. Now we are ready to concentrate on this factor which is called picturization—the second fundamental element of directing.

Picturization is the visual interpretation of each moment in the play. It is the placing of characters in a locale that suggests their mental and emotional attitudes toward one another so that the dramatic nature of the situation will be conveyed to an audience without the use of dialogue or movement. It is the outer action that, in turn, makes the audience understand, at times contrary to the dialogue, the inner meaning or subtext existing within and between characters. This visual interpretation of the play should be developed as fully as the auditory.

Composition and Picturization

Composition contributes the rational arrangement of technique and the mood of the subject whereas picturization contributes the meaning or thought to the stage group. One might say that picturization is the concept, and composition the technique. Concept is the author's creation—his thought, meaning, or subject. It is his imaginative contribution without technique. It is his own personal expression or invention of the mind.

Concept and technique in any art should be related, with composition expressing the feeling or mood of the concept. For instance, if a good picture is stripped of its picturization or storytelling elements of the emotional relationship of character to character, leaving only its arbitrary line, mass, and form (the composition), an emotional quality or mood of the subject matter will come across to the audience.

In the teaching of painting, the instructor frequently turns a picture upside down when analyzing its composition. He does this in order to remove all meaning from the painting so that the class will consider only the composition and its mood and not confuse both with the subject. In the teaching of play directing this process is impossible, but the way to obtain an analysis of the composition in a stage picture is to have each person on the stage eliminate all facial expression and communication with the others —in other words, to become an inanimate figure.

Body Expression and Relationship to Other Characters

In life the relationship of one person to another and the body expression of the person himself have a definite storytelling value. Instinct keeps us away from those whom we dislike, suspect, oppose; near to those whom we trust, endorse, agree with, love. This picturization of the emotional state tells the director where to place each character in a scene in relation to the other characters. You will notice that under the section on Composition we have always talked of "figures," never of person or character. Now for the first time we begin to talk about characters, since we are considering the character in emotional relationship to another character. (See Plates 1–3, 7–13, 24, 27–29, and 34–37.)

We shall begin first with storytelling positions by means of which two people through their body reactions and body relationships will recall to us certain experiences in our lives that will tell us what they are acting. We shall then bring character into the exercises in order to establish an emotional relationship.

In the following exercises notice how certain scenes pictured around one piece of furniture will vary considerably in their power to convey meaning to the audience when played around another piece of furniture. Be certain, therefore, to choose the right piece of furniture for each scene.

Exercises Using One or Two Areas

1. Storytelling pictures.
   SET: *One table, two chairs, and a sofa.*
   CAST: *Two people.*
   Picturize

   (*a*) A scolding.   (*b*) A quarrel.

(c) Telling a story.

(d) Whispering.

(e) Equally divided quarrel.

(f) A confession.

(g) A formal conversation.

(h) An expression of grief.

(i) A surprise.

(j) A gossiping scene.

(k) A conspiracy.

(l) Congratulations.

2. Character and storytelling pictures.

SET: *A door.*

CAST: *Three people.*

Picturize farewell:

(a) Husband and wife saying good-by to

   i. Friend.

   ii. Son who is going to school.

   iii. Son who is going to college.

   iv. Son who is going to war.

   v. Son who is going to prison.

   vi. An unwelcome guest.

(b) Father ordering son out of house.

(c) Farewell of two lovers.

3. Character and storytelling pictures.

SET: *1 and 2.*

CAST: *Two characters.*

(a) Two whose children have quarreled.

(b) Two greeting each other after a long interval of separation—vary relationships as brothers, sisters, friends, business associates, etc.

(c) Two saying goodby to each other—vary relationships as above.

   i. When the separation is to be short.

   ii. When the separation is to be long.

Frequently we have a more difficult emotional relationship to picturize, as, for example, one of a mixed emotional state: love and anger, as when two lovers quarrel; or hatred superimposed upon two who originally loved.

To gain a clear understanding of picturizing a mixed emotional state, let us work out the picturization of the two lovers who have quarreled. This becomes a problem of projecting the mixed emotional states through body positions and expressions.

The way to approach the problem is to make a picturization of the one basic emotion which in this case is love. Let us place the characters close together on a sofa. The connotation of such a background setting is helpful in itself. Now move each as far apart as possible; this separation helps to put the element of quarrel into the picture. Next have them turn their backs to one another. This last move has emphasized the element of quarrel too strenuously, so an added touch must be given the picture by having one or both run the downstage hand back toward the other and rest it on the edge of the seat.

Title of the Scene (Concept)

So much for exercises in simple picturization. We now turn to the process of applying the principle to the play. We spoke of picturization as embodying the author's concept at each moment of the play. In order to express the concept we should understand what each moment of the play has to say. This brings us to a discussion of the scenes of a play.

Scene Divisions and Titles

A play is composed of many scenes or basic situations. Each scene represents an idea that is either incidental or pertinent to the main story or idea. A scene (in the French sense) is often marked by the entrance of a new character who changes the subject matter as a part of the progressive thought in the unity of the play. It is possible, of course, that two subjects or thoughts may be carried on in a scene by the same group of characters. A scene of this kind must be necessarily treated as two basic situations, but the division is an arbitrary one made by the director according to each individual idea or purpose put there by the author. The director must analyze the author's purpose along with character objectives and attitudes, because without a knowledge of these, picturization cannot be created with meaning. The purpose or subject of each scene can then be given an overall title expressive of its general intent.

The director cannot be urged too strenuously to analyze the basic purpose, objectives, and attitudes underlying each scene in a play, because now, under picturization, he must express graphically the dramatized situation by placing his characters on the stage in storytelling positions and emotional relationships. In many an absurdist play where the meaning rests in its totality, the moment to moment relationship of characters though not specifically related to prior or subsequent actions, still must be rendered with a meaning coherent with the total idea. Often to accomplish this purpose the meaning must be projected by giving the actors objectives that for the moment seem to have no connection with the text.

The basic situations of a section from Act I scene 1 of Molnar's *Liliom* expressed in synopsis form indicate the kind of analysis necessary for arriving at the basic picturization.

CHARACTERS: *A*—Julie; *B*—Marie, her friend; *C*—Mrs. Muskat; *D*—Liliom. SET: A bench.

Basic situations:

a. *A* defiant against someone approaching; *B* frightened, trying to persuade *A* to run away. (*C* enters.)

b. *A* on the defensive opposing *C* on the offensive, unjustly accusing, with *B* defending *A*. *C* is jealous of *A*.

c. *D,* arrogant and annoyed, enters followed by several girls, admiring, flirting, and pleading. Others look on.

d. *D,* dominant, quarreling with *C* over *A* who is agitated but adamant for an answer. *B,* frightened, tries to help *A.*

e. *C* and *D* in angry confrontation with *A* and *B* siding timidly with *D. (C* exits.)

f. *D,* bragging and assertive, with *A* and *B,* concerned and in awe, trying to please *D. (D* exits.)

g. *B,* embarrassed and defensive, confessing love to *A* who tries to be superior, not realizing love for *D.*

Supplying an overall title for the general intent of each scene, we have:

a. Defiance
b. Unjust accusation
c. Flirtation
d. Argument and plea
e. Angry confrontation
f. Two concerned over one
g. Confession of love

Exercise

1. Title the remainder of the basic situations in Act I scene 1 of Molnar's *Liliom.*

Classification of Scenes (Technique)

The author not only has a purpose for each scene in his play but has also decided by what technical manner he is going to convey that purpose. Some playwrights create intuitively, in which case concept and technique are inparable parts of the creative process. Any scene in a play falls into one of the four kinds of technical arrangements.

Scenes of Incidental Action

Some scenes not pertaining to the main action or idea are nevertheless scenes of activity through which exposition, atmosphere, or presentation of characters is woven. They are scenes of a social gathering, a game of cards, preparation for a meeting, a cocktail party, a reporter obtaining news, and so forth, in all of which the action, although fully developed, is of itself not important as the dialogue that runs through it, leaving aside the "how-do-you-do's," "two lumps," "your deal," and so on. Once in a while they may contain main action dealing directly with the main story, but more often they are scenes of irrelevant action with which exposition of great importance is interlaced.

In the old days scenes of incidental action were pure declamation, for the audience's benefit, of a long expositional dialogue between an important character and her maid companion or confidante. In the later drama they became scenes between two servants (one new and one old) dusting furniture while they laid the foundation of the story or elaborated on the characteristics of the principals. In time the exposition became more cleverly handled, and we had scenes between a secretary and a newspaper reporter or scenes in a waiting room. There has been a definite improvement in the treatment of exposition until now, in the present-day drama, it is usually incorporated into real action and often carried by the principal characters.

These scenes, often void of strong dramatic interest, are nevertheless important scenes that demand careful analysis and control.

They are scenes where the author:

a. Introduces characters and situation.
b. Establishes basic relationships.
c. Relays antecedent actions.
d. Sets groundwork for building of basic situations.
e. Defines atmosphere, mood, and locale.
f. Establishes tone and basic attitude.
g. Establishes relationship of world of play to audience.

For his part, the director:

a. Clarifies character relationships.
b. Sees to it that the actors point up the important situation lines.
c. Points up foreshadowing.
d. Breaks up expository speeches for pointing and variety.
e. Creates variety in composition, since actions are most likely in parallel with no significant conflicts to bind the interest of the audience.
f. Establishes business to reveal important character traits.
g. Establishes rhythm of basic situation.

In general, the problem in the control of incidental actions is to focus attention where it should be and to excite and maintain interest. Often they are ensemble scenes requiring the kind of compositional control discussed under Diversified Emphasis. For example, in a cocktail party the several characters would be generally positioned to take or bring focus easily as set by the text. Then, through the business of pouring and passing drinks, essential lines are pointed, characters brought together, relationships established, and so forth.

Scenes with Background Action

Some scenes establish the locale or time, and the dialogue and emphatic incidents carry the main thread of the story.

Examples:

1. A scene on a dock or bridge where there is continual movement of people passing by, traffic noise, and so on.

2. A retiring room at a large reception with guests passing in and out.

3. A restaurant with bar where the diners and drinkers at the bar come and go.

4. At an airport just before flight.

5. A scene at a fair.

Background scenes are established by the playing of the minor characters during and after the principals play the main scene. Sometimes the background action continues through the principals' scene, although it is always diminished. The problem in staging these scenes is the subtle and careful control required in shifting emphasis to the key characters. For gaining variety and enrichment, the several methods of obtaining emphasis deserve special consideration.

Scenes of Main Action

Scenes of main action contain the main situations of the play in graphic or dramatized form. In such scenes the background, if present, thins out while the attention focuses on the graphic unfolding of the story.

They are the critical scenes where:

a. The balance is upset.

b. Inciting factors and disrupting elements enter into actions and behaviours.

c. Changes in character relationships occur.

d. New characters are introduced.

e. Complications develop.

f. Tensions begin to build with their accompanying stresses and strains all demanding careful analysis of text and vividly delineated picturizations of the various forces at work.

Directorially:

a. The inciting factors and elements of disruption are pointed up.

b. Transitional scenes are carefully rendered.

c. Changes are picturized.

d. New relationships to characters and story emphasized.

e. The inner meaning of basic situations, often implicit, are picturized by significant character actions and reactions.

Scenes of Dramatized Emotional Relationship

Finally, some scenes show mental and psychological states and attitudes; they actually may occur in any of the above actions. In them the play of character upon character, the picturization of the mental and emotional attitudes of characters upon each other, can be graphically rendered as discussed later in the chapter on Movement (section on Character Pattern) when it becomes important to bring added emphasis to the conflicts involved, especially in scenes of major crises where events reach a state demanding decisive action and procedure.

Inherent Mood Values on the Stage

After we have determined the subject and title of a scene and analyzed it for its technical classification, we would seem to be ready to place our characters onstage, but before we do this we need to know more facts about the stage than we have learned so far.

In Areas (see Plates 1, 6, and 12.)

Upon a more acute examination of the areas of the stage we find that each area not only has its own value in terms of strength and weakness, but also seems to have a definite feeling or mood value. There may be no psychological reason for this, but from long history of stage practice we find that a mood value does exist for areas. These mood values of areas, like color, line, mass, and form, have a tonal quality that can be described.

We find, moreover, that the subject of each scene in a play has an inherent mood which can also be expressed in tonal qualities. Furthermore, we know that each scene will convey this mood more convincingly if it is played in an area with the corresponding mood value. Although the mood of the subject of the scene should harmonize with the mood of the area, the following classification of the mood values of areas *should not* be taken to imply a rigid, unbreakable rule concerning where a scene must or must not be played. Mood values of areas, expressed in terms of tonal qualities and scenes that the mood value suggests, are given more as a guide. Also, although we can appreciate the part that color and atmospheric lighting play in creating mood, we must, for the same reasons as in composition, relate them to actual stage production and not consider them in this analysis.

The best way to appreciate the subtleties of inherent mood values of areas on stage is to arrive at your own conclusions through demonstration. To select two obvious examples:

1. Contrast the intensity of a strong argument placed DC as against its placement UR.

2. Contrast the tone of a memory scene of departing lovers placed DC as against its placement UL.

In deciding where a scene should be played many factors governed by the particular script must enter into final consideration.

Mood values of areas in terms of tonal qualities and suggestive scenes.

Tonal Qualities in Each Area	*Scenes Suggested*
1. Down center: hard, intense, harsh, strong, climactic, great formality	Quarrels, fights, crises, climaxes
2. Up center: regal, aloof, noble, superiority, stability	Formal and romanticized love scenes, scenes of domination and judiciary nature, royalty
3. Down right: warm, informal, tender	Intimate love scenes, informal calls, confessions, gossip, long narratives
4. Down left: not so warm as down right; distant intimacy, introspection	Conspiracies, casual love scenes, soliloquies, formal calls, business matters
5. Up right: soft, distant, romantic	Romance
6. Up left: Infinity, ghostliness, depression	Supernatural scenes, background scenes, scenes of isolation and despair

Exercises in Coordinating the Mood Value of Area and the Subject or Title of Scenes

1. Two people compose a picture suggested in the chart for each area of the stage successively and show the suggested mood of each area.
2. Repeat each picture in an area different from the one suggested in order to evaluate the subtle difference or conflict in mood values between content of scene and area.

In many plays the same idea expressed by a particular character or the dominance of a particular character keeps recurring. In such cases the character can wisely be placed in the same area, usually on the same piece of furniture, for each recurrence of idea or dominance. The audience will gradually associate this area with the particular character or idea. Such use of area, however, cannot be handled too blatantly but should be disguised in order to avoid obviousness. One way to do this is to have another character or other characters use the same piece of furniture for a short time in the course of the play. This also contributes the definite value of variety.

If often happens that an identical situation occurs at the beginning and at the end of a play, showing a complete cycle of a day or of a character. The same principle as expressed above applies here: The use of the areas, the positions of the characters, the dialogue, and the movements are approximately duplicated to accentuate or make clearer the idea of the play.

In Planes (see Plates 2, 17, and 21.)

Planes are so tied in with the mood values of areas that a word should be said about them. The stronger the emotion in a scene and the more important the scene the farther front it should be played, using the downstage planes. The upstage planes, aside from scenes that suggest softened areas, are good for background scenes or for unimportant characters in a scene of main action. Scenes of extreme physical violence, such as shootings and stabbings, are usually placed upstage, when the major focus of the scene is not on the physical violence itself, but on the reactions resulting from the deed.

Frequently a director has a scene in which there are many people who for atmospheric purpose carry on dialogue that should not be heard by the audience, but who are necessarily near the important characters. The director should take this into account in his ground planning and conferences with the designer and arrange an alcove or a small room into which the audience may look. This area beyond the normal stage planes may be a reception room, a cocktail bar, and so on. Its position may be center or, better still, up left. This establishes these added upstage planes as a place for the withdrawal of characters, left without lines, to *ad-lib* in silence. Their business has to be carefully worked out when added upstage planes are used in this manner. The convention we establish that people in these planes cannot be heard is quickly accepted by the audience. To safeguard this illusion, we must take great care to see that no one in the "nonhearing" planes speaks aloud or speaks to somebody downstage of these planes. If the character must speak, he should come forward and step out of the nonhearing planes.

There are cases when so much necessary dialogue has to take place away from the minor, or background, characters that the directing of such a scene has been solved only by having the main set become the withdrawing room, with a large opening in the center showing the reception room in which the background action takes place. The main set, then, becomes a withdrawing room into which the principals and a few others may stray to carry the story of the play. In cases of this kind the full business of continual background action has to be directed minutely. An example of this is the third act of Chekhov's *The Cherry Orchard* where background actions continue in the ballroom seen through the UC arch while the retiring room in the downstage planes is the major acting area for the main actions between Madame Ranevskaya and others.

The upstage planes in the form of alcoves or other similar recesses are excellent places to set dreams, return of the dead, ghosts, and other supernatural scenes. In all these instances the beginning of the scene should start in these upstage planes even though, as the scene progresses, it is better to bring the characters forward by degrees in order to utilize the center planes.

In Levels (see Plates 20, 24, and 26.)

Levels, as can be readily seen, also have a definite feeling, or mood value. An actor's level can often correspond to the emotional tone of the character —a humble character can be in a low level, and a regal one on a high level. Often the changing use of levels can represent the building or diminishing of the emotional state of a character.

In a certain production of *Oedipus Rex* the changing use of level corresponded with and brought out the progressive steps of the king's downfall. The production was staged on an immense flight of steps. At the opening of the play we saw the king on the highest level—grand, prosperous, master of himself. As each tragic implication bore down upon him we saw his gradual descent from step to step, although at times he ascended again as the obstacles diminished. Not until the end, when the tragic downfall had reached its depths, did we see the king on the lowest level nearly prostrate on the stage floor.

Exercises in Placing Scenes in Their
Proper Mood Area, Plane, and Level

1. Place in its proper areas each of the picturization exercises on page 166 and 167.
2. A mother talks to her dead son.
3. A captain, disgraced by defeat, reports to his superior.
4. The king enters and denounces the superior for treason which brought about the captain's defeat in battle.

Creating Full-Stage Picturization

With a complete understanding of the many considerations of the title or subject of a scene and its technical classification, of the mood values of composition, of the stage itself, and of the emotional qualities of body expression and relationship, as well as the imagination to dramatize, the director is ready to practice full-stage picturization.

The thought process of combining the director's imaginative concept with the several technical considerations is one that will vary considerably.

From experience it is found that the beginner had best separate the many steps and do each in turn. As he acquires more experience, the steps in the thought process become blended until a fully experienced director will think of the expression of the situation directly in terms of mood values and technique. It will seem to be only one creative process.

With the strong belief that a director should begin with a separation of concept and technique, the following procedure is offered for the working out of picturization and composition, both of which should ultimately come together in the total expression of each scene in a play.

Seven Steps in Creating Picturization

1. *Analyze the scene for purpose, character objectives, and attitudes so that it may be definitely titled:* a scene of struggle, of love, of forgiveness, of oppression, of suspicion, and so on.

2. *Determine the mood qualities that are inherent in the title:* if it is a title of suspicion for a situation in which six people are each suspecting the others, we should have awareness, unrest, nervousness.

3. *Express the nature of the mood in terms of mood value of composition such as line, mass, and form:* whether the composition is compact or diffused, large or small, regular or irregular, flat or deep, and so forth, with all the different combinations of these. In the situation of six people suspecting each other, we have isolation in space, diffused mass, and irregular line and form. Now express these in the technical terms of composition, which in the situation under analysis means: diversified emphasis, uneven sequence, and a great deal of counterfocus together with irregular body positions.

4. *Visualize the background of the situation, characters, and setting:* the forces and circumstances about the situation, the social standing of the characters, the environment where the situation takes place, and frequently the time of day and season. The situation of the six people who suspect each other has been brought about by a robbery. The characters might be people of high social standing, and the environment might be the drawing room in the home of one of these people; or the characters might be gangsters, and the environment a hide-out, murky and hot. In this second instance the picturization would assume totally different qualities from those in the first.

With a clear knowledge of what the situation is, of the mood qualities inherent in the situation, of the mood values of composition that will express the nature of the mood; and with a clear conception of the entire background (situation, circumstances, characters, and setting), we may now transfer our mental picturization to the actual stage.

5. *Place your characters in roughly the proper areas of the stage* and in a manner that expresses their emotional attitude in terms of their cultural and environmental background.

6. *Apply the factors of composition* that will, in particular, stress the emphatic characters or objects.

Having approximately related our characters, we now work for an articulate and clear-cut quality. We make definite use of our technical knowledge of composition, applying the proper emphasis and the necessary stability, sequence, and balance, with a careful eye to avoiding monotony and achieving an enriching variety.

7. *The last step is the attitude of the individual actor.*

Have your actors give their emotion body expression and reaction. Individual picturization is more or less instinctive with the actor, as a result of the emotion that he is striving to portray, or it may often be the result of technical skill resulting from his observation. According to normal expectations, if he is defiant, he will express this physically with feet firmly planted and the body erect and forward; if frightened, he will cringe; if humble, he will relax with head bowed. This physical accompaniment of emotion in man is a universal language that he speaks and, as with the picturizing arrangement of the group, arouses in the audience an immediate conception of the emotions and emotional relationships that are in action onstage.

In arriving at our final picturization we have worked from the general to the specific. We first made known to ourselves the title for which we would work, and then through a series of steps starting with a rough sketch we have arrived at a detailed visualization of it.

After the picturization is completed, check on each individual factor, and make sure that the picture tells the title, the story, and the background.

Precautions

Make certain that

(*a*) Your composition is not obvious but is subtle and varied. The placement of your emphatic characters should correspond to the mood of the area, and the center area should not be used in every picture for the emphatic figure. Esthetic balance should be used more frequently than physical.

(*b*) The treatment of the picturization is not trite and too conventional but shows an imagination, an individuality, and a richness in detail which come from acute observation of life.

(*c*) The actors react in character and in terms of content of the scene.

(*d*) Disorder is avoided in the picturization of great emotional stress. Disorder comes from violation of the principles of composition, with no regard for emphasis. No matter how disorderly a mood may be inherently, you cannot be disorderly in your composition. Whenever the object is to portray confusion onstage, it must be orderly, or composed, confusion.

Summary

Analyze

1. The title of your situation.
2. The mood inherent in the situation.
3. The mood expression in terms of composition.
4. The background.

Then

5. Place the actors onstage to express the emotional relationship between them.
6. Apply the elements of composition for emphasis and articulation and for pleasing and varied effects.
7. Have the characters express their individual attitudes.

Application from Title to Complete Visualization

Now let us work out together the steps in this thought process from title to complete visualization, using a definite situation.

Example: two women before Solomon, each claiming to be the mother of the child.

1. The title of the situation is two people seeking justice of a third: Solomon is justice; the two women are the seekers of justice; the child is the claim.

2. The mood values inherent in the title are impartiality, firmness, appeal, anger, and hatred.

3. The mood values of composition are those of strength, stability, balance, and loftiness of justice, as well as those of vigor and intensity of excitement. One feels a seemingly conflicting note from a diagonal line crossing a broad and strong perpendicular line.

4. The background of the situation is a mother's struggle for the possession of her child whom another women has claimed as her own. The two women are of low birth, and the scene takes place in Solomon's court.

5. The placement of the figures in the proper parts of the stage and the expression of their emotional relationships are as follows.

Solomon should be placed dead center, high on a level (throne), and should be strongly emphasized by repetition of line coming from guards standing behind him. The mothers should stand before Solomon as far as possible from each other, with their body positions in antagonistic attitudes to each other yet leaning forward toward Solomon (their appeal). One of the women should have an arm raised to give the prolonged diagonal line. The women should be equidistant from Solomon to bring out his impartiality toward them and his inability to decide which is the mother. The child should lie horizontal to Solomon on the floor of his throne; in this position the child is equidistant from the two women and in possession of Solomon; since the child is the motivation of the scene, it should receive secondary emphasis.

6. Application of the factors of composition for emphasis and articulation:

Solomon should have the dominant focus. The mothers should have strong equal emphasis yet in varied methods. In addressing Solomon they will have to steal on their body positions so as to open up. In the entire scene there can be additional details of councilors, and so on. Any raised arm must avoid covering the face. In most picturizations there is the need for slightly added changes to vary the triangle and obtain balance, but in this one the basic form is necessarily symmetrical.

7. The individual attitudes of the characters: This picturization presents more common problems than is ordinarily supposed. The mothers have two basic emotions to portray at one time—their hatred toward one another and their appeal to Solomon. These two conflicting emotions are expressed by having the body leaning and focused toward one another, while the arms point toward another. The head may turn toward either object. As we have already mentioned, the arm of one woman *A* may be raised toward Solomon, while her head may be turned toward the other woman *B*. As the raised arm gives great emphasis, with the bodies of both *A* and *B* leaning toward Solomon, *B* may have her head toward the king, but her arm may be pointing toward *A*. In this way we get variety between *A* and *B* without duplicating exact positions, and yet each is of equal strength and importance.

With these steps we have completed our picture of the emotional relationships and have expressed visually the meaning of the scene; composition has been used for its technical unification and form for its mood contribution. We have used that moment in this story when each woman is putting forward her case at the same time, just before Solomon makes his decision. Continue the story in two or three pictures to the point where Solomon makes his decision by having the baby held up in a feigned attempt to cut it in half. Notice the slight but telling changes in the dominance of the women and Solomon. Continue with the picturization of the whole story. Analyze in each case what you have done.

In this approach to directing a play we have a picture for every scene; but as soon as we add movement (our next fundamental element) to picturization we have a picture that is ever changing. In the finished product, therefore, the pictures does not remain static during the entire length of a scene but changes slightly as the action or the emotional reaction of the principal characters changes. The motion pictures is a series of static pictures which pass so quickly, one after the other, that the eye does not notice any break between. So it is with the stage picture within a particular scene. There is a definite, constant kaleidoscopic, small movement reflecting the general progressive values in the scene. Nothing is more peculiar than to watch a play in which the director has arrived at a picture and held it continuously until it is time to change and then all the people suddenly rise or move and form a new picture, only to hold this until it is time to move again. The small changes in a picture often alter the meaning of a scene entirely.

Referring once again to the Solomon story, we can tell the whole tale with very little movement between a series of individual pictures and show who is, and who is not, the mother. The picture remains practically the same, yet by small changes of strength and weakness, by change of emphasis, by climactic movements we may hear the story from *A* and from *B*; make it seem as if *A* were the mother, as if *B* were the mother, as if both might be the mother; show the varying doubts and certainties of Solomon; show his decision; show the women's reactions to the decision; show Solomon pronounce his decision by starting to cut the baby in half; show the real mother's reaction, the false mother's reaction; show him bestowing the child on the natural mother; show him reprove the false mother. There may be possible even further minor adjustments which would show more minute changes in the story. Each one of these is a picture. Running one slowly after the other, we have the complete dramatization of the story which would be understandable to a deaf person, even if he did not recognize the Biblical tale.

An excellent picturization does all this: It tells the story in visual terms so that someone who was either deaf or a foreigner could understand the story and characters of the play.

Degrees of Picturization
Related to Mood Values of Composition

Beyond the actor's individual control of the character, it is within the director's control to deepen or lighten an emotional moment to the degree that he picturizes and composes the action. How fully should an action be picturized? What use should be made of the connotative values of composition? Answers to these are naturally dependent on the inherent dramative values of the play itself and the interpretation brought to it by the director. A play like Chekhov's *The Cherry Orchard* has run the emotional gamut from comedy to farce to tragedy in the many interpretations given it since its first production by the Moscow Art Theatre. For demonstration a brief scene from Act I of this play will serve the purpose.

Trofimov, the former tutor of Grisha, enters unexpectedly to pay his respects to the mistress of the house, Lyubov, who has just arrived home after a long absence. As implied in the dialogue, Lyubov's child Grisha was drowned—one of the reasons for her departure from home.

LYUBOV [*Looking out the window with Gaev.*]: What a wonderful orchard! Masses of white blossoms, blue sky . . .

TROFIMOV: Lyubov Andreyevna! [*She turns to him.*] I'll just pay my respects and leave at once. [*Kisses her hand.*] I was told to wait till later, but I couldn't wait any longer. [*Lyubov continues looking at him.*]

VARYA [*In tears.*]: This is Petya Trofimov.

TROFIMOV: Petya. . . . Grisha's tutor. Have I changed so much?
   [*Lyubov weeps quietly.*]

GAEV: [*Embarrassed.*] There, there, Lyuba . . . don't cry.

VARYA: I told you, Petya, to wait till later.

LYUBOV: My Grisha, my little boy . . . Grisha, my son!

VARYA: Please, don't cry, mamma . . . it was God's will.

LYUBOV: My boy was lost . . . drowned. Why? Why?

Figures 31, 32, and 33 show a progression in staging the scene from compositional control to more intensified picturized control.

SET: *A sofa, window above sofa, door DL.* CAST: *L—*LYUBOV, *T—*TROFIMOV, *V—*VARYA, *G—*GAEV.

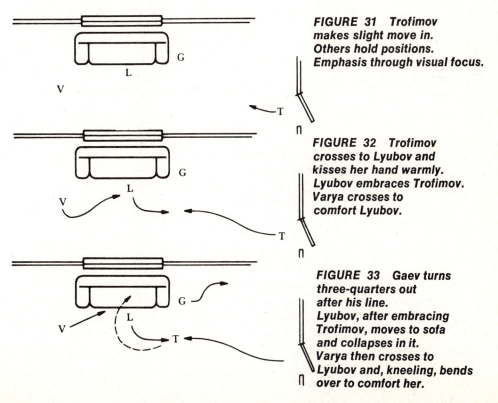

FIGURE 31 Trofimov makes slight move in. Others hold positions. Emphasis through visual focus.

FIGURE 32 Trofimov crosses to Lyubov and kisses her hand warmly. Lyubov embraces Trofimov. Varya crosses to comfort Lyubov.

FIGURE 33 Gaev turns three-quarters out after his line. Lyubov, after embracing Trofimov, moves to sofa and collapses in it. Varya then crosses to Lyubov and, kneeling, bends over to comfort her.

In the third staging (Figure 33) the picturization is composed in such a way that it accentuates the deep inner feelings of the characters. It is related to the basic situation and circumstances of the scene and gives extension to the inner processes of thought and feeling. Trofimov's entrance revives memories of a tragic event. For fullest intensification, Lyubov, unable to contain her tears after embracing Trofimov, moves toward the sofa near her and collapses in it. After a moment she cries: "My Grisha, my little boy . . . Grisha, my son." She gives complete release to her emotions as Varya, kneeling by her, bends over to comfort her. Stirred by the brutality of her fate, Lyubov moans: "My boy was lost . . . drowned;" then in full grip of defiance cries out: "Why? Why?" The emotional impact is further accentuated through the connotative use of composition such as compact form and heavier massing through use of weak body positions. As we shall see later under Movement, further accentuation comes from the negative use of movement in Lyubov's approach and collapse and in Varya's cross to her.

In contrast to this let us assume that we wish to lighten the emotional impact of the scene as we might do in a comedy. Now, rather than picturizing extensively with the kind of intensification indicated above, the characters, still responding with the same emotional thrust, would instead be positioned as in the second staging (Figure 32) with Lyubov and Trofimov sharing the scene throughout while Varya and Gaev focus on them.

In the first staging (Figure 31) the business of kissing hand and embracing has been eliminated and the staging kept quite arbitrary in its compositional control. Note that rigidity in positioning with emotions kept in restraint projects in itself an entirely different quality—a control that might be applied to a play like Pinter's *The Homecoming*. Compositional treatment, rather than extended picturization, can lessen the emotional content of a scene as in Figure 32, but contained in line and form as in Figure 31, the severity and isolation depicted elicit a mood distinctly different from that projected through the sort of control exemplified in Figure 33. If we can appreciate the distinction, we can understand the importance that a director's control of the fundamental plays in the interpretation of each moment in a play.

Demonstration

1. The members of a house party suspect one girl of having committed a theft. (She is innocent.)
2. A boy's club at an election, when they are waiting for the returns from the voting for a new president. The ballots are being counted in the next room.
3. A conservative suburban family at home in the evening; the eldest son returns

from the Far East and introduces his new wife to them. Although neither the son nor his wife knows it, the family sees that she is covered with scales.

Exercises in Picturization

1. SET: *Six pieces of furniture.*
   CAST: *Six people.* Establish attitudes and circumstances for each. Then repeat changing attitude and circumstance.
   Example: (*a*) A scolding.
   1. Attitude—serious. Circumstance—one has mistreated another.
   2. Attitude—pretence. Circumstance—covering up a misdemeanor.
   Picturize:

   (*a*) A scolding.
   (*b*) Telling a story.
   (*c*) Whispering.
   (*d*) Equally divided quarrel.
   (*e*) A confession.
   (*f*) A formal conversation.
   (*g*) A quarrel.
   (*h*) An expression of grief.
   (*i*) Surprise.
   (*j*) A gossiping scene.
   (*k*) A conspiracy.
   (*l*) Good news.
   (*m*) A dinner party.
   (*n*) A death scene.
   (*o*) A Shakespearean death scene.
   (*p*) A rebellion.
   (*q*) A cross-questioning scene.
   (*r*) A pleading scene.
   (*s*) One suppressing five.
   (*t*) One boring five.

2. Title the photographs on pages 102–162.
3. Work out the pantomime for sustaining a role on page 90.
4. Have each member of the group create one original picturization based on a scene from a play. Have the rest of the class title each scene.

Movement

Movement, the third fundamental element of directing, is the stage picture in action. It comprises the moments of picturization in their ever changing aspects. Although movement exists in the passages from picture to picture, it must have of itself a definite picturizing value. In discussing the situation of Solomon and the two mothers (Chapter 8) we have incorporated the smallest amount of movement during the changes from one picture to another. By degrees this increases until we arrive at a great deal of movement, movement that becomes an important factor in staging and must be considered an active contributive quality of a play in performance. Just as we learn the principles of composition and picturization from painting, so we learn the contributions of movement to the stage play from the principles of movement in the dance.

Like composition, movement has both a technical value and a mood value. Movement, such as exits and entrances or the hiding of an object, is supplied by the author for the necessary action in the progression of the story. There are other movements, however, supplied by the director for character evaluation, emphasis, variety, and mood expression.

Movement Values

As with body positions, areas, planes, and levels, stage movements have certain definite values. These must be learned and thoroughly absorbed by the beginning director so that any wrong movement will be immediately sensed by him.

All movement may be generally valued as strong or weak, but again we must point out that these terms do not mean good and bad. They are merely the evaluation of movement; there is a right time to use strong or weak movement, as well as a wrong time, depending upon the character, his line of dialogue, and the situation.

Body Movement

A strong movement of the figure is stepping forward, straightening up, placing the weight on the forward foot, rising from a chair (lower to higher level), raising arm, or walking forward.

A weak movement is stepping backward, slouching, placing the weight on the rear foot, sitting down, lowering the arm, walking backward, or turning around and walking away from a figure or object.

In the general flow of movement, the value of the final movement before a pause, as for the delivery of a speech, becomes the dominant impression of the full movement. For example, if we desire a figure to be strong, while the script requires it to sit and yet at the same time be strong, the figure sits (weak movement) and then suddenly becomes strong by sitting very erect or by executing a large gesture. The reverse of this is also true: If a child is sitting on the floor and her mother enters to admonish her, the child rises (strong movement); but since under the admonishment she should be weak, she may hang her head and put her weight on her rear foot.

In this movement from strong to weak or weak to strong is evident the first influence of the dance. The increase in the amount and size of these strong and weak movements is of itself a dance.

Stage Movement

Not only does the movement of the figure have its strong and weak values, but the lines of movement of the figure onstage have their own values as well.

RELATIVE STRENGTH OF MOVEMENT The following charts give the value of lines of movements of the moving figure not only in the strong and weak stage movements but also in their relative degree of strength and weakness.

Here, again, we notice that a strong stage movement followed by a weak body movement is made weak. For example, if a figure walks from upstage to down center and sits, the general value is weak unless he makes a strong body movement after sitting. Likewise, a weak movement followed by a strong body movement will be made strong, for example, walking from downstage to upstage and turning full front for the final lines. This is the only possible way of making a final exit definite, strong, and emphatic.

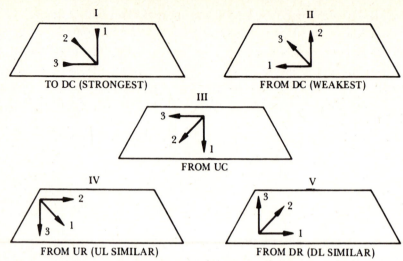

FIGURE 34   *Charts showing relative strength of movement*

Movement from a weaker to a stronger area is very strong. This is an excellent way to strengthen important dialogue and business or to make a figure emphatic. As a matter of fact a figure kept unemphatic until the crucial moment will become stronger if you give him a strong movement, going from a weak area into a strong area, than if you keep the figure in a strong area continuously. This principle is basically true in many phases of directing. For instance, there is a limit to the time that a director can keep the focus of emphasis on an actor who has few or no lines of dialogue, no matter how important he may be as a character or how much he may be acting during his period of silence.

There are those who do not believe this fact and want to take attention during all moments they are onstage. A few years ago a very fine director kept a star in unemphatic positions during stretches of dialogue in which she did not have occasion to be in the focus of the scene. Then when she did "take scene," he brought her into focus by using strong movement which brought her from a weak to a strong area. By having her take scene in this manner he made her doubly emphatic. The star, however, did not like her direction. A few days after the opening performance she began to edge nearer and nearer toward focus with each performance. Within a fortnight she had redirected herself in the whole play so that she was constantly the center of attention whether her part at the moment was emphatic or not. There she sat or stood at center stage the entire time. When she had no lines, she gesticulated and used facial expressions for mental reactions, acting very much like a jumping jack. This star never appreciated the value of the unemphatic position which allows strong movement to an emphatic position in the composition.

Occasionally there are plays like Arthur Miller's *After the Fall* in which the central character is onstage the entire time or nearly the entire time. In such cases the director simply has to find moments in which the actor will be unemphasized during long stretches of time. The resulting build from weak to strong can then be handled excellently for dramatic purposes.

MOVEMENT RELATED TO LEVEL   Movement from a lower to a higher level is strong. This is apparent not only in the simple cases of the body slouching and then straightening out but in movement up flights of stairs as well. An interesting phase of movement with level is exemplified by a weak movement that becomes neutralized by a strong one; the weak movement of walking directly upstage to a raised exit is balanced by the strong movement of going up steps. The figure will not gain dominant strength unless it turns before exiting.

LENGTH OF MOVEMENT   Walking long distance ordinarily weakens a movement, especially an exit. For this reason it is wise for the director to move his figure fairly near the exit before the actual exit movement. The weakening value of the long walk may be neutralized by making it more rapid than usual, or a long walk for entrance or exit may be built up for royalty by a formalized procession of guards and courtiers.

There are other ways also by which a weak exit movement may be strengthened. All of us have seen the leading lady take a gentleman's arm to support her exit. Both figures *turn in*; but although she has his arm, she keeps as far as possible away from him, usually a little ahead, talking violently to him as they make an exit from down to up center. Such an exit strengthens an inherently weak movement.

MOVEMENT RELATED TO GROUND PLAN   The values of these stage movements must be considered in the placement of entrances and exits in the director's ground plan for the designer. In general, important entrances should be made through upstage openings—up center being the strongest position for entrances, since it allows the entering figure full-front body position, possibility of strong movement coming downstage, and focus of emphasis from the other figures downstage. Important exits should be made through down-right openings, because the moving figure's profile is stronger than his back and the line of movement from center to right is stronger than from center to upstage.

Final exits of figures are usually more important than entrances, as they frequently stress the keynote of the character in the play. In considering the ground plan this importance must be decided, especially if there is only one door in the set, as is often the case, or if the figure must exit by the same opening through which he entered. Exit openings, therefore, should have preference over entrance openings. Accordingly, if we have one door only and the exit of the heroine going out to commit suicide is the climax of the play, the exit becomes more important than the entrance. In studying the chart of relative strength and weakness of movements (page 186) to decide the placement of this exit, we find that I-1 is excellent for an entrance but bad for an exit as in II-2, whereas II-1 is better for an exit than for an entrance as in I-3. The openings for this exit, therefore, should be placed down right.

Exercises in the General Evaluation of Movement

SET: *Doors DR, UR; fireplace on R wall between the two doors. Door UC with two steps leading into room. Window at center of L wall; door DL Stool in front of fireplace; sofa facing front at right angles to fireplace; chair at C, L of sofa, facing fireplace. Desk in front of window with chairs at L and R of desk. Bookcases UL and UR on rear wall.*

Problem: Have one member of the class execute each direction, and have class decide whether the movement is strong or weak.

The movements should be performed by someone who has memorized each one so as to show the direct relation of stage movement to the dance. The speed of execution in this demonstration should vary.

1. Figure *A* enters DR, Xs to chair C, sits.
2. Rises, Xs to door DR, closes door as he turns toward C.
3. Xs up to door UR, opens door.
4. Xs to US, stops, turns toward UL.
5. Turns toward DR.
6. Xs to chair C.
7. Turns toward UC door.
8. Xs to US door, going up both steps; turns on top step toward DL.
9. Sits down on top step and then straightens up.
10. Rises, Xs to window L, and looks out.
11. Turns around toward desk.

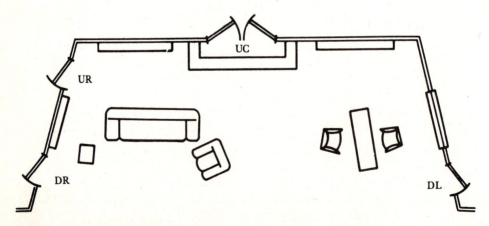

FIGURE 35   Ground plan for exercise in evaluation of movement

12. Sits in chair L of desk.
13. Buries his head in his arms on desk.
14. Rises, Xs to bookcase UL, and takes out book.
15. Xs to sofa.
16. Sits on sofa.
17. Stretches out on sofa.
18. Sits up.
19. Rises, Xs to stool.
20. Sits on stool.
21. Rises.
22. Turns toward fireplace.
23. Turns toward C.
24. Xs to C, then turns toward UR.
25. Turns front, then sits on arm of chair C.
26. Rises, Xs to door DL, and looks out.
27. Runs and Xs to chair R of desk, looking toward door UC.
28. Xs to above sofa and turns front.
29. Xs to right of desk, then sits on desk with feet on chair right of desk.
30. Xs to L above desk, stands on chair left of desk, and looks out window.
31. Jumps off chair and turns toward UC.
32. Turns and then Xs to below chair C.
33. Xs to stool, then sits with back toward audience.
34. Turns front, then buries face on knees.
35. Rises and Xs above sofa to door UC.
36. Xs to C and then turns toward UR.
37. Xs to door UR, turns toward DL, and exits by door UR.
38. Enters door UR.
39. Xs to door DL.
40. Xs to door DR and exits.

Values of Movement from Left Stage to Right; Right Stage to Left

Repeated experimentation has shown that a figure or group passing from left stage to right stage gives the effect of stronger movement, as well as a greater amount and force of movement of the figure, than movement from right stage to left. Of the many possible reasons why this is so, one is convincingly understandable: The normal movement of our eyes is from left to right. In looking at a panorama, whether it is actual or photographic, we begin at our left and follow through to our right.

We do the same thing when looking at the stage. When a figure or group walks along the normal direction of our vision, there is a certain ease or harmony between the eye and the moving figure. The figure goes along with us until he is offstage. With our eye going from left to right, it means that the figure is passing from right to left stage.

L to R

When, on the other hand, the figure goes from left to right stage there is a certain clash with the follow-through of our eye which, as we have seen, naturally travels from right stage to left. This clash, or resistance, in vision makes us feel that the figure is stronger than when it travels along and in harmony with our vision.

The sense of harmony, or ease, with our movement and sense of resistance to the other create definite values of weakness and strength respectively which, in turn, express definite mood qualities.

If the figure or group, therefore, is to enter with a sense of strength, it should enter from left stage and go to the right. Processions, groups, or lines of figures imply with this strength that they are going to something definite or important with an anticipation of success. Also, if a group comes from victory or success, it enters from the left stage.

R to L

In contrast to this: If the figure or group goes from right stage to left, it is weaker and, therefore is retreating or going to defeat or to something indefinite and uncertain. If the group returns from defeat, it comes from the right stage toward the left.

Peculiar as this phenomenon may be, it becomes clear and evident from demonstration. In a short time the beginning director will readily sense the degrees of strength and weakness in the two movements and will apply the proper movement when called for in a scene.

Demonstration

SCENE: *An army storming a castle.*

Problem: Is the castle on stage right or stage left?

    1. Decide its position from the principles described above.

    2. Try the castle on stage L.

    3. Try the castle on stage R.

For the mob storming the castle use about nine members of the class; space them at intervals with majority on stage L when the castle is at R, and vice versa. Have each take a different position of hurling a rock, shooting an arrow, using a battering ram, shaking fist, etc. Each should be in a different body position. Place one figure on a level behind and at the top of the castle which may be two flats.

This demonstration will show clearly that when the castle is on stage right the fighting appears much fiercer.

Exercises in Left and Right Movement

Picturize the following lines of people, and see that the line of movement faces the right way:

L to R   1. Going to your new exciting job.

L to R   2. Going to war.
R to L   3. Waiting for free bread and soup.
L to R   4. Climbing a difficult mountain.
R to L   5. Going to a grave.
R to L   6. Coming home and dreading to go in.
R to L   7. Leaving a house forever, sadly.
R to L   8. Arriving at a summer hotel, tired out after a day's trip in an automobile.

Closely allied with left and right movement and its implication is movement of an entering figure crossing to a stationary figure either standing or sitting. We have here the basic conflict of which is stronger—the movement or the stationary figure. The placement of the chair or desk around which the rest of the ground plan is often designed depends upon which figure is to be victorious. The figure moving from left to right stage is stronger than a figure placed right center. In such an instance the entering figure is more important and emphatic than the figure at right center whom he is approaching. In contrast to this when the stationary figure is more important, he should be placed left center, as that position is stronger than the one of the entering figure coming from right to left stage. In both these examples the movement has greater value than the area. The strong movement is stronger than the strong area; and vice versa, the weak movement is weaker than the weak area.

Demonstration of Movement Related to Stationary Figure

Place a figure on a chair LC facing R; have three figures offstage R enter one at a time, cross stage to LC, bow, speak part of the alphabet, and depart off R.

Reverse chair and figure to RC; have the three figures enter one at a time from the L repeating the same movement and exit L.

Which of these movements emphasizes the sitting figure, and which emphasizes the entering people?

Exercises

Picturize and see which is the better line of movement:

1. One figure approaches a king.
2. One figure appears before a judge; another waits to go before him.
3. Two children who have misbehaved come to their mother to confess.

Diagonal Movement

Diagonal movements from down right to up left or from up left to down right or from down left to up right or from up right to down left have four different values and implications.

As a general rule they are less strong than lines of movement parallel or perpendicular to the footlights, but the diagonal line is longer and seems much more so than these others. It seems to traverse a great distance and even seems to extend offstage. Whenever an exit or an entrance is so vitally important that it practically becomes the subject or title of a scene, the diagonal line is properly and wisely used.

Demonstrations

1. Test out for the class, singly and in groups of three, each one of the four diagonal movements, and decide their relative strengths and weaknesses.
2. Decide the exist of *A*, *B*, and C under the following conditions:

A room in *A's* house. *D* has come to visit and stays on and on, fighting with the servants and asserting himself until *A* can hardly call her home her own. After many minor situations which are unbearable for *A*, her daughter *B* and her son-in-law *C* come to help *A* pack and to take her from her own home, leaving *D* alone. They think that by this stratagem *D* will leave shortly; but instead *D* is delighted, as she has some relatives whom she wishes to have visit her in *A's* house. *D* is victorious; and *A*, *B*, and *C* are defeated.

So important was this scene that the doors were purposely designed into the set in order to dramatize the departure of the defeated.

Find the diagonal exit for *A*, *B*, and *C* and the position for *D* who cheerfully says good-by as each of the three departs with a short pause between each exit.

3. The same situation, except that this time *D* does not want her relatives to visit her. She is left alone, sad. In this situation *A*, *B*, and *C* are strong and victorious; *D* is weak and defeated.

(Check your results for 2 and 3 with the findings on page 219, under Direction of Movement.)

Summary

These four divisions of movement are all concerned with the values of sheer movement: first with body movement, then with general stage movement, next with right and left movement, and finally with diagonal movement. Just as in areas, we have seen what the values are and then what action or sort of scene these values suggest.

Movement and Dialogue

As in picturization, the use of movement depends upon the script. Later on under Effect of Movement on Mood we shall see the manner of choosing the amount and kind of movement.

With an understanding of the values of sheer movement our next problem is to find the relationship of these values to the lines of dialogue. In contradiction to the often heard lament of beginning directors that they can find no legitimate reasons for interpreting movement out of dialogue, the motivation for much of the movement in bringing a play to life arises from the meaning or mood of the line of dialogue which in turn relates to character. More than this, all movement should be related directly to the line, except in those instances where movement has a connotative value.

Dialogue Values

Just as in the case of body positions, areas, planes, levels, and so on, so too we find that lines of dialogue may be classified as strong or weak. The point to remember, however, is that weak speeches or lines may be as important and as emphatic as strong ones. In so far as they are strong or weak they have a definite relation to movement; every sentence of a play has an inherent movement. In this respect a play, speech by speech, may be likened to a dance. The inherent movement may be strong or weak, or it may be a rest in movement that is as much a part of movement as movement itself. A rest in movement, as in dance, is the timed pause; it corresponds to a rest in music.

The line, moreover, may be made strong or weak according to the movement given it, or we may change the meaning of a line by the movement given it. What, then, determines our evaluation of a line and the interpretation that we give it? The interpretation of any one element in a play—the character, the scene, the dialogue, and so forth—depends upon what dramatic value can contribute most to the main purpose of the play. Therefore, in determining the evaluation of any line it is considered not in itself but in relation to its dramatic value within the entire text.

It is necessary to learn to sense the values of lines. To a large extent, this is an intuitive faculty, but we suggest below the possible kinds of lines with their appropriate movement:

a. The absolutely positive and strong line of dialogue should be used with strong movement only. These are lines of command, determination, defiance, optimism, threat, and so on, the characteristics of which are positive. "Look here: I'm not going to stand this!" "Do as I say or you go out!" "There's no question about it, he'll win." These are lines positive in connotation demanding strong movement.

b. The negative and weak line of dialogue should be used with weak movement only. Lines of doubt, defeat, introspection, fright, hopelessness, frustration connote a negative quality. "What a mess I've made of it!" "I swear to you I feel the whole weight of the denunciation." "I am disgraced, impeded, and baffled here . . . and I have no way out." These are negative lines demanding weak movement.

c. The line that is partly strong and partly weak, either beginning weak and ending strong or beginning strong and ending weak, demands movement to correlate with the strong and weak parts of the line.

"If I stay, we'll go on making ourselves miserable . . . we must call it quits now!" The first part of the line takes a weak movement; the second, a strong movement.

"Sir, you must believe me. . . . Ah, yes, I can tell, it's all quite useless." The first part of the line takes a strong movement; the second part, a weak movement.

An exception to the use of a strong movement on a positive line or a weak movement on a negative line is found in comedy where for incongruity we may make use of a strong movement on a weak line or vice versa. It is a common stock in trade of the comedian's technique to make a weak movement like backing away as he calls out: "I'll punch you on the jaw!"

Demonstration

Demonstrate on stage the examples given above. First do the line with the correct use of movement as illustrated; then do it with the opposite value of movement. You will find that the correct use of the movement reinforces the sentiment of the line.

d. Many times in order to emphasize the correct interpretation of a line it becomes necessary to evaluate that line by the movement given it. The line can be made positive or negative according to the movement related to it. For illustration let us take: "I'm the one that's being made a fool!" By giving a strong movement to the line a positive statement is made by which the character asserts his indignation: "I'm the one that's being made a fool! (And I won't allow it!)"

But by giving a weak movement to the line the character assumes an ineffectual and self-pitying attitude of mind: "I'm the one that's being made a fool! (And there's nothing I can do about it.)"

e. Related to the foregoing are those lines whose meaning depends on the movement given them. "Yes, it's wonderful!" Give a strong movement to this line, and the character means what he says. Now give a weak movement to the line, and the opposite effect is achieved: The character does not believe that it is wonderful. The movement has changed the meaning of the line. It becomes evident that before we can decide the movement required by a line we must first make clear to ourselves the right interpretation of the line in reference to the character and the situation.

f. Sarcasm is a positive line with a negative meaning and will take either a strong or a weak movement according to the meaning.

Demonstration

Work out the movement for the lines of sarcasm spoken by Henry in the following dialogues:

1. SHE: He longs to be free . . . he said so himself.
   HENRY: Yes, so as to be able to see you again . . . having been touched by your pity.
2. SHE: He'll talk her out of her fright.
   HENRY: She's not afraid, doctor. Don't you believe it. The thing bores her rather.
3. SHE: History says—I don't know whether you know it or not—that . . .
   HENRY: Yes, I know. You are most faithful to history, my dear.

Do each line of sarcasm first with a strong and then with a weak movement. In each instance decide which is the more effective.

Movement on, before, and after Lines

a. When possible the movement should come *on* the line. As a rule lines are never held for movement unless, of course, the pause is used for a definite dramatic effect. Lines that do not need particular pointing up should have movement come on the line when movement is called for. A movement that is illustrative of the line should come *on* the line. Sometimes when movement is boldly illustrative of the line, a movement separated from the line will soften the general effect.

b. The movement is made *before* a line when it becomes essential to attract attention and emphasize the line as the important thing. This is an instance of "pointing" the line. The actor first attracts attention to himself by making a strong movement and then stops or holds the movement just before speaking, thereby giving the line definite emphasis. Such a movement may be standing or making a strong stage movement or gesture with the hand. Important lines and words that contribute directly to the story or idea or both demand this kind of pointing. Movement is only one of many ways of pointing a line. Often for greater emphasis or variety it may be used with one or more methods of line pointing, such as

1. A pause in movement, business, or voice before the line or the important words.

2. Taking an important position, such as coming down into a stronger area.

3. A contrast in the quality of tone when speaking the important line or words, as going from a full tone to a whisper.

4. Raising or lowering the pitch of the voice.

5. Speaking the important words with staccato.

6. Retarding the tempo of the line.

When pointing a line with proper movement and business it is important to do it with precision, especially in the playing of comedy. Apropos of this, all movement should be definite and simple in execution, for movement, more than anything else onstage, attracts the attention.

Usually the movement before the line must be strong if the line is to be emphasized; but if the movement itself is to be emphasized rather than the line, then the movement before the line must be weak. A character who turns upstage (a weak movement) and then delivers his line is emphasizing the movement.

c. The movement *after* the line will likewise emphasize the movement. The delivery of the line attracts attention and gives emphasis to the movement immediately following. Here again, as a rule, the movement after the line must be strong if it is to receive emphasis; otherwise if it is weak, the line receives emphasis. Lines that follow movement are those which have finality.

Exercises in Relating Movement to Dialogue

1. Study any play and having determined the evaluation of lines of dialogue, find two lines of each of the following:

(*a*) positive lines requiring movement.

(*b*) negative lines requiring movement.

(*c*) lines partly strong and partly weak.

(*d*) lines that are positive or negative according to the movement.

(*e*) lines of sarcasm.

(*f*) lines that you can move on.

(*g*) lines that you can move before.

(*h*) lines that you can move after.

2. Execute these lines on stage with their respective movements.

3. Show ten different ways of pointing a line or the important words.

Important as movement is to a play, it is a dangerous and difficult element. Like the old saying about fire, it is a fine slave but a bad master. If as a director you can conquer it, your play benefits; but if you are at a loss how to handle it, it will destroy your play.

Movements Related to Emphasis

MOVEMENT AND DIALOGUE Movement commands a great deal of attention. It will make the audience look at it rather than listen to a speech. No matter how much a director builds up the emphasis of the speaker, a small movement from an unimportant figure will distract the audience's attention.

What little of directing we have covered so far boils down to the audience's looking at what we want it to see and hearing what is necessary for an understanding of the play. Let one of the minor female characters appear with a fan and unconsciously use it when she feels that it is in character, and your work of hours crumbles like a house of cards. For this reason, hand props, in all circumstances, must be used selectively on the stage.

Like the fan, small doodads on dresses, handkerchiefs, and jewelry also can prove distracting. They are small, but they are typical of the danger arising from any unwise movement. In plays with many characters, it is difficult to obtain the necessary reaction and movement and still protect important lines.

DIALOGUE AND BACKGROUND MOVEMENT   The technique required by a player of Cyrano in the fencing scene, where the actor has one of the most beautiful passages in poetic drama and must fence throughout before many spectators, presents a problem in control of movement. In fact, all the action of background crowds in circumstances as in *Cyrano de Bergerac* can be so obtrusive that one has to carefully control the movement and business in these scenes, oftentimes almost freezing the crowds on passages of important verse.

ACTOR'S INDIVIDUAL DIALOGUE AND MOVEMENT   Because of the power of movement in attracting attention, it has become the custom in the theatre for an actor to move on his own lines rather than on those of someone else unless the lines being spoken by the other actor are very unimportant. This is wise because in many instances an actor can judge the best of several lines to move on and can decide the relation of the line to the movement.

The easiest line on which to make a movement, such as a cross or exit, is one in which the line describes, explains, or is expressive of the movement.

Examples: Execute me, but I've got to go.

Come on, I'm in an awful hurry.

We'll go ahead slowly, and you can catch up.

Good-by, everybody, good-by!

The actor can cross to an exit on all these. In spite of the distracting movement, enough of the words will be heard, and the movement itself is explanatory of the line.

ENTRANCES AND DIALOGUE   This is equally true of an entrance. Unless there is a very definite reason for not doing so, an entering figure should begin to speak immediately. Many actors feel that they should walk to their position after entering and then begin to speak. When this is done, there is a break in the flow of the scene. When an act has several entrances in it, such as a first act, the general effect resulting from pauses for unimportant speeches is one of hesitation and jerkiness. Actually an entrance speech is seldom so important that it needs a holding of the figure. When it does, it is better to hold the actor by the door for the full pointed effect and then have him move on his second speech. But lines like the following can be spoken while the character moves:

I just stepped in with some magazines for poor Mrs. Jones.

Hello, Anna. How do they like your patio?

How do, Mr. Neil? Mrs. Neil? Ellen?

An entering figure nearly always has a speech. It is much easier for an actor to have the first speech on entering. Only occasionally does a person onstage have a speech to a person entering. When this is so, the entering figure should keep moving to a position onstage while the actor onstage is addressing him. This prevents the entering character from being *suspended* any longer than possible before he gives his first line.

CROSSES AND DIALOGUE   Crosses and movements are usually made in front of the other figure with whom the character is conversing. That is another reason why the speaker should move on his own line. When a cross is made behind another actor, the moving figure passes out of focus and breaks his power of holding attention. By moving on his line and crossing in front, he can still hold this attention until he has finished and at the same time allow the other figure to pick up his cue and continue the attention and interest in the scene. Minor characters, like servants, do make crosses upstage of the principals.

EXITS AND DIALOGUE   When a figure leaves the stage, it is nearly always best for him to be near the exit for his last speech. A usual method is for an actor to give part of his speech, make his cross, and then give the rest at the door. Even if a figure does not proceed with his exit in this manner but must deliver his last speech, let us say, near center stage and then exit, the director should see to it that the figure is fairly near the exit door so that the cross to the exit is not too long and does not hold up the lines and flow of the scene.

If an exit is very important or if it has value as comedy in line or business, the people remaining on stage should hold their lines for the exit. Also, they should hold their lines if the character exiting is not supposed to hear what is said after he leaves. The smooth flow of a scene is so important that unless there is a definite and important reason for an emphatic exit, dialogue should not be held for actors leaving the stage.

Relation of Movement to Dialogue in a Pacing Scene

In a pacing scene the relationship of movement to dialogue must be carefully considered, and the movement planned so as to preserve the lines. Its control, manner, and variation depend on the nature of the situation.

In execution of a pacing scene movement must be organized into a definite pattern. This is most important so as not to confuse the audience. A disorganized pacing scene makes the audience wonder where the actor is going next, and thus detracts from the lines. The pattern established for the scene may be a repetition of definite planned movements in the form of a triangle or straight lines or any regular form that best expresses the nature of the situation. By unobtrusively establishing this pattern, we draw the attention of the audience to what the actor is saying and not to what he is doing.

The pacing may be done by the person speaking, in which case he points his own lines either by stopping before he speaks or by speaking on strong movements only. The others, if they have lines, speak while he is taking weak movements.

Or the pacing may be done by the nonspeaking person, in which case the pacer points the speaker's lines by his movement.

The following outline gives the general procedure for pacing scenes:

PLACEMENT OF ACTORS   The nonmoving actor is placed in a strong downstage area as far as possible from the mover. The mover is placed in weakened areas; his movement may be roughly from up center to down left.

LINES OF THE NONMOVING ACTOR   His lines are spoken loudly and while the mover is making a weak movement or while the mover is in a weak body position. To bring enough emphasis to himself, the nonmoving actor should make a slight movement before or after his lines, as the case may be. In instances where the lines of the nonmoving actor are particularly important, the mover should stop pacing, often occupying himself with business.

LINES OF THE MOVER   He emphasizes his lines by stopping and holding the movement for the line and then picks up his pacing in a faster tempo. Or he emphasizes them by speaking on strong movements, like coming downstage or going from left to center. Or he may speak as he opens up or just before a turn if he is going into a weak movement. He should get variety in the pointing of his lines by using all the methods mentioned.

PLANNING OF THE MOVEMENT   In the pattern of the movement he will use a regular form like a triangle. The movement may go from up center to down left to up left and back to up center. It must be subordinated to the lines. Once the pattern of movement is established, he should use a movement out of the basic form for variation. This, however, should not be carried too far; otherwise the pacing becomes disorganized and confusing. For variety again the actor may use different body positions and different positions within the pattern for the delivery of speeches. As the scene progresses the speed of movement should be increased or decreased, depending on whether the scene calls for a build or for a diminished ending.

Demonstration

1. Let each group work out the technique outlined above, using letters of the alphabet for lines. Each group should present a different pattern of movement.

   a. Do one scene where the speed of the movement increases as the scene progresses.

   b. Do one where the speed of the movement decreases as the scene progresses.

Exercises in Pacing Scenes

1. Let each group work out a pacing scene where the pacing is done by the non-speaking person. Use letters of the alphabet for lines.

2. A pacing scene from *Bell, Book and Candle* by John Van Druten, Act III, scene 1. Copyright 1951. Reprinted by permission of Carter Lodge Productions, Inc.

NICKY: Well, darling, how do you feel now?

GILLIAN: [*Inarticulate with rage.*] Feel? Feel?

NICKY: Feel like coming to Natalie's party with me?

GILLIAN: Maybe. But I've got a little job to do here first.

NICKY: Old Bianca? [GILLIAN *nods grimly.*]

MISS HOLROYD: You know, you're wrong about her, Gillian. She was very nice about you tonight. She really was.

GILLIAN: Yes, I'm sure she was. "Dear Gillian, I'm so fond of her. Just an amateur, of course, but really quite gifted in her way." Wasn't that it?

MISS HOLROYD: Well, sort of—yes. But . . .

GILLIAN: Amateur. I'll show her.

NICKY: That's my little sister.

GILLIAN: She and her five thousand dollars. With her potions and her . . . I wonder why he said it tasted bad. I suppose she thought if it didn't, he wouldn't feel that he was getting his money's worth. It must have tasted revolting for that.

NICKY: Maybe she gave him a candy, after.

GILLIAN: It'll cost her a lot more than five thousand to get out of what I'll do to her. She's got a lot of valuable Chinese rugs, you once told me. And that mink coat! Well, we'll start with some *moths!*

MISS HOLROYD: Gillian, you mustn't!

GILLIAN: Come to that, there's Merle, too. [*Furiously.*] "Be as thou wast wont to be." And how was that? In love with Merle Kittredge. No. She's not going to get him back. Not if I have anything to do with it. Where's Pyewacket? [*She opens the kitchen door and calls.*] Pye—Pye—Pyewacket? Pye, where are you? [*She goes into the kitchen.*]

MISS HOLROYD: I've never seen her like this before.

Problem: Gillian is angry and expresses this in pacing. Nicky, her brother, is amused while Miss Holroyd, her aunt, tries to appease her.

a. Determine the placement of the actors and kitchen door.

b. Determine the lines on which Gillian can move to preserve her own lines and the lines of her aunt and brother.

c. Establish a pattern that will subordinate movement to the lines.

d. Get a continual flow in her movements.

e. Get a build in her movements.

f. Obtain variety in her form of movement.

g. Get the laugh lines across.

Movement and Picturization

In the demonstrations of Solomon and the true and false mothers, as we proceeded with the various pictures that told the meaning of the whole story, we found that movement crept into the process of going from one picture to another. In this case the movement was of secondary importance, and the resulting picture the dominant part of the exercise. It is true that in many plays the movement between scenes is of secondary importance, but usually the movement itself between pictures is just as important as the pictures. Not only does it relate itself to the overall mood inherent in the pictures, but it is as telling as the pictures themselves.

Storytelling Quality of Movement

Under Areas we have seen the storytelling quality that is conveyed by figures at a distance from each other or in close relationship. Now, the actual strong movement that brings *A* from stage right to *B* on stage left has a storytelling quality. The distance between two figures cuts down the emotional intensity between them. There is not a close or strong emotional relationship. As they draw nearer to each other in any emotional condition, their positions grow stronger, more intense, and therefore more climactic; the love grows more fervent; the anger, more vehement; the situation, more intense. The change in this emotional relationship is known as "low to climactic position."

Under Breaking Up we saw the opportunities for a variety of positions. This also holds true in picturization; as the figures draw nearer to each other during a scene, the emotional intensity of the movement increases and contributes to the climax of the scene and at the same time makes clearer the meaning of the scene.

Planning Pattern of Movement to Obtain Storytelling Quality

We have already seen how placing our characters to picturize the emotional relationship helps us with the positioning of the people for a scene. We shall now see how the changing of the emotional relationship of character to character gives us the movement for an entire scene.

THE SCENE   Let us imagine a scene between the supervisor of a rehabilitation center and one of the boys. The supervisor has caught the boy in a position that leads him to think he was attempting to steal. The boy is at first belligerent, and the supervisor is firm and severe. The latter, not being able to get the boy to confess by this means, next tries to persuade him to tell, offering him his confidence and doing him a friendly act by putting a blanket around him, as it is night and he is cold.

The boy does not respond but turns on the supervisor and tells him what he thinks of him, the center, and life in general. He is thoroughly denunciatory. He is bold and frank because he knows that he will receive severe punishment in any case.

The supervisor then tries to win the boy's confidence by telling him of certain events in his own life. The boy becomes interested. The supervisor's disclosure shows him that this supervisor was once in the same situation. The boy softens, relents, and confesses. The supervisor professes his affection and future personal interest in the boy. The latter agrees to do the right thing and be the supervisor's friend and supporter.

THE ANALYSIS   Upon close analysis we find that there are five distinct changes of emotional relationship in this scene—five major phases. Accordingly, there are five distinct picturizations of the scene, and the transitions from one to the other will give us the movement.

1. First we have the two opposing characters who are obviously placed opposite each other on the far sides of the stage.

2. The first change of emotional state is when the supervisor pleads with the boy. He comes over to the boy. Meeting with no success, he returns to his own side.

3. The boy's next state is one of attack upon the supervisor. Accordingly, as this part of the scene progresses, he approaches from his place by degrees, going over to the supervisor; and since, at the end, he is still antagonistic, he will return to his former position.

4. The next state is when the supervisor tells the boy the story of his life. He comes part way toward the boy but turns away from him because the narration is so difficult for him that he cannot give it to the boy directly. He comes part way because he is more sympathetic than he has been heretofore. As the supervisor tells the story, the boy, at first indifferent, gradually becomes absorbed and is drawn closer to the supervisor. Accordingly, he begins by being in an aloof picturization and slowly turns and walks over toward the supervisor.

5. Then in the final lines in which they are in mutual understanding, they are together in the same area at the center of the stage, possibly shaking hands.

From this example we see that the change of the emotional relations between two or more people on the stage leads to a definite pattern, a definite combination of emotional picturization and movement. We shall discuss this point further under the section on motivated movement through character pattern.

If an actor is put physically into a picture with the correct relationship to the other people in the scene, in the correct body position for the mood in which the speech is to occur, and given the correct movement for the transitions and changes in emotional relationship, he will instinctively read the speeches of that scene with greater intelligence and emotional depth than if he is in the wrong picture or there is no picture at all.

Technical Details of Movement

Building a Scene Solely by Movement

METHODS   In building a scene to a climax, voice and tempo as well as movement are important. Our problem at the moment, however, is to practice building a scene by the use of movement only. Movement will build a scene if we increase the amount and size; change the value, placement, and tension; and use contrast.

The following is one arrangement in the use of these methods:

1. Increase length of movement from shorter at the beginning to longer toward the end.
2. Increase number of people moving.
3. Use contrasting movement.
4. Use shorter movement.
5. Go from weak body positions and levels to strong.
6. Increase tension of the movement.
7. Use stronger areas.
8. Increase the number of people crossing one another.
9. Increase the amount of small movement.
10. Go from individual to group movement.

Exercises

Variations on these methods of building a scene are being effectively used in contemporary dance choreography and by experimental theatre groups.

1. Work out the arrangement outlined above in building a scene solely by movement, using seven people.
2. Using the text as a basis for creation and motivation of movement, apply variations of these methods to one of the choral scenes from a tragedy by Sophocles or Euripides, Eliot's *Murder in the Cathedral,* or van Itallie's *The Serpent.*

CONSERVATION OF MOVEMENT   In a scene that demands a build you will find that the inherent interest of the situation usually holds in itself so that the amount of breaking up required in the beginning is small compared to the amount and acceleration of breaking up necessary in the latter part of the scene. The control of the methods of building and the proportion of breaking up are also dependent on the characters who, in themselves, may or may not be able to hold scenes. In building a scene, therfore, we must be careful not to unload all our means at one time but to work out a progression that will give a smooth build in relation to situation and characters. This is necessary for conservation and variety. For a reminder on general principles of conservation and build both in reference to scenes and the entire play, we refer the student to page 88.

Parallel and Countermovement

As a rule, parallel movement and countermovement, that is, two persons moving in identical or directly opposite directions at the same time, are to be avoided. These movements, however, are sometimes effective in comedy or farce. A slight retarding of one person's movement will break up parallel and countermovement. This, as in other such rules, has exceptions.

Contrasting Movement

This movement can often be used to great advantage. Compare a mob going off to the right in victory with a lone figure going off to the left in defeat. The contrast of the movements heightens the value of each.

Handling Violent Scenes

Unless we are intentionally doing a scene of this kind for its horror element, all violent scenes should be softened and blended into the whole of the play.

In a murder the scene preceding the actual killing should be built up, very often by movement, and the killing should follow rapidly. Generally, the actual death execution should be muffled by using a weak area. The body should fall behind furniture or somewhere so that it will be partially covered unless it is important to have it visible to the audience in the following scene. The same holds true for suicide by shooting, which in most cases should also be carefully muffled by having the actor's back toward the audience and by placing the scene in a weak area. Refer to what was said in Chapter 4, Elementary Stage Technique for the Actor, regarding the actor's handling of violent scenes.

Handling Love Scenes

GENERAL PRINCIPLES   With amateurs it is necessary to take advantage of the connotative value of the softened upstage areas for love scenes. The actors will blend into the picture, add more of a romantic flavor to the scene, and feel less self-conscious than if they were downstage in close contact with the audience.

The director should keep constantly in mind the fact that a sense of the emotion of love should be stimulated in the audience rather than in the actors. This can be done by means of romantic picturization. We need to picturize most graphically, as that will hold the interest of the audience in the sheer beauty of the picturization and will tend to make the actors less self-conscious by keeping their minds on the business. In romantic positions they will also read their lines with more feeling.

The third principle to consider in a love scene for purposes of conservation and variety is the postponement of the actual embrace which the actors reach at the end of the scene. Far too often directors place the actors downstage, either standing center stage or sitting on a sofa, for an entire scene; whereas a love scene can begin with the actors somewhat apart. The movement, then, that accompanies the scene can be such as to draw them slowly and by degrees closer and closer together from the farther sides of the area used for the scene. In this way we have built to the embrace while maintaining interest by a progressive picturization of the love scene.

EXAMPLE IN PROCEDURE   As an example of these principles, let us block out the picturization and movement for a love scene.

Let us play the scene around a sofa placed slightly upstage at right center. (If the scene has to be played standing, it can be done behind a chair or table but in any case in a softened area.) The girl can sit on the center of the sofa early in the scene, with the boy standing at right when the scene first begins to take on a love interest. He can cross from where he is standing to the right end of the sofa. He can hold his position there for several speeches. Then he can move along behind the sofa until he is leaning over from behind the girl. From this position he can come around the left end of the sofa and stand there. He can then sit on the arm of the sofa and then on the left end of the sofa itself. The girl can easily find lines that will allow her to move over to the right end of the sofa. The boy can then move toward the center, then closer to the girl until he is by her. He can then place his arm upon the back of the sofa, then take her left hand in his left. He can bring his arm from the back of the sofa down to her shoulder, and finally he can kiss her.

This manner of handling a love scene is possible in many cases, whether the scene is played around a sofa or not. Love scenes are often played about a piano, a mantelpiece, an armchair, a table, a window, the lower steps of a flight of stairs, or a mantelpiece and sófa together, and so on. But in all cases the actual embracing should be postponed by the building up of romantic positions that increasingly bring the lovers closer together.

A good principle to follow is to have the love scene played about a piece of furniture rather than standing center stage. Furthermore, it is a good policy to have the embrace come from a sitting rather than a standing position. Refer to what was said in Chapter 4 regarding the actor's technique in embracing and kissing.

Exercises in Technical Details of Movement

1. Build an abstract scene solely by movement.
2. Each group pantomime a murder scene, using a weapon.
3. Each group pantomime a love scene—different from the sofa example.

General Kinds of Movement

Story

Movement may be used to express the story or attending circumstances of a play. As such it is usually indicated by the playwright and covers such actions as entrances and exits of characters, handling of objects, dressing, going to a window to look out, serving meals, fighting, and dancing. They are obvious movements for the necessary action in the story progression. Movements illustrative of the lines belong to this kind of movement. Examples: "Help me with this packing"; "Close the door, dear"; "Drink up."

Demonstrations

1. Entrance of the refugees in Wilder's *Skin of Our Teeth*.
2. The Common Man's preparations in Bolt's *A Man for All Seasons*.
3. The duel in *Hamlet*.
4. Julian's presentation of the clothes in Hellman's *Toys in the Attic*.

Background

Background movements establish locale and atmosphere. They are often supplied by the playwright, but more often than not it is up to the director to supply them when essential for a fuller realization of the scene. Scenes such as the sidewalk cafe in Ionesco's *Rhinoceros*, the police headquarters in Kingsley's *Detective Story*, the bar and street scenes in Sackler's *The Great White Hope*, and the theatre in Rostand's *Cyrano de Bergerac* contain examples.

Character

These movements portray the type of character or the character's state of mind. To express the temperament of a high-strung, restless character we should give him plenty of movement: rising, sitting, rising again, moving about from one side of the stage to the other—movement on the slightest provocation, but a kind of movement that demands careful control (Jimmy Porter in *Look Back in Anger*). The sluggish type of character, on the other hand, would be portrayed with very little movement (Lennie in *Of Mice and Men*). Impatience, confusion, uncertainty, fear, torment, and the like may be expressed by proper movement (Serafina in *Rose Tattoo*).

Movement is never neutral. For example, a character may sit in a manner that depicts anger, despair, relief, exhaustion, or whatever emotion the moment demands. Remember, then, that any action on stage makes an impact on the audience. No action can be performed perfunctorily.

Technical

On stage there are technical as well as emotional reasons for movement. By this we mean that movement may be made for esthetic reasons of good composition or out of sheer necessity of opening up an area for an entrance or an exit. But though the movement may be necessary for technical reasons, nevertheless it must come out of a motivation which ultimately, whatever the reason for executing the movement, relates to character.

COMPOSITIONAL   The movements for obtaining emphasis, as discussed under Composition, come under this description of movements for technical reasons. So also do movements for obtaining stability, sequence, or balance in the composition. *Taking* or *giving the scene* is a purely technical movements to achieve a balanced composition—in these instances the subtle manner of execution should make the movements unobstrusive. The movements for variety, as the arbitrary breaking up of a scene; movements to stimulate the attention of the audience or to relieve tension are technical movements. In realistic plays technical movements must be motivated by the actor and director and must be related directly to the lines and character.

TRANSITIONAL   Transitional scenes are usually those of entrances and exits. During these we may move the actors to effective positions for the ensuing action. In addition, such scenes demand some fill-in movement at this time such as crossing to a piece of furniture to keep them vital.

Motivation of Movement

Movement used to express story, background, or character may be motivated out of either inner or arbitrary considerations, depending upon the script that is to be directed. What is motivated out of arbitrary considerations is of a technical and intellectual nature whereas movement motivated from inner considerations has a more emotional basis. For this reason we say that, as a general rule, the movement of comedy is more arbitrary than that of tragedy.

There are several ways in which motivation for movement on stage may be found. The first is that related to purely arbitrary consideration. The second is the inner motivated type of movement which includes realistic follow-through, psychological follow-through, and the movement that is the result of character pattern or fundamental design.

However, we must not be misled by such terms as "arbitrary," "character pattern," or "fundamental design," since we cannot stress too strongly that motivation for movement must ultimately seem to come from character —whether it is need, desire, or drive. For this reason, in blocking a scene the director should learn to give directions for movement in terms of motives and objectives—to get something, to be near somebody, to stretch, and so on. In this way he justifies the movement for the actor by explaining the impulse for it, rather than giving an arbitrary direction such as "cross from DR to L," even when his main intention is to have the actor move to stage left for technical reasons.

The ground plan, which is a result of analyzing the many requirements of the situations for determining placement of doors, chairs, table, and so on, ultimately brings about its own logic for movements. (See page 337, Designing the Ground Plan.) Since the placement of doors and furniture already is determined, the direction to the actor is simply "Lay your package on the table," not "Cross from door at DR to table at L."

Arbitrary Considerations in Using Movement

Arbitrary movement is created by the director or actor for a script that is inherently static or talky. For example, we enhance the play of wit in such comedies as those of Oscar Wilde, Noel Coward, Terence Rattigan, and Neil Simon by movement calculated to emphasize the significance of the line. The movement may be one of ennui, sarcasm, pretended joy, overdone sorrow, mock fatigue, and so on. In any event it springs from the intent of the line and the desire to increase its laugh-provoking power. Likewise, character movements may be made for the same reasons, or the movement may be made for sheer variety which is arbitrary movement at its best. The clever director who inserts movement of this kind into the performance is always careful to rehearse it over and over again so that it is smooth and definitely related to situation or character, thereby presumably projected out of the given circumstances or inner motivations. As a result, this "arbitrarily" created movement, although not an intrinsic part of the script, seems to be so. In some instances business is created to justify movement such as taking out a cigarette, but crossing to a sidetable for the lighter. In this way the movement is used for an essential pointing of a line or for necessary variety. Similarly, incidental actions may be created to encompass an entire scene. Normally, the playwright will set up these scenes with functions that permit a great amount of business, as discussed under scenes of incidental action in the chapter on Picturization.

Overused or not, these functions serve their purpose not only in keeping this kind of scene alive, but also in opening up opportunities for movement to bring emphasis where necessary. Let us say the host carries the weight of a scene where discussion centers around principles of belief in a moral issue. And, let us say, that his views must relate to several characters. The setting may be a patio or any drawing room. For a function the director introduces cocktails with which to work for clarification and delineation of the topic under discussion. Though movement will be created out of arbitrary considerations, its execution must be motivated. The host's motivation to rise is justified: he must go to the bar to get or replenish drinks. On his way over he stops to deliver a line or two of dialogue to one of the characters, thereby pointing up his line; on the guest's reaction the host continues his cross and starts to fix drinks while the center of interest may shift elsewhere. The emphasis returns to the host for an off-hand but important remark as he moves in, possibly stirring the beaker of liquor. Next, the host serves the drinks, passing from one character to another, and each time pointing up a part of his argument that has special significance to the character he is with at the moment. Serving drinks becomes sufficient motivation for the host to move to another guest and the fact that he is with that character sufficient motivation to point up what concerns the guest only. Throughout these actions emphasis on conversation must remain uppermost. In summation: by careful analysis of the text to note the order of speaking and by the proper positioning of the characters in a diversified composition, we can make each move, each relationship, each bit of pointing become the logical thing to do. Subtlety of control has made it appear logical and motivated, besides vitalizing an otherwise talky scene.

Arbitrary movement selects its end and proceeds to it with dispatch and neatness. The result is a well-paced, clean-cut movement unhampered by minutely worked-out detail. Such movement is admirably suited to the playing of comedy.

In farce or farce comedies where geometric movements like parallel and countermovement are continually introduced to enhance situations, we find still another instance of the arbitrary use of movement, which again must be related to character needs.

Nothing is more disconcerting than stage movement which an audience recognizes as being completely and thoroughly unrelated. For this reason the director should be careful to have the arbitrary considerations for movement become pertinent to the character within the situation.

Inner Considerations for Use of Movement

REALISTIC FOLLOW-THROUGH   In realistic follow-through, movement must have an objective to which it is directed. In this the motivation is obvious and thoroughly worked out. Realistic follow-through demands that an actor present every step of the movement so that there is nothing false about it. This is appropriate to the plays of Chekhov, of O'Neill, of Arthur Miller, of Tennessee Williams—plays that depend upon the richness and truth of character and situation. Many melodramas employ highly detailed realistic movement due to the exigencies of the situation.

In such plays even purely technical movement must have realistic follow-through. Consistency demands that technical movements not become purely arbitrary. In the example above the host's move to the bar could have been primarily for the technical reason of having him cross from one area to another. To give a realistic follow-through to the movement the director has the character start toward the bar, presumably to get a drink, but stop on the way to speak, leaving the motivation unfulfilled. If not a bar, the director could have the character start toward the bookcase, this time presumably to pick out a book. The director has motivated a movement executed solely for technical reasons. Actually, this is an arbitrary movement, but motivation has been supplied to blend in with the overall realistic follow-through of the entire play. In a realistic play every movement must be motivated in some way, even though the objective of the motivation is never reached nor the motivation fulfilled. This motivation, as we have seen, may be the beginning to go somewhere, to sit down, to leave, and so on. Background movements in realistic plays must also have a realistic follow-through of movement.

PSYCHOLOGICAL FOLLOW-THROUGH   These are the movements motivated by the emotional and intellectual content of the line or by character expression. They have already been discussed under relation of movement to the kinds of line and under movements that portray the character's state of mind. They illustrate changes in thought of the character, in character relationships, and picturize the mental and emotional attitudes of characters toward one another.

MOVEMENT AS A RESULT OF CHARACTER PATTERN   Associated with and dependent upon psychological follow-through of movement are character patterns. These show graphically the interplay between two or more characters, either in one scene or during the whole play, when the story and theme rest upon such interplay. Character pattern is achieved by the combination of changing picturization of emotional relationships and connotative movement. A scene worked out thus will have a definite pattern in movement that is clear to the observer and can be drawn in graphic form.

Demonstration

Romeo and Juliet, Act III, scene 5—scene beginning with the entrance of Capulet and Nurse. Work out scene without learning lines.

In this scene Juliet makes three appeals: to Capulet, to Lady Capulet, and to the Nurse. Each time her appeal is rebuffed. In the interplay of the four characters the motivation to action comes from Juliet. We immediately see that in order to project the greatest dramatic value of the scene we must interpret the action from Juliet's point of view. The pattern for the scene, then, must graphically show this play of action and reaction, or, in terms of this particular scene, appeal and rebuff. Certainly, if we have each of the three go to Juliet, we shall lose the significance of the scene. The diagram shows the pattern that will best express the nature of the situation. Lines drawn designate the movements of Juliet.

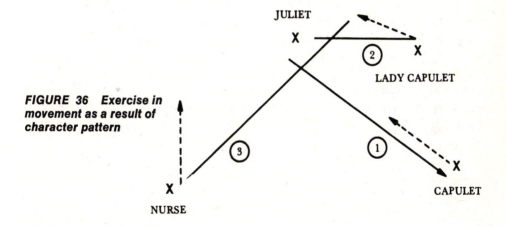

FIGURE 36   *Exercise in movement as a result of character pattern*

By now we have probably accepted the fact that the blocking of a scene varies from director to director, not so much in projecting the intent of a scene, as much as in the execution of that intent into stage terms. However, at this time we are not concerned with blocking per se, but with the process of thought that brought the blocking into being. The overall structure comes first, blocking is the detailing.

Character pattern, as a projection of the interrelation of character actions and reactions through picturization and movement, structures a design that is expressive of the meaning of the content.

Demonstration

From: Act III, scene 3 of *Othello* by William Shakespeare

OTHELLO: [*Seated bench DLC.*] Give me a living reason
    she's disloyal.

IAGO: [*At DRC.*] I do not like the office:
    But sith I am enter'd in this cause so far,
    Prick'd to't by foolish honesty and love,
    I will go on. I lay with Cassio lately,

                                           X to O, slightly behind (1)
                                           him

    And, being troubled with a raging tooth,
    I could not sleep.
    There are a kind of men so loose of soul
    That in their sleeps will mutter their affairs:
    One of this kind is Cassio.

                                             sits to O's left from (2)
                                           behind bench, whispers

    In sleep I heard him say, "Sweet Desdemona,
    Let us be wary, let us hide our loves!"
    And then, sir, would he gripe and wring my hand,
    Cry "O sweet creature!" and then kiss me hard,
    As if he plucked up kisses by the roots
    That grew upon my lips; then laid his leg
    Over my thigh, and sighed, and kissed, and then

                                             touches O's thigh

    Cried "Cursed fate, that gave thee to the Moor!"

OTHELLO: [*Tightening up.*] O monstrous! monstrous!

IAGO: [*Rising*] Nay, this was but his dream.

                                             Xing DL (3)

OTHELLO: But this denoted a foregone conclusion:
    'Tis a shrewd doubt, though it be but a dream.

IAGO: And this may help to thicken other proofs
    That do demonstrate thinly.

OTHELLO: [*Almost down on his knees.*] I'll tear her all to pieces!

IAGO: [*Xing above bench.*] Nay, but be wise; yet we see nothing done; (4)
    she may be honest yet. Tell me but this:

                                             Xing RC, touching
                                           pocket (5)

    Have you not sometimes seen a handkerchief
    Spotted with strawberries in your wife's hand?

OTHELLO: [*Looking up.*] I gave her such a one; 'twas my first gift.

IAGO: I know not that; but such a handkerchief—
    I am sure it was your wife's—did I today
    See Cassio wipe his beard with.

OTHELLO: [*Rising.*] If't be that—   /1/

IAGO: If it be that, or any that was hers,
     It speaks against her with the other proofs.
OTHELLO: [*Pacing between DL to DLC then to above bench.*]   /2/
     O! that the slave had forty thousand lives!
     One is too poor, too weak for my revenge.
     Now do I see 'tis true. Look here, Iago:
                               — *X to Iago at DRC*   /3/

     All my fond love thus do I blow to heaven
                               — *with gesture*

     'Tis gone.
                               — *X to UC, full back*   /4/
     Arise, black vengeance, from the hollow hell!
     Yield up, O love, thy crown and hearted throne
     To tyrannous hate. Swell, bosom, with thy fraught,
                               — *opening up, full front*

     For 'tis of aspics' tongues!
IAGO: Yet be content.
OTHELLO: O! Blood, blood, blood!
                               — *Xing to DC*   /5/

IAGO: Patience, I say: your mind, perhaps, may change.
                               — *Xing to O*   (6)

    In this scene Iago through indirection and insinuation continues his objectives of inciting Othello to take action in his growing mistrust of Desdemona's fidelity. Othello's pent up anguish finally bursts into a passion for revenge.
Key to Movements diagrammed in Figure 37
    for Iago—(1) to (6)
    for Othello—/1/ to /5/

FIGURE 37
**Diagram of the detailed
blocking**
                            **Basic design upon which
the blocking is based**

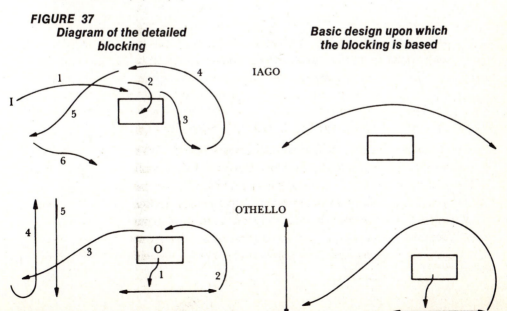

IAGO

OTHELLO

Thought process in developing the basic design:

For IAGO: keeps on the periphery to study his victim;
is observant and objective; probes, thrusts,
and retreats.

Translates into movements around and behind Othello.

For OTHELLO: feels ensnared; storms within; concentric
until his pent up anguish bursts.

Translates into holding within area and
finally breaking out.

Technical considerations:
  a. Conservation of movement at the beginning with Othello seated
     for later contrast in
  b. building scene with pacing and enlargement of movement for Othello's
     emotional outburst.
  c. Use of negative to positive movements at climax of scene.
  d. Contrasts in vocal dynamics—Iago's whispers when seated by Othello as
     contrast to Othello's final outburst.

Violent or bestial imageries in text for mood evaluation:

For IAGO: pricked, raging tooth, gripe and wring,
plucked up

For OTHELLO: monstrous, monstrous; I'll tear her all
to pieces; black vengeance, hollow hell,
aspics' tongues; blood, blood, blood

These imageries for Iago could translate into the *stealth of a serpent* accounting for movement around and behind Othello; for Othello, into the *rapaciousness of a tiger* which could account for his posture of almost kneeling and wanting to tear into the ground.

Staging the *Othello* scene as a metaphor

In line with some of the contemporary trends in physicalization, we could abstract the meaning and imageries of the scene into a metaphor. Without roots in reality, physicalization and abstractions can become meaningless, but proceeding from what has already been established, the staging of the metaphor could be as follows:

For IAGO: sound—sibilant, movement—serpentine
For OTHELLO: sound—guttural, movement—tigerish

Maintaining the basic design, enact the scene using only sounds to project the meaning and feeling within the lines of dialogue; physicalize the blocking and business into indicative gestures and movements of serpent and tiger. Also, consider compositional and rhythmic controls. This process can be used for an entire play, as in some recent experimental productions of Greek and Shakespearean plays.

MOVEMENT AS A RESULT OF FUNDAMENTAL DESIGN   Similar to character pattern is fundamental design which is usually extended to a whole act rather than restricted to a scene. Furthermore, it shows pictorially not so much the changing relationships of character to character as the relationship of a character to a group or a force. The picturization of this usually places the character in a particular location on the stage and shows by connotative movement the opposing forces coming toward or away from him, or it may show the protagonist in movement demonstrating his relationship to the more or less static force.

In arriving at the fundamental design we first determine the meaning of the act and then interpret this meaning in terms of areas, levels, lines, emphasis, and so on, so that the composition of the act is expressive of the idea. This in movement will give the design for the main action of an act or a whole play. There will be minor scenes that will deviate from the main design; but these scenes of themselves, it will be noticed, are inherently deviations from the main idea of the act. Moreover, the design must have variations so as not to make it too obvious. The blatancy, or clear-cut quality, of such a design in a play varies proportionately with the abstruseness of the writing. Strindberg's *Dream Play*, O'Casey's *Within the Gates*, Beckett's *Waiting for Godot* will be made clear to the audience through a strong fundamental design. Fundamental design, therefore, is a symbolic pattern.

Demonstrations in Movement as a Result of Fundamental Design

Sophocles' *Oedipus Rex*

Under Picturization we discussed the changing use of levels as treated in a production of Sophocles' *Oedipus Rex* to bring out the progressive steps of the king's downfall. The fundamental design, planned for the entire play, shows pictorially the changing relationship of Oedipus to the forces bearing down on him. Refer to this section in Picturization for the treatment of the design.

In graphic form on paper demonstrate this treatment of the fundamental design for *Oedipus Rex*.

Brecht's *The Good Woman of Setzuan*

This play tells the story of gods who came down to earth in search of a good person. They wandered through the byways of the world and finally found a good human being in the prostitute, Shen Te, who in order for her goodness to prosper creates a cousin, Shui Ta (herself in disguise). The cousin enacts the practical man with business acumen. But here rests the puzzlement: "To be good to others and to myself—I couldn't do both at the same time," says Shen Te to the gods.

The fundamental design of the play comes out of this circularity; the struggle between good and evil and the gods' search through all the corners of the world. The globe, abstracted constructivistically, allowing movements over, down, and through it in several directions, epitomizes both the circularity of the struggle and the unending search for goodness. (See Plate 21.)

Effect of Movement on Mood

Connotative movements have a picturizing value of their own like those suggested earlier in this chapter. These movements are also contributive to mood expressions, as in nonverbal theatre, where effective use is made of pure movement for projection of mood, or as in the staging of the *Othello* scene as a metaphor (page 214). For a better appreciation of this fact let us consider movement as an extension in time of line, mass, and form which in their various arrangements create a mood or arouse an emotional re-

PLATE 21   **The Good Woman of Setzuan** *by Bertolt Brecht*
Set concept arrived at out of fundamental design. Note secondary emphasis on figure on highest level UL reinforced through actual and visual lines.
Carnegie-Mellon University Theatre. *Director:* Lawrence Carra.
Designer: Paul Trautvetter. *Photographer:* William Nelson.

sponse in the audience. When discussing the mood effect of line, mass, and form in composition, we considered it from a static point of view. A play in performance, however, is action, and the mood effect achieved must be visualized dynamically by seeing these lines, masses, and forms in movement. The grace portrayed by the use of curved lines on stage exists more often in the sweep of the real movement than in the static form. So it is with mass or form in movement. In all cases the mood effect achieved exists in the composition, but in actual execution onstage it becomes a composition in flux which is movement.

A good example of composition in flux for mood values is the actions in rituals and ceremonies, which include formalized activities and often repetitive patterns of movement with connotative significance.

Line, Mass, and Form in Movement

LINE EXPRESSED IN MOVEMENT Stage movements, as well as line in composition, may be classified as horizontal, perpendicular, and diagonal, and may be treated in a straight, curved, or broken manner to obtain the various mood effects desired. We have only to refer to Line under Composition to analyze the mood effects of these different movements with their variations. For they are nothing more than these lines in action. The perpendicular movement, however, in execution onstage can exist only as movement from level to level; movements to higher levels, which are strong movements, have the same connotative values as those discussed under Perpendicular Lines. Such movements may also be from higher to lower levels in which instances we express defeat, loss of aspiration, frustration, loss of grandeur or dignity—in other words all that is implied by weak movement.

MASS EXPRESSED IN MOVEMENT The effect of mass in composition depends on the number of people included and on the handling of space intervals between members of the group, as well as upon the body positions that they assume. In movement we have the additional factor of this mass in action. A heavy mass moving in one direction creates power and determination; in contrast, the same mass milling about in diverse directions connotes restlessness, instability, or turmoil.

FORM EXPRESSED IN MOVEMENT The different arrangements of form in composition also exist in action. Stage movement may be regular or irregular in execution; it may extend through all the planes of the stage, or it may be confined more or less to a single plane; it may be spread over all the areas, or it may be restricted to one or two. Consider the stage movements in Weiss's *Marat/Sade*. Characters move in irregularity of form; they extend their movements from upstage to downstage; their actions spread over most of the areas. Compare these stage movements with those in a play like *The Way of the World*, a Restoration comedy of manners. The wit, the sharp delineation of character, the artifice of situation are best captured in movements that are regular, that are confined to a few planes, and that cover definite areas of the stage. In all cases the mood effects achieved by form in movement are those which we have analyzed under Composition.

Connotative Values of Movement

Along with the various effects of lines, masses, and forms in movement are the connotative values of the different ways in which movement may be executed. In the total mood expression the amount, strength or weakness, length, direction, intensity, and rhythm of movement are important considerations.

AMOUNT OF MOVEMENT Is the movement to be constant or occasional? Plays of continual excitement, of characters requiring no detailed characterization, of dialogue lacking innuendoes, of antics, of sharp contrasts in mood—plays like melodramas, rowdy farces, or many of the propaganda plays—demand constant movement. But the play of rounded characterization, of ideas, of infrequent climactic moments, of protracted moods, takes only occasional movement. We sense immediately that the amount of movement used is directly dependent on its appropriateness in expressing the mood of the play, the situation, the character, the locale, and the atmosphere.

STRENGTH OF MOVEMENT Is the movement to be weak or strong? Here we must take into account the evaluation of body movement and stage movement in terms of strength and weakness which we outlined at the beginning of this chapter. Certainly the variations in these values are contributive to the mood effect and, as we found under Values of the Lines of Dialogue, are definitely related to the ultimate impression of the sentiments in the lines. In determining the overall effect of strong and weak movement and whether a greater amount of one or the other is used, we must consider the kind of play, the nature of the situation, the characters, and the atmosphere. Chekhov's plays of futility are abundant in weak movements, since the mood of futility can be visually portrayed only by the use of weak movement. On the other hand, the overall mood quality of plays of positive and open action like G. B. Shaw's plays demand strong movement.

LENGTH OF MOVEMENT Is the movement to be long or short? Here, again, we must go to our play, our situation, and so on. You will find that long movements convey impressions of composure, deliberation, futility, languor, lack of emotional strain; whereas short movements are expressive of excitement, sharpness, irritability, impulsiveness, gayety. Long movement has a legato, or smooth, quality; short movement has a staccato, or sharp, quality.

DIRECTION OF MOVEMENT   Shall we have the character move toward the left or toward the right? For this we refer you to what was said under Movement Values from left stage to right stage and vice versa where the connotative effects of each were discussed.

Closely related to these are the diagonal movements from down right to up left and down left to up right and vice versa. The connotative value of these we analyzed in the demonstrations under Diagonal Movement. If we analyzed these correctly, we found that for Demonstration 2 the diagonal exit for *A*, *B*, and *C* is from up right, where *D* cheerfully says good-by, to down left—a movement that is not only long but also weak, as it follows the course from right to left, leaving *D* victorious and *A*, *B*, and *C* defeated. In the reversal of this, *A*, *B*, and *C* in leaving strong and victorious would start up left where *D* stands and leave by down right, thereby making not only a strong movement from a weak area but a movement that goes from left to right. As regards the mood effect of these diagonal movements we find that the movement from down right to up left is the weakest of them all and therefore a movement that implies utter defeat, uncertainty, a departure into the unknown, or a farewell.

INTENSITY OF MOVEMENT   What degree of intensity should we give the movement? This depends on the emotional content of the scene and the emotional status of the character. Heightened emotion is conveyed by greater intensity in movement as well as in voice. Highly emotional utterances coming from a character who makes ineffectual, lax movements are not convincing. Such movement often accompanies a scene for farcical or comic effects.

RHYTHM OF MOVEMENT   What about the rhythm of the movement? Is it to be strongly accented? Is its tempo to be slow or fast? Is it to accelerate or diminish? An answer to these questions demands a chapter in itself.

Exercises in the Effect of Movement on Mood

1. Redo the exercises on the effect of the composition on audience emotions on page 164. Describe the mood effect, and explain the method of conveyance of this mood in terms of movement of line, mass, and form.
2. In doing the following exercises use the amount, direction, and kind of movement that will be expressive of the mood and characters:

(*a*) Three condemned prisoners await sentence. The verdict of death is announced. The condemned are led out.

(*b*) Four workers are trapped in a coal mine. Rescuers enter, and the miners are led out to safety.

(c) Six actors are in a dressing room just before curtain time on the opening night of a premiere. They return—the play is a grand success. They return— the play is a "flop."

(d) Four tourists are about to cross a frontier on their way to a winter carnival. Their passports are being inspected. War is declared, and the tourists are ordered back.

Summary Exercises in Movement

1. Take any play, and find five lines with movement dictated by the story. Execute these lines on stage with their respective movement.

2. For the following, work out the scenes giving the movements a realistic or a psychological follow-through or both, as the situation may warrant. Choose scenes from realistic plays.

(a) Each group work out a scene that calls for background movement.

(b) Each group work out a scene in which movement is used to portray the type of character.

(c) Each group work out a scene in which movement is used to express the state of mind of the character or to illustrate changes in character relationships.

(d) Each group work out a transitional scene where movement is necessary to keep the scene alive.

3. Each group work out a scene from high comedy demanding arbitrary use of movement.

4. Create a scene in which the connotative value of movement expresses a mood of grief, of joy, of loneliness, of turmoil, of oppression, of peace.

5. Each member of a group work out a short scene from a play that will demonstrate at least ten points discussed under Movement. The scene should be approximately five minutes long. Do not have the actors learn lines.

Exercises in Character Patterns and Fundamental Design

1. Each member work out on paper the character pattern for a scene from a play of his own choosing. Explain how you arrived at the basic design.

2. First explain in writing and then work out the fundamental design of any play that you think will be illuminated by this kind of design concept.

10
Rhythm

With rhythm, our fourth fundamental element of directing, we come to the area of play directing that is most difficult to analyze and project in writing, even though rhythmic experience and expression can be appreciated and understood by most. The exercises under rhythmic pattern and tempo are meant primarily to further this appreciation and sensitivity to rhythmic experience rather than to give the student an instant technique that can be applied mechanically to the subtle dynamics of directing.

Rhythmic Experience

Rhythm is an experience we receive when a sequence of impressions, auditory or visual, has been ordered into a recurrence of accented groups. This experience is marked by a willingness to adjust ourselves emotionally and muscularly so as to conform with the accented groups we see or hear. Dependent upon the intensity of the impressions our experience is expressed by degrees of emotional and muscular reaction ranging from pure inner feeling to bodily movement.

Two special features are common to all rhythms—vitality and power of attraction. The pulsing quality in rhythmic experience is related to two fundamental life processes in nature. One is the beating of the heart, and the other is the breathing of the lungs. Both function in a rhythm of expansion and contraction which follow in endless sequence. Things that are rhythmic are associated with these processes, and thus have vitality.

Whatever the rhythmic experience, it is marked by an effortlessness and ease which are impossible to resist because they, somehow, seem to persuade us to fall in with them. The secret of our esthetic pleasure in rhythmic experience has probably a more practical basis than we suspect, for rhythm seems to satisfy the natural longing for progressive movement which is ordered rather than chaotic and haphazard. To fall into rhythm with something represents an adjustment and an adaptation for which most of us are very grateful. Since we seem to be naturally inclined toward it, we speak of its power of attraction.

When we see a rhythmic performance on stage, we become aware of a person in rhythm with his surroundings and performing with ease what seems complicated. It is an action that we are willing to follow wholeheartedly, and so we find our rhythms conforming with those of the performance on stage either in feeling or in actual physical movement. Our sensation of pleasurable surprise when discovering this fact is one of the joys of rhythmic experience.

The Characteristics of Rhythm

To fulfill our needs we must look further into this rhythmic experience and determine the characteristics of rhythm out of which we can form the basis for the practical aspects of directorial control.

Rhythmic Pattern

Technically, as we stated above, rhythm is a regularly recurring accent. This means that there must be an equal space or time-interval between the accents, since a succession of accents coming at irregular intervals of space and time does not give a feeling of rhythm. In sensing a uniform recurring beat, the individual has a tendency to collect the beats into units or groups. This grouping is a true rhythmic experience, felt rather than spoken. It is the experience of this grouping which makes us sensitive to *rhythmic pattern*—the first characteristic of rhythm. To maintain the sense of rhythm the pattern must occur at fixed relations of time. For example, the feeling of a waltz rhythm comes out of a continuing pattern of three beats to the measure with the accent on the first beat.

Tempo

Pattern alone does not fully explain rhythm. If we refer again to our heart beat, we know that, though the heart may maintain the same pattern of beat, something happens to that beat when we do any strenuous bodily activity or when we are in nervous tension—the heart beats faster. The tension of our nerves may even cause the heart beat to slow down as when we are in imminent danger and the heart pounds like a one-cylinder pump engine. The rate, then, of the rhythmic pattern may vary. This rate, or tempo, is the second characteristic of rhythm.

To sum up: the two characteristics of rhythm are pattern and tempo. However, along with rhythmic pattern and tempo we must understand the meanings of two other words frequently used and even interchanged in reference to rhythm—these are *timing* and *pace*.

More than a matter of semantics is involved here, for it is the awareness of the true significance of each—rhythmic timing and pace—that gives actor and director a basis for control of the dynamics of performance. More will be said about timing and pace under Application of Rhythm and Tempo to a play.

The Role Played by Association

Rhythm is one of the most important elements in creating impressions and emotions. The reason for this rests for the most part on our powers of association. When again and again throughout life we find that the sensations of rhythm within us are the result of definite bodily and emotional excitements, we grow to associate the rhythms that happen outside us with definite inner emotions or impressions; and finally, when we read a scene of emotional tension, we are able to sense its rhythm.

Association, therefore, plays an important part in the relationship between rhythm and the resulting emotion. On this the director and actors, consciously or unconsciously, depend in their creation of impressions and emotions. And it is in terms of the pattern and tempo of these associations that a director controls the rhythm of a character, a scene, or the whole play. What are these associations? Certainly they are as varied as the sensitivity and experience of the individual. If the rhythm of a play appeals to one director as the rapid driving impacts of a steel riveter, while to another as the swift flashes and the crackling thunder of a lightning storm, it is because each is more sensitive or impressed by an experience the sensation of which he now recaptures through association. Our impression of the rhythm of a play, a character, or a scene may summon up associations which will be expressive of the inherent mood quality in that rhythm.

Previous statements indicate that the audience adapts its emotional responses to the rhythm experienced. This is the basis of an important control for the director. In order to unify his audience's responses to the basic rhythm of his play, he must establish his rhythm at the outset, and give time for the audience to adjust to it. Then throughout the play he must re-establish it periodically. His use of variations, of slightly different tempos for different scenes is an important control and will be discussed later.

Exercises in Association and the Resulting Emotion

Have each student express in terms of associations his emotional reaction to a play; then do the same for a scene and a character in the play which lend themselves to such expression. Hand in your findings.

Rhythm and Emotion

Though the resulting emotion from rhythm is dependent on association, it is not true that for each rhythm that stimulates us we must first consciously or unconsciously bring to mind a previous experience to which we associate the rhythm and then from that arrive at the emotion. Whether or not it is because we eventually become conditioned in our response to rhythms, nevertheless we know that rhythms directly stimulate emotions through their pattern and tempo. There is not necessarily any question of association in recognizing the differences in feelings stimulated by a funeral march and a waltz. Rhythmic pattern and tempo have definite connotative values which can be readily analyzed.

Rhythmic Pattern and Its Connotative Value

Rhythmic pattern which we shall designate as the fundamental beat of rhythm in a play has the same function as metrical form in music and poetry. The number of beats and the variations in the placement of the accent are factors of pattern which affect the ultimate mood impression.

Even though a director may not consciously analyze his reactions to a play in terms of such measured rhythm, the fundamental beat does exist. Oftentimes it becomes most important to know the measured rhythm of the fundamental beat, particularly when actors are not sensitive to rhythms.

The exercises at the end of this section based on the following analysis can prove very helpful and enlightening to the student both in stimulating rhythmic sensitivity and in eliciting response to various rhythms; the value of the analysis rests primarily in this, since rhythmic sensations can only be realized through experience. In the exercises and analysis we assume the tempo to be the normal tempo of life.

a. Three beats to a measure convey gentleness, smoothness, restfulness, quiet. An accent on the first beat gives a sense of formality and definiteness; accent on the second beat gives a lilt and glide; accent on the third beat gives a lift.

b. Four beats to a measure, and its multiples, convey regularity, heaviness, impressiveness, or even a steady dying force. Accent on the first beat gives a downward, heavy, deadening effect. Accent on the fourth beat is heavy, deeply impressive, and then has a lift. The accent on the third beat is lighter than the others and has a flow and lift.

c. An odd number of beats to a measure such as five and seven convey irregularity, uneasiness, restlessness, or, perhaps, the unreal.

d. Six beats to a measure may give a sense of grandeur when the accent is on the last beat, or of excitement and tension when the accent is on the fifth beat.

In the placement of an accent we find that regular stress generally soothes and controls while irregular stress conveys restlessness and excitement. A stress at the beginning of a measure generally conveys regularity without opposition, a degree of heaviness, and a sense of steadiness. Stress at the other parts of a measure encourages different degrees of a lift, a turn, pleasantness, or unpleasantness; it may give the feeling of the unusual, the unexpected, or even the undesired.

Tempo and Its Connotative Value

Tempo, for our purposes, is the variation of the rhythmic pattern. It is based on the rate of the rhythmic pattern and on the multiples or divisions of the beats in the pattern.

The use of any one of these singly or in combination results in the variations which we know as tempo variations. Tempo, then, is variation in time duration. Tempo variations, moreover, are expressive of different moods and are more evident in their effect than pattern alone.

a. Considering the variations as multiples or divisions of beats in the pattern we find that:

1. Shorter beats or pauses convey an element of excitement, elation, gayety, irritability, sharpness, impulsiveness, staccato quality, driving force, and so on.

2. Longer beats or pauses convey an impression of languidness, composure, futility, dullness, lack of emotional strain, deliberation, and so on.

The duration of a pause gives a greater effect of rate than the duration of a beat.

b. Considering the general effect of time durations we find that:

1. Slow tempo conveys solemnity, mystery, wonderment, sublimity, apathy, submission, and all such moods that we associate with deeper feelings. Slow tempo adds weight and significance to a movement or a thought.

2. Medium tempo, which is normal for activity, is rational, self-controlled, calm, composed, sober, and serious.

3. Fast tempo conveys animation, fancy, gayety, irritability; excitement, tension; any kind of strenuous action finds true expression in accelerated movement or utterance.

Again, the exercises that follow will prove helpful in clarifying rhythmic pattern and tempo variation and in stimulating a sensitivity to rhythmic sensation, and hopefully the application of this to actual scene control.

Exercises in Rhythmic Pattern and Connotative Value

In working out the following exercises, the people onstage are to be arranged without any emotional relationship but in arbitrary design. The tempo must be the normal tempo of life and is to be kept the same throughout the exercise. The beats of the pattern must be executed in unison.

Example: Four beats to a measure with the accent on the fourth beat.

Figure *A*: Position at L facing front. Action: clap hands on a 1-2-3-4 pattern, giving the greatest stress to the fourth beat.

Figure *B*: Position at R facing front. Action: arms outstretched side to side at beginning, then fold one arm, fold other arm, extend both arms forward, outstretch both arms to first position, and so on. Outstretching the arms becomes the accent.

Figure *C*: Position UC facing front. Action: walk three steps forward, turn facing upstage, walk three steps forward, turn facing front, and so on. The turn becomes the accent.

Figure *D*: Position DR facing UC. Action: walk from DR to UCR to DC to UCL to DL, and return by same path. Walk on a 1-2-3-4 pattern, giving the greatest stress to the fourth beat.

a. Maintaining uniformity in beat, accent, and tempo, have each begin their actions in this sequence:

A on 1st measure
B on 3rd measure
C on 5th measure
D on 7th measure

continue for sixteen measures.

b. With A setting the rhythm for one measure, have A, B, C & D execute each of their actions simultaneously for the following twelve measures.

c. Vary the accent of the first beat as follows:

A give greatest stress to the first beat
B start with both arms extended
C be at full back position, then turn on first beat
D gives greatest stress to the first beat

then with these starting positions, repeat exercises a and b. Have the class give their emotional reactions to the several patterns.

Example: three beats to a measure with accent on the third beat:

Maintaining same positions and uniformity as in four beats to a measure:

A clap hands on 1-2-3 pattern
B arms outstretched at beginning, fold both arms together, extend both arms forward, outstretch both arms to first position
C walk only two steps before turn
D walk on a 1-2-3 pattern

Execute the following exercises in fashion similar to the examples; work out the design appropriate to the pattern; have the class give their emotional reaction; have them analyze the pattern.

1. Three beats to a measure with accent on the first beat.

2. Three beats to a measure with accent on the second beat.

3. A measure of your own choosing with regularity in the placement of the accent.

4. A measure with irregularity in the placement of the accent.

Exercises in Tempo and Connotative Value

These exercises are to be worked out in the same manner as those given under rhythmic pattern. It is important that the majority carry the fundamental beat unvaried. Have the class give their emotional reaction to the rhythm and then have them analyze the pattern and the tempo.

Example: maintaining pattern given for four beats to a measure—

a. vary the pattern by having two subdivide a beat. For example, B and D execute measures in eighths.

b. vary the pattern by having one subdivide a beat in eighths while another holds a beat.

c. vary the pattern by taking shorter pauses.

d. vary the pattern by taking longer pauses.

e. vary the rate of the pattern. For example, in (a) under exercises in Rhythmic Pattern and Connotative Value accelerate tempo of pattern on measures 3, 5, and 7.

1. Establish a pattern of your own, then with variations in tempo build to a climax stopping abruptly at a point of high intensity.

2. The same as above, except that at point of high intensity begin diminishing slowly.

3. Vary a pattern of your own choosing with tempo variations of your own selection. Note your conclusions.

Determining the Rhythm of a Play

Each play has a fundamental rhythm that can be determined by the kind of play, the nature of the situation, the dialogue, the characters, the locale, and the atmosphere.

Kind of Play

Basic attitude becomes one of the main considerations in determining the rhythm of a play: whether the play is a tragedy, a comedy, a melodrama, or a farce, or the many variations of these as serious comedy, comedy of manners, sentimental comedy, satire, farce-comedy—each calls for the rhythm that will create the proper emotional response. In working out the exercises under rhythmic pattern and tempo we found that certain rhythms are more connotative of heavier moods, others of lighter moods. The basic attitude of a play may stimulate us as directly as these exercises in sensing its rhythm; on the other hand, as we have discovered, the rhythm of a play may be sensed through association by choosing impressions that will be expressive of the whole tone of the play. One way or the other, the director's talent depends on his sensitivity of rhythmic response to a play's basic attitude.

Nature of the Situation

The situation determines the rhythm. Tempo of speech and movement varies with the changing thought and emotional content of the situation and the attending circumstances. In the exercises under Composition (page 164) we found that it is possible to imagine the mood effects of a situation by the mere mention of the scene. Then, we expressed this feeling in terms of line, mass, and form and in turn, under Movement (page 220), expressed these in movement. Now if we are acute to the mood value of rhythm we see that rhythm can express and add to this same mood by the *manner* in which the movement is executed.

The Dialogue

For the dialogue to be a determining factor the lines must have been written in the contained rhythm of the play, the characters, the locale, and so forth. Frequently many lines of dialogue are not written within the contained rhythm—at such times the director must solve the problem of blending that part of the scene into the whole rhythmic structure of the play. Rhythm of comedy dialogue, for example, must be clear-cut and must allow for proper pointing, timing, and building.

The connotative power and sound value of the words, and the phrasing of the dialogue aid in the ultimate feeling and, therefore, in the determination of the rhythm. Pinter, Beckett, Mamet, and Stoppard create rhythmic impulses through dialogue that is elliptical, oblique, and supercharged. Long and short phrasing, for example, affects feeling: excitement of any kind demands short phrasing; calmness is expressed in longer phrasing. More important than this, however, are the understanding and interpretation of the thought to which the above are complimentary and which largely determine the rhythm of the dialogue. In manner and rate of utterance, we necessarily seek for the vocal rhythm appropriate to the intellectual and emotional content of the situation, thus making the rhythm of utterance an essential part of meaning and mood. Sustained legato utterances and movements create a totally different rhythmic effect than do sharp staccato utterances and movements.

Continuing experiments in nonverbal theatre, as demonstrated in staging the *Othello* scene as a metaphor (page 214), are opening up new channels for theatrical expression in the use that can be made of vocal sounds, words, and phrases used for their prime connotative values in conjunction with the connotative power of composition, movement, and rhythm. The Open Theater's productions of *The Serpent* and *The Mutation Show,* Grotowski's production of *The Constant Prince,* and the New York Public Theatre production of *Agamemnon* are indicative of this trend.

Characters

The kind of characters help in determining the rhythm of the play. Rhythm of speech and movement varies with the kind of character as well as with the attitude of that character in the situation. Once we have analyzed the characters and established who they are we find that they have their own particular rhythm: if we compare the sophisticates of a Noel Coward comedy with the farmers of a Paul Green folk drama it becomes evident that each group demands a different treatment of rhythm. Coward's sophisticates are sharp, rapid thinking, and poised, while Green's folk characters may be dull, slow thinking, and plodding.

Locale

The locale in which the play is laid becomes an important consideration in determining the rhythm, either for a particular scene or the whole play. Each locality and country has a distinctive rhythm. We know that a totally different rhythmic sensation is experienced when we arrive at a metropolis after a stay in the country. This sensitivity to locale makes us acute to the differences in rhythm of locales that become essential to the play's action.

Closely related to locale are the people associated with it. Race and nationality determine rhythm. People move in their own individual rhythm. This should be definitely determined in studying a play in which racial or national characteristics are particularly important, as in Chekovian and other distinctively foreign plays. French, Italian, Russian plays demand the characteristic rhythm of their people in order to project the semblance of the nationality or race; catching the correct rhythm is especially important when the play is being acted by persons of another nationality or race.

Atmosphere

Along with the other determinants of rhythm we must be sensitive to atmospheric details as well as to locale, both of which lend a three-dimensional quality to the total impression of a scene. The time of day, the season of the year, the kind of climate or weather determine rhythm when the atmosphere they create is a contributing factor to the understanding and action of the play. A scene at the breakfast table has a totally different rhythmic feeling from a scene at dinner time. A scene at the waterfront in a thick fog has a different rhythmic feeling from the same scene played in full sunlight.

Exercises in Determining Rhythm

Bring in short scenes taken from:

(*a*) A tragedy.
(*b*) A serious comedy.
(*c*) A comedy of manners.
(*d*) A sentimental comedy.
(*e*) A black comedy.
(*f*) A melodrama.
(*g*) A mystery play.
(*h*) A satire.
(*i*) A farce.
(*j*) A play by Ionesco or Beckett.

Read the dialogue to the class and have them analyze from what kind of play it was taken.

Functions of Rhythm

Rhythm is primarily the factor which gives life to the play. A review of the more important functions will clarify its special values.

Rhythm Establishes Mood

Mood reduced to its lowest terms consists of a degree of tone evaluation, such as hard and soft or light and heavy with myriad gradations. It is the dominant emotional characteristic of a play.

In our work up to now we have seen that mood can be established by the connotative form of composition as well as by the connotative value of movement. We have suggested that the connotative value of words both through the sound of the word and the association induced by the thoughts of the dialogue lend to the creation of mood. Finally, we have analyzed the connotative value of rhythmic pattern and tempo. In our creation of mood, therefore, we may use one or more of these methods depending on the needs of the scene: for example, when the lines of dialogue fail to carry the mood of the situation, it is possible to bring it out by stressing the connotative values of composition and movement or by emphasizing the words that have particular connotative value. Or as in Robert Wilson's exploration of time, space, and silences, we can project varying degrees of tone quality by the dominant use of rhythm in movement through space, in extension of pauses, and in shifts of tempo. But whatever method we use, rhythm is always present to unify, to blend, and to strengthen.

While on the subject of mood it would be well to mention the important contribution of vocal quality to mood. The pitch of the voice, the resonance with which lines are spoken, the projection behind the pitch and resonance, and the rhythm of utterance all contribute to it.

This short review of the methods of obtaining mood ought to emphasize the fact that there are other ways of projecting "tragic mood" than by a slow rhythm.

Rhythm Establishes the Kind of Play

Once we have decided on the play and determined its rhythm, we then establish the kind of play through proper rhythmic control. Any movement is rhythm in motion, but the manner of executing the movement depends on the type of control we have established for the particular play and, repeating what has already been said in this matter: the manner of movement, gestures, and delivery of lines must be performed in harmony with the fundamental beat. To this extent we can say that rhythm blends comedy scenes in serious plays and, vice versa, blends tragic scenes in comedies. The porter scene in *Macbeth,* to give a popular instance, must not be played for comedy to the extent that it will disturb the mood of the whole. In the opposite vein, quickening the tempo of an emotional scene in a comedy will lighten the depth of the scene.

Rhythm Establishes the Nature of the Situation

Once we have established the fundamental beat that will control our play then the tempo variations of this fundamental beat will vary according to the nature of the situation. We learned from picturization that in a play we may have scenes of love, of jealousy, of argument, of reconciliation, of deceit, of death, and so on. Each of these scenes has its own inherent mood quality. The mood for each must be within the control of the whole play, yet as we discovered in doing the exercises under tempo and its connotative value, each demands its own variation in the use of the fundamental beat. Whether we are putting on a tragedy or a farce, there cannot be nor should there be an even tenor of rhythmic dynamics. Such control would deny the inherent nature of each scene besides resulting in monotony.

Rhythm Establishes Characterization

Every person has a characteristic rhythm in his movement and speech. This rhythm is the result of his personality and environment and its variation depends on his state of mind, on the situation in which he finds himself, and on his surroundings. Under General Kinds of Movement we saw that movements portray the type of character and his state of mind. Rhythm now establishes the manner of executing these movements. Though a weak movement may illustrate the change in thought of a character, it is in the execution of that weak movement that we consider its appropriate rhythm.

It is well to point out here that in ordinary conversation speech tends to be rhythmic although the cadence does not remain regular for long. In dramatic writing, however, selection and economy of writing, especially in scenes of emotional tension, tend to give dialogue a greater regularity of cadence. We shall find that the actor who must give vent to intense passions will project a greater truth of character if his movement and utterance are kept within rhythmic control rather than permitted the abandonment which we know as "tearing a passion to tatters."

Rhythm Conveys an Impression of the Locale and Atmosphere

No more need be said here than was pointed out in determining rhythm from locale. Since localities, countries, races, and nationalities have their distinctive rhythms it is important for the director to acquaint himself with them. Photographs, travel films, contact with people who belong to the nationality, locale, or race in question will give many cues to the control of rhythm that conveys the proper impression.

Rhythm Conveys a Change in Scene

Change in scene should not be left solely to the scenery. A true change in locale and atmosphere is accomplished when we make the corresponding change in rhythm that is inherent to the new locale or is affected by the new atmosphere.

Rhythm Ties the Actors Together into a Coordinated Group

When the star system was prevalent to a greater degree than today and when ensemble acting was a thing of the future, little or no attention was given to the coordination of roles. Each actor was interested in the projection of his part and did not bother about such things as blending the rhythm and tone of his acting with the acting of others in the cast. Today we rightly expect coordination in acting. The "warm up" sessions before rehearsals and performances as practiced by some groups have proved their merit by achieving a coordination in the interaction of actor to actor which is so essential for an ensemble feeling. This harmony or ensemble acting is brought about through rhythmic control where each actor is sensitive to the fundamental beat of the play and is careful to discipline his acting within this framework. To this extent it is important that "warm up" sessions be keyed to the basic dynamics of the play.

Rhythm Brings the Audience Together

One unique characteristic of rhythm is its ability to bind individuals together. An effective control of rhythm does much to bring the audience together into one common reaction. As we know from mob psychology, large groups of people are susceptible to rhythm—crowds demonstrating under rhythmic exhortations of their leaders offer a good example. For this reason, a play should begin at the rhythmic flow of the audience, particularly in emotional scenes coming right at the opening of a play or at the opening of an act. Time must be given the audience to adjust to the emotional tonality of the play; otherwise a sudden dominance of rhythm from heightened emotions can be so alien to the emotional state of the audience that it will not be psychologically ready to accept the scene or rise to it. The result is usually lack of emphatic response and at times even laughter in a scene that should be serious.

Rhythm Ties Together and Blends All Parts of the Play

Parts of the play such as scenes, movement, gestures, dialogue, and entrances are colored by the overall tone of the whole, and in turn the whole takes its tone from the nature of the parts. We must always remember that unity and harmony belong to all good art.

1. Rhythm controls the flow of movement achieved through proper regulation of attention and through proper control of the flow from strong to weak movement and vice versa.

2. Rhythm will tie a scene together when the composition of the scene fails to do so.

3. Rhythm bolsters up transitional and parallel scenes, and ties them in with the whole. It keeps these scenes alive by holding the interest of the audience.

4. Rhythm determines the timing of entrances and exits, of all movement, of cues, of pauses, of the building of scenes, of interpolations, of scenes of low intensity, and so on. It determines the timing of offstage noises and effects, of music, and other such problems.

5. Rhythm ties together scenes of diffused effect. Seemingly unrelated elements, as the groups in a naturalistic play like *The Lower Depths* where at times no one pays attention to anyone else, can only be brought into control by a harmony of rhythm in the variation of these unrelated parts.

PLATE 22 Everyman, *a morality play.*
A workshop session in preparation for rehearsal.
University of California, Riverside. *Director and Designer:* Robert Benedetti.

6. Rhythm supplies tonal unity when the development of the play denies such unity. Shakespeare's *The Winter's Tale* offers a well-known example of this. The two parts of the play offer two completely different tonal impressions: out of the tragic impact of the first part densely crowded with incidents that are violent, abrupt, severe, and hurried rises the leisurely pastoral lyricism of the latter part where the general effect is soothing and composed and where romantic beauty is blended with comic drollery. If we are to have unity and harmony in the production of this play, we must achieve a kind of rhythmic control that will color the first part of the story so as to blend it in with the lighter vein of the latter part which culminates in a happy ending to the story.

The Application of Rhythm to a Play

The director will prefer to have rhythm come into his play through the unconscious reactions of his sensitive actors to the rhythms of the lines, the characters they are portraying, the locale suggested by the script, and the action of the play. However, if rhythm does not come into the production by the actors' response, the director must make the actors consciously aware of it. Here our understanding of the connotative value of rhythmic patterns and tempo variations have immediate application. We may bring out the proper rhythmic response by mechanically beating out the rhythm such as slapping hands. The use of appropriate music as an accompaniment during rehearsals or the working out of impromptu scenes of common understanding where the rhythm is similar to the one desired but more obvious, are other ways to bring out the proper rhythmic response. The use of one of these methods becomes especially necessary for rhythms unfamiliar to the cast.

Timing

Timing is an essential technique of an actor's control in the delivery of a line of dialogue or in the execution of an action. Some believe that an actor's sense of timing is an innate talent. Be this so or not, a rhythmic sensitivity to phrasing, auditory or visual is involved. It implies proper preparation, proper delivery or execution with the proper length of pause and proper emphasis. Timing considerations are probably more obvious in comedy, but any performance whether a comedy, a tragedy, or other type of play is a continuum of timing. There is only correct timing effectively rendered or incorrect timing that disrupts the flow of a scene.

Pace

The pace of a performance may be designated as slow or fast, heavy or hectic, beautiful or intolerable, and so on. Whatever the term, a sense of time and response from the audience's point of view is implied. The duration of time, as we know, can vary according to circumstances—a passage of one minute can be excruciatingly long or imperceptibly fleet for someone who is thoroughly engrossed in an action. Pace of a show, therefore, is more related to an audience's responses than to the actual duration of the performance. Pacing involves the dynamics of rhythmic control and timing. It involves holding the audience's interest in all aspects of performance. As to tempo, an action may be enacted very slowly, but if this control, properly rendered, holds the audience from moment to moment, then the play is effectively paced. Inversely, quickening the tempo of a scene to play it fast does not necessarily bring about effective pacing.

Controlling Rhythm: Points to Watch

PHRASING OR "BEATS"   be aware of where a scene begins, how it develops, where it is going, when it reaches its most telling point, and how it is resolved. Meaningful phrasing is the building unit in the dynamics of playing a scene.

INNER BEATS   be alert to each segment of dialogue for an exacting definition of its thought in order to project its meaning, distinctly and colorfully.

DIALOGUE   make sure the phrasing of the dialogue is within the contained rhythm of the play and that its tempo is expressive of the intellectual and emotional content of the lines and the situation.

SCENES   keep the fundamental beat of the play flowing through the scene even in the minor changes where the demands on phrasing make a change in timing essential.

ACTORS   make sure the actors are within the contained rhythm of the character and the situation.

TRANSITIONS   watch the rhythm in transitional and parallel scenes. Keep up the tempo of the movement and dialogue in harmony with the fundamental beat.

CLIMAX   make sure the tempo of building and the height of the climax are within the rhythmic range of the whole, and that the dominance of the rhythm is in proportion to the intensity of the emotion. In life, increasing intensity of emotion, which in turn implies the lessening of reason, brings an increase in the dominance or definiteness of rhythm. We find that strong emotions tend to fall into a regular rhythmic order, but that as thought increases rhythm becomes less evident. The deeper the feeling of a scene or the higher the rise of emotional intensity, the more dominant will be the rhythm.

PAUSES   watch the length of pauses—length is determined by the rhythm.

ENTRANCE AND EXITS   be careful about pauses during these. Gauge hubbub on exits according to the rhythm.

MOVING OBJECTS AND RECURRING NOISES   pay attention to the rhythm of such movements as a rocking chair, recurring noises on- and offstage, and so on.

LAUGHTER   when rehearsing comedies and farces watch the lines and business that are most likely to arouse laughter; allow for this laughter in establishing the rhythm. Laughter lengthens the duration of a scene and if the director in timing a scene has failed to take this into consideration he will find that in performance the actors will lose control of the scene— rushing lines, destroying builds, and so forth.

AUDITORIUM   note the acoustics and size of the auditorium—both must be considered in the final adjustment of the rhythm.

Maintaining the Rhythm: Special Points to Consider

(a) The actor holding the stage from one scene to the next is the one to maintain the rhythm.

(b) Reestablish the rhythm at the beginning of a scene with the entrance of a new character.

(c) Carry through the rhythm and reestablish it at the end of the scene.

(d) Hold the fundamental beat by a stronger or louder accent than the variations.

(e) Hold the fundamental beat by having it projected by the majority.

The Application of Tempo to a Play

A play should contain as many variations of the fundamental beat as is practical. A production in which the fundamental beat remains unvaried and is continuously pounded at the audience becomes monotonous, tiresome, and uninteresting. The variations, however, must not break or violate the fundamental beat, for the proper harmony between tempo and fundamental beat creates the true impression of rhythm. Tempo, besides being an inherent part of the rhythm of the whole and dependent on it, is further determined by the attitude of the speaker, the earnestness and intensity of his feeling, the importance and weight of his thought, and the mood induced by such thought. Within certain limitations imposed by the length of words and the facility of bodily activity, rhythmic pattern may be rendered in any tempo. We have already studied the several ways of achieving tempo variations. Now we are interested in their application.

Variation of the Fundamental Beat for Characterization

After the basic rhythm of a play has been established, each character should act in a rhythm that is the fundamental beat itself or a multiple or division of it. Certain characters will have relatively fast or slow tempos that will be revealed through movement, speech, and gesture. Once the variation is established for each character, then each character will develop consistently with the rate of tempo as it varies with the changing mood or situation. Change in characterization may of course alter this proportion.

Variation in Rate of the Fundamental Beat

Lengthening or shortening the time duration of the beat or the pause is determined by the emotional intensity of the scene. As the duration of either is shortened in time, the tempo is speeded up and the intensity of the scene increased. As the duration of either one is lengthened, th tempo will slow down. This variation of tempo is entirely dependent upon the fundamental beat of the play, and the maximum and minimum development of tempo are set by this fundamental beat.

A play of basically slow rhythm will have a slower minimum than a play of fast rhythm—which is to say, that tempo in a farce should never become as slow as the slowest tempo in tragedy. The play of slow rhythm, on the other hand, will never have as rapid a climax or maximum—that is, the tempo in tragedy should never be as fast as the fastest tempo in farce. These considerations are important in judging how high a scene should be built or how low it should be diminished.

Closely associated with the above is the variation in the rate at which the fundamental beat recurs. For example, offstage noises which may be used to strengthen a build will intensify the final effect of the climax if they recur more and more frequently as well as increase in tempo.

Acceleration

This is the manner of spacing the breaking up or pick up of a scene and is based on tempo.

(a) Acceleration may refer to the gradual breaking up of a scene for variety without change of speed in movement or delivery of lines. This would be a variation in the multiple or division of the pattern where the greater number of movements used and the great number of people moving would produce an increase in tempo.

Not much breaking up is necessary for the first quarter of a scene. This is a result of the inherent interest in the start of a scene. The remaining three-quarters of the scene should break up increasingly so that the second quarter is broken up more than the first, the third quarter more than the second, and the fourth more than the third. This is often called breaking up in accelerated form. This kind of acceleration contributes to the build of a scene.

The following diagram illustrates graphically the breaking up of a scene.

In breaking up a scene in accelerated form the amount of inherent dramatic material must be definitely taken into account. The more dramatic the material the less need there is of breaking up the scene, and vice versa. The director must sense the holding power of the dialogue and not under- or overestimate it. Besides the dramatic content of the scene, the other factor that controls acceleration is the place of the scene in the progression of the play. Later scenes generally demand greater acceleration than earlier scenes.

(*b*) Acceleration also refers to the gradual pick up or speed in the execution of movement and the delivery of lines during a scene. All that has been said regarding breaking up in accelerated form holds true here. But where the gradual *breaking up* of a scene may be done for sheer variety to keep the scene alive, the gradual *picking up* of a scene becomes the build of that scene. This kind of acceleration is discussed in full under "Building the Scene."

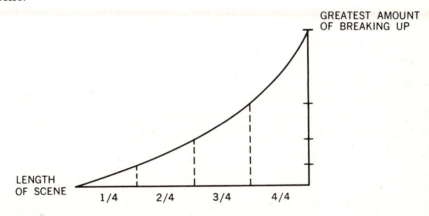

GREATEST AMOUNT
OF BREAKING UP

LENGTH
OF SCENE

1/4   2/4   3/4   4/4

FIGURE 38   *Diagram showing the breaking up of a scene*

Telescoping

Telescoping is the picking up of cues in dialogue or movement before the other has finished speaking or moving. It is one of the techniques used in building a scene and is based on an acceleration of tempo—it is an accelerated give and take. Each actor must always emphasize the first or keynote of each bit telescoped. Telescoping must be led into gradually and continued to a climax; an abrupt telescoping is confusing. Conventional elements, however, like goodbyes or greetings do not need this gradual leading into since the impression of the scene will in itself carry over to the audience.

Telescoping in a serious play must be carefully controlled. It is important to watch that it does not break the rhythm for this may often result in comedy.

When scenes are overwritten telescoping will help in keeping up the tempo.

Exercises for Breaking Up in Accelerated Form and for Telescoping

1. Refer to the exercises given under Composition in Variety within the area and between areas. Work out the scenes to show breaking up in accelerated form.

2. Have four people on stage speaking successively eight letters of the alphabet; gradually telescope the speeches to a climax.

Building the Scene

Under movement we discussed the problem of building a scene by the use of movement only. To this we now add tempo and voice. Any or all of the the following methods may be used in building a scene.

1. Accelerate the tempo to build it to the highest point permitted by the fundamental beat. This includes all the means used in the breaking up and picking up of a scene.

(*a*) Build vocally by differences in tone, increased volume, changes in pitch, increased intensity or emotional strain, and increased tempo by shortening the length of speeches; by increasing the rate of delivery, by making the speeches staccato, and finally by picking up cues with greater and greater speed until speeches overlap and the peak of the scene is telescoped.

(*b*) Conserve movement at the beginning of the scene and then increase the amount and size of movement; strengthen its value, placement, and tension; increase its contrast and tempo.

(*c*) In sound and effects increase the volume, intensity, and tempo of off-stage noises, effects, music, and so forth as well as increase their recurrence.

2. Increase the dominance of the fundamental beat by bringing out the pattern and accent through greater formalization.

3. Increase the number of variations used in executing one or all of the methods listed above. This may be done by varying the kind of tempo, the type of breaking up, the degree of formalization, and so on.

Demonstration of Building a Scene

1. Have four people on the stage speaking successively, each says the first five letters of the alphabet, then four, then three, then two, then one, as an example of increase in building.

2. Ask four people on the stage to take turns in delivering three letters of the alphabet so as to demonstrate the different forms of building by voice.

3. Have one individual take seven letters of the alphabet and say them in seven different speeds, beginning with the slowest and working up to the fastest, as a demonstration of increase in tempo by speaking lines faster.

4. Take fifteen people offstage. Have the first one enter on the count of one. Two people enter five counts later; three people enter four counts later; four people enter three counts later; five people enter on that last two counts. The instructor will count from one to fifteen. This is an example of the increased intensity that results from an increasing number of people in a scene.

5. Take a pattern of four beats to a measure worked out in the exercises under rhythmic pattern. First, use the rhythm without stressing the beats or acccent, but keep within the rhythm harmony; gradually bring out the pattern through greater and greater stress on the beats and accent. This is an example of increase in the dominance of a fundamental beat.

6. Have a group of ten use the alphabet for speech, and build an imaginary scene using as many of the methods of building as possible.

Exercises in Building a Scene

1. Without learning lines, rehearse the *Othello* scene demonstrated in the section on Character Pattern, apply to it several of the techniques in building a scene.
2. Do the same with a scene of your own choosing.

Timing in Pointing and Delivery

An actor may or may not have as an inborn asset a sense of timing, but long exposure in performance, especially in comedies, can develop acute sensitivity to audience response, which is an integral part of timing. Timing in itself, however, will mean very little unless other factors of control work together harmoniously. Once we understand the material we can plan our control which combined with proper timing will get the sought-after response.

In comedy, for example, the control in delivery for getting a laugh includes the following:

1. The plant or feed lines are carefully rendered and emphasized. The acting team of Lunt and Fontanne stated it in this way: "You have to make your feed line clear, in order that the other person tops you and so that the funny line gets the laugh."

2. To intensify the contrast or incongruity, the tone that best expresses the humor is employed. Should the tone be imitation or exaggeration? Should it be nasal, aspirate, dry, drawled, and so on? Oftentimes, as in certain comedy characterizations, the delivery of a line with an unusual tone of voice helps project its humor. Comedy is also obtained through the contrast or incongruity between thought and delivery, for example, shouting: "Quiet! The baby's asleep!"

3. The correct pitch and inflection are used. Some laugh lines depend on a drop or rise in inflection on the last word. The "throw away" and

"punch" come under this control. The "throw away" is an immediate lowering in volume to a level that appears unprojected; the "punch" is led to with clear pointing, pause, and then punching the key word.

4. The most effective facial expression is used.

5. Business is precisely determined in relation to the line: whether it should come before or after delivery. Unless line and business serve the meaning, business executed as the line is delivered will either detract from the impact of the line or "kill the line."

6. Finally, the proper rapport is established with the audience through exact timing such as cue pickup, correct phrasing, and the precise sensing of the length of pause before the word or words that bring out the laugh. Drama critic Brooks Atkinson commenting on a performance by Alfred Lunt had this to say: "Lunt takes a funny line and sort of pursues it around the room until he corners it where it can't escape, and then he just takes it and shakes it like a terrier until there is nothing left of life and he has gotten everything out of it."

These are the major considerations that enter into comedy reading. How, or to what extent, they are used depends on the motivation for the comedy. In any case the legitimate goal is to get the laugh. Once the laugh comes, however, another important control in timing must be considered.

Holding for a Laugh

The reasons for holding for a laugh are obvious. If the actors continue their dialogue, either the laugh is cut short or the audience fails to hear the next lines. The solution is not simple. To have the actors hold or freeze for the laugh creates a static stage which can prove dangerous to the vitality and pace of the scene, particularly if a laugh is expected and does not come. The experienced actor, adept at timing, keeps his stage alive by a follow through of gesture, business, or movement to fill the interval between start of laugh and attack on the next line. For the tyros a director should initiate his cast into this technique during the latter stages of rehearsal. Some directors will actually applaud at places where laughs are most likely to occur to give his cast a feeling of audience reaction. Previews, of course, accomplish this same end more effectively.

The hold for a laugh is broken immediately after the laugh has reached its climax and not before. If the hold extends well beyond, the tempo of the scene slows down which, if repeated whenever laughs occur, dampens the comic momentum and pace of the scene. The dynamics of comic performance are at their best when laugh feeds upon laugh. The best comic writers like Kaufman and Neil Simon take this into account when structuring their scenes, but are at the mercy of the proficiency of directors and actors to make full use of the indications in the script, for they remain indications only until put to work in performance. To keep up the pace, then, the laugh is never permitted to die out and the audience will still be laughing when the dialogue is picked up. This means that the actor with the line pickup must punch the first words in order to arrest the audience's attention and bring the laughter which is slowly subsiding to a halt. There is psychological reasoning here, too. An audience that is not permitted to exhaust itself on any one laugh remains stimulated and eager to burst out on the next provocation. We find here a valuable clue to generating and building up the audience's verve for laughter. Similar to the warmup sessions at live entertainment in television studios before the show is taped, we warm up our theatre audience by setting the tone at the beginning of the play. Adding to the actors' esprit and tempo, we generate a greater spirit of comedy by cutting laughs short. Technically, it means spacing the laughs which is one of the really challenging methods of changing a willing but cold audience to a warm one. If the writer has failed to give us the means, then we must achieve it ourselves through business and the other techniques of pointing and delivery. While on the subject of laughter, a word should be said about uncontrolled spasms of laughter which can prove destructive to a performance. Usually they come from stimuli other than the characters in the play —a mishap, an awkward reaction, an amateurish reading. Legitimate or not, uncontrolled laughter can in the long run be detrimental to the pace of the play if not brought firmly under control.

Types of Scenes and Their Tempos

The structure of a play must be carefully analyzed. There should be awareness of where the major crisis and climax occur; recognition of which scenes are expository, which scenes are ones of conflict, and so forth. For phrasing and the other many technical reasons, it is necessary to determine where a scene begins and where it ends. Ultimately, structural understanding of a play determines how, for example, we compose, picturize, and proportion the amount and intensity of such elements as movement and tempo.

Play structuring and the point of view exercised by playwrights in their theatrical outputs have a long history of ever changing form and conventions with new vistas opening up for each generation. A study of the many genres and styles of playwriting and theatrical expression and the directorial controls involved is without question important in the schooling of a director. However, although these studies are for later, after the beginning director has a firm grasp of the many factors that are basic to acting, playwriting, and directing, there is every reason for him to be cognizant of both the present trends in playwriting and the more traditional forms. He should be aware that in some of the present climates of playwriting: motivation that comes from developing a scene from cause to effect may be nonexistent; that linear progressions in plotting have given way to portraying states of condition; that exploration of events or actions precedes conception or structure; that events, characters, and ideas are transposed into metaphors which in turn are transformed into whatever limits the playwright's imagination may reach. Notwithstanding, a study of the plays of writers in the forefront of recent playwrighting trends like Adamov, Albee, Arrabal, Beckett, Frisch, Handke, Shepard, Genet, Ionesco, Stoppard, Mamet, Mrosek, and Pinter shows that certain structural controls more or less fall into the types of scenes discussed below.

Parallel Scenes

Parallel scenes are scenes of preparatory action primarily occurring at the beginning of the play. They are usually scenes of exposition and atmosphere that give the audience information essential to understanding subsequent actions. The characters are going along in the same direction, presenting little or no conflict, either mental or physical. The forces out of which conflict will arise are in equilibrium. The fundamental beat is established, and the tempo maintains a more or less even pace. If a parallel scene comes late in the play, as in many contemporary plays where the playwright involves an audience immediately in conflict in the opening scenes, the director has to resort to a forced acceleration of breaking up, an increased tempo, or a marked dominance of rhythm to bolster the dynamics of the scene. Whether parallel scenes occur early or late in the play, the challenge to the director is to maintain interest, point up the significant lines of dialogue, and picturize the essential relationships so that the audience can digest the important information of the scene. Out of parallel scenes comes a change in equilibrium by the introduction of inciting factors leading to scenes of conflict.

Scenes of Conflict

In scenes of conflict the minds and bodies of the characters are in direct conflict, propelling the action toward the climax. Through the actions that are set in motion, character relationships are altered or complicated, leading to a greater unbalancing of forces. These scenes have minor climaxes of their own, presenting to a lesser degree a beginning, a rising action, an expected conflict, and a climax. The thrust in the unbalancing of forces makes for an accumulative build from one action scene to the next. These scenes are built to a climactic point by use of breaking-up movements and an increased tempo, which varies with the changing thoughts and attitudes of the characters and with the changing nature of the situation. The director must bring out the inherent dramatic values in the scene, such as the elements in conflict, alterations in character relationships, and new inciting factors. He must control the various tensions of the scene so they fit the overall dynamics of the play. Overstressing a build beyond the requirements of a scene may be exciting for the moment, but can prove damaging to succeeding scenes.

Transitional Scenes

In transitional scenes, void of dramatic action and usually of entrances and exits, an even steady rhythm is applied so that they may serve their purpose of tying together two other scenes. The dominance of rhythm provides vitality and interest so that the audience is unaware of the break between one scene and the next and retains its interest in the play even though there is little apparent action. The handling of tempo during these scenes depends on their position in the main design of the play.

Climactic Scenes

Climactic scenes have inherent dramatic force; the emotions are increasing in intensity and building to a crisis or climax. Such scenes present the problem of building the scene as outlined above.

Diminishing Scenes

A diminishing scene is one in which the dramatic intensity of the preceding climactic scene decreases slowly. A scene is diminished by droppng off in reverse order the steps that were used one by one to build the scene. Diminishing a scene should not take longer than approximately one-third the time it took to build the scene.

Drop Scenes

In a drop scene there is a sudden change from a point of high intensity to a much lower level. If a drop scene precedes a scene that builds to a climax, it helps to intensify the build. A drop scene may evoke considerable emotion in the audience by the suddenness of its contrast to the high pitch of the scene which preceded it.

Suspense Scenes

These are scenes of tension in which suspense is prolonged so as to include several rises and falls of intensity within the situation; this variation is intended to arouse a state of expectancy about the outcome. In many situations suspense is held by introducing *teasers*—tricks of business and movement that arouse suspense and delay the ultimate discovery. Another term applied to such teasers whether they are in the writing or in the business is *stretching,* in other words, getting out of the scene all the suspense possible before exhausting the audience.

The suspense scene usually begins at a higher intensity than an ordinary climactic scene, then drops and rises several times in order to draw out all the anticipation possible. Its nuances exist within the scene itself. The speeches or movements upon which the suspense element depends need special attention in emphasis; the drops immediately following can be considerably lower. The build of the final portion of the scene must be higher than any previous part and its height of intensity must be determined by its relation to the main build of the play.

Exercises in Types of Scenes and Their Tempos

1. Bring in short scenes from any play, past or contemporary, that demonstrate the several types of scenes. Read the dialogue to the class and have them analyze the type of scene. A brief introduction to the scene may be necessary.
2. Without learning lines, rehearse one of each type of scene according to its requirements for control of tempo.

The Main Build of the Play

The rhythmic pattern through its change in tempo produces the main build of a play, not on one continuous line of development, but in a progression of nuances, thereby achieving richness and variety. These nuances are the shadings resulting from the change and contrast in the tempo of the various scenes. They are the rise and fall in intensity of an action or actions within a scene and become the dynamics of the performance, contributing to the ascending propulsion of the scene toward the climax. Though plays vary greatly in the structuring of act and scene divisions, particularly many contemporary experimental plays, the following breakdown gives the basis for an understanding of the factors that are usually involved in the main build of a play.

After the planting of the exposition in which we have
the atmosphere and locale telling us place, time, and so on,

the establishment of mood and basic attitude,

the antecedent action telling us the present and past relations of characters,

the main idea out of which conflict will rise,

the lining up of the forces, the inciting factors,

and the carry-over scene which gives us the first suggestion of conflict and precipitates us into the struggle,

the main conflict of the play begins by giving us the rising action resulting from the clash of forces. The scenes that make up the rising action are minor climaxes which are alternated with transitional scenes and scenes of low emotional intensity until the major crisis is reached which propels actions directly to the main climax or obligatory scene. Out of this follows the denouement, resolution, or falling action to the end of the play, which usually is made up of diminished scenes. The increased build of the minor climaxes to the main climax is the means by which tempo contributes to the main build of the play.

Below is a diagram of the main build of a play showing the intermediate scenes and their rising and falling emotional intensity:

FIGURE 39 *Diagram showing the main build of a play*

In the play's progression of action the climaxes become longer in duration of time and greater in emotional intensity. The scenes of low emotional intensity such as diminishing scenes, drop scenes, transitional scenes, and parallel scenes that may occur late in the play, become lower each time in proportion to the preceding climax, but actually they should never fall as low as at the beginning of the play. They also become shorter as the action of the play progresses.

It can be appreciated from the above analysis why the overall rhythmic control of a play is a major challenge to the director, let alone an area difficult to express in writing. Unfortunately, the dynamics of a play's rhythm cannot be projected as a pattern in space like composition and viewed as a whole, but rather as something to be experienced within onself making it possible to orchestrate these dynamics which by the nature of plays extend over a long span time. For this reason a director's sensitivity to rhythm becomes a most important attribute to have and develop.

Handling Interpolations

The principle of handling interpolations of dancing, music, and specialty acts in a play not presentational in any of its aspects is to blend the interpolation into the rhythm of the scene in such a way that it does not stand out as a specialty number or an individual bit of entertainment. The interpolation must be part of the whole. Applause and any break between the interpolation and the scene must be avoided. Otherwise it resembles a vaudeville number when rightfully it should remain within the illusion of the play.

Several additional principles, along with many we have discussed previously, must be considered in the handling of interpolations:

1. Have the actors and performers gradually get into their new positions during the dialogue preceding the interpolation. Make sure there is no break or silence between the dialogue and the interpolation while they reach their positions.

2. If there is to be accompaniment to the dancing or singing, this should start before the number. The accompaniment should begin during the dialogue, continue through the number, and on into the dialogue again. It should begin very quietly and at the end trail off unnoticed. If music is offstage and the dancing onstage, have the music begin before someone says "There's music" or some such remark.

3. Always motivate the source of accompaniment. If it is radio music and the radio is turned on in view of the audience, cover the action of turning on the switch and dial and allow a definite time for the radio to warm up, if necessary.

4. Begin the song or dance quietly, smoothly, with little motion, and let it die off at the end.

5. Have the person singing, dancing, or playing begin definitely in a weak area and position. If it is dancing, have it trail off into a weak area.

6. Never let the interpolation get spectacular. Do not emphasize introductions and have the actors who are supposed to urge the performer on use as little persuasion as possible.

7. Do not let the number stop with a climax. If there is one, build up to it, but then allow it to diminish, possibly by repeating the first few measures.

8. Keep the interpolation as short as possible.

9. Have the other characters begin the dialogue before the interpolation is over, and speak out loudly so as to attract attention from the interpolation. If possible, have the performer begin his own lines first.

10. The performer must relate to the people onstage rather than to the audience.

11. Watch the footwear of dancers making sure that it is in character. It should be what the character would be wearing in the scene.

12. Do not use familiar music, otherwise the audience will be humming the tune or associating the music with some past experience, thereby taking them emotionally away from the play.

13. The number must fit into the rhythm of the play, the timing of the scene, and the rhythm of the characters in the scene. It should be appropriate to the occasion meeting all requirements of time and place.

Exercises in Rhythm

1. The following exercises are to be devoid of any pantomimic action. The people on stage are to be arranged without any emotional relationship but in arbitrary design. The exercise should show the basic rhythm strongly by having the larger proportion of people carry the fundamental beat and the other people supply variations of the pattern. Use as many variations as possible.

(a) A protest meeting of angry citizens.
(b) Teenagers at their favorite weekend haunt.
(c) A farce.
(d) A black comedy.
(e) A tragedy.
(f) A city newspaper office during a big scoop.
(g) A waterfront during a fog.
(h) A street corner in a shopping district during rush hour.
(i) That same street corner on Sunday morning.
(j) A harmonious political rally.
(k) A revival meeting with new converts.
(l) A small-town library.
(m) A board meeting of a conservative organization.
(n) Breakfast with three of the children late for school.

Have the class analyze each rhythm.

2. Have each group do an original rhythm.

3. Scenes of building: These are to be abstract in design and devoid of emotional relationship. Use as many methods as possible in building.

(a) Scene built and diminished.
(b) Scene built and dropped.

11
Pantomimic Dramatization

The importance of pantomimic dramatization to the performance of a play is evidenced by the psychological fact that most people are visually minded and therefore are more deeply impressed by what they see than by what they hear. This fifth element of directing is most valuable in giving a play distinction, warmth, richness, vitality, and an illusion of life.

Definition

To arrive at a general understanding of the term *pantomimic dramatization* it is best to define the word *pantomime*. Pantomime is action without words. By action is meant a sequence of facial expressions, gestures, hand operations, and body positions and movements that, observed from life, is used imaginatively by the actor and the director to tell something about the elements of character, situation, locale, and atmosphere of a play. If these elements are made clear without the use of dialogue, they are dramatized by pantomime. This process is called "pantomimic dramatization." It is in this particular limited sense that the term will be used in this chapter.

A wider meaning of pantomimic dramatization is the complete visual performance of a play and, as such, includes the use of composition, picturization, movement, rhythm, and pantomime to convey, without the use of words, all the elements of a play. A solo performer may dramatize a simple story by means of pantomime, movement, rhythm, and picturizing body positions. The presence of several characters in a play demands the full use of composition and picturization as well as pantomime, movement, and rhythm to convey the complete content of story, character relationships, and theme. The exercises at the end of the chapter, which involve a group of characters, demonstrate this wider use of pantomomic dramatization.

Before proceeding to the general characteristics, application, and use of pantomomic dramatization, it is well to point out two things: the distinction between pantomime and business, and the relation of pantomime and business to properties.

Business means going through the motions of actually opening and closing doors, wrapping bundles, dialing a telephone, pounding a table, writing a letter, putting on eyeglasses, and making other movements, gestures, and reactions without dialogue or in synchronization with dialogue. The old meaning of pantomime was prolonged action without words. Since the terms are in many ways interchangeable pantomomic dramatization includes both business and pantomime, and all these terms will be used interchangeably. Movements unrelated to properties, gestures, and body positions are also called *pantomime* or *business*. They may be related to and involve the use of properties and still be called pantomime or business.

It should also be noted that a particular use of the term pantomime during early rehearsals without properties is the direction "Pantomime the business." This means that the business is to be executed without the actual use of properties.

Determining Pantomimic Dramatization

The imaginative use of good pantomimic detail comes from an understanding and observation of life, but the springboard for this imagination is the play. In order that we may at the outset give free scope to our imaginative flight, we should, when reading the play, look no further than the general title of a scene and disregard the author's detailed directions regarding actions, modes of expression, descriptions of characters, and so on. This is not to say that the author's directions are not essential to the final choices. But as the first source of inspiration, the situations themselves allow full play to the director's interpretation, imagination, and creation, which often bring new insights beyond the indications and descriptions set down by the author. However, this release does not mean the director is at liberty to superimpose concepts, interpretation, business, or anything else to show off his cleverness. The director's responsibility is to explore the text and be sensitive to all indications that serve as catalyst in revealing the life that is in it. Following this unrestricted visualization comes the restriction of selecting, arranging, and controlling the things visualized in terms of situation, kind of scene, pacing of the play, emphasis, and the many other controls that will be discussed in this chapter.

The springboard for our imagination, then, is the play, and the elements of the play that give it support are story, dialogue, character, properties, locale, and atmosphere.

Story

The story or any one situation will tell us that certain business is essential in the action of the play. The playwright will usually have prescribed this, but before reading his detailed description we should visualize for ourselves the elaboration of the necessary action.

Essential business is inherent in the action: the revelry in the wine cellar in *Twelfth Night*, the burial of Ophelia in *Hamlet*, the boxing scene in *A View from the Bridge*, the poker game in *A Streetcar Named Desire*, Alison's ironing in Osborne's *Look Back in Anger*. These are the obvious examples of business prescribed by the story or the content of the scene. There are instances, however, where business that is inherent in the action is the creation only of the director's imagination. For example, in the second act a character gives the summary of a book that he has just read. We have here a suggestion for business that might be given this character in the first act, that is, the reading of that book. For business to be used in one act, look for suggestions in other acts through which you might create continuity.

Possibilities for business may come from actions that are happening offstage and to which the situation onstage may be directly related, though at the moment no reference to it is made in the dialogue. A murder by poisoning is being committed upstairs. We are to learn about this later on in the scene, but at the actual moment of the deed one of the characters onstage knows what is taking place. Immediately we have suggestions for pantomimic business to give this character in the run of the dialogue onstage. Such use of pantomime not only plants the seed for coming developments but also enriches and gives added dimension to the scene.

Dialogue

One of the greatest sources for inspiration in the creation of pantomime is the dialogue. The business suggested may be merely illustrative of the line, as the handling of the duel scene in *Cyrano de Bergerac* where the business is suggested in the ballad that Cyrano improvises, or Hamlet's handling of the skull in the graveyard scene, or Molière's Mascarille showing off his costume.

We give life, clarity, and emphasis to a line by the use of gestures or bits of business. Falstaff describing the attack on his person will give life and humor to the description if he re-enacts all that presumably took place. In creating such business from dialogue we go to the imagery behind the language and then translate this imagery in terms of action. If the language gives no imagery, then we must seek action out of nouns and verbs themselves.

Often the imagery comes out of the symbolism implied by the text, as in Ibsen's *A Doll's House* and *The Wild Duck* or in Chekhov's *The Cherry Orchard*. In these plays the symbolism serves as catalyst to business that reveals the character's attitude and state of mind to the situation and in turn expresses the implied symbolism. In *The Cherry Orchard* the manners, gestures, and deportment of Lyubov and her brother Gaev can be reflections of the cherry orchard over which Lyubov delights ecstatically: "What a magnificent orchard! White bursts of blossoms . . ."; but in the words of Lopakhin "the old cherry orchard must be chopped down."

For fuller imagination we must often create situations that bring out or might bring out the particular dialogue. This is no more than saying that you must picturize to the fullest the implication of the dialogue, thereby giving that dialogue fertile ground out of which it flowers.

Characters

Characters offer us an abundance of possibilities for business. Their external traits: bearing, age, mannerisms of voice and walk, mannerisms of gestures, costumes, and make-up; their internal traits: background, culture, nationality, race, beliefs, morality, state of mind, and so forth—all these offer us numberless suggestions for business. It is important, however, that such business, besides being pertinent to the character, be first of all pertinent to the action. For a more complete study of the creation of business from character, refer to Study of the Role in Chapter 5.

Properties

The significance of properties, hand and others, can lead to business that enriches the action. In the Act I scene 2 from Shakespeare's *King Lear* the letter as a symbol of Edgar's "treachery" is equivalent to a third character in the scene:

GLOUCESTER: [*With "Edgar's" letter in hand.*] O villain, villain! His very opinion in the letter! Abhorred villain! [*Throws down letter in disdain.*] Unnatural, detested, brutish villain! Worse than brutish! [*As Gloucester in anger points down at the letter.*] Go, sirrah, seek him! [*Gloucester grabs*

Edmond's arm as Edmond starts to pick up letter.] I'll apprehend him.
[*Gloucester picks up and crumbles letter.*] Abominable villain! [*Gloucester
throws letter away in disgust.*] Where is he? [*Pacing.*]

EDMUND: I do not well know, my lord. [*Edmund surreptitiously picks up crum-
bled letter and pockets it.*]

Locale

The scene in which the action takes place is replete with suggestions for
business. Here, as always, we should visualize unrestrictedly the possibilities
offered by the locale to give us an abundance of material from which to
choose when we begin to select, arrange, and control. Consider the possibilities offered by these locales: a bar (*No Place To Be Somebody*), a hairdress-
ing parlor (*The Women*), a pawnshop (*American Buffalo*), a table being
set for family dinner in a small town (*Ah, Wilderness!*).

Atmosphere

The strata of society; the culture of the period; the customs, social conduct,
manner of living, and fashions of people; the characteristics of a place; the
time of day; the season of the year—these are the many sources from which
we draw inspiration for business. Whether a play belongs to a historical
period or is modern in setting, the consideration of atmosphere is inherent
in each situation. When the atmosphere is that of our own time and place,
we enrich our imagination through observation of life. However, to capture
the atmosphere of foreign lands and former periods in history we must study
the general characteristics of these lands or historical epochs by studying
their arts, culture, modes, manners and literature.

Exercises

Using the plays suggested above or plays of your own choosing:

1. Find instances of business inherent in the action. Write out an elaboration
of the action without reference to the author's detailed description.

2. Find passages of dialogue where use of gestures and bits of business will
give life, clarity, and emphasis to the lines. Act out these passage, using your
own imaginative contributions.

Act out, using your own imaginative contributions:

(*a*) Falstaff describing the attack on his person in Act II, scene 4 of *Henry
IV, Part I*.

(*b*) Cyrano's improvised ballad in the opening duel scene.

(*c*) Hamlet's handling of the skull in the graveyard scene.

(*d*) Mascarille showing off his costume in Molière's *The Affected Young
Ladies*.

3. Write out an elaboration of the possibilities for business of a character in a play that you have studied.

4. Find instances of locales that offer possibilities for imaginative contributions of business. Write out an elaboration of the business.

Think over the possibilities offered by these locales:

(a) The amusement park in *Liliom*.

(b) The lobby in Wilson's *The Hot l Baltimore*.

(c) The common room in Wasserman's *One Flew Over the Cuckoo's Nest*.

Write out in full your contributions.

5. Find instances in plays where the atmosphere—customs, society, fashions, season, time, and so forth—is necessary to the complete realization of the scene. Write out in detail the business that you would use to achieve this atmosphere.

Contributions of Pantomimic Dramatization

Once he has given full power to his interpretation, imagination, and creation of pantomime from the context of the play, the director, in plotting the business, should keep in mind the special contributions that use of pantomime gives the play.

Establishes Situation

Obviously, pantomime helps to establish the situation. Just as the director is able to establish this rhythmically, so, too, through pantomime he can plant definite facts that an audience is eager to know about the play either at the opening or in the later development of each scene. Suggestions for business mentioned earlier under Story open avenues in the search for business that would further enrich the situation and establish whatever attendant circumstances may seem pertinent to the scene.

Much of the opening situation of an act or scene can be expressed through details of pantomimic business which will tend to make the exposition of the situation much more vivid.

Establishes Character

The first impressions of a character in the first scene in which he is revealed are most important to the audience. Drawing from the wealth of material that they have gathered from the intellectual study of the role, the director and actor should establish at the outset the delineating marks of the character. The business of putting on eyeglasses, for example, could be used to reveal aspects of character. We could have him fumble for his glasses, wipe them carefully, adjust them slowly to his eyes, and deliberately arrange the material to be read. The choices are many, as against doing the business without embellishment, but the final selection should serve the requirements of the text.

Costumes and accessories, hand properties, and manners of a period become valuable tools when the time comes to select the most effective means of enriching and expressing a particular trait, thought, feeling, or attitude. In Chekhov's *The Cherry Orchard* Gaev has his cape, gloves, and cane; Lopakhin, his watch and chain: Trofimov, his spectacles and rubbers; Varya, her ring of keys; Charlotta, her rifle and cards; Epihodov, his guitar. Gaev's manner of removing his gloves and his use of the cane as a billiard cue, Lopakhin's fiddling with his watch, Charlotta's juggling and card manipulation, Epihodov's guitar playing—all reveal a state of existence that creates depth for the picture. Carried to an extreme, business and pantomime can become a "glorification of accidental detail," which may have strong fascination for an audience and bolster the director's conceit, but actually offer little illumination of character or situation. Its excessive or over-emphasized use steals interest away from the true content of the scene.

It is important to say here that many of the internal traits of a character are revealed through the development and unraveling of the story. As suggested by the study of his role, the actor should know the appropriate time to perform each bit of revealing business and each gesture or expression that will enrich and give understanding and progression to his characterization. This timing is important for conservation and variety. In the handling of amateurs the director will discover that a more convincing performance results from giving them "something to do."

The working out of characteristic behavior and action cannot be over-emphasized, for it is a contributing factor to the life of a production. Although the beginning director should plan on paper his positions and movements, he should not become too set in his ideas of how he wants a scene to be played, for he will often receive ideas for business and interpolation from what his actors contribute. In the course of rehearsal, good actors begin to "feel their parts" and often insert bits of detail that are exactly right. The director should keep a sharp lookout for this, especially since the actor may make these contributions quite unconsciously. Give and take of this kind between actor and director constitutes an ideal relationship, and a director should stimulate his cast to make these creative suggestions. In this way the richest character detail is frequently developed.

Establishes Locale

At the beginning of a scene, the locale should be immediately established. Pantomimic detail is one important means of achieving this. The richness of such pantomime is vital to the illusion of the play. It gives a conviction of reality, showing people living in a definite place, reacting with the responses of life and not merely acting in front of a set to which they have no relation. This pantomimic relationship should be incorporated into the action of the play. An excellent example of pantomime establishing locale is found in *Our Town,* where through the careful rendering of business in pantomime the audience's imagination is stimulated to see a kitchen with its appliances, a garden, a soda fountain, a graveyard, and so on.

Establishes Atmosphere

It is impossible to establish place without qualifying it in some way with atmosphere. Let us take as an example the locale *city street.* Now let us give it atmosphere. Let us qualify this street. It is nightfall in the heart of Algiers; the temperature is stifling; the streets are empty except for one or two furtive figures that scurry from one doorway to another. Now we change the facts to New York, just before Christmas, Fifth Avenue, Saturday about three in the afternoon, snow falling; we could continue to qualify this locale in terms of all that atmosphere implies regarding strata of society, historical period, and so on. Or the street might be a city street in the play *Julius Caesar* or in Brecht's *The Good Woman of Setzuan* or again in the Restoration comedy *The Way of the World.* We immediately sense here how important atmosphere is in arriving at the distinctive quality that gives our play fullness, maturity, and color.

Aids in Establishing Kind of Play

The use of pantomime helps to establish the kind of play. This is not the place, nor is it within the scope of this book, to go into an analysis of the four main types of plays and their many corollaries, past and present; nor is it the place to detail controls in play directing that merit consideration under each type. A few words, however, are necessary to distinguish the kind and quality of pantomimic business that each type, irrespective of style, demands.

TRAGEDY   Since the emotional contact between audience and play is strongest in tragedies and serious dramas, and since the characterization is at its highest development, we find that we must use business that is simple, direct, honest, and less developed than in the other kinds of play. Our attention must go to the dramatic significance of the character or dialogue, and whatever business is used must not attract attention in itself but must be used as a further means of clear delineation. We must not spend time on the details of business but must choose only the significant and essential.

COMEDY   In comedies, limiting our frame of reference to those plays dealing with the lighter aspects of life, we have a more objective point of view; laughter needs objectivity. The amount and kind of business varies inversely with the comedy's intellectual value. In high comedy the business is apt to be small, seemingly trivial, and arbitrary; there should be great selectivity and precision. As our comedy becomes broader, our business assumes greater and greater proportions. We must remember, however, that many of our comedies today face abrupt changes in attitudes running rampant between melodrama and farce, as in comedies by Feiffer, Shisgal, and Stoppard. We should also note that with today's audiences, at least the more sophisticated, laughter usually comes from the meaning of the line, or the gesture if the gesture speaks as a line of dialogue, rather than from the situation itself. What carries is the suggestion and not so much the actual doing.

MELODRAMA   Here we must distinguish between old melodramas and new. Though melodramas are more or less the externals of tragedy with emphasis on situation, today ideas and character as found in *Petrified Forest, The Bad Seed, Victims of Duty, The Birthday Party,* and *Sleuth* largely replace the teasers of the earlier forms of melodrama. Business in melodrama is detailed, carefully executed, and deliberate, and is used primarily to strengthen the situation rather than characterization. In mystery plays we find much use of *plants* (see page 61) to foreshadow things to happen and in the suspense scenes use of *teasers* to build up suspense and anticipation, like the business of stripping the pages of newspapers in *The Birthday Party.* A teaser may also be any kind of delaying action that heightens the suspense of the outcome by its intrusion in the build towards a climax.

FARCE   Farce like melodrama is based on situation. It has the externals of comedy and emphasizes antics more than language or character. Its primary intention is to amuse by its invention of situations and incidents which embroil the characters in a way that excites laughter. The true farce like *Flea in Her Ear, Three Men on a Horse,* and *The Matchmaker* structures its story on a foundation of "possibility, but improbability." The events could happen, but probably never would. The range is wide: from sheer tomfoolery (*Charley's Aunt*) to satire (*The Madwoman of Chaillot*) to grotesquerie (*What the Butler Saw*) to absurdism (*The House of Blue Leaves*), or to some plays with more completeness of character (*The Taming of the Shrew*). In the farce, where situation is more emphatic, the business is exaggerated, lively, and executed in bold simple strokes. Its timing should allow no pauses for reflection on the part of the audience as incidents, created primarily from immediate emotional reactions, pile up and push forward the action with accelerating speed. It is important to remember, however, that the build-up of momentum in farce must have a starting point.

ity. This is due in part to the complete absence of unnecessary intermediate steps. Rehearsing an actor in a piece of business should tend to make him an "expert" at what he does and help him to obtain similar results.

Another important point concerning the precision of business is the timing of the action with the lines of dialogue so that neither are blurred. Usually a piece of business, unless it is very small, comes before or after the delivery of the line unless it is intended that the line be "thrown away." Cigarettes may be lighted, table set, cocktails served, and so on, during mere "Yes, sirs" or "No, ma'ams" or "I'll see" and unimportant lines of this nature. Yet the moment something is said that has to do with plot or character, that is, something that affects the understanding and advancement of the play, all business must be subordinated or stopped entirely.

Rhythmic Appropriateness

A special consideration must be given to the amount of pantomime that is appropriate to the over-all rhythm of the play, to the tempo of the individual scenes, and to the rhythms of character, locale, situation, etc. Overall the business of the characters in a comedy will have a different rhythm from that in a tragedy, although the characters may have identical business to do. Within the play itself, the change of tempo affects the amount and kind of business. Therefore, although much business may be found in the expository party of a play, it diminishes rapidly as the tempo of the scenes picks up. Detailed business will invariably slow up tempo.

Proportion

Closely related to the rhythmic appropriateness of pantomime is its proportion. Proportion of pantomime is controlled by the kind of scene and the position of the scene within the play. Parallel scenes, transitional scenes, and the like should be enriched and made interesting with pantomimic detail. As a scene builds, when and how much to include, diminish, or eliminate must be evaluated in relation to the overall dynamics of the play. Through control of pantomime you can either slow down or quicken the pace and build of a scene.

Control

"Imagination," says Stanislavsky in his book *An Actor Prepares*, "creates things that can be or can happen, whereas fantasy invents things that are not in existence, which never have been or will be." As we have hinted all along, imagination works to combine all the possible memories that we have of fact—in other words, the things that can be or can happen. The director's ability to recall and to present this recollection in a provocative manner is imagination at its best. Every actor who has to perform a stage death uses his imagination; the more vivid and realistic the death the more details or combination of details the actor must be able to recall from his memory. Many directors whose plays are laid in the South Seas or in the arctic must recall what hottest August or coldest January was like and proceed from there to the workings of the imagination. In all these cases, fact must act as the springboard for imagination.

To speak of controlling imagination does not contradict our emphasis on richness of detail. But definite problems arise in the unrestrained use of detail in which a play can be swamped by an overactive imagination. A certain recognizable convention, or norm, is absolutely demanded by an audience. Furthermore, every attempt should be made to avoid the fantastic, unless, of course, the play calls for such effects. Unrestrained imagination tends to go in these two directions: toward an overabundance of detail or toward the introduction of fantasy. In either case the results are confusing for the play rooted in reality.

Interesting Ground Plan and Setting

Essential to good pantomimic dramatization are an interesting and practicable ground plan and setting. As in creating business, a director should first plan out his setting with complete freedom of the imagination, disregarding the directions of the author. Later the author's ideas about the setting added to those of the director should make possible a richer and more interesting one than if the director had slavishly followed what had been suggested. The final selection, rearrangement, and control come from a consideration of the characters living there, the kind of play, the locale, the atmosphere, and other factors—refer to the chapter on Directing the Play for the process involved in creating the groundplan.

Furthermore, the director may find that the action calls for two or three important elements that need to be emphasized. These elements may be particularly expressive of the locale or the character of the people, or they may be essential to the action, but in all cases the emphasized elements must be properly placed to suit the demands of action.

The director should be very particular not only about the exact layout of the stage setting but about the offstage surroundings as well, for the development of business is dependent both upon the setup onstage and upon where the characters come from and where they go. From his study of climactic movements and general patterns of important scenes, the director decides where the windows, doors, and furniture can be placed most advantageously. In this respect the arrangement of all these elements should be created for movement. Arrangements that force actors to follow complicated movements or interfere with the action of the characters are definitely bad.

A play that is set outdoors or in an abstract realm of levels and platforms gives the director a certain amount of freedom in preparing a ground plan, since there is an irregularity to nature and an indefiniteness to the abstract. The instant that he goes indoors, however, he is dealing with walls and is faced with the problem of introducing variety in the well-known layout of the average home. Therefore, as a conclusion to this section devoted to the essentials of good pantomimic dramatization let us set down certain facts that govern the arrangement of furniture in the realistic play.

GENERAL PRINCIPLES Great care should be taken to avoid the conventional placement of a soft on one side of the stage and a table and a few chairs on the other. For years this arrangement constituted the main form of stage furnishings; but it was overdone and has become timeworn, conventional, and unreal.

It is basically sound to make your stage look as much like a real room and the placement of furniture in that room as natural as possible. Furniture should be placed in relation to the walls. If these walls happen not to be a square box set but on a triangular formation, then it must be arranged in relation to this shape. This means that sofas cannot be placed casually on the right or left center of the stage but must bear relationship to a fireplace (either perpendicular or parallel to it), a table, a wall, or a window, since that is the way sofas are placed in a real house. Chairs should not be placed facing the audience but in relation to other chairs or other pieces of furniture or to the room itself. One of the best ways to arrive at a good stage setting is to draw all four sides of a room and arrange the furniture as it would be in that room. Then remove one of the walls and see if, with a slight readjustment, it is not suitable for a stage setting. This will lead to irregular and unusual form. One can take a room in a house that he knows, or one can take pictures from magazines. Remember that in the final adjustment and selection the necessities to be kept and stressed are dictated by the action of the play.

PLOTTING THE GROUND PLAN The furniture on a stage should be placed in groups, each one constituting an acting area. A group is made up of one main piece of furniture like a sofa and the small pieces that go with it; for example, there can be a footstool, a floor lamp, an end table or a rear table, a newspaper rack, or a smoking stand. Another group could be a large armchair with a side table or floor lamp by it or possibly a stool. Still another example of an area would be a table with two or three chairs about it, with magazines, a bowl of flowers, or a lamp on it. Usually each stage set should have at least three areas of furniture. This allows for one or two clear areas.

The groups of furniture should usually have places for at least two people. When using a sofa and table, this is easy. In the case of the armchair, it is possible for someone to sit on its arm and play a scene with a person sitting in the chair or to sit on the stool and talk to a person in the chair. These three groups should also be placed so that an actor can sit in one area and have a scene with someone sitting in another group or area. The groups should bear relation to one another.

DISTRIBUTION   At least one group of furniture should be placed downstage, either on the left or on the right. If a fireplace is on the side wall downstage, a stool can usually be placed alongside it on which an actor can sit and join in conversation with people in another area. Generally, chairs downstage on the left or right do not face the audience but are in profile to it.

The best places for mantelpieces are along the side wall, because only when they are so placed can an actor play looking into them and still be seen by an audience. If a fireplace is upstage along the back wall, it is difficult to use because an actor in facing the fire has to turn his back on the audience.

Windows take careful consideration. They are usually best along a side wall, as it is easier to let the audience imagine what is outside than to make the exterior convincing with the use of props. Furthermore, if a window is important in the play (that is, if a person has to look out of a window and describe what is outside) , it is easier for him in this position to convey what he says to the audience than it is when he has his back to the audience (as he might if the window were on the rear wall) .

The placement of doors or entrances has already been discussed under Movement. A set should never have an entrance that is not used. The more entrances there are in a set—within limitations of textual requirements, of course—the easier it is for the director, because then it is possible for him to have an actor enter at the most convenient point onstage for his relation to the group. But few rooms require more than two or three points of entrance. Accordingly, the director should not have more doors in a set than would be likely in a room. The problems that arise when there are only one or two entrances revolve mostly around congestion at the entrance and finding motivation for characters entering to cross to the other side of the stage.

MOTIVATION   The director should establish each exit onstage so that the audience will know where it leads; and he must see that the actors are consistent in always using the same exit when they are going to the particular place that that exit designates. He should be sure that every character who has left the stage by a certain door always returns by the same door unless it is clearly explained in the script why he does not. One of the best ways for a director to keep in his mind where the doors lead is to draw a plan of the entire floor of which this particular room is a part. In that way he will see this room in relation to the different exits.

Never use the spaces between the proscenium arch and the tormentors for an entrance or exit.

MISCELLANEOUS DETAIL   In addition to the two or three main areas of furniture, there are other pieces that we call trim. These are knickknacks, small tables and chairs against the walls and in the farther corners of the room, which are not used for the big scenes of the play or may not be used at all, especially if the stage is large. If it is small, these chairs along the side walls and far corners may be used for the minor characters in a scene.

If one scene occurs at night, each area of furniture must have its own natural source of light; that is, there must be a lamp for each group unless a group is near a fireplace which will flood it with light or near wall brackets which will be sufficient motivation for light on the group.

In arranging the furniture on a stage, one should be careful to achieve balance, although a symmetrical arrangement is often dull and should be avoided, except where the style demands it. One can arrive at balance without symmetry by having the areas of furniture evenly distributed over the whole stage.

Careful consideration should be given to the set to make it look real and convincing in its reproduction of the place that it is supposed to represent. The more natural the arrangement of furniture the easier the directing and the more tasteful the effect.

Not only should an attempt be made to arrive at originality in the settings of one interior, but if the play has two or three sets, care should be taken to obtain a radically different arrangement of furniture for the remaining act or acts. If there is only one set, a certain amount of business and interest will result from the change of ground plan from one act or scene to another. This change may be motivated by passage of time, introduction of a new tenant, essentials of action, or design. This last may need explanation: It is often possible to obtain variety and interest in a one-set play by changing the angle of vision of the set from one act to the other. Where in the first act the main entrance was up center and the alcove at right, in the second the main entrance may be shifted to the left and the alcove to up center. Such shifting of the angle of vision should be used, however, only when the importance of a particular area or of a particular entrance may shift from one act to the other.

Application of Pantomimic Dramatization

The Italian *commedia dell'arte* productions of the sixteenth and seventeenth centuries were enthusiastically received over all western Europe. "Because," to quote a contemporary critic, "they make a strong point of gesture and represent many things through action, even those who do not understand their language cannot fail to understand the subject of the piece."

This is precisely the point to keep in mind in applying pantomimic action to a play. Let us pretend that the play is to be given before an audience that does not understand the language. Consequently, the characters, locales, atmospheres, and situations will have to be accurately portrayed if there is to be an understanding of what is taking place. We assume that there can be no explanation by word of these things and that everything must be conveyed by gesture, facial expression, and movement. Those of us who have sat through the stiff posturing and broad gesture of the earlier vintage operatic performance realize how possible it is to obtain nothing of a play's content from the acting. Here we have the use of pantomimic detail at its stock minimum. The result is, of course, a performance that, except for the delivery of the music, is at once bland and uninteresting. What we miss completely are the details of individuality—in short, something that reveals these people as actual beings. Pantomimic dramatization supplies these details. Based on what is said or implied in the script, it represents in action the facts of character, locale, and atmosphere.

General Procedure

We refer the student to Chapter 15 for the overall considerations in approaching the direction of a play. This section on general procedure relates to those considerations as well as to pantomimic dramatization in directing the realistic play.

The director with a good visual sense begins to see the play "in action" during his first readings. Rereading it creates in his mind more definite pictures, movements, positions, and business. These need not be connected and continuous at this time but merely high spots in the script. It is not advisable for him to become lost in details during these first readings; rather, he should concentrate on the general overall progress of the entire play.

His next step is to plot out the business more definitely with the script at his side and, as we mentioned earlier, disregard the stage directions until later so as to allow free scope to his imagination. Inserting his own business in this way, the director does what he considers best for the interpretation of the play, and he judges the business by what is natural and appropriate to the characters, locale, and situation. At all times he must consider his use of pantomime as an element that will lend richness, depth, and reality to the script. This tests a director's keenness of observation of people, places, and things.

In filling in a set of characters, a locale, or situation with pantomimic detail his ability of observation becomes especially evident. First of all, he recalls from his own experience what he knows about these elements. His next step is to filter this detail through his imagination. In other words, he takes a fact and by rearranging, eliminating, heightening certain of its features produces what is more effective, more stageworthy for his particular use. This is, of course, the "rearrangement of nature" followed by any artist. Apropos of this someone has said that there can be nothing in art that was not first in life. We see how this applies directly to pantomomic dramatization; it is the imaginative use of details that the director has first observed from life. This is the keynote of this chapter. All our detail is drawn from the question "What would such and such a character do in such and such a locale and atmosphere?" and we make the first test of the pantomime that we use not its originality but its truth to the circumstances.

The greatest care should be taken by the director to control and blend his imaginative contributions so that the audience is unaware of any trick effect for the effect's sake. Once it senses sheer acrobatics, an audience becomes suspicious and even antagonistic.

A steady concern for the overall flow of his production will keep the director from losing his way in a maze of detail. Frequent and uninterrupted run-throughs help in keeping his perspective on the play.

Selection after Pacing of Play

In the matter of pacing the play we may find that much of the business that we liked when we inserted it during early rehearsals may have to be taken out. This should be done unhesitatingly, since such detail cannot be of value if it harms the overall dynamics of the play. The procedure of filling up the play with details and then selecting what is wanted when pacing the show is good training, especially for beginning directors.

Control of Business at Opening of Play

The play should not start at too high a pitch of business and general action, for an audience is easily bewildered at the beginning and may react unsympathetically as a result. A director should "ease" into the opening situation. This becomes especially important in directing farce or melodrama, where things happen quickly and suddenly. Just as at the rise of the curtain we allow an audience time to adjust itself to the rhythm of the play, so we must give it time to adjust itself to the opening scene and avoid shocking it by firing guns, screaming, exaggerated movement and gesture, and so on. Furthermore, opening scenes are usually replete with exposition, and it is important that business either keep clear of these lines or be used to point them up, so there will be no distraction from them.

At the commencement of a play the playwright will often have several characters onstage, including principals and minors. It is important to focus attention as soon as possible on the principals, if this is not done by the writing. They should be emphasized by directing and relating the business of the minor characters to them. In a party scene, for example, besides emphasis through composition, there can be a difference in both detail and timing in the way the main characters are served. Moreover, depending on the scene, the principals may be served first or last.

In a scene of this kind, the attention is at first general. Then out of this diffused attention we gradually bring our focus to the main characters. The opening scene in Rostand's *Cyrano de Bergerac* or Weiss's *Marat/Sade* offer excellent examples of going from diffused to specific emphasis.

Control of Business at Middle of Play

Here, where conflict is under way and the drama of the situation holds by its own intensity and interest, we must be careful not to cloud such scenes of conflict with too much business. The business must be apportioned, usually not more than two incidents to a page of script. In a comedy or farce, where business is introduced for laughs, it should either be cumulative in its effect, leading up to one big laugh, or else it should be apportioned. For example, too much business for laughs in any one situation at the beginning or middle of a play will eventually hurt the play by tiring the audience or by making the end tame in contrast.

In climactic scenes as the situation builds in emotional tension the amount of pantomimic details should be reduced, except in suspense scenes where the build depends directly on the use of teasers; but care must be taken to avoid losing the start of a suspense scene by too much emphasis on the unemphatic.

Control of Business at End of Scenes

The end of a scene should receive a finishing touch of pantomime to tie off the whole progression of the scene. This can be done by introducing a deft bit of appropriate business.

Control of Business According to Style

We mentioned earlier that the kind of play controls the type and quality of business used. We shall not elaborate on this aspect of control any further but refer you to that section, Aids in Establishing Kind of Play. There is another consideration that enters into the control of business, and that is style. For a discussion of this important subject and its relationship to the principles of directing we refer you to the chapter on Directing the Play.

Control of Business for Emphasis

In our application of business to a play we must take into account the fact that business reinforces a character, a line, or a movement. A sentiment of love, a burst of anger, a threat, a curse, an expression of repentance, and so forth, can be accentuated by immediately following it with a characterizing and appropriate bit of business.

Control of Business for Locale and Atmosphere

Business to establish locale and atmosphere need not be continually pounded out. After both have been clearly fixed in the audience's mind by emphasis at the beginning, then in the development of the scene or act such business may be gradually thinned out and re-established periodically when necessary or even dispensed with altogether, as the attention of the audience is drawn into the action of the play. When the business that establishes locale and atmosphere has been carefully emphasized and controlled, dispensing with it later will not destroy the illusion of reality.

Sound effects can do much in establishing both locale and atmosphere. However, they must not call attention to their artificiality. Rain, wind, thunder, street noises, trains, planes, bells, and music, must remain as a background to the action of the play and must be carefully timed in the play's action so that they will not drown out the delivery of lines. Sound effects often play an important part in the action of a play, as in *Rhinoceros* and *The Glass Menagerie*.

Control of Business Related to Use of Properties

As long as the play is placed in a realistic setting, various kinds of props can be introduced for the purpose of giving the characters a chance to do some business. The tea routine and the mixing of drinks have long been reliable stand-bys and will probably continue to be so. As for the everlasting "cigarette business," it has been said of some directors that their only ground plan is a generous distribution of cigarette boxes, matches, and ash trays. The use of properties presents again the problem of getting the director and the actor to use imagination. Arranging and rearranging decor; sitting, lying, and even standing on chairs and sofas if seemingly appropriate; dressing or planning a variety of hairdos in the mirror while arguing and pleading with another character—such business effectively executed with the lines redeems an otherwise talky and static play.

Developing Business in Historical and "Static" Plays

It was stated earlier in this chapter that a director should postpone looking at his author's suggestions for business and detail until he has exercised his own imagination. Therefore, the information in this section pertains to the directing of all plays. In this regard there are two general groups that afford him an excellent challenge in the matter of creating business. These are the historical play and the "static" play where ideas or mood are most emphatic. In these plays all the pantomimic dramatization is, in a sense, introduced, since there is little or no indication of it in the script itself. Let us examine each group.

The Historical Production

The absence of detailed reference and stage direction in the Elizabethan drama is misconstrued by some to mean that all pantomimic business was lacking in these plays. It is difficult to believe that their popularity could have resided solely in the delivery of the language. That mere declamation would have been criticized is evident in the remarks of a contemporary who compared the *commedia dell'arte* performances with the French theatre in this fashion:

There is always a happy blend of gesture and inflection with the discourse . . . and the actors come and go, speak and act as informally as in ordinary life. Their acting gives a far different effect of naturalness and truth from what one sees in the French theatre, where four or five actors stand in line like a bas-relief at the front of the stage and each declaims his discourse in turn.

It is generally believed that business was not indicated by the Elizabethan playwright because he wrote his parts with definite actors in mind who were given the business directly or who had their individual pieces of business for which they had achieved a certain fame. This latter is a practice not unlike that used in the *commedia*.

One of the great helps in directing a historical play is to determine whether or not there are any places where characters may sit down. This is important not only from a standpoint of composition and picturization but also because it enriches the play with a familiar and human piece of business.

We have insisted all along that our pantomime is based upon an observation of life. In the historical play we are faced with the problem of presenting a life that we must observe through report and document. But simply because these historical figures are of an age remote from our own, they need not be the pale, wooden, impossible personalities that so often repeat their lines from the stage. It seems necessary to remind a director and actor constantly that the people they are portraying were of flesh and blood with all the passions, faults, and virtues of present-day characters. So even though details of costume, manner, custom, even speech separate us from a Greek king or a Danish prince, still we are interested primarily in their similarities to us as human beings, in their character and personality, and in their response to given situations. Furthermore, they must move in a locale and atmosphere vivid and possible to conceive. Even in the types that appear in comedies we want to know that if there is exaggeration it is the exaggeration of an actual human quality and not of something freak and impossible. The following suggestions indicate the possibilities of developing pantomimic detail in the historical play—detail which is not only rich and imaginative but human, real, plausible, and therefore truthful.

LOCALE   The scene of action, no matter how distant in time or space, should have certain definite characteristics that convince an audience of its existence. Pantomimic detail will help to establish these. There are long passages in historical plays that accurately describe the setting. Pantomime can make this description more convincing. If scenery is used, as is usually the case in a modern production, then many of these passages can be deleted. In any event the interpolation of detail is important to the vividness of these surroundings. Consider, for example, *Romeo and Juliet* (Act I, scene 1: Verona, a public place. Enter Sampson and Gregory). Without making a huge spectacle of the piece, it is important to introduce something of the activity of a public place before Sampson and Gregory begin their speeches. There may be one or two vendors; one or two purchasers; a fop; people in general talking, singing, and laughing; lords and ladies from court, and so on.

In the tragedies the detail of locale is never so full as in comedy. However, even at the start of a play like *Oedipus Rex* there ought to be a moment or two before Oedipus enters in which the priest and his suppliants gather about the altar. Their business will not be minutely detailed, but the effect of the local will be enhanced if, by their actions, they give evidence of being before an important palace and in a holy spot which they deeply respect. Consider, for example, the possibilities of introducing a formalized dance around the altar, a gesture of blessing by the priest, an attitude of reverence toward the door through which Oedipus is about to step.

Act II, scene 1, of *Othello* is played with the seaport of Cyprus for a locale. Much can be done through the attitudes of waiting attendants to suggest such a place. A strong wind is blowing; gunfire is heard; there are shouts offstage and on. These scene builds to the arrival of Desdemona, Emilia, Iago, and others, so that as well as establishing locale, pantomime contributes to the excitement of the situation. This anticipates what we have to say in the next section. For pure locale, however, business such as shading the eyes, looking out to sea, wrapping cloaks firmly about the body, sitting on bales of goods, and so on could be used.

ATMOSPHERE AND SITUATION   Just as appropriate business is introduced into modern plays, such as reactions to murkiness, clear sunshine of a winter day, tenseness, excitement, relaxation, and so forth, the characters in the historical play also are expected to react to conditions about them. Modern conveniences such as scenery and lighting suggest a great deal of the atmosphere and the circumstances of the situation, but a director must not count on these elements for emotional effects. No matter how magnificent the scenery or how significant the lighting, a performance that is bland and uninteresting puts its stamp on the whole production.

Several drama departments and regional theatres have constructed replicas or modifications of Elizabethan stages for performances of plays along the open stage convention of Shakespeare's time. (See Plate 23.) This implies no change of setting for the various locales and atmospheres and requires broad, flat lighting to suggest the daylight of the courtyard theatre. Effects of damp, murky dungeons; night on a battlefield; ghosts in the still of night; splendid banquet halls depended for their atmosphere on how well the poet painted them with his words and how convincingly the actor conveyed his reactions to such places under such circumstances. These open stages provide a challenge to the imagination of both director and actor of suiting the action to the words of the playwright so that an audience believes in the existence of what is described.

The following scenes from *A Midsummer Night's Dream* require atmospheric detail:

> Act I, scene 1: Athens.   The place of Theseus.
> Act I, scene 2: Athens.   Quince's house.
> Act II, scene 1: A wood near Athens.

In the more traditional conventions of staging the atmosphere surrounding each of these scenes can be suggested by appropriate business. For instance, the attendants who usher in Theseus and his train will do so in dignified, majestic, formal manner. The company that enters Quince's house will sit, move, stumble, shout in the manner of workmen without much breeding. The woods near Athens, on the other hand, should convey the feeling of another world, and the business of Titania and the fairies could, in contrast to the first two scenes, be tenuous, fleeting, and exaggerated in detail.

PLATE 23   Modification of an Elizabethan theatre
Oregon Shakespearean Festival. *Designer:* Richard I. Hay. *Photographer:* Hank Kranzler.

Recently historical plays have been recreated with varying concepts and schemes of production in an attempt to make them more immediate and meaningful. (See Plates 4, 24, 25, and 26.) Peter Brook's production of *A Midsummer Night's Dream* turns the play from its traditional fairyland magic to the open magic and "nothing up our sleeves" frankness of a one-ring circus with all its physical trappings, giving an entirely new environment for experimentation in stage business. In New York City the Performance Group's production of Euripedes' *The Bacchae* transformed the work

PLATE 24 *Julius Caesar by William Shakespeare*
New concepts and schemes of production in staging historical plays.

American Conservatory Theatre. *Director:* Edward Payson Call. *Designer:* Richard Seger.
Costumes: John Conklin. *Photographer:* William Ganslen.

into highly energized gestures, movements, and choral acrobatics, diffusing activities over a multi-area environmental theatre that allowed the audience to view the performance from several perspectives. This is an instance of a thrust toward a total sense of theatre that is meant to be more organic in the interchange of actions between the actor-character and the audience, and, in its own way, opens up opportunities for stage business according to the exigencies of the moment.

CHARACTER Pantomimic detail of locale, atmosphere, and situation is usually a matter of ensemble business. In other words the director inserts effects that are meant to suggest the background and milieu. Individual actors may put in their own suggestions, but on the whole it is a matter of ensemble effect. Individual business is important to the enrichment of character. The director should make suggestions, but he will often prefer to let an actor give what he can at first and then, only if the results are not satisfactory, inject his own ideas. With most amateurs it is necessary for the director to conceive something for them to do, or else they "go dead." Although individual business is important to the enrichment of character, the director must always motivate it out of the needs of the text.

PLATE 25 *Julius Caesar* by William Shakespeare
New concepts and schemes of production in staging historical plays.
Great Lakes Shakespeare Festival. *Director:* Lawrence Carra. *Designer:* Milton Howarth.
Costumes: William French. *Photographer:* joseph e. karabinus.

We can get almost all our facts for character delineation and intentions by a careful examination of the text in which characters describe themselves and are talked about by others. For example:

Petruchio's speech in Act II, Scene 1 of *The Taming of the Shrew* immediately before Katherina's entrance contains the clues to his behaviour with her and his method of wooing.

The Way of the World: Mirabell's description of Mrs. Millamant in Act II, scene 2, gives an excellent suggestion of detail appropriate to this character:

Here she comes i'faith full sail, with her fan spread and her streamers out, and a shoal of fools for tenders . . .

It is perfectly possible to use this as the model upon which to base the character detail of many Restoration women. Furthermore, it suggests not only the flippancy and coquetry of these women but their costume and walk and the kind of people with whom they surround themselves.

DRAMATIC ACTION FROM THE LINES THEMSELVES   Much that is rich and imaginative in detail can be obtained from close examination of the language of the play. Whenever there is opportunity to accompany the lines

PLATE 26 'Tis Pity She's a Whore by John Ford
New concepts and schemes of production in staging historical plays.

Carnegie-Mellon University Theatre. *Director:* Radu Penciulescu. *Designer:* James Carhart. *Costumes:* Jean Teuteberg. *Lighting:* Kathleen Lewicki. *Photographer:* William Nelson.

with appropriate pantomime, we have again that "double richness" which pantomimic dramatization brings to a production. For example, these lines indicate the possibility of action accompanying the word.

Marlowe's *Edward II:* Act I, scene 1:

EDWARD: Throw off his golden mitre, rend his stole,
      And in the channel [gutter] christen him anew.

Edward addresses these lines in derision of the hated Bishop of Coventry. Taking his cue for action from the verbs themselves, he can tear a part of the bishop's garment, hurl it on the floor, and give him a violent shove at the same time.

Ben Jonson's *Volpone:* Act I, scene 2:

VOLPONE: My caps, my caps, good Mosca. [*Mosca tosses him his skullcap and nightcap with tassle.*] Fetch him in. [*As Volpone crosses to bed while putting on skullcap.*]

MOSCA: Stay, sir; your ointment for your eyes. [*Mosca pulls out a tray of oint-ments and powders from the cabinet.*]

VOLPONE: That's true; [*Sitting.*] dispatch, dispatch! [*Mosca runs to him with tray.*] I long to have possession of my new present.
[*During the following lines Mosca anoints Volpone's eyes and cheeks with expertise to make him look drawn and sickly.*]

MOSCA: That, and thousand more, I hope to see you lord of.

VOLPONE: Thanks, kind Mosca.

MOSCA: And that, when I am lost in blinded dust, and hundreds such as I am, in succession—

VOLPONE: Nay, that were too much, Mosca.

MOSCA: You shall live still to delude these harpies.

VOLPONE: Loving Mosca! [*Mosca finishes the makeup with dusts of powder.*] 'Tis well! [*As he leaps out of chair.*] My pillow now, and let him enter. [*Mosca quickly puts away the tray, adjusts the pillows in bed, and exits running. Volpone coughs, limps, and staggers on his way to bed as he names each ailment.*]
Now, my feigned couch, my phthisic, and my gout.
My apoplexy, palsy, and catarrhs,
Help, with your forced functions, this my posture,
Wherein, this three year, I have milked their
    hopes.
[*Stomping and voices outside.*] He comes; I hear him—Uh! [*coughing.*] uh! uh! uh! [*Leaps into bed, sits up, pulls up covers, and feigns exhaustion as he collapses.*]
O—
[*Reenter Mosca, introducing Voltore with a piece of plate.*]

In this example we have taken the implications in the text and the words "stay," "dispatch," "delude," "well," and "feigned" as cues for the business.

So much for the means of developing business in the historical play. Note how in every case we have depended upon the script to give inspiration to our imagination. Actually we have at all times been putting into effect what Hamlet so wisely advises the Players when he says: "Suit the action to the word. . . ."

The "Static" Play

Many plays written during the late nineteenth century are of an introspective nature. Introspection may have a talky quality such as one finds in the contemplations of Chekhov and the preachments of Shaw, or it may take the form of "mood" as in the writings of Lenormand and Maeterlinck. Then there are those plays, not exactly introspective, which present a problem that was vital once but must today be treated through the interest of the characters, such as the plays of Ibsen, Pinero, or Brieux. This being so, it becomes important in all instances to detail character values and circumstances.

The same considerations can be applied to contemporary plays with similar qualities. Examples are found in the more reflective moments in the plays of Tennessee Williams or Edward Albee; in the mood plays of Saroyan or Beckett; in the social plays of John Osborne or Gore Vidal; and in the existentialist plays of Sartre or Pinter. Very often these writers have themselves indicated elaborate bits of business, for they are aware of the necessity of supporting their characters and situations with enriching detail.

Plays of these types in which it is important to introduce business to maintain the dynamics and sense of rhythmic flow we call *static*. By this we do not mean that they are without dramatic content but that the action is of a mental and psychological nature in which the builds are gentle, far between, and not obvious. In directing such plays, every effort is made to bring as much intensity into the builds as possible. But as we have observed by now, business drops off as a scene builds. It is rather in the scenes of exposition and transition that we take the opportunity of enlivening the script by superimposing business and bringing action to an otherwise talky or mood play.

If a play is full of mood and atmosphere, we make every effort to heighten and capitalize on all the activities and detail that the script will allow, subordinating the mood and atmospheric touches, unless their use in the text brings out a meaning as clear as the delivery of a line of dialogue. Bathing a scene with atmospheric details weighs the balance of values toward moods and feelings and not toward the conversation which, though it may be set off by the atmosphere, should be listened to for content. This is especially true in plays where ideas are foremost. The calm and cool evening atmosphere of the exterior scene in Shaw's *Heartbreak House* should be bright and lightly colored; if it is drenched in moonlight and shadows the audience will sit in partial reverie through long passages of talk.

In a play like Ibsen's *A Doll's House* it is no longer necessary to emphasize the idea that a woman has a right to freedom and equality of thinking with a man. What does interest us today is the kind of woman Nora is. Above all, in directing this play now, it becomes important to make her as rich and as interesting as possible. Details of her treatment of her children; of managing the household; of how she reacts to flattery, to resistance, are all important to the establishment of character. The business of locale is important, since it is Nora's world, the house in which she lives. Furthermore, Nora must set the atmosphere of each scene, since her character predominates—the way she tidies up, the greeting that she gives Mrs. Linden, and, of course, the manner in which she dances the tarantella. By this means we are emphasizing the importance of detail in order to compensate for the overabundance of idea and problem that fills the writing.

Exercises in Pantomimic Dramatization

These exercises employ from six to ten people, and are to be planned in advance by each member of the group. The pantomimes may have a simple story, or they may have a few disconnected incidents or they may be atmospheric studies. They should not run longer than five minutes. The action, however, should have sufficient business to cover a thirty-minute act. In other words, the business should be much more concentrated in these exercises than it would be in a play. Do not hesitate, therefore, to create a great amount of business and to encourage contributions from the group, leaving final choice to the director of the exercise.

Be sure to establish the locale and time of day and to consider the arrangement of the ground plan as well as all the five fundamental principles of directing which must be used to convey the content of the pantomime. If there is a story, be certain that all important characters and facts are clear and emphatic and that it has development, proportion, build, and a conclusion.

The following are intended as suggestions:

1. Meeting of a student senate.
2. An opening night party.
3. A ship's saloon in mid-ocean.
4. Waiting for departure at an international airport.
5. An overworked housewife in a scene with her family.
6. A city newspaper office receiving a scoop.
7. A television studio before telecast of a live panel show.
8. An environmental art exhibit.
9. A folk sing.
10. A drawing-room scene without tea, cards, or cocktails.
11. Before a funeral.
12. An informal concert by a popular combo.
13. The sundeck of a resort hotel.
14. Sitting up with the dead.
15. Getting ready for an important guest.
16. A trial.
17. A rehearsal.
18. Arrival of family with flowers at a grave.
19. An automobile accident.
20. A carnival.
21. A company picnic.
22. A lunch counter—1 P.M., midnight.
23. A hotel lobby.
24. A wharf.

Plan, prepare, and rehearse a pantomimic dramatization of an act from a basically realistic play, compressing its visual demands into an approximately five-minute scene. Incorporate all essential dynamics. In the planning stage, break down the act into its basic situations. Write these out briefly in the most explicit terms. Also, work out a ground plan to scale. In the selection of plays try to cover the major types such as those listed under the exercises on determining rhythm.

4

Central Staging

12
Central Staging

Though the fundamentals of play directing have been discussed in relation to directing and staging for the proscenium stage, most of what has been written has direct application for the theatre-in-the-round. However, differences do exist, and adjustments have to be made when going from one to the other.

Between the two extremes of the proscenium stage and the central or arena stage, there are a number of variations in the relationship between the area occupied by the audience and that occupied by the actor. In addition to our more traditional proscenium-oriented stage with or without apron, abbreviated or extended, we have open stages with apron, thrust stages with upstage acting areas, amphitheatres, multiple stages on three sides of an audience, peripheral stages surrounding the audience, and flexible theatres where the entire space can be converted into any form and relationship between acting area and audience. Each form of stage has its advantages and disadvantages. The proscenium stage may be more adaptable in creating a greater degree of illusion and offer greater opportunity for elaborate scenic and lighting effects, but one of the attractive advantages of thrust and arena stages is that the intimacy they offer in seating arrangement can be combined with a larger seating capacity. This feature, along with the lesser technical requirements, is an economic advantage that has encouraged the growth of theatres with these stages.

Whatever the relationship of stage area to audience, the important consideration in directing is to stage the play completely in terms of the intrinsic demands of the existing relationship rather than to favor, for example, proscenium staging when directing in-the-round. No greater disservice can be done to the play, the audience, and the particular stage–audience relationship than to force the staging of one form of theatre onto another. Having mastered the techniques of staging for the proscenium and the central stage, the director will not find the adjustments to open, thrust, and other forms of stages an overdemanding task.

Without question, the business and scenic requirements of certain plays can strain the limitations of central staging, but on the other hand the theatrical conventions of in-the-round (in which no one side is favored) can open up other aspects of staging that can find release from the proscenium stage's conventions.

This all-important characteristic of the theatre-in-the-round—the stage area favors no one portion of the audience—offers a great challenge to actors and directors trained in the tradition of the proscenium stage. Unfortunately the tendency of the beginning actors or director is to orient actions

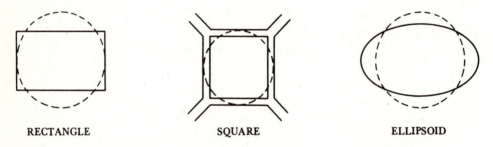

RECTANGLE   SQUARE   ELLIPSOID

FIGURE 40 *Diagrams showing circular acting area for central stages of several shapes*

toward the portion of the theatre that tends to become the focus of staff activity or toward the part of the house that holds the largest amount of seats. The latter happens in situations where the central stage has been adapted to the physical limitations of an auditorium. In musicals particularly the tendency is to overrelate actions to the segment of the stage area that outlines the orchestra pit—the conductor becomes a too strongly attracting force to resist, both from custom and musical demands. Actually, the musical that is given careful rehearsal and directed according to the intrinsic demands of central staging requires no more orientation to any portion of the theatre than does the play.

In this study of central staging the application of the fundamentals will be related to directing in-the-round as a form of theatre that has its own theatrical conventions. Again we remind the student that the present emphasis on these five fundamentals of play directing is not meant to diminish the importance of acting requirements in the total expression of the play nor of the interpretive values of play analysis.

PLATE 27 **An Enemy of the People** *by Henrik Ibsen*
Central Staging: *Notice placement of properties at aisle areas and positioning of actors to open up stage picture to all segments of the audience.*
Arena Stage, Washington, D.C. *Director:* Zelda Fichandler. *Designer:* Grady Larkins. *Costumes:* Marjorie Slaiman. *Photographer:* Image.

The Central Stage

By its very nature the central stage varies in its form more distinctively than the proscenium stage. Auditoriums have been constructed or adapted for central stages that are square, rectangular, ellipsoidal, and circular with any number of variations in between. Sizes are as varied as the size of stages to be found in proscenium theatres. As to form, the slightly ellipsoidal and rectangular central stages offer certain advantages which are discussed later under ground plans. Regardless of the form and size of the central stage, the beginning director will find it to his advantage to describe all such forms in terms of a circular acting area and thereby not favor any single portion of the audience. (See Figure 40.)

With the circular acting area as our point of reference, any sharp variations in the central-stage–audience relationship can be readily realized and proper staging adjustments made when necessary. However, keeping the principle of the circular acting area in mind, regardless of the form of the central stage, the director will find that he can control the dominant visual aspects of his staging in reference to three major vantage points.

These three major vantage points, however positioned, make a workable field of vision for observing actions. To reduce this field to any smaller degree only complicates and restricts the openness needed for composing in-the-round. The vantage points are based on the normal range of vision that the eyes take in, roughly 120°. Whether a stage is thrust, open space, or in-the-round, this range of vision remains the same. However, the major difference between the proscenium and central stage is the changing perspective of the spectators from different sections of the auditorium. The difference rests in the actor's distance and body position—for one spectator the actor is near and in one body position, while for a spectator at the opposite end of the auditorium, he is distant and in the opposite body position. This discrepant perspective must be taken into account continually. There is no question that it must have its effect on the spectator, making the same scene more "intimate" or more "objective."

By superimposing these three major vantage points on any of the forms of the central stage and taking advantage of the particular physical setup in which you are working such as permanent positions of entrances, you will be giving yourself ready reference points from which to check your sight-lines, compositions, and so on. In practical terms you will not be favoring any one portion of the audience. (See Plates 27, 28, 29, and 30.) This applies as well to extreme thrust stages and amphitheatres. Note that in Figure 41 staging actions for the three vantage points is equivalent to staging in-the-round. In practice, however, many directors, consciously or unconsciously, tend to favor the same two-thirds portion of the house thereby directing the play more in line with proscenium staging.

Basic Technique for the Central Stage

Stage Positions

Of course, there is no right and left stage, no downstage and no upstage; there is no above, no below. The stage areas are designated as in Figure 42.

Designations of stage areas are made as though they were the markings of a clock lying face up on the central stage. It is best to place the clock facing the control room booth so that the same acting areas can be used to designate lighting areas and read from the point of view of the control room for quick identification. The diagram above shows the acting areas divided into center, three, six, nine, and twelve o'clock as major areas and the remainder of the numerals for more specific divisions. It is up to the director to establish his identification of areas. Entrances established by the physical

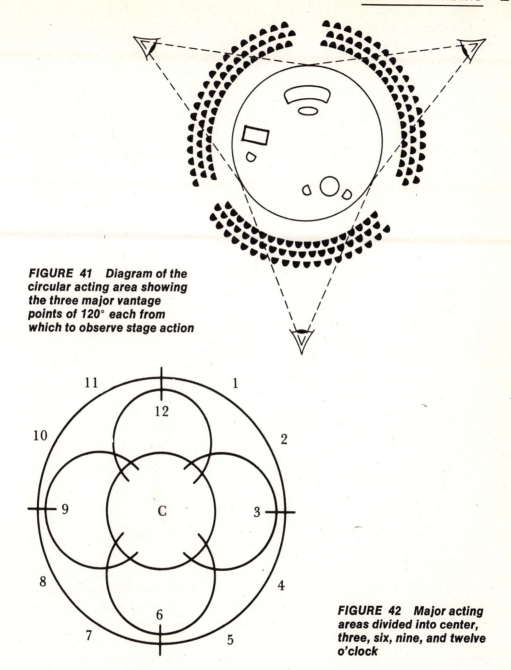

FIGURE 41 *Diagram of the circular acting area showing the three major vantage points of 120° each from which to observe stage action*

FIGURE 42 *Major acting areas divided into center, three, six, nine, and twelve o'clock*

setup of the auditorium may determine that two, four, eight, and ten become more serviceable acting areas for major identification, and so forth. Some directors have used points of the compass for labeling of areas, though experience shows that actors adapt more readily to the clock division system.

In giving directions to area positions, the setting itself can prove most helpful by relating the directions to furniture or parts of the setting.

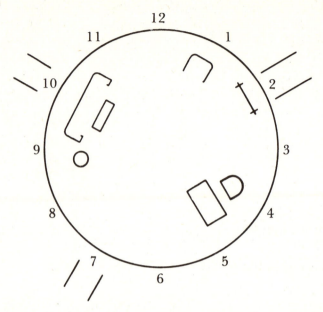

FIGURE 43 *Relation of furniture and setting to clockwise designation*

Exercise in Central Stage Positions (See Figure 43.)

Armchair at 1, window at 2, sofa at 10 with coffee table in front and taboret at 9, desk at 5 with chair at 4, entrance at 7. Have actor enter 7, cross to armchair 12 side, cross to coffee table, cross to window and look out, cross to desk C side, cross to 6, cross to taboret, cross to back of sofa, cross to front of sofa by 11 and sit.

Body Positions

Referring to the section on Body Positions for the proscenium stage on page 34, we find that for central staging the body positions of the actors relate primarily to other actors. There is no full front or quarter position or profile, and so on, as these body positions relate to the audience, and since the actor is always opened up to some portion of the audience these terms no longer apply. The actor, however, can turn in or close in toward the center of the stage; turn out away from center; move forward by walking in the direction he is facing; move back by stepping back from the exact position in which he is standing; blend in for better relationship to other actors.

Positions in relation to other actors, described beginning on page 37, only hold true relatively, as the audience surrounds the acting area. The *shared* and *profile* positions have no significance in reference to the whole audience, but to relate in the *given* position becomes most advantageous in a scene between two actors. In the round the *give* and *take* relationship places each actor facing a different segment of the audience, thereby giving the entire audience face-to-face contact with one of the two actors. Applied to central staging this relationship does mean sharing the scene with the entire house. Keeping distant from each other to a minimum of some four feet also helps to open up the scene to all members of the audience. (See Figures 44 and Plates 27, 29.)

THIS: NOT THESE:

(shared)

(profile)

FIGURE 44   Central staging—playing position for two actors

The shared and profile positions in proscenium terminology can block the actors from a large percentage of the audience, depending on the area used (except in peripheral areas with the actors open toward center stage). (See Figure 48.)

Demonstration on a Central Stage of Position of One Actor in Relation to Another

Two actors, following proscenium terminology, share a scene in area one, first *turned in,* then *turned out.* Play the scene in *profile* in area one. Repeat at C: first profile; then shared position *turned out* toward the 9 side, then the 3 side. Repeat at area 7.

Two actors, maintaining the same basic relationship, play a scene in the *give* and *take* relationship at C, then at areas 5, 11, 3, and 9.

We can see that in the peripheral areas, the shared position opens the actors out to a smaller or larger portion of the audience, depending on whether the actors are turned in or turned out, but that at center area their backs are to half of the house. The profile position places one actor with his back to a good portion of the audience meanwhile blocking the other actor from the same portion of audience. The give and take positions keep the actors in face-to-face contact with the audience while the peripheral positions open up one of the actors to a larger portion of the audience.

These facts become vital when considering emphasis on the important speaking actor. (See Figure 45.)

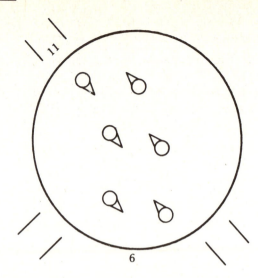

FIGURE 45 *Give and take positions at area 11, C, and 6*

Dressing stage and *stealing* can be applied quite directly to central staging. *Covering* of one actor by another, however, is one of the major problems in central staging; it cannot be avoided, especially for those seated in the front rows. Placing two actors on a central stage will unquestionably partially cover each for some member of the audience; because of this it is wise to avoid holding any position for an overly long time. A subtle change by shifting within area in the course of reactions is usually sufficient to make the audience feel that they are never being deprived of a complete view of the actions. Seating one of the actors is another way to help uncover the scene. If two people must be seated in a sofa (low back essential), both should sit far apart in positions that keep themselves and the scene more open. (See Figure 46.)

THIS: NOT THIS:

FIGURE 46 *Two actors seated in low back sofa*

Covering of business or properties that are being faked must sometimes be solved in other ways than those described on pages 54–59. An actor can cover the reaction to a dagger or gun by doubling over or turning into a sofa or chair (it is important to aim a gun toward the stage floor and in the direction of an aisle entrance). He can cover the action of lighting a lamp, if it is to be controlled from the switchboard, by holding his hand under the shade. It is difficult, however, for him to cover the action of playing a piano, unless he is well blocked in by actors on each side which unfortunately creates a rather solid wall of backs to a section of the house. The many demands of covering called for by the play need other solutions which will be discussed later.

In sitting, rising, kneeling, and in making turns and gestures when playing in peripheral areas, it is necessary to consider opening up of body positions to the larger segment of the audience.

Approaches

The curved rather than the direct approach is, with few exceptions, the maneuver to use when approaching another actor or object. The curved approach keeps each actor more consistently in contact with a larger portion of the audience and avoids the continual covering of an actor for one segment of the house that occurs in a direct approach. (See Figure 47.)

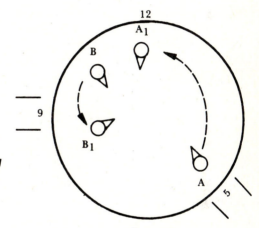

FIGURE 47 A crosses to B moving in a curved approach from 5 to 12, while B dresses stage to 9 to keep scene open to largest portion of audience.

In general, as in the proscenium stage, the preceding technique of movement and positions is planned primarily to have as many members of the audience in face to face contact with the actors and at the same time keep the correct relationship of character to character. With this in mind ready adjustment can be made to central staging of the techniques included under Basic Actor Technique for the proscenium stage.

Body, Voice, and Role

The acting demands for truth of portrayal and expression on the central stage are no different from those of the proscenium stage. The same demands are made on the actor in regard to his voice, body, and role. There is no question that the smaller theatres-in-the-round can accept subtler intimacies in acting, but so can the smaller proscenium theatres. The fact that in central staging some members of the audience may sit quite close to the acting area does not alter the fact that certain other members are distant and that at any one instant a portion of the audience must hear an actor's dialogue while his back is to them. Granted that the smaller theatre-in-the-round creates an atmosphere of intimacy, the actor should not be misled into thinking that he need not project his words. As in all structures, the level of projection, disregarding sound reinforcement, must be adjusted to the size and shape of the theatre.

The nature of the central stage possibly places greater demands on the actor's concentration, since he can never turn away from the audience. But more than this is the need to relate to other actors which in itself generates greater concentration. The effectiveness of in-the-round acting comes out of this deep engagement in communication.

Stylistically, some believe that the central stage adapts itself better to the realistic play form. Let us say rather that the audience accepts the conventions of central staging as much as it has those of the proscenium stage and that experience shows that it will accept plays that require romantic acting as well as acting that is highly formalized. Given truth in communication it seems that any form of theatre will accommodate any style.

The Director's Media

The characteristics of the central stage differ markedly from those of the proscenium stage.

The Actor

The actor on the central stage does not have a changing tonal quality in respect to the entire audience—a full back to one member of the audience means a full front to an opposite member. However, if the actor is in a peripheral area, turned in toward center which is generally the normal relationship, he will be opening himself up to a larger segment of the audience and, vice versa, if he turns out from center he will be turned away from the larger segment. Relatively, then, under these circumstances and limitations there can be some changing tonal quality in the control of the actor's body position.

The Stage

AREAS   As a working terminology, we have divided the central stage into the twelve parts of the clock plus a center area. The twelve parts become peripheral areas.

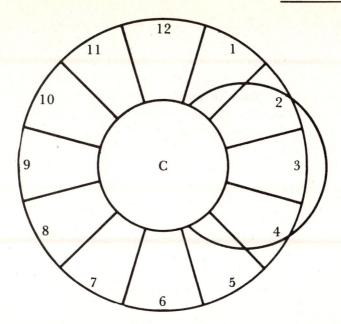

FIGURE 48 *The clock system using a center area plus twelve peripheral areas*

The size of the stage will determine whether the twelve subdivisions of the clock are necessary. More than not, as in the diagram above, combining areas, 2, 3, and 4 will make a workable acting area which for purposes of directions could be designated as area 3.

Again we have no right or left stage, nor is any area stronger or weaker than another in its effect on the entire audience. Center becomes the strongest area since it attracts the eyes of each member of the audience with equal focus. Its strong focal pull, however, is deceptive—a point that the director needs to prove to the novice. At center stage the actor has command of only half of his audience at any one moment; nor do continual gyrations at center to reach each member alter this physical fact. However, the more an actor, facing center, plays off center, the more audience he brings into his command. At an open-aisle position in a peripheral area, the actor facing center can, by slightly turning to his right and to his left, be in easy contact with his entire audience.

Planes

In relation to the entire audience we have no downstage or upstage planes, but as in the actor's body position, where full back to one segment is full front to an opposite segment, we must consider the changing perspective.

For one spectator the actor moves from near to far (downstage to upstage); simultaneously for the spectator seated directly across he moves from far to near (upstage to downstage).

The movement through planes presents a changing tonal quality differing for each segment of the audience. This problem must be solved by other controls involving positive and negative evaluations. The sections to follow on the control of levels and the fundamentals applied to central staging offer some suggestions.

Levels

Levels can be used as effectively on the central stage as on the proscenium stage for variety, relative strength, emphasis, and positive and negative evaluations. The continual need to keep the picture open to all parts of the house requires a variety of levels in furniture as well as architectural elements such as steps and platforms. Moreover, the opportunity for change of levels offers one solution to the problem of changing perspective discussed under Planes. A sit, a rise, or a bow of the head is a change in level having the same impact on each member of the audience and can be used effectively to designate a positive or negative tonal quality.

Demonstration

With the class seated around a central acting area and using the ground plan in Figure 43, have one person, standing at area 6 and turned in, move forward to area 12; turn in, take a curved approach to window; turn in, cross to sofa and sit, turned partially out toward 9; rise, cross to desk, center side, and with both hands on edge of desk bow head and then slowly sit in desk chair, head bowed low; then straighten up, rise, and cross to area 8; turn in and exit 7. Discuss the findings from different sections.

The Five Fundamentals of Play Directing Applied to Central Staging

The three major vantage points for observation of stage action, described at the beginning of this chapter, have practical application to central staging when we come to analyze it in terms of the fundamentals of directing. Actually, the view of the central stage from a single vantage point is like viewing the action on a proscenium stage, provided you relate the immediate view to the other two points. If you consider a major vantage point as being a seat at the center of the house, the audience included within your 120-degree angle of vision is oriented toward the stage in the same way as in an auditorium of a proscenium theatre. Using the three major vantage points from this frame of reference gives the director a constant control in staging the dominant visual aspects of the play. The fundamentals of directing as studied for the proscenium stage have with some obvious exceptions direct application to central staging. In this study we shall deal only with these exceptions. Adjustments of these exceptions to the thrust stage involves, basically, an understanding of the angle of vision seen from the extreme seats near the wall framing the upstage portion of the tongue.

Composition

An advantage of the arena stage is the circular seating arrangement. By setting the actor against a background of audience, it creates an ambience of intimacy, warmth, and involvement, and more than the proscenium-oriented stage it heightens the three-dimensionality of the acting space. In any composition the opportunity is there to compose for the sculptural impact as against the pictorial effect of the "picture frame" stage.

Emphasis in central staging is obtained primarily through space, level, and direct focus. Furniture becomes an effective means of bringing emphasis by reinforcement or contrast of line. Repetition has value in a limited way. When playing a scene with two or three actors, the use of body positions and contrast for emphasis have meaning for a larger portion of the audience if the actor who is being emphasized is placed in a peripheral area, particularly at the aisle positions where no member of the audience is directly behind him.

Positioning an actor in line with the aisle entrances makes the most of the opportunity to open up more sightlines. As the actor plays closer to the edge of the stage, his position in line with the aisle entrance becomes all the more essential.

The triangular formation comes into its own in central staging in scenes with more than two actors. (See Figure 49.) It puts each member of the audience in direct facial contact with one of the actors and offers opportunity for the many variations analyzed on pages 116–119. The use of different levels in the triangular form becomes an obvious way of bringing emphasis and opening up the stage picture. (See Plate 28.)

In large groups, think of positioning the actors to create several triangular formations—a positioning in diversified emphasis whereby the actor–audience facial contact is distributed as equally as the situation permits. Here again, off-center positioning—facing center area—is, as a rule, the more advantageous relationship. Turning out at any peripheral area would serve as a counterfocus.

When dealing with larger groups the need for variety in levels in order to open up the stage picture becomes obvious. Various sitting and standing

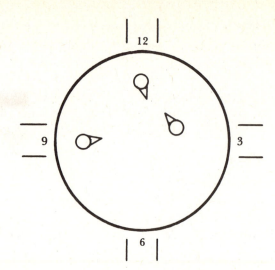

FIGURE 49 *Triangular positioning of actors, opening them to major portion of audience and allowing each member of the audience direct facial contact with at least one actor. Note positioning in line with aisles for optimum sightlines.*

positions are used whenever the situation permits it. Oftentimes minor characters in the situation are positioned in the aisles adjacent to the stage areas when their presence needs to be felt, as in crowd scenes. When use of the aisles is impractical in these scenes, it becomes essential to make levels an intrinsic part of the ground plan. More will be said about this when we discuss the ground plan for the central stage.

The application of variety in the use of emphasis and the stage space continues to be a contribution that the director can make toward enriching compositions and avoiding monotony of treatment.

Stability, sequence, and balance, both physical and esthetic, are as essential in central staging as they are in any other form. The same holds true for the effect of line, mass, and form on mood. Obviously adjustments have to be made to suit the particular circumstances, but basically the applications are the same.

Exercises in Composition

Redo the exercises on page 164 for central staging. Notice especially the effects of line, mass, and form on mood. The impact on all sections of the audience should be essentially the same.

Picturization

Outside of the fact that the inherent mood values of areas and planes can be disregarded, with the possible exception of the center area which would be equivalent to its use on the proscenium stage, all that has been written about picturization has direct bearing on central staging. Of course, the thrust stage offers a certain flexibility over and above theatre-in-the-round since it presents some opportunities for proscenium staging and design, limited though they are by distance and the problem of sightlines from the extreme side portions of the auditorium.

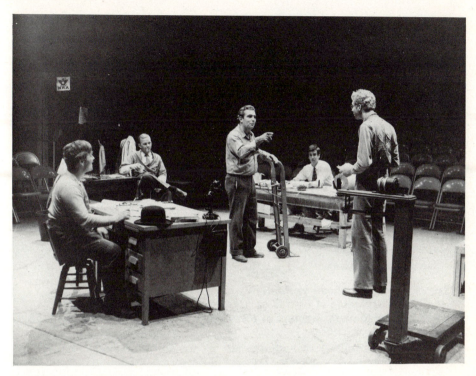

PLATE 28 **Memory of Two Mondays *by Arthur Miller***
Central Staging: *Notice placement of desks and other set props to vary use of acting areas and to open up stage picture to all segments of house.*
California State University, San Jose. *Director:* Hal J. Todd. *Designer:* Irle White. *Costumes:* Kevin Seligman. *Lighting:* Kenneth Dorst. *Photographer:* James Lioi.

Movement

How we evaluate movement in central staging depends on its relationship to other figures and not on the direction of the movement itself; and how strong or weak it is depends primarily on the manner of execution by the actor, for as we noted earlier, movement away from one section of the audience is movement toward the section seated opposite. Body movements, length and rhythm of movements, and movements related to levels have effective evaluations, but movements from one acting area to another must be related to other figures. Circular arrangements of furniture and patterns of movement can be particularly effective in the three-dimensional space of

PLATE 29 **The Bridgehead *by Frederick Bailey***
Thrust Stage: *Positioning of figures as in central staging opens up actor–audience contact to each segment of the house. Linear outline suggests an overhanging roof.*

Actors Theatre of Louisville. *Director:* Charles Maryan. *Designer:* Paul Owen. *Costumes:* Kurt Wilhelm. *Photographer:* David S. Talbott.

in-the-round. Acting too becomes more effective out of the need to relate continually to other actors rather than favoring the audience, the convention in proscenium staging. With this in mind the greater part of the chapter on movement has direct application to central staging.

We must get rid of the notion that central staging demands more movement from the actor than a proscenium stage in order for him to face all members of the audience with reasonable frequency. There are some techniques, such as moving in a curved line, to keep the scene opened to as many as possible. As always all the movement must be motivated, but the direction in which the movement is executed will oftentimes have technical considerations. For example, in a triangular formation if actor *A* is to move and the movement can justifiably be made toward actor *B*, or toward actor *C*, or to the opposite side between actors *B* and *C*, this last choice will bring actor *A* to an area that opens him up to an entirely new segment of the audience. Actors *B* and *C* would dress stage or focus accordingly, thereby continuing the scene with each, however, now opened to other sections of the house.

PLATE 30   A Month in the Country by Ivan Turgenev
Thrust Stage: *Notice placement of furniture to vary the use of acting areas and to open up stage picture to all parts of the house.*

Cincinnati Playhouse in the Park. *Director:* Michael Murray. *Designer:* John Lee Beatty.
Costumes: Elizabeth Covey. *Photographer:* Sandy Underwood.

Demonstration

Place actor *A* in area 6, actor *B* in area 3, and actor *C* in area 9. Have actor *A* cross to actor *B,* then to actor *C,* and then to area 12 with actors *B* and *C* giving focus.

Using various triangular formations, try out several movements similar to the above in different parts of the stage.

In the scene where actor *A* is to enter, the others already in the scene will have cleared the entrance area. Actor *A*'s entrance completes a triangular formation. After actor *A* has been established, on a motivation for action, he moves to an opposite area, thus facing the section of the house which was originally behind him. The others in the scene relate accordingly.

Demonstration

Entrance at 1. Actor *B* at 10, actor *C* seated at 8, actor *D* at 4. Have actor *A* enter at 1, the others focus on him. Have actor *A* cross to 5 as actor *D* dresses to 2. All focus on actor *A*.

The subtle use of these and other technical considerations in movement will create the feeling for any single member of the audience that all actions are being played to him.

PLATE 31 All The Way Home by Tad Mosel
Thrust Stage: *Showing vomitories for entrances at DR and DL positions. Notice flexibility in staging added by levels in upstage areas.*

Hartford Stage Company. *Director:* Paul Weidner. *Designer:* John Conklin.
Photographer: Lanny Nagler.

Rhythm and Pantomimic Dramatization

The material written up in Chapters 10 and 11 on these two fundamental elements of directing can be applied to any form of staging provided that the obvious adjustments in ground plan as noted below are made.

Exercises in Central Staging and the Thrust Stage

1. Rework some of the exercises in Pantomimic Dramatization on page 281, adjusting them to central staging.
2. Using the same exercises make the necessary adjustments for staging on a thrust stage of your own dimensions.

The Ground Plan and Setting for Central Staging

The selection, arrangement, and control of a ground plan should accomplish all that it does for proscenium staging. It should have workable acting areas distributed and balanced so that the blocking of movements and

PLATE 32 Charley's Aunt *by Brandon Thomas*
Thrust Stage: *Notice selective use of scenic elements.*

Indiana University, Brown County Playhouse. *Director:* Howard Jensen.
Designer: Stephen M. Zapytowski. *Photographer:* John Underwood.

changes in positions for technical considerations can be derived out of the placement of furnishings and scenic elements which should be grouped in logical relationships to the entire ground plan, allowing for easy maneuverability and unobstructed views. As mentioned earlier, slightly ellipsoidal and rectangular central stages have certain advantages. In contrast to circular and square stages, the end areas of ellipsoidal and rectangular stages offer opportunities of creating more confined acting areas. Oftentimes dramatic actions or the need to separate locales demand strongly delineated areas which can be achieved more readily in the narrower ends of these slightly elongated stages. Moreover, their longer sides open up a flexibility in the placement of large units like settees and long tables not possible in the strict circle or square. In short, more variety can be achieved by the two longer and the two shorter sides.

The ground plan should be expressive of the characters living there,

PLATE 33 *Safehouse by Nicholas Kazan*
Modified Thrust Stage: *Multiscene split level setup of four living areas.*
Berkeley Stage Company, California. *Director and Designer:* Angela Paton.
Photographer: Jerald Morse.

of the kind of play, locale, and atmosphere; it should allow for sufficient seating elements to permit opening up of sightlines when several characters are in a scene—usually minor characters can be seated on the periphery of actions; it should accomplish everything else written about the dramatic significance of good ground plans, such as interest, variety, selectivity of the more expressive elements called for by the action of the play, and finally, proper placement of exits and entrances for dramatic needs.

In planning exits and entrances distribute them at more or less opposite areas to balance use of stage space in the progression of the play. For example, in a play of several scenes vary the area positions of the major entrances and exits. In a one-set play position entrances in opposition—areas 1 and 7 as against areas 1 and 11. These considerations in planning help to keep a balance in the use of areas rather than favor any one side. Also, it is important to establish each exit so that an audience knows where it leads. A ramp leading from the aisle or vomitories in some theatres to a stair unit positioned on the stage area can indicate an entrance from upstairs, if the stair unit adds a more effective value to the scene for reasons of its elevation. Otherwise, if the entrance itself has been established as leading to the upstairs, then that is sufficient.

The great limitation of the central stage is the sightline problem. Ideally, each member of the audience seated around the playing area should have an unobstructed view of the actions, besides feeling that the play is being performed specifically to him. These are two objectives that should be in the minds of actors and director at all times. Each action and the follow through from action to action should be constantly evaluated from the three vantage points.

We can help in other ways to open up the picture from all parts of the house. Eliminating unnecessary scenic units is one way to free the picture. Scenic units such as windows can be suggested by using a window seat only, provided the actors relate to it with consistency. The audience will accept the nonexistent window as they will accept any suggested scenic element that the actors themselves honestly bring into imaginative existence.

The basic idea is to avoid solid pieces in front of the audience. For example, in selecting a desk and chair, use a variety with open sides and backs. Place the desk with its end toward the edge of the playing area— not only does this arrangement place less frontage directly before the audience in the nearest rows, but it also places the actor seated at the desk in an open position. The same consideration obtains in the placement of tables. Of course, whenever possible, large units such as tables, settees, cabinets, and pianos should be located at aisle positions when those aisles are not used for entrances. Oftentimes, a unit as large as a piano can be played completely offstage and out of sight, especially if the playing is to be faked. Or the aisle position adjacent to the stage area can be used as a playing area and the piano positioned here at whatever angle called for by the action of the play.

The stage floor in the arena theatre is so strong a focal area that it should be toned to the mood of the play and definitely not draw attention

PLATE 34 Mother Courage *by Bertolt Brecht*
Flexible Stage: *Space at the Performing Garage converted into an environmental setup of acting areas and seating arrangement.*
The Performance Group. *Director:* Richard Schechner.

to itself with tape and other obtrusive markings. To facilitate shift routines for multiscene plays and musicals, the stage floor is often designed with appropriate patterns that serve as markings for the positions of furniture and other pieces.

Heights of backs of sofas, chairs, and the like should be kept well below the shoulder of the person seated to keep him open to all parts of the house.

Levels such as raised portions of a room or an area in an exterior help to open up the stage picture and add variety to the basic ground plan. The employment of raised areas, steps, and ramps can do much in creating added areas for positioning people and in extending the compositional control of scenes. Here we have an indication of the flexibility that is possible in the ground plan for the central stage and of the flexibility of central staging itself.

The Flexibility of Central Staging

An audience's readiness to accept what is presented to it as theatrical truth, provided the presentation is honest and consistent, is one of the delights of the theatre. The audience's willingness to believe expands the range of central staging in all directions, esthetically and physically. Establish the darkened area of the stage as being behind a curtain with a character eaves-

PLATE 35 Oedipus *by* Seneca
Flexible Stage: *Space at the Performing Garage converted into a circular arena filled with three feet of dirt.*
The Performance Group. *Director:* Richard Schechner. *Designer:* James Clayburgh.
Photographer: Clem Fiori.

dropping, and the audience will accept the reality. Or let us say the setting is a living room: establish the entrance at the edge of the stage area, with or without indications of a door, and the audience accepts it as an entrance; establish the entrance to the room at a position in line with the first row of seats, and the audience accepts this; now establish the entrance at the back of the aisle behind the last row of seats so that the actors can speak their lines as they walk down the aisle, and the audience still chooses to believe. This flexibility in establishing the limits of the playing area opens up many possibilities for staging actions that would strain audience belief were they to be performed within sight. For example, circumstances present the victim trapped behind locked doors; the rescuers break down the door to force an entrance. With the solid door established earlier offstage at the rear of an aisle, the sounds of pounding and breaking are sufficient to stimulate the audience's imagination to the actuality of the action. In *Dial M for Murder* positioning both the French doors and the main entrance doors offstage at the rear of their respective aisles not only heightens tensions, but brings the force of the scene to concentrate on the actions of character on character.

Once the threshold of the acting area is decided, whether on stage or off, entrances and exits to and from the area should be as unobtrusive as possible so as not to disturb the audience's concentration on the stage. Character limps, use of canes, and so on should only come into prominence as the actor is about to cross the threshold.

The primary test of whether or not it is necessary to have the actual scenic element within sight is whether the dramatic value of the scene depends on the operation of the element itself or on the actions about and reactions to it. Even with a multiple scene where an interior and an exterior may be viewed simultaneously, it is enough to indicate the exact position of the door by a free overhanging frame or by outlining the base of the frame and the audience will accept the imaginative barrier.

If the structure of the theatre house permits it, a walk around above and behind the last row of seats as well as auxiliary stages positioned in the upper sections of the seating area can also extend the playing area. These and the use of aisles as acting areas are particularly advantageous in multi-scene plays and musicals permitting an uninterrupted flow of action during scene shifts on the main stage. The effectiveness of playing musicals in-the-round comes from the added flexibility offered by these multiple areas, as well as the possibility of movements up and down aisles. A good example of adapting a scene to this enlarged scope is to be found in the musical *Brigadoon* where the chase brings the actions before, around, and between sections of the audience. Experimental groups who are reaching out for new theatrical experience are in many ways bringing this wider scope of in-the-round staging to bear on their own productions of participatory theatre.

Central staging has its limitations and its flexibility. There are very few plays that will not require adaptation to its limitations and its flexibility. Flexible staging can reduce the limitations when, for example, one end of the central stage including the part of the house behind it is blocked off and used as a scenic background. Furthermore, flexible staging in itself allows for any variation of the playing space in relation to the audience. (See Plates 29–35.) But the purpose of this study has been to analyze the fundamentals in terms of the true theatre-in-the-round. A knowledge of the techniques of proscenium staging and central staging will prepare the student of directing to make his own adjustments to the many other relationships of stage area to audience.

5

Production Procedures

Production Procedures

There is no attempt in these next three chapters to cover the many variables for procedures in tryouts, casting, rehearsals, and play interpretation and directing. Many directors and theatre organizations in theatre centers everywhere have established their own individual approaches. New organizations with new beliefs about what theatre should be are continually being spawned. Participation in some of these groups has more to do with sociological, philosophical, or activist leanings than with specific role playing.

In general, however, granting these variables, certain basic requirements are still involved in any production. The following chapters discuss some of the more salient points for the beginner to know. Like the five fundamentals they are here for you to use according to the circumstances and the play.

Again, final selection of a play comes out of many considerations: objectives and status of the group; experience of players; restrictions on staff, money, and time; place of performance, nature of audience, and community standards; educational factors, and so on. Selection of a play must take all these factors into account.

The fourth chapter in this section on production procedures discusses the additional considerations that enter into directing musical comedy beyond the demands of a straight play.

13
Tryouts and Casting

After the play has been chosen and announced, copies of the script should be made available. When the actors have had sufficient time to read it, the director may hold either private interviews or general tryouts or a combination of both methods for casting.

Tryout Procedures

Personal-Interview Method

In using the personal-interview method the director should try to be as informal as possible and do everything that he can to put the actor at ease. At first, the interview may consist of talk about the play in general, the plot, the characters, and the theme. The actor should be urged to discuss all points freely. Then he should be asked to read for a certain role. After a first reading, the director should make suggestions to help his interpretation. To the extent that it is possible, the director should hold the interview in a place that will allow the actor absolute freedom of movement and emotional expression. During the entire interview he should, without making it too obvious, study the actor and try to see him as the character in the play. This method of tryout is useful in casting a small number of parts, or it can be used after a general tryout when eliminations have been made and the number of prospective actors greatly reduced. The professional theatre director, whether working through agents or through personal contacts, uses the personal-interview method of casting almost exclusively.

General Tryout Method

The regional non-professional theatre or college director may find it more expedient, for the sake of impartiality and a variety of other reasons, to hold a general tryout, open to all interested. Here he first makes sure that all have read the play. If, for some reason, the script has not been made available, he may, by asking everyone to read in turn, have the group read the play. (No one should be allowed to think that he is reading for a particular part.) In the first reading of a play it is essential that all prospective members of the cast have the opportunity to give spontaneous and uninhibited reactions to the play as a whole.

After the play has been read, the director should clear up any questions regarding the plot, theme, or kind of play. Then he should give thumbnail sketches of the characters and answer any questions about them. Sketches or models of the scene and costume designs and ground plans may be shown to indicate the scheme of production. This creates interest and enthusiasm and helps the actors to get into the spirit of the play. An effective method of helping them capture the emotional qualities may consist in having them, as a group, sing songs in the mood of the play, listen and move to music in the mood of the play, or work out pantomimic improvisations. This procedure also aids the actors to achieve physical and emotional relaxation and freedom—absolute essentials for the best results in tryouts.

In this informal and relaxed atmosphere actors are asked to read for certain parts. It is not necessary to begin with the first line of dialogue in the play and read to the end. It is best instead to pick out certain scenes. The reading of crucial scenes which will outline the character patterns is the most advisable procedure. When the director has allowed everybody to read (and, to avoid any hard feelings, everyone should be given a chance), he can then reduce the number to those who are definite cast possibilities.

Improvisational Approach

In contrast to the above methods of tryouts, some directors prefer that the actor present himself without any knowledge of the play. The actor comes prepared to present a selection of his own choosing or is given a short scene of dialogue to look over or is told a set of circumstances upon which to improvise. In any of the three methods the director may ask the actor to use more or less the same lines of dialogue but under changing attitudes and circumstances.

This improvisational approach allows the director to gauge the actor's responsiveness, spontaneity, and flexibility, though for some actors the method can prove inhibiting.

Casting the Individual Actor

As a basis of elimination from the general tryout, the director, keeping each character clearly focused in his own thought, should consider the actor's (1) physical appearance in general, (2) age, (3) voice quality and diction, and (4) sense of movement and rhythm.

In further determining the suitability of an actor for a part, the director must carefully consider his (1) sense of theatre and background, (2) sensitivity and imagination, (3) audience appeal and power of projection, (4) acting experience, (5) personal tonality, and (6) playing ability for kind and style of play.

Sense of Theatre and Background

The director has various means of arriving at an estimate of an actor's mental facility and general sense of theatre. Knowledge of prior training and experience offers some indications. Ability to understand the play and respond to suggestions for character interpretation demonstrates both general intelligence and sensitivity to theatre requirements.

Sensitivity and Imagination

An actor's reading and his sense of movement and rhythm indicate his sensitivity and imagination. In making suggestions and generally coaching him, the director can arrive at a further appraisal by setting up for him pantomimic improvisations, with or without music. Interesting the actor in a given set of circumstances and inducing him to concentrate puts him in a position to demonstrate his imaginative ability.

Audience Appeal and Power of Projection

To judge an actor's audience appeal and his ability to project it, the director should consider general appearance, voice quality and diction, grace and precision of movement and pantomime, and general personal magnetism from the spatial and esthetic distance of auditorium to stage. The director sits in the auditorium of the theatre, tries to imagine himself a representative of the audience, and determines whether or not the actor gets his personality across and commands audience attention and interest.

(The use of at least general distribution of light on the stage makes the task easier.) This consideration is important, for it must be realized that an actor always creates character out of his personality.

Acting Experience

If the director has seen the actor onstage in various roles and knows his acting experience, he will be aided in imagining him as a particular character. Moreover, experience and actual technique often weigh heavier than personal, physical, and emotional qualities.

Personal Tonality

As a final check in casting, the director must consider an actor in terms of personal, physical, and emotional tonality in relationship to other characters in the play and the actor's rightness for the particular kind of play and its style. The actor's suitability in this respect is most important in the conveyance of the play's dramatic values. His personal "tonality" means his inherent degree of softness, hardness, lightness, heaviness, genuineness, artificiality, and so forth, irrespective of his use of technique to achieve a particular tonality of character. The director must be ever mindful of this personal tonality.

Playing Ability for Kind and Style of Play

Personal tonality may make an actor right for a particular kind of play, but he may not be able to use the special technique of playing demanded by the play. An actor's ability to use the particular skills necessary for tragedy, drama, melodrama, comedy, and farce is an important consideration. It involves his quality and use of voice, his physical flexibility, and his general emotional and intellectual adaptability.

The actor's ability to play in the style demanded by the play presents another question that the director must answer. Different styles of playing make demands on the actor's ability to control voice and body and to convey the various manners of character behavior. Playing in particular styles as well as playing in particular kinds of plays requires a special suitability, experience, and training.

Casting the Ensemble

Before definitely setting the cast individually, the director should see the entire group onstage. He should then go into the auditorium and look at it as the audience might.

Contrast

First of all he must visualize the actors as the ensemble of characters demanded by the script. Then he must so place them onstage that they relate to one another individually, to one another as groups and to one another as representatives of conflicting forces. He can thus see contrasts in physical appearance; and on having them read, he can hear the voices in contrast and in concert. The emotional tonalities of characters will also be evident. Remembering that the basis of the dramatic lies in contrasts that create variety and conflict, the director will sense the need to try to cast for contrast in physical appearance, voice, and emotional tonality, as well as for balance in the ensemble.

Unity

However, the director in casting for contrasts must not lose sight of the necessity for contrast that does not disrupt unity. For example, a naturally high comic voice and appearance are obviously out of place in a serious play.

Individual Cooperation

In addition to an actor's apparent ability to play a part and make the right tonal contribution to the ensemble, the director must consider his ability to work with the group in rehearsal. This depends upon a willingness and an ability to function as a unit within the composite whole. Many excellent solo performers are absolutely incapable of subordinating and molding themselves into an ensemble. A sense of emotional, mental, and physical cooperation and adjustment is essential. This qualification of the actor must be duly weighed when the director considers the desired ensemble effect.

14 Rehearsals

Only carefully planned and organized rehearsal schedules and intelligently administered individual rehearsals can lead to finished productions. Not all the exigencies of rehearsals can be anticipated and forestalled; but certain pitfalls are characteristic of all, and these can be expected and guarded against. Also, the procedural details of conducting rehearsals, as outlined here for an average realistic play of three acts, can be helpful in understanding the essential planning and organization involved in the rehearsal process. However, the student should know that procedures in conducting rehearsals are manifold and depend on the aims and philosophy of theatre of both director and organization.

Organization

Proportion of Rehearsals to Parts of Play

For one thing, an organized period of rehearsals can help the director avoid the mistake of spending a disproportionate amount of time rehearsing the first part of the play and neglecting the middle and end. Paradoxically enough, the first act, which is often overrehearsed, is usually the simplest in the play and needs less rehearsing than the other two. It merely presents the characters and their status quo and points toward the direction the play is to take, but the second and third acts consist of the development of character and situation and the denouement. Actually most of the drama in a play lies in the last two acts. It is true that there should be a good beginning to make the audience come back after the first intermission, but it must be remembered that the audience is more likely to overlook deficiencies in playwriting, acting, and directing at the beginning of a performance than it is later on in the evening when the theatre seats seem harder and fatigue has set in. A good beginning may create impetus, but the good ending is what brings satisfaction.

Thoughtful planning and an intelligent division of rehearsal time according to the demands of the play, act by act and scene by scene, will safeguard the director against one of the gravest errors of rehearsal procedure.

Total Number of Rehearsals

To plan the total number of rehearsals necessary for a production, the director must consider, first of all, the play itself in terms of act and scene division, number of characters, dramatic values, style, and general stageworthiness. Plays of many scenes, large numbers of characters, complex structure, and unconventional form require long rehearsal periods. Period and stylized plays need more rehearsals than the average realistic type. Rehearsals for an original script which is subject to constant revision must exceed in number those necessary for a tried play.

The schedule of rehearsals may be affected by the total number of plays to be presented in a season and the consequent time allotment. If all plays are selected in advance for the season, the director can analyze the rehearsal demands of each play and can thus apportion the rehearsal periods of each. Experimental and subsidized theatres may have the luxury of rehearsals extended over a period of months, but unmitigated circumstances may force some directors to rehearse within a prescribed time—such as the three afternoons a week in schools, the week-end rehearsals in community groups, weekly stock, or the three- to five-week rehearsal schedule of resident and commercial theatres.

The training and experience of the actors and the time that they can devote to rehearsals obviously affects the rehearsal time period. Inexperienced actors who can rehearse only part time necessarily require more rehearsals than do professionals. The director must meet the demands of the particular conditions.

Although it is hazardous to prescribe a rule, most plays require an overall rehearsal period of four to six weeks, six days a week. It is seldom advisable to try to do the average play in less than four weeks with an amateur cast. More than six weeks of rehearsal may succeed in wearying a cast and may cause it to lose interest. Even though the director may be inventive and generally brilliant in his direction and extremely stimulating to his cast, a long rehearsal period can gradually dim the enthusiasm of actors. Amateurs, especially, are under too much of a strain physically and emotionally to make long rehearsal periods advisable. Short, concentrated ones achieve the best results.

Time Period for Each Rehearsal

The time period for each rehearsal with the acting company is usually longer than a concentrated period for coaching the individual actor. Coaching may be effective in periods of thirty minutes to an hour. After an hour's work the actor needs a rest. For the acting company, the two- to three-hour rehearsal period is more productive than a shorter or longer period. Little can be accomplished in less than two hours. After three hours of rehearsal without a break for rest, actors, both professional and amateur, because of general fatigue begin to show less and less responsiveness to direction. Overlong technical rehearsals may be necessary to coordinate the scenery, lighting, costumes, and sound effects with the action of the play, but the director cannot expect anything but strained or mechanical performances from the actors. In professional productions, of course, because of union regulations these technical rehearsals cannot exceed a five-hour span without a break for rest.

Costume Review

In addition to the play rehearsals, the director must plan reviews and rehearsals to check on production matters. A costume review is usually helpful. This is particularly advisable for costumes that are not modern. All the actors should wear their complete costumes and appear on the stage individually, then together with related characters, and then finally together with the entire cast. Thus the designer and the director are able to study the effect of each costume on each actor in these various static situations. The next step in the costume review is to direct the actors to go through the crucial movements and bits of business of the play, making entrances, exits, and long crosses, opening and closing doors, and so on. A separate costume rehearsal simplifies the director's problems when the time for dress rehearsals arrives.

Technical Rehearsal

At this rehearsal the actors should make all entrances and exits and learn the proper use of doors, windows, and other "practical" parts of the settings. They should also go through all business and learn to handle the actual properties to be used in performance, though there has been practice with substitute properties during the latter part of the rehearsal period. They need not go through all speeches but should merely give the cues necessary for movement and business. The director must warn them, in making entrances, to keep out of sight lines and keep away from lighting instruments that may cast shadows; in exiting, to close doors for masking purposes and go offstage in the proper direction; and, while in the acting areas, to keep within the focus of the lighting instruments. A preliminary checkup on the distribution, intensity, and general mood of the lighting of each scene or act is another job for the director. He must also see that the sound effects are convincing and that their cues are properly timed. After each scene or act, the position of the furniture should be adjusted and then painted on the floor cloth. Although the supervision of details of the technical rehearsal is usually left to the technical director, the play director must make sure that these details are quickly and smoothly coordinated. The routine of scenery shifts is explained in Appendix A.

The wise director checks all properties, sets, and costumes periodically in the process of building and assembly, and does not wait to be surprised at the technical rehearsal. Sizes, colors, textures, intensities, shift routines, and so on should all be checked before technicals to avoid time-consuming delays that can prove frustrating to everyone involved.

The technical rehearsal is the first attempt to blend acting and the purely technical elements of scenery, properties, lighting, and sound effects. The greater the coordination achieved at this rehearsal and at the costume review the smoother and the more finished will be the first dress rehearsal.

First Dress Rehearsal

The first dress rehearsal is a complete run-through at which all sound cues, light cues, costume changes, entrances, exists, important movement, and business should be coordinated. Costumes and make-ups must be adjusted to the lighting and to the actors' characterizations. Dialogue offstage and behind scenery should be checked for audibility. Each "curtain" must be timed exactly with the dialogue and business. At the end of the performance, curtain calls should be coordinated with the last curtain.

During this rehearsal, corrections should be made only at the end of scenes or acts. There should be absolute continuity within each scene and act. This is necessary to maintain the rhythm and unity of the production. Because of the necessary interruptions between scenes and acts, the actors may not be able to give emotionally consistent and unified performances. However, their efforts at continuity will help to tie in all the essentials of production with the action of the play.

Second Dress Rehearsal

The second dress rehearsal should be a tryout performance before an invited and selected audience. Friends and the backstage crews, except the light and sound-effects crews who are needed backstage during the running of the performance, can make up this audience. They will stimulate the actors and help them to get the feel of playing to a house. If the play is a comedy, it is essential to have an audience because a comedy often loses its spirit and spontaneity in rehearsal and can be brought to life only through the stimulation of audience response. Also, the director often loses his perspective on a play in the course of the rehearsal period, and an audience helps him to check the laughs and note any comic dialogue that may fail to click. He can also gauge the effect of each scene and the effect of the play as a whole.

In order to allow the crews to shift scenery and properties and also see the show it is necessary to go through the following procedure:

1. The stage manager takes up the curtain on each scene or act and has the actors play for two or three minutes.

2. He calls: "Cut. Crews out front."

3. He calls: "Curtain." The actors then begin the scene over again and play to the end of the scene or act.

4. On cue, he calls: "Curtain."

5. Then he calls: "Crews on stage and in position for the shift."

6. He gives the actors a line near the end of the scene or act, and they play to the curtain which is brought down on cue.

7. After the *strike* and *setup,* the stage manager takes up the curtain on the next scene or act and repeats the procedure itemized above until the play has ended and the actors have taken their curtain calls.

If there are to be pictures of the production, they should be taken at this rehearsal. Pictures for publicity, which are usually tight shots of the major characters, will have been taken earlier at special photo calls. For the sake of performance it is better to take the production pictures at the end of the show. This means taking pictures of the last act or scene first and working toward the first act or scene. If the shifts are complicated and difficult, the pictures may be taken at the end of each scene or act as the rehearsal progresses from the beginning to the end. This second procedure is harder on the actors and the continuity of the play but easier on the crews.

During the second dress rehearsal, corrections and adjustments are made by the various production departments at the end of scenes or acts while the crews are getting ready for the following scene. All changes should be made quickly and expeditiously to avoid long breaks in the rhythm of the performance. In spite of the interruptions necessary to allow the crews to see the show and also carry out their duties, and in spite of the necessity of taking pictures, everything should be done to achieve continuity and unity.

Third Dress Rehearsal

The third dress rehearsal should be in the nature of a performance rehearsal. It is wise to have an invited audience for this performance. The play is presented, without any interruptions or stops whatsoever, from the beginning to the end. Then follow the curtain calls. This should be a performance complete in every detail. The director and the technical staff make corrections and give instructions only at the end of the performance.

At least three dress rehearsals are necessary to achieve a smoothly running production. The *preview* system developed in New York merely telescopes dress rehearsals with tryout showings for plays that are not toured prior to the New York opening. The amateur theatre, if it is to set worthwhile standards for itself, will see the necessity of holding more than one dress rehearsal, for any attempt at coordination requires sufficient time for corrections, adjustments, and trials. Play production depends upon a large number of different workers, each responsible for different artistic activity, and dramatic effectiveness depends upon the unification of all efforts.

Rehearsal Schedule

No schedule of rehearsals can be considered set and inviolable. The director may find it necessary to make changes from day to day to meet contingencies that may arise. It is important to note here that a play, realistic or otherwise, has its own characteristic structure and emphasis requiring its own approach in scheduling rehearsals. The following is only a general working schedule for the average realistic three-act play with a cast of not more than fifteen, based on the act to act approach of play directing.

Rehearsal	*Procedure*
1	Reading and study of whole play
2	Reading and study of whole play
3	Reading and detailed study of Act I
4	Blocking out of Act I
5	Adjustments and addition of simple business for Act I
6	Study of Act II
7	Blocking out of Act II
8	Adjustments and addition of simple business for Act II
9	Run-through of Acts I and II
10	Study of Act III
11	Blocking out of Act III
12	Adjustments and addition of simple business for Act III
13	Continuing study of characterization and memorization of lines for Act I
14	Run-through of Acts I, II, and III
15	Continuing study of characterization and memorization of lines for Act II
16	Run-through of Acts I and II

17 Continuing study of characterization and memorization of lines for Act III
18 Run-through of Acts I, II, and III
19 Detailed work on Act I for characterization, line reading, additional business, rhythm
20 Detailed work on Act II for characterization, line reading, additional business, rhythm
21 Detailed work on Act III for characterization, line reading, additional business, rhythm
22 Run-through of Acts I, II, and III
23 Rehearsal of special scenes for business, line pointing, and transitions
24 Run-through of Acts I, II, and III
25 Rehearsal of climactic scenes for tempo and ensemble playing
26 Run-through of Acts I, II, and III for rhythm, unity
27 Costume review and technical rehearsal
28 First dress rehearsal
29 Second dress rehearsal
30 Third dress rehearsal

It will be seen from this schedule that the actors learn the play as a whole first and afterward learn the parts of the whole. Thus they approach their characterizations through a knowledge of each character's relationship to the play as a whole. They also see the relationship of each situation to the rest of the situations in the play. Only through emphasis on the whole play can the director achieve a sense of proportion and relativity. Frequent run-throughs give the play continuity and unity.

Current with this schedule are coaching periods arranged with each member of the cast.

Roughly speaking, the rehearsal schedule is divided into four periods of work: (1) study, (2) blocking-out, (3) enrichment period, and (4) refinement and coordination.

Study Period

During the study period, the director, first of all, should help the actors to grasp the story, or plot, of the play, the basic attitude, purpose, and major interest—the general outline. Each member of the cast should be able to tell, not in detail but in general, the sequence of the plot development. If the actors underscore the plot lines in the script, they will be able to memorize the plot more easily, and they will also realize the need for emphasizing these lines through line reading and pointing. The next step is to make them understand the character relationships. Then, each member of the cast should ask questions about the character that he is to play and round out a thumbnail sketch of the character. (See page 87 on the actor's intellectual understanding of the play.) The theme, or idea, of the play must be made clear. A study of the play's structural values should be a natural outgrowth of the discussions on character relationships and theme. After this preliminary discussion and study, the director should explain his general purpose, concept, scheme, and style in producing the play.

A further study of character to learn the "spine of action" of each is the next step for the cast. A detailed study reveals the smaller units of action, the motivations, and the subsequent sequence of stimuli and responses in terms of mental images and physical action. In this study of character the director aids the actors in line reading, emphasis, and inflection and in pantomime and movement.

Blocking-out Period

The cast is introduced to the ground plan, the costume and scene designs, and becomes generally acquainted with the characters' specific environment. The costumes and accessories, character properties, settings and atmospheres are explained in detail—their use or relationship to each other and the play. The blocking of entrances and exits, areas of playing, and main directions of movement are sketched in. This blocking-out period of rehearsals consists of finding the general pattern of movement and large bits of business necessary for a revelation of the plot and of the character relationships. This overall physical pattern results from the director's clear understanding of each character and its relationship to other characters and situations. This is dramatization by visual means, mainly by the use of composition, picturization, and movement.

Enrichment Period

The enrichment period of rehearsal is devoted to the invention of pantomime and business, action and reaction, variety and shading of line readings. During this period the director works with the individual actor, and, by dividing the actors into groups according to scene, he works with the actor group. Together with the actors he makes a further and more detailed study of the script. He tries to squeeze every last drop of drama out of each word, line, piece of business, movement, or grouping. He and the actors add to and build up each character and situation. At the same time he also injects a slight modification and rearrangement of positions for technical considerations such as variety in area, emphasis, asymmetrical balance, third-dimensional effect, sight lines, and other considerations in composition.

The static moments are now varied by arbitrary breaking up, by changes in character relationship, or by the demands of mood and the kind of play.

Refinement and Coordination Period

The refinement and coordination period of rehearsal involves the selection of the significant, the elimination of the unnecessary, and the unification of all aspects of the performance. During this time the director tries to shape his production according to its style. He must sense and determine the kind and amount of the various elements of performance necessary for consistency, harmony, and unity. This process involves throwing out certain business that may be out of key, eliminating distracting or inessential movement, changing line readings, and sharpening visual and aural emphasis. After these refinements and attempts at articulation, the director focuses his attention on the tempo of the various scenes and the overall rhythm of the play. He works for timing in pauses, picking up of cues, building speeches and scenes, and the blending of scenes to obtain a rhythmic flow. In *building* scenes great attention must be paid to the pitch of each in relation to the others; that is, the extent to which each scene is built must be relative to the intensity and key of the other scenes. Thus the performance becomes refined, rhythmic, and synchronized.

Other Rehearsal Procedures

Sequential

The act-to-act rehearsal procedure outlined above is a common practice among many directors, each adapting it to his own particular approach and way of working with a cast. Sometimes in the course of rehearsals actors are asked to improvise scenes by having them change attitudes and circumstances as a means of opening up new possibilities for enrichment and interaction between characters, stretching their imaginations, and in general extending their range of expression. It is a sequential kind of approach, working from scene to scene according to the script.

Nonsequential

A contrasting approach would be: after preliminary study and discussion of the play, segments from the beginnings and endings of scenes are rehearsed first for the purpose of gauging the differences of emotional levels and attitudes between the beginnings and ending of scenes. This is true especially for important scenes such as the major crisis and climax. These segmented rehearsals are meant to throw full emphasis on the content of each scene for richest illumination—all related, of course, to the entire play's meaning which has been absorbed by the director and discussed with the cast. The belief here is that by knowing and experiencing the endings of scenes and juxtaposing them with the beginnings, the actor gains a firm sense of direction for selecting and shaping his controls. We might call this the nonsequential approach to rehearsing a play.

Improvisational Based on Familiarity with Script

Using either sequential or nonsequential procedure in rehearsing, an important variation is the use of improvisations based on familiarity with the script. Again, following preliminary studies and discussions, the actors thoroughly explore the characters to gain as complete an understanding as they can at this stage of development. Next, they break down each basic situation involving their characters into synopsis form, noting down intent, circumstances, character objectives and attitudes, and overall title of scene. From here on the actors rehearse by improvising each scene, following in general the events set down in the script, but using their own words. Rehearsals proceed in this fashion until the entire play is improvised close to performance level. Meanwhile, study of script and author's dialogue has been continuing outside rehearsal hours with actors left free to use or not use the author's line in company rehearsals. In period plays like those of Shakespeare dialogue is carefully analyzed for meaning and then paraphrased by the actor.

Improvisational without Knowledge of Script

Another procedure in the improvisational approach requires the actors to improvise the moods, atmospheres, circumstances, and objectives that are analagous to those in the script, but without any knowledge of the script itself. Rehearsals may even be held in actual locales similar to those in the play. These may be improvisational games based on various moods depicted by the circumstances of the play. In the later phases of rehearsals the games are extended to include situations in which the plot and text of the play are introduced, but without assignment of roles. The next stage in this approach is the designation of parts.

    The director's purpose in this improvisational approach is to give free rein to the imagination of the actor before introducing him to the actual script. This period of improvisation is followed by an intensive study of the script, after which more improvisations are conducted together with controlled rehearsals where the actor's motivation for business, movement, and behaviour develops out of the content of the play. The final stage in this process is the learning of the playwright's lines.

Approach Based on the Emphatic Element

Another approach involves study and rehearsal of the element that moves the play along at the beginning of the rehearsal schedule. (See Chapter 15 for comments on the Elements of a Play.) Directors who follow this approach feel it establishes a foundation on which the student actor can build and to which he can relate all that he does when focusing his attention on the essentials of character, idea, situation, or whatever else may require it. Thus the director does not make each scene or act a thing unto itself and restrict the actor's creative process within these limits.

THE PLAY OF SITUATION   Where all factors contribute to the development of situation, it is best to adopt an act-to-act procedure, since it follows the sequence of events as written. But, even here some directors, after the usual opening discussions and studies, will sketch in the blocking of the entire play rather quickly with the actors taking down general blocking. Then, after a few rehearsals he will have the company run through the play roughly at least twice in order for the actor to experience the thrust of the situations, the space and relationship with other actors, and the mechanics of traffic. After this the scene to scene work is intensified.

THE PLAY OF CHARACTER   Demanding as it does a penetrating study and exploration of character-traits, social environment, relationships, and so on —places the director's primary concern immediately with the actor. The play is broken down into small rehearsal units for analysis and discussions. Actors are encouraged to hold their own practice sessions with other members of the cast for further explorations of character. The results of their work are reviewed for comments and suggestions. After this study period the actors are introduced to the ground plan, settings, costumes, and properties with discussions on the locales, atmospheres, moods, use of accessories and properties, and given basic blocking to acclimate them to the areas and general relationships to other characters. Even at this stage of development some directors will hold two or three run-throughs to round out the initial studies. After this period of assimilation, each scene is rehearsed to note intensities, builds, and moments of direct conflicts in preparation for intensive investigation and work on the main critical scenes. The play is now broken down into sequences of scenes: those that are bound together by the follow-through of one or two principal characters, or by a strong emotional line, or by a group relationship. These scenes are rehearsed in sequence to give the actors a sense of continuity, the idea being that, in a play of character rehearsing scenes as a unit sets the role, dispersed throughout the play, into a unified sequence and brings it boldly into contrast with the rest of the play to provide a more sensitive awareness of essential controls such as dynamics, and so on. Finally the play is ready for rehearsal in the more sequential order of act to act.

THE PLAY OF IDEA With its principle interest not on characters for themselves, but on the ideas put forth by the characters, requires first of all a study of the architecture of the entire intellectual concept in order for director and cast to disassemble the play into its logical units of action. In this approach the first phase of the work is devoted to round-table discussions of the ideas—their interpretation, relation of each character to them, and lines that need special emphasis. At one point each actor may be asked to summarize and evaluate the argument step by step as related to his role. The points of view assumed by each character are clarified as beginning steps in characterization. During the period that these sessions are being conducted, lines are studied and memorized. The play is finally acted out, without scripts in hand, usually standing, but with no attention given to movements or business. Full concentration is on ideas, attitudes, and the handling of dialogue and dynamics. Specific blocking and all other aspects of production are not worked on until this phase of the rehearsal process is firmly in hand.

As mentioned earlier, these few examples in no way exhaust the many possible approaches to conducting rehearsals, nor has there been an attempt to detail the procedures involved in each. The beginning director should keep in mind that procedures are only as effective as the experience and talent of the director and the acting group.

15
Directing the Play

The Whole Experience of the Play

Although there is, of course, no standardized formula for directing a play, repeated productions have taught us not to start by working out the particular details of a scene—its composition, picturization, movement, rhythm, or business—but first to get a feeling of the play: its general tone, qualities, and emotional values and how they may be sensed by an audience. Only by helping the actor to convey these qualities in a performance will the director be able to direct several plays a season and not mark each production with the same rubber stamp. His own creative contributions that have been inspired by the text will thus be freed and expanded.

The Mood Conveyed by Movement and Rhythm

The mood of the script, therefore, is the first element to consider, because it is the most difficult to recapture after one becomes involved in the technical aspects of acting and the production. Accordingly, after the first reading it is necessary to pause to let the mood penetrate, to feel the play as if it were music, and then decide how this emotional quality may best be translated into rhythm and movement. We determine the basic rhythm and the predominant timing of the production; we sense the intensity and number of emotional climaxes and whether these are to be based on character or on theatrical effect. However, mood is not conveyed by rhythm alone. The amount and kind of movement contribute to the emotional tone as well. Here, as we have seen, the director can learn much from developments in the dance and cinematic techniques. Is the mood to be expressed by constant or little movement? Do we want to add as much as possible or to eliminate all but the absolutely necessary action? Is the contemplated movement to be long or short, rapid or slow, vibrant or relaxed?

Take, for instance, an exciting, devastating, many-scened drama of violence demanding a dominant constant basic rhythm as rapid and driving as a steel riveter and a movement that is constant, short, quick, and divergent. In directing such a play, no time should be taken for detailed characterization, no pauses for innuendo or for picturized effect. It must have continuous rises and tense drops in tempo. It must have bold, broad, and erratic moving about, even possibly stop action and slow motion for startling contrasts. Compare this mood quality and its execution to a play with light, leisurely rhythm with only occasional climactic moments where the movement is easy, long-flowing, and infrequent. Here are entirely different patterns of movement and rhythm, each projecting its own special mood.

The Image Conveyed by the Play

Mood is only one aspect of the "feel of the play." The whole experience of response to a play comes packaged with other ingredients which for purpose of discussion need to be separated, even though *image* more than *mood* is difficult to confine within definitions. Where mood is better expressed in tonal qualities and feelings for dynamics, image can be explained as the shaping in visual terms evoked by the "feel of the play" or by its intrinsic meaning.

The image that takes shape in the mind of the director may be a mental picture or a metaphor—associations reflective of nature, of sounds, of color, of ideas—associations that are limited only by the director's experience. The play's title and names of character, either in the literal meaning, sound, or symbol, also contribute their share in the total image conveyed by the play. In *The Cherry Orchard* the title itself becomes a symbol of a fading generation, delicate, ornamental, but without function, like the fruits of the orchard of which Lopakhin says, "what good are they, you do nothing with them." Earlier, in our discussion of character patterns and fundamental design, we mentioned the circularity of *The Good Woman of Setzuan* and the animal imagery of *Othello*. These are the kinds of images that grow out of the whole impact of the play and begin to shape a director's concept; later, if so desired, they are transformed into actual designs—scenery, lighting, costumes, ground planning, and patterns in directorial controls.

Type of Play

Another dimension to the whole experience of the play is the basic attitude assumed by the playwright toward a life event. The type or genre of a play titles this basic attitude. The author may look at the event from a farcical, comic, tragic, or melodramatic point of view, or he may change his basic attitude completely and from the tragic move to the comic in the final scenes of his play. Or the writer may observe the event philosophically and see it as quite *absurd* and express this absurdist world by juxtaposing farce and tragedy. Not all plays clearly show their basic attitude or attitudes, but then these are the plays that need special care and planning. The important fact is that the playwright's basic attitude, besides underpinning the work, sets the tone of the play and creates its fundamental rhythm and mood. Moreover, tragedy, melodrama, farce, comedy, and the various combinations of these have distinctive qualities which must be considered. How much farce can the actors put into this comedy? How much melodramatic effect can be allowed in this tragedy? How much characterization may be developed in this melodrama? Are the comic possibilities to be emphasized as much as or more than the serious thematic scenes? How can two opposite qualities be blended? How abruptly can we go from farce to tragedy? There are innumerable questions of this type that need answering. In summation: type of play or genre is the guide to the emotional control of the play through which we achieve tonal unity.

Emotional Values and Casting

Whether the play's emotional quality rests in the determination of its mood, its imagery, or its type, a general consideration of casting arises at this time. Versatility in characterization is found in actors both professional and amateur, but almost never is it possible to find versatility in mood and tonal quality. So, at this stage of studying the script, one should determine what qualities of voice, body, and personality the actors must have in order to convey the musical tone of the play.

Style

The next major problem is the style. This will determine the manner of the direction, which perhaps more than any other factor leads to variety in the productions of a single director. No other subject connected with the theatre is so difficult to express in a few words, because, although terminology has been given to a few of the major schools of writing—classic, romantic, realistic, naturalistic, surrealistic, impressionistic, expressionistic—a contemporary play seldom has a pure style. We should distinguish style of play from other methods of theatrical presentation such as ritual theatre, theatre of the absurd, theatre of cruelty, and many other nomenclatures including participatory, environmental, improvisational—all of which incorporate one or more stylistic manners.

Style is the degree and kind of lifelikeness that a playwright has used in his writing, the degree of his selectivity in dramatic form and structure. It is the reality of the text defined in its own terms and influenced by the climate of the times in which it was written—the modes, manners, theatrical and literary conventions, and so on. In more general terms—style is the *manner* of dramatic expression that the author chooses to use. But to define style in these terms is to reduce the complex artistic process of creativity to a simple voluntary line of action. Style does not necessarily come out of the artist's conscious desire to put things in a certain way; nor does all expression, dramatic or otherwise, have style. Style also implies distinction in the manner of executing the very attributes that give the work style. Style signifies that the work has achieved an identity brought to full realization by the exacting delineation and clarification supplied by the creator out of his own convictions. The manner of expression is not applied superficially. Imitators may apply style, fashions may attach themselves to style, but true style comes out of the individual artist's basic belief and point of view about himself related to the world around him, and out of his creativity in making form and meaning come together into one artistic statement. A refreshing viewpoint, a new way of looking at nature, a searching for deeper truth, the freeing of oneself and breaking of all shackles imposed by tradition, conventions, and social morality—these "unconventional attitudes" are the sort of catalysts that spark artistic explosions and open up new vistas in the ways of expression.

Given this conception of style, we can say that the author's basic attitude toward his subject may be comic, but the manner of expressing the comedy may be realistic or romantic, to cite two fundamental manners of dramatic expression. In these terms *The Lady's Not for Burning* by Christopher Fry is a romantic comedy, while *Volpone* written by the seventeenth-century author, Ben Jonson, is a realistic comedy. The purely realistic play is perhaps the easiest to direct, but within the scope of realism there is a wide range—from the arbitrariness of Shaw's *Getting Married* to the seeming actuality of O'Neill's *Ah, Wilderness!*; from the picturesque reality of Housman's *Victoria Regina* to the lifelike illusion of Gordone's *No Place to be Somebody*. Polonius' combinations of tragedy, comedy, history, and pastoral are sheer baby talk in comparison to the combinations of styles from classicism to expressionism to surrealism in plays today.

Style will control the directing of the play's form and the image that it may evoke. It will distinguish the theatre of illusion from presentational theatre—whether we are to believe in a world where character confronts character or one where character communicates directly with audience or in a world of open theatricality where audience participates with actor. The determination of style will tell the degree, kind, and amount of composition, the simplicity or complexity of form to be used in the groupings. It will settle the actors' body relationship to the audience, the use of area and levels. For instance, are the stage pictures to be closed in, as if the fourth wall had been removed; or are they to be flat and open to an audience to connote a more artificial form? Are only the front areas to be used for the most part, or is every inch of the stage to be utilized? Are the actors standing about on a stage or moving around in an actual place? Is the setting to be a mere pictorial background, or is it to be used by the characters as part of their actions? Is the movement to be arbitrary or highly motivated? Is the business to be scant or rich in its inventiveness and "follow-through"? Answers to these questions and many more of the same kind determine the definite style or manner that the play is to acquire from the direction. Style, ultimately, becomes the controlling guide to the manner of acting, the design and use of setting, properties, lighting, costumes, and the controls of the fundamentals of play directing—in short, it sets the limits within which all phases of production are unified.

Purpose behind the Writing

The awareness of the playwright's purpose in his writing is another aspect of the "feel of the play," and is inseparable from the response to mood, type, style, and any image the play may convey.

The purpose behind the writing may be none other than to entertain the audience with a story. A farce, for example, entertains by whatever hilarity it generates and a melodrama by its stress on suspense. Some authors inject a purpose that goes beyond the entertainment value. The author's devilish intent to ridicule or satirize may jab the farce along, giving us the *satiric* farce or comedy; or the melodrama, driven hard by the author's prejudices, may attack the viciousness of society. By adding the author's purpose to our other dimensions we then have *social* dramas, serious in their basic attitude; *thesis* plays; comedies of *manners* where the author neither ridicules nor satirizes, but exposes the ways of a society by truthful revelations. The purposes are many: story telling, character portrayal, wit and manners, projection of ideas, philosophical and social discussion, propaganda, satire, burlesque, travesty, and so on. The important thing for the director is to recognize the purpose in order to know where to focus the emphasis and what controls to exercise.

The Elements of a Play

In understanding the purpose behind the writing and the type or genre of play we have had to consider the several elements of the play—the characters involved; the plot or action presented; the language used; the general idea in the play, directly or indirectly expressed; the environment in which it all takes place; and finally the overall dynamics and mood generated by the interplay of these components. We should here recognize the fact that the total experience of a play does not rest in these separate elements nor in the manner in which they are structured—a play in totality is more than its parts. Possibly we may find that these elements are essential components of any play regardless of intention and structure, if we state them simply in these terms:

a play is about someone
involved in some kind of
situation or action
who communicates   (can be in pantomime)
something   (may be himself)
and is somewhere   (even if on a platform, empty stage, or
           auditorium with or without appurtenances)
and in some kind of tension (rhythm or dynamics)

The last of these, rhythm, holds the key to what is "dramatic." Rhythm contains opposition which implies dynamics at work whether it be conflict, tension, suspense, or just stimulation—intellectual or emotional. Another interesting observation about these elements is that, although they are contained in all plays—the author may have enriched one, or two, more than the others, which then become the major interest or emphatic and unifying elements. In a good mystery play anxiety and curiosity are aroused by how it will all turn out, and the main interest is in the situations and events. In tragedies we are primarily concerned with characters and everything else becomes an extension from character. In some plays ideas are of foremost importance, while characters and story serve primarily to bring out these ideas. In a few plays our enjoyment rests as much on the brilliance and wit of the language as on the characters or story. In other forms of theatre where logical causality is rejected only feelings and states of conditions are presented, fascinating us by the totality of the situation that creates a mood and a rhythmic coherence and depends on them for unity of impact. For some of our contemporary playwrights the movement in writing is away from the prosaic world and toward the poetic realm of metaphor and myth, where causal relationships are often nonexistent and where the statement of the moment and intuition, not explanation, make reality. Writers like Shepard, Durang, Stoppard, Mamet, and many of their contemporaries are forsaking social and psychological dramas of the school of Inge, Miller, and Williams in the mold of the "well-made play" and opening up new vistas.

Through this understanding of the elements of a play and the channeling of interest into these areas, the director is able to evaluate each for what it offers or lacks. A play that is strong in situation or overly heavy in ideas may need enrichment in character. A play of mood may need to be vitalized by making more of the circumstances within a situation and by strengthening the conflict in the confrontation between characters. The considerations are numerous. Is it a play with story but little plotting? Are the characters one-dimensional or fully realized? Is it a subjective exploration of character or a documentary statement of character? Analyzing and understanding the emphatic element or elements in a play give the director other important measures of control.

The Meaning and Structure of the Play

The meaning of the play and our understanding of it become our points of reference in delving into the details of the play. At this point we should work as if we were the dramatist, analyzing the theme and the way that it is to be expressed and the meaning of each scene in relation to the whole play. It is now that we want to go over each scene to gauge its length, its purpose, and its achievement; whether or not it accomplishes logically what it should, whether or not the psychological states of the character in each scene are clear. We should analyze the structure of the play—its handling of exposition and inciting factors, its development, its treatment of conflict scenes, crises, climax, and how it resolves its actions. We should give close study to the type of scenes and the overall dynamics in the flow of actions. We should study the critical scenes and the interrelation of forces in preparation for ground planning. With original scripts there is always considerable rewriting to supervise, in order to eliminate repetiton, to accomplish progression, and to insure consistency of characterization. Too often the beginning writer confuses his issues, and there is always much work in clarifying and emphasizing the important parts and adjusting the proportions of the play. Although many errors in writing are bound to turn up at rehearsals, many more can be detected from the written script than is ordinarily supposed.

Theatrical Conventions and Period Influences

The whole experience of understanding a play knowledgeably remains incomplete without full consideration of two more important areas that exert influence on the playwright. *Theatrical conventions* refer to the conventions of a particular age that are directly operative on the structure of the play, the technique of acting, and the mechanics of staging. *Period influences* relate to the manners, culture, tastes, and other features of an age. Many people may not perceive these conventions and influences in contemporary plays, since they are of our times and are produced in our own milieu in whatever form of theatre is currently in favor.

In the Elizabethan era the conventions of direct communication with the audience and of unlocalized areas in the flexible open stage had direct bearing on the structure of Shakespeare's plays; in the same way the conventions of our generally proscenium oriented theatre and its stage machinery and instruments have their effect on contemporary playwriting. The staging of Maxwell Anderson's romantic drama *Elizabeth, the Queen,* is evolved out of our own theatrical conventions and not out of Shakespeare's, even though the play is about his contemporaries. Stylistically, *Elizabeth, the Queen* is a *romantic* work, but the conventions of acting and staging relate to the proscenium stage. Stylistically, Shakespeare's *Richard III* is also a *romantic* work, but, in this case, the conventions of acting and staging relate to the open stage of the Elizabethans. This is all quite obvious, yet many find it difficult to accept Shakespeare's *Measure for Measure* as a *realistic* dark comedy because of the questions raised by differing theatrical convention. In the same frame of reference we can relate the intimacy of the Restoration Theatre with its large forestage and adjoining box seats to the brilliant tete-a-tete conversations of its comedies, and contrast this to the vastness of the Greek amphitheatre, open to the skies, and the monumental confrontation of characters and choruses in their symphonic plays. These examples are not meant to advocate attempts at archeological reproductions, which, in production before a contemporary audience, can exhibit fascinating decor, but prove meaningless in exploring and projecting the inner dramatic values of the play.

The confusion in separating stylistic concepts from theatrical conventions becomes further aggravated when, for example, the term *classicism,* as a style of playwriting, is applied to works as distinctive as Anouilh's *Antigone,* Miller's *A View from the Bridge,* and Sophocles' *Oedipus Rex.* To distinguish theatrical conventions from period influences derived from art, culture, modes, and manners, and these two from stylistic considerations are further responsibilities in the process of play analysis and preparation. In researching the historical background of Anderson's *Elizabeth, the Queen* for authenticity and enrichment we would study the art and culture of the Elizabethan era to capture the spirit and flavor of the age; we would also study the modes and manners of the time for ideas in handling costumes, duelling, social etiquette, and so on. Unquestionably, it is important to recognize the elements that distinguish style from theatrical conventions and both of these from period conventions; only then can we place each part in proper perspective within the requirements of the play. These matters are mentioned to remind the beginning director that these studies in the fundamentals of play directing only cover basic working techniques and by no means encompass the entire range of play directing.

Procedure in Directing

Designing the Ground Plan

Having absorbed the whole experience of the play in all its details, the director is ready to transpose his concepts into practical terms—and ultimately must arrive at a ground plan. Although the various approaches to the direction of a play affect procedures in planning, the processes toward the evolvement of the ground plan remain rather basic:

A ground plan is evolved out of a complete plan of the play.

It is evolved out of the director's visualization of the life within the play.

It is evolved out of the dramatic needs that will project each scenic moment to its fullest dramatic value.

It is evolved out of a dynamic design in the flow of a pantomimic choreography that fully expresses all relationships of character to character, charac-

PLATE 36 Death of a Salesman *by Arthur Miller*
Directorial concept for scheme of production.

Arena Stage, Washington, D.C. *Director:* Zelda Fichandler. *Designer:* Karl Eigsti.
Costumes: Marjorie Slaiman.

ter to theme, character to story, character to mood, and character to atmosphere.

Rereading and reworking the script will create in the director's mind definite pictures, movements, positions, and business. These need not be connected nor continuous, but should be critical moments in the play and descriptive of the interaction of forces. The climactic movements and patterns of the important scenes that have been planned will tell the director where the various objects—whether doors and windows or benches and tree stumps—can be placed most advantageously. Mentioning these objects should remind us that the ground plan is only the floor markings of the setting. The mental picture of any scene to the visually minded director is a three-dimensional one that more often than not includes all elements of production.

Relationship with Designers

Closely associated with the director in the entire planning process are the designers. At an early stage in this process when concept, style, scheme of production, and ground plans have been resolved, there comes the time for final technical adjustments of the setting in its relation to the architecture, the sightlines, and the general flow of movement, both in and out of the field of action. In Appendix A are listed the duties and responsibilities of designers and production staff and their relationship with the director.

Scheme of Production (see Plates 36, 37, and 38.)

In discussing the image conveyed by a play we mentioned that one of its transformations could come from design. In discussing style we mentioned that among its control it could serve as a measure of design and use of setting. To these we can add theatrical conventions. The scheme for a production comes from many sources and can extend to the horizons of a director's or designer's imagination. However, on the interpretive level it must not be extraneous to the play's basic attitude, style, and meaning. It is best explained by example.

Shakespeare's romantic comedy *As You Like It* can be realized through several schemes of production without subjecting it to artistic disservice. It can be staged on a replica of its original theatrical surroundings, like the open flexible stage of the Elizabethans; or placed within the confines of the proscenium stage with a scheme of wing and borders for the court and forest-scenes; without destroying its romanticism it can be given life on a space stage enveloped by a cyclorama with rear projection of romantic stylization of trees; it can be treated as an enormous child's storybook standing upright on stage with pages serving as scenic cutouts like the old valentine cards that popped out on opening; it can be the scheme of a forest in movement from upstage to downstage as Rosalind and her companions penetrate deeper into it; or the play can be set on an arena stage with flying ribbons outlining the scenic elements. Certain plays do not permit this wide range of schemes of production—for example, a naturalistic play, where its physical surroundings and atmosphere give it substance, probably finds its truest life in the fourth-wall tradition of the proscenium theatre that first nurtured it.

Wilder's concept for his play *Our Town* offers a fine example of relating scheme of production to theme. The bare stage, love scenes on ladders, the smell of nonexistent coffee brewing and nonexistent heliotropes in the garden form an integral part of the playwright's concept—our failure to see,

PLATE 37   Death of a Salesman *by Arthur Miller*
Directorial concept for scheme of production.

Cincinnati Playhouse in the Park. *Director:* Michael Murray. *Designer:* Neil Peter Jampolis. *Costumes:* Annie Peacock Warner. *Photographer:* Sandy Underwood.

PLATE 38 The Trial by Franz Kafka
Scheme of Production: *Bird's-eye view of multiple setting in a modular theatre, an environmental theatre concept of staging. The script was broken down into fifteen scenes of equal length with each scene repeated on a ten-minute interval as audience groups of twelve passed through the funhouse.*

California Institute of the Arts. *Director:* Robert Benedetti. *Designer:* Greg Kollenborn. *Photographer:* Rumio Sato.

feel, and sense every living moment and everything around us, which otherwise can become nonexistent.

Approach to Rehearsal

The approach to the rehearsal of a play should be determined by its intrinsic needs. For example, the rehearsal procedure in directing a contemporary comedy of idea, highly selective in its realism, would be quite different in approach from directing a mystery thriller. Although in Chapter 14 a general working rehearsal schedule is set down as a guide to the beginning director, the lead-in paragraph should be noted. Arbitrary rules and divisions set down for rehearsal procedures governing all plays would be as illogical as outlining the same procedure for painting a watercolor, oil, or a mural in gesso. Where one play might justify an extensive period of probing into a character's background with visits to the actual environments, as practiced by some directors, alternating with periods of improvisations to enrich the actor's perception of his character; another play might require preliminary round-table discussions not on character but on the ideas promulgated by the playwright, with early rehearsal emphasis on lines. While some casts are put on their feet immediately to sketch in movements and business, establish space relations and external circumstances in order to give the actors a frame of reference for study; others may require concentrated study and intensive rehearsals of major critical scenes in the latter part of the play before work begins on the early scenes. Some styles of writing call for a particular approach to rehearsals which in turn develop schools of philosophy about the process of bringing these scripts to life on stage. We are not thinking here of the actor-director-writer collaboration where performances are the outgrowth of a long process of improvisation, but of approaches more in line with the "method" or the "Brechtian" approaches which seem to come alive best when they are applied to the styles of writing that gave them conception.

The type and style of a play call for their own distinctive approach in direction, but by the same token the approach in itself does not create the type or style of play. For example, an improvisational approach to rehearsals might be undertaken for a farce or a tragedy without altering its basic attitude and mood. Ultimately, it is control of the acting and the fundamentals of play directing that create the basic attitude and style of performance.

Relationship with the Actor

The relationship between director and actor unquestionably varies according to the personalities, philosophy of theatre, background, and circumstances involved, even accepting the talent, creativity, knowledge, and dedication of both. Whatever the balance may be, we still should expect from the director a compassionate understanding of the actor's problems, a facility for communicating his concepts of the play and its values, and a talent for inspiring actors and eliciting their best efforts. Indicated here is a trust and respect for each other. In practical working relationships: we have the situation where the actor responds freely to the director's wishes, trusting and obeying his concepts and interpretations and following each direction exactly; or, from the more collaborative point of view, we have the director who encourages discussions, allows time for exploration and improvisation, is amenable to ideas, offers several choices along with suggestions for actions and interpretation before final decision, is subtle in his own suggestions, and generally runs a very free course before shaping and pruning the work. Be it one or the other, the director must show patience for whatever limitations, tensions, and struggles an actor may have as he works on his role. The director should study and know his actor, understand his strengths and weaknesses; he should give him confidence and encouragement by respecting the actor's own feelings and opinions, and by giving him constructive criticisms upon which the actor can build.

At this point, the beginning director may well ask about preconceived directions for blocking. We refer the student to Chapter 14 for these discussions in conducting rehearsals. However, for the beginning director the procedure of planning positions and movements on paper can give a solid basis for preliminary blocking. When he has had considerable experience and his ideas come more quickly than the actors can absorb them, then it is safe to discard premeditated detailed directions within the larger concept of scene control. No director, on the other hand, should become too set in his ideas of the way he wants a scene to be played if he is to stimulate and receive ideas for business and interpretation from the actors themselves, granted that the suggestions are not in contradiction to the main conception of the play.

Director's Perspective at Final Run-Throughs

Only when the actors are in secure control and command of their roles, when the director has finished working on details, and when the pace and overall dynamics of the play are reasonably set can the director sit back and watch the final run-throughs in perspective from several points of view. These include four main ways of looking at the run-throughs: they are the auditory, the visual, the empathic, and the audience points of view. They are not necessarily assumed individually at different run-throughs nor are we necessarily concerned with all of them for each play. The needs are relative to the play itself—its type, style, period, emphatic element, and the demands made by each of these on the cast. What is important, however, is that we have this knowledge at our command to put to use as necessity dictates.

FROM THE AUDITORY The director hears the run-through from the speech point of view giving attention to elements such as pronunciation, diction, line delivery for clarity, proper emphasis, force, variety, and so on. He listens for definition in pointing, for balance of emphasis on lines that point up idea, story, or character understanding. He also listens to the musical flow and poetry of the play; he gauges the balance and contrast in voices; is sensitive to the rhythm with its tempo variations in the rising and falling actions, the drops, and the tonal values of voices; is alert to cue pickup and pace.

FROM THE VISUAL   The director sees the run through as a painter and choreographer, studying the compositions for their points of emphasis and mood connotations; studying picturizations for proper expression of story and emotional relationships; making sure that movement expresses the character, atmosphere, and mood choreographically; studying business to see that it is appropriate, explicit, and in proportion.

He looks at the play from the point of view of pantomime to be sure that story, character, and atmosphere are visually readable.

Oftentimes it is advantageous to the actors to run through the play without speaking the dialogue, but retaining the visual elements. The actors think the lines while carrying out the movements and business, progressing without pause from action to action and in so doing compress the visual flow of each scene. This is equivalent to a run-through of the lines without movement.

FROM THE EMPATHIC   The director gives himself fully to the emotions and moods at play, sensitive to the sincerity of their projection. He is sensitive to the truth of characterization and scene belief, and to the consistency of the esthetic distance established for the play.

FROM THE AUDIENCE   The director does his utmost to watch the play as if seeing it for the first time. He must remember that an audience's understanding of story, theme, and characters develops scene by scene, that an audience cannot look beyond what is being acted at the moment, and that therefore a relatively unimportant scene in the play is nevertheless all important to an audience as it is being performed. We can understand, then, why it becomes necessary for the director to keep every element in proper balance and proportion, knowing what to emphasize and what to subordinate, and maintaining, meanwhile, the audience's interest in each moment of every scene.

Such an analysis as this on the approach to directing the play necessarily places the stress on the purely intellectual and technical aspects of directing. In no way, however, is it intended to lessen the value of pure imagination or intuitive creation. All art, as we have seen, must have both the purely creative impulse itself and the technique of conveying it. Any experienced artist blends these two, the creative along with the technical, so that he creates in form. It is the same with the director and actor.

Preparing the Production Script

The following outline is one suggested step-by-step breakdown of the process involved in preparing a script for production:

Character and text	Basic situations	Graphics
Statements relating to character and text with identifying business. Thematic analysis.	Statement of basic situation with illuminating business regarding circumstances, locale, atmosphere. Analysis of structural values — inciting factors, crises, climax.	Statement of fundamental design, if applicable. Character patterns: (see **Romeo and Juliet** scene on page 211) 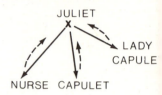

Composition:

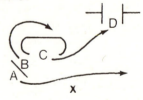

Text

Character A

xxxx xxx xxxx xxxxx, xxxxxxxx
xxxxxxxxx xxxxx xxx x xxxx xx
xxx xx xxxxx!⌐xxxx xx xxxx, xxxxx ⎤— Rise
xx xxx xxxx. xxxxxxx, xxxxxx⎸xxxx x⎦
xxxxx xxxxxxx.   X——ch——DR

Major blocking indicated with full or partial ground plans:

Character B ———————— enters LC

xxxx xxxxxx?

Character C

xxxxx xx xxxx xxxxx xxx.⌐xxxxxxx xxx — X—tab—LC
xxx....

Indication of forces in action

Explanation of Symbols for Blocking

X——ch——DR = cross below chair to down right.

X—tab—LC = cross above table to left center.

xxxxx xxx, etc. = words to be emphasized.

Write down statements of:

1. "Feel of the play" analyzed in terms of personal emotional reaction; sensual response of taste, color, texture, sound; images and associations evoked; mood.

2. Type of play.

3. Style of play.

4. Purpose behind the writing.

5. Emphatic element or elements.

6. Idea of play—what is the play about?

7. Basic action of the play—the spine.

Describe and analyze:

8. Major characters—internal and external characteristics; background; major objectives of each; relationship to each other and to the basic action.

9. Structural elements—starting point of major complications, crisis, climax.

Consider director's approach:

10. Problems involved.

11. Director's concept.

12. Scheme of production.

13. Actors' control—speech and movement.

14. Use of fundamental elements.

Work on ground plan:

15. Reasons for it.

16. Stage space available; sightlines.

Do specific script analysis and preparation:

17. Divide scenes into units with brief statement of basic situations. (See Title of the Scene in Chapter 8.)

18. Underline lines of dialogue that point up emphatic element or elements—story, character, theme, language, mood. This is a matter of selectivity of key lines that must be given proper emphasis.

19. Use of whole or partial ground plan to designate major positions and movements in character relationships.

20. Use action diagrams to indicate major action emphases.

21. Write in focal directions of movement, business, and interpretation.

22. Notate important points of character analysis.

16

Directing Musical Comedy

In common usage the term *musical comedy* means a type of musical performance consisting of songs, dances, and dialogue with a thin plot, called a book. A wide application of the term *musical* could include operas, operettas, comic operas, revues, extravaganzas (*Folies Bergère*), rock operas (*Jesus Christ Superstar*), musical fantasies (*The Wiz*), musical dance dramas (*West Side Story*), musical dramas (*The King and I*), and the more recent clinical musicals like *A Chorus Line,* to indicate some of the variations.

In the earlier musical comedies like *Anything Goes* and *No, No, Nanette* the song, dance, and dialogue fell to a large extent into easily divided sections, which in turn simplified the organization of rehearsals for the music director, choreographer, and book director. The formula with slight variations was simple: a bright song and dance opening followed by a dialogue scene, leading to a song, solo or duet, picked up by the singing chorus, and building to a dance number by the dancing chorus with possible specialties by the lead dancers. For the dances clearing the stage of all other performers and flying set pieces allowed the dancers ample space. The finale to the dance number, depending on its position in the production, could include the return of the singing chorus and principal singers. From this point would follow a change of scene into dialogue usually played in "one," the downstage area, while behind the drop new scenery would be set up for another spectacle of song and dance. So it proceeded, with a thin plot threading the components together.

Historically, in the American musical comedy the integration of song, dance, and dialogue into an inseparable unit began with the production of *Oklahoma!* In the contemporary musical, the songs and dances are there to advance the story and enrich actions and character. Whatever element of spectacle they contribute grows out of the needs of the action.

The purpose of this chapter is to discuss the additional considerations that enter into directing musical comedy beyond the demands of a straight play. To a lesser or greater degree these considerations apply to the other varieties of musicals.

A wide variance exists in the assignment of responsibilities to a director in staging a musical—from setting the concept, having complete artistic control, and organizing everything to directing only the dialogue sequences. In the latter instance the producer may set the concept of the production; contract with composer, lyricist, book writer, music director, chorus director, choreographer, book director, and designers; jointly cast singers and dancers; and supervise the work of each along with the other responsibilities of promotion and management. In other instances the director works along with the producer in the initial stages and in production carries on the artistic part of the work, while the producer runs the promotion and business management of the operation. Where dance carries the weight of the production, as in *A Chorus Line* and *West Side Story*, the choreographer may assume all the functions of a director. In contrast, the Metropolitan Opera Company on several occasions has given overall artistic control of the opera to a stage director. The functions and responsibilities of a director of musicals, then, vary according to his experience, reputation, range of talents, and circumstances of production. For our purpose we shall assume that the stage director is somewhat knowledgeable in music and dance, though not necessarily a practitioner of either one, and that his function in a musical comedy is equivalent to that in a play—artistic control of the production.

Organization

Before continuing into details of production we should note that one of the major challenges in directing musical comedy is *organization,* beginning with planning to rehearsals to performance. The charts detailed later in the chapter are absolute requisites for the planning phase of production. This need becomes obvious when we consider the many components that make up a musical comedy production: to the dialogue and physical aspects of production of a play, add songs, dances, routines, and musical accompaniment, plus the enrichment in sets and costumes; and to these add the extra personnel involved, including music director, chorus director, choreographer, rehearsal accompanists, musicians, singers, and dancers, besides other assistants required by the larger musicals.

Ability to organize is also a requisite for the esthetic side of directing musicals. Though to facilitate rehearsal and make the most of available time, the several components of a musical are scheduled out of continuity, the director must keep the whole context (music, songs, dances, and text) of the work in mind when evaluating any part of it for any reason. The

Organizational Chart

Director
Stages dialogue sequences, songs with principals, routine and ensemble numbers; * uses rehearsal pianist; has overall supervision.

Music Director
Rehearses principals with songs, singing chorus, and dancers when involved in singing numbers; rehearses and conducts orchestra; supervises work of the librarian; uses rehearsal pianist; may use a chorus director.

Chorus Director (if used)
Rehearses singing chorus and dancers when involved in singing numbers; uses rehearsal pianist.

Choreographer
Stages principals in dances, dancing chorus, and singers and actors when involved in dance numbers; stages routine and ensemble numbers when assigned by the director; uses rehearsal pianist.

Designers
Scene, costume, and lighting designers may also prepare special effects.

Sound Engineer
Prepares special effects, reinforces sound for performers.

---

* Routine numbers, like the "Tin Horn Fugue" quartet in *Guys and Dolls*, and ensemble numbers are often assigned to the choreographer, though many stage directors prefer to stage routine and ensemble numbers that do not require the discipline of dancing. A choreographer also may stage all songs and musical material in situations where the stage director works only with the dialogue sequences.

real challenge in directing musicals rests in this ability of the director to maintain the feeling for the context of the entire work in a process of production that breaks up into many sections over an extended period of time.

Planning the Production

The budget, place of performance, available rehearsal time, and other circumstances of production affect the number of singers and dancers in the choruses, the number of musicians and the make-up of the orchestra, the doubling of roles, and the use of members of the choruses in minor roles, besides the usual physical aspects of production. The early musicals make heavy cast and scenic demands that can be judiciously reduced with no appreciable effect on the enjoyment of the performance. The degree of reduction in numbers and simplification of production are matters that should be resolved in conference, jointly or individually as circumstances warrant, with the producer, director, music director, choreographer, and designers. Musical accompaniment, for example, can range from one piano to a string, horn, and percussion combo, to a fifteen-piece orchestra, to a full orchestra of forty or more pieces. Important is a well-chosen and well-balanced group of instruments to meet the needs of the musical. When budgets are tight it is not unusual for one musician to handle two or three instruments. Though the principal singers and dancers are set by the requirements of the musical, the number of people in the choruses can vary; conditions may permit a reduction to four singers and four dancers or an extension to a singing chorus of eighteen voices and a dancing chorus of twelve, to set limits.

Initial Conferences

At the initial conferences the director should set the concept and scheme of production, space requirements for ensemble and dance numbers, number of set and prop changes and the time allotted for each in the musical transitions, and number of costume changes and the time allotted for each in musical transitions or between musical numbers. The director will have studied these factors in arriving at a scheme of production. Granted that music to allow for set and costume changes is in the original score, for reasons of budget, concept, rehearsal time, or other limitations, music for transitions now may be eliminated or extended. A unit set with suggestive use of scenery allowing continual flow of action will certainly justify cutting transitional music formerly used for shifts. Along with other cuts or editing for songs and dances, and possible transpositions of music to adjust to voices, these matters must be settled before rehearsals, for they affect preparation of the score for later rehearsals with the orchestra as well as for the immediate need of the singers and dancers.

Preparation

With the music director, discuss:

Vocal requirements of singers—principals, singing chorus, dancing chorus.

Concept and tempi for musical numbers (include choreographer in routines and numbers with dancers).

Breakdown of each musical number—cuts, repeats, cast (include choreographer in routines and numbers with dancers).

Musical transitions—cuts or repeats for technical reasons (shifts, costume changes).

Cueing requirements—dialogue, songs, chorus numbers, technical (shifts, light cues, entrances).

Cuts and editing in general.

Special requirements.

With the choreographer, discuss:

Concept for each dance and routine number.

Tempi (include music director).

Breakdown of each dance and routine number—cuts, repeats, cast (include music director).

Division between director and choreographer of those routine numbers involving only singing principals and singing chorus (this arrangement depends on the rehearsal schedule and the ability of the director to routine a musical number).

Ensemble numbers involving dancers.

Space requirements for each musical number involving dancers, including routine numbers to be staged by choreographer.

Analysis of ground plans that involve dances and routines; points of entrances and exits.

Set, property, costume, and lighting requirements for each dance and routine number (include the designers if possible; otherwise transmit information to them).

Cueing requirements—musical, technical.

Special requirements.

Rehearsal Considerations

THE BOOK   Staging the dialogue sequences in musical comedy involves the same disciplines as staging any comedy. Because it is a presentational form of theatre, the performers may be staged more opened up to the audience than in a straight play, but not to the extreme of static full-front body positions, the convention in the early days of musicals.

In pacing a scene the director should be aware of the dynamics relating the scene to what has preceded and to what follows musically as well as to the overall structure of the work.

Often dialogue sequences are underscored with musical accompaniment, either to reinforce a sentimental moment or to heighten moments of tension and turmoil. Special attention must be given to these scenes to see that proper balance is maintained between the volume of the accompaniment and the projection of the performers with or without sound reinforcement. Particularly with orchestral accompaniment, not only the volume, but the varying tones and pitches of the instruments can interfere with understanding lines of dialogue. Here the performer has as much responsibility in maintaining proper projection and articulation as the conductor has in keeping the orchestra in balance.

THE MUSICAL NUMBERS   It is not uncommon to find singers who, though they know the music and lyrics of a song, have not actually delved into the *meaning* of the song's text. This problem should only happen with the untrained, but regardless, the text of any song should be analyzed for its story, ideas, attitudes, and emotional values. The ideas for actions and reactions, attitudes, picturization, and imageries come out of this kind of analysis. Fitting gesture to meaning to music with proper projection and articulation is the way to master the continual challenge of having the lyrics come across to the audience.

There are obvious musical entrances when the singers and dancers must keep a subtle eye on the conductor for *cueing*. The director and choreographer must know these moments and position the performers accordingly. However, this does not mean full-front body positions with all eyes staring at the conductor. After all, everyone has been rehearsed and can be subtle in making contact when necessary. The director must be in constant touch with the music director for the less obvious cueing needs that crop up during music rehearsals, either for intricacy of musical notation or for personal reasons of the performer, and be ready to make staging adjustments during his own rehearsals. Attention to details of this kind will go far in eliminating surprises during run-throughs with the orchestra, which in commercial ventures can mean costly overtime. It is usually the insecure and inexperienced conductor and singer that require constant eye contact with each other, which in turn generates static staging and stiff positions.

The best preparation for *staging* a musical number, besides the preliminary study of music and text, is to attend the later rehearsals of the singers held by the music director or the chorus director. Besides absorbing the feeling of the music, it is the time to notice the dynamics, measures of rest, essentials of breathing and cueing, and any personal adjustments, all of which affect the staging of the number. Important to note are the measures of rest in the songs that may need to be filled in with emotional follow-through, movement, business, or gesture. Staging rehearsals should not take place until the numbers are fully in hand musically.

Beginning staging or *blocking* should be done without accompaniment, piano or otherwise, so that the performers can concentrate on the meaning of the text and the execution of the movement, business, and gesture. Some singers prefer to speak-sing the lines softly rather than use straight speech, which can prove rather cumbersome because of the repetitive nature of many lyrics and actually hamper delivery for meaning and phrasing. Later in this chapter a procedure is outlined for staging routines that applies in part to staging songs.

In staging differentiate between those songs that are sung character to character like a love song or are introspective and those that play directly to the audience.

When rehearsing just for staging, guard against the tendency of some singers to sing out fully when accompaniment is used. Not only is it an unnecessary expenditure of energy, but it takes concentration away from the primary purpose of the rehearsal.

Be sensitive to those actions that run counter to the natural limitations put on a performer by the demands of singing, such as excessive movement, movement running counter to the phrasing in the music, business that can restrict the free release of the voice in climactic moments (such as embraces in duets), actions that interfere with the needs for breathing, and moments that require repose after heightened vocal outbursts.

When possible and in accord with the music director have singers, at least the principals, attend an orchestra rehearsal before dress so that they may hear the score instrumentally. Many precious minutes have been lost due to singers not recognizing a cue in the orchestra.

THE DANCE NUMBERS   As we mentioned earlier, the responsibilities of a choreographer can include the many functions of a director. In any event, overall concept and scheme of production, casting that involves dances, concept of each musical number to be staged by the choreographer, ground plan for each, and requisites for setting, props, lights, and costumes are matters for preliminary conferences before rehearsals.

During the rehearsal period the director should check:

1. The progress in the development of the dances for story, character, and mood consistency.

2. The use of available space for the dances—it is not unusual for dances to expand beyond the space available.

3. The use of levels and other parts of the setting.

4. The points of entrances and exits and their direction for story consistency —again it is not unusual for dancers to confront other performers on exits or entrances during the first full run-through.

5. The timing of each number.

Rehearsal clothes equivalent to the actual costumes should be used in the early stages of rehearsing dances and routines to check any hindrance to movements as well as specific needs for proper fitting. This is the time to make adjustments to avoid frustrations during dress rehearsals.

The music director should attend the final rehearsals of dance numbers to check tempi before meeting with the orchestra.

GENERAL Check music and dance rehearsals daily near the close of the rehearsal hour for any problems or new developments. Though this is a responsibility of the production stage manager, it is good policy for reasons mentioned earlier for the director to do so himself periodically.

Check the progress in set, prop, and costume construction or assembly periodically for problems and developments, particularly those that are crucial to staging and use by the performers.

When attending these rehearsals and a run-through of a number is taking place, get a timing even if rough. A rough estimate of the length of performance, including the dialogue portions, becomes a valuable guideline for the overall pacing of a show before dress rehearsals.

Time, energy, and money can be saved if costume fittings (not measurements, which are taken during the first days of company calls) are organized into groupings, especially when there are several changes, and called as each group of costumes is ready for fitting. Men and women dancers deserve first call, because their needs are often critical. The next largest groupings, usually with several changes, are the men and women singers. The principals can normally be scheduled individually around the rehearsal calls, and so can the supporting performers. It is important to accomplish all fittings well before dress rehearsals.

Run-throughs, Technical Rehearsals, and Dress Rehearsals

Organization with checks and counterchecks in all phases of rehearsal and production is the key to a smooth dress rehearsal with orchestra. Accomplishing it is the responsibility of the director, who is the only one to hold within himself the whole of the separate parts. If he has done his work properly, he will have had: a run-through of all dialogue sequences apart from musical numbers; a run-through of all musical numbers except the dances; a run-through of musical numbers that include dances; and a run-through or two of the entire show before technical, dress, and rehearsal with the orchestra.

Whenever possible he will have added essential props and parts of setting, or substitutes for each, to the separate run-throughs. Also, whenever possible, and in accord with the music director, he will have had the principal singers and dancers at an orchestra rehearsal, the one when all scoring and difficult passages have been cleared up.

Technical rehearsal with sets, props, lights, and sound control should be held apart from cast and orchestra. However, circumstances may allow a particularly complicated dance number to be checked on set at a break during technicals.

The aim in each run-through is for the director to maintain a feeling for the dynamics of the entire performance, since often the economics of production permit only one or two rehearsals with full company and orchestra.

Staging Routines

Under routines we include those musical numbers that do not require dancing, but only movements and business that must be phrased and executed in rhythm. Directors knowledgeable in musical phrasing often stage routines that do not involve dancers, saving precious rehearsal time for the choreographer to work with the dancers, who need as much rehearsal time as is available under the schedule, whether six weeks or one week as in stock productions.

Preliminaries

Before staging a musical number it is expected that the performers have already memorized and rehearsed the lyrics and music, and that the director is fully acquainted with their musical work. With this much accomplished, the initial routining can be done without musical accompaniment or outright singing. Actually, there should be no full-bodied singing until the routine is set. Attention must go to the physical execution and not the vocal. This restraint is not easy to achieve with singers and a musical director whose primary commitment is to the music.

Steps in Routining a Musical Number

1. Analyze the lyrics as a text to arrive at the one or more basic situations as outlined in Chapter 8 under Title of the Scene.
2. Still working on the lyrics as you would on the text of a play, picturize the moments in movement, gesture, and business.
3. Count out the number of measures in the musical composition. Note the measures of rest. Phrase the measures according to the musical demands. The lyrics, of course, will be in accord with the musical phrasing.

4. Phrase your patterns of movement according to the phrasing of the music.

5. For the performers, before working on the details of staging, sketch the general outlines of the number.

6. Establish a count for each pattern of movement. Execute each gesture, movement, and business to the count.

7. In developing the number eliminate all extraneous gestures, movements, and business.

8. At certain points in the development of the number perform the routine to music with its proper phrasing, but in a comfortable tempo. However, in smoothing out any rough sections do this slowly to the count without accompaniment.

9. Once the routine is set and comfortable to execute for each member, rehearse the number to music in the proper tempo.

10. Work out any final polishing to a count before bringing in the musical accompaniment.

Charts

The following charts are an important part of the preliminaries in planning the production.

The chart on scene and cast breakdown, besides listing the roles in each scene, is used for the assignment of subsidiary roles among singers, dancers, and extras. It also serves to record the number of costumes assigned to each performer. Other notations can be made on the chart, such as a performer's participation in a scene: song (S), dance (D), routine (R), lines of dialogue (L). Also, the musical numbers performed in the scene can be noted at the bottom of the column or along the side next to the group involved.

The chart on the breakdown of scenes and musical numbers is a more specific division to facilitate hourly scheduling of rehearsals of book, dances, songs, and routines clear of one another. Rehearsal calls can be readily listed individually or in the following groups.

Songs rehearsed with music director:
    with principals only
    with singers only
    with principals and singers
    with principals and dancers
    with dancers only
    with ensemble
Dances rehearsed with choreographer:
    with principal dancers only
    with dancers only
    with principals and dancers
    with ensemble

Title of Production

Scene and Cast Breakdown

SCENE / PAGES / PLACE / TIME	I·1	I·2 and so on				II·1	II·2 and so on				Comments
PRINCIPALS Character names											
1	X^1	X	X^2		X	X^3		X^1	X^2	X	
2				X^1	X^2		X^3	X	X	X^1	
SUPPORTING Character names											
1		X	X		X		X		X	X	
2	X^1			X		X		X^2	X	X	
SINGERS — M Names											
1	Role 1	Role 2		Role 2		Role 3	X		X	X	
2	Role 1	X		X			X			X	
SINGERS — W Names											
1	Role 1	Role 2		Role 2		X	X			X	
2	Role 1	Role 2	X		X		Role 1			Role 3	
DANCERS — M Names											
1	Role 1	X	*Dance*	Role 2			X^2		X	X^3	
2	Role 1	X		Role 2			X^2		X	X^3	
DANCERS — W Names											
1	Role 1	X	*Title of*	Role 2			X^2		X	X^3	
2	Role 1	X		Role 2			X^2		X	X^3	
EXTRAS Names											
1			Role 1		X		X	*Title of Song*		X	
2			Role 1			Role 2			Role 3	X	

$x^1, x^2 \ldots =$ number of costumes

X following a numbered X indicates same costume

Title of Production
Breakdown of Scenes and Musical Numbers

DANCES AND ROUTINES

SC	TITLE OF NUMBER	PRIN	SUP	S—m	S—w	D—m	D—w	EXTRAS	TYPE	STAGED by
I-1	Title	Char	Char	Names or nos.	Names or nos.	Names or nos.	Names or nos.	Roles	Dance or Routine	Dir or Chor
I-2	Listings					X	X		Song & Dance	Chor
	X signifies entire group									

SONGS

SC	TITLE OF NUMBER	PRIN	SUP	S—m	S—w	D—m	D—w	EXTRAS		REH. with
I-1	Title	Char	Char	Names or nos.	Names or nos.	—	—	—		Mus Dir
I-2	Listings......			X	X					Mus Dir
	X signifies entire group									

DIALOGUE

SC	PAGE NOS.	PRIN	SUP	S—m	S—w	D—m	D—w	EXTRAS		STAGED by
I-1	pages	Char	Char	Names or nos.	(Names or nos.)	—	—	—		Dir
I-2	Listings......									
	(Name) signifies no lines of dialogue									

Routines rehearsed with director or choreographer:
  with principals only
  with singers only
  with principals and singers
  with ensemble
Book rehearsed with director:
  with principals, supporting players, and others not called for song or
    dance rehearsals
  (also includes songs that are ready for staging)

Technical Plots and Ground Plans

The technical plots for properties, costumes, and lights in musical comedy may contain more items than straight plays, and may be more complicated when dealing with musicals that require many changes of setting, but the general requirements in planning remain the same. The same may be said for the rendering of ground plans. However, the multiscene musicals with interiors, exteriors, backdrops, scenes in "one," full-stage scenes, and scenes in limbo, offer certain traffic and shift complications that can have drastic effect on the pace of the performance.

Preliminary planning with the designers must take many factors into account, such as the placement of set and prop units for shifts, the traffic pattern of principals and choruses on entrances and exits, the positioning of quick-change booths for fast costume and makeup changes, and the flow of movement from scene to scene for a smooth transition.

For these multiscene musicals a layout in miniature (about $1\frac{1}{2}'' \times 2\frac{1}{2}''$) of each ground plan on a single board can give a bird's-eye perspective of the traffic patterns and interrelation of scenes for planning and immediate reference.

Appendixes

Appendix A

The Proscenium Stage, Setting, and Stage Management

Listed in this appendix are a glossary of terms for the stage and its equipment; detailed information about set, lighting, and sound equipment; backstage terminology; a description of the duties of both the technical staff and the stage manager and his assistants—essential information for everyone connected with the theatre. Check the index for alphabetic listing of terms.

Equipment from Auditorium to Backstage

House. The part of the theatre that includes auditorium, box office, foyer, and adjacent spaces in front of the curtain as separated from those backstage. The front-of-house personnel includes house manager, box-office people, ticket takers, ushers, and maintenance staff.

Pit. Originally the term referred to the entire lower floor, or what is now known in America as the orchestra and in England as the stalls. Today it refers solely to a sunken area before the stage in which the orchestra plays.

Proscenium, or Proscenium Arch. The open frame in the solid wall of the auditorium which discloses the stage.
    a. *Proscenium width.* The horizontal distance of the opening from wall to wall.
    b. *Proscenium height.* The vertical distance of this opening from the stage floor to the uppermost part.

Apron. That portion of the stage extending out into the auditorium beyond the line of the proscenium arch; also called *forestage* when it extends out far enough to serve as an ample acting area.

Footlights, or Foots. The row of sections of low-wattage colored lights in a metal trough or compartments usually sunk in the stage floor at the front of the apron. Metal reflectors prevent the light from striking the eyes of the people in the house and send it back onto the stage. Footlights are usually wired in three circuits, one color for each. This row of lights should not extend the full width of the stage. When it does, the end bulbs cast an unfortunate shadow on the downstage end of the setting. If the stage manager finds in his theatre that the footlights do extend too far, he should loosen, or "black-out," the end bulbs up to the point where the light no longer shows on the end flats. Footlights are out of fashion in many theatres. Their major function is to blend and tone the light from the spotlights and remove shadows from under the eyebrows and noses of actors.

Asbestos. The fireproof curtain directly behind the proscenium, usually made of asbestos, occasionally of steel. When it is raised, it goes completely out of sight. The law in some states requires every theatre with a seating capacity of over 299 to be equipped with one. It must be lowered before the theatre is opened for a performance and the audience admitted. Generally it is raised (by the stage carpenter at the stage manager's signal) in full view of the audience five minutes before the performance starts. Actors would do well to know, and stage managers must know, where the rope is for the lowering of this curtain. The law requires that a knife be fastened to the stage wall near the emergency rope which, when cut, will lower the asbestos. The emergency rope is at either side of the proscenium. The asbestos is not required in some states where new theatres have adequate exits.

Grand Drapery. Painted canvas hung permanently in the upper part of the proscenium arch just behind the asbestos curtain. It consists of a crosspiece which fills in the proscenium when it is any shape but rectangular and has two side pieces dropping to the stage floor. Usually it is painted to represent folds of rich velvet with many tassels, hung profusely around painted marble columns. Seldom used in our theatres of today except in revivals, it is still found in old theatres and opera houses on the road.

Act Curtain. The curtain directly behind the grand drapery. It is used when necessary to conceal the stage from the audience before, during, or after the play. It is either drawn up and let down vertically, a fly curtain; or parted in the center and drawn horizontally one-half to each side, a draw curtain.

Curtain Line. The location at which the act curtain strikes the stage floor when lowered or slides along the stage floor when drawn.

Center Line. A line marking the verticle center of the stage from curtain line to the rear wall, used for marking off groundplan and general centering.

Tormentors. A framework directly behind the act curtain that cuts down the size of the proscenium opening to the exact proportion that the scene designer desires for his setting. The height of this inner framework varies in different theatres and is used with flats from eight or nine to twenty feet in height. In old theatres the tormentors were the side pieces of this inner framework.

They are the first flats behind the act curtain. There is one on each side, coming out onto the stage and parallel to the footlights. Their position is adjustable in that they are made to be placed farther onstage or drawn off according to the width of the set.

Teaser. The very first crosspiece of canvas between the two tormentors. In design and color it matches the tormentors and with them forms an inner picture frame. In the older theatres it cut down the proscenium to a smaller opening than the grand drapery. The teaser is fastened to ropes above so that it can be raised and lowered to varying heights.

Box Teaser. Another form of the teaser in the shape of an L, with the vertical side facing the audience and the bottom part serving as support for lighting equipment.

Inner Proscenium. Today the grand drapery and the old teaser and tormentors have for the most part disappeared. In their place, a framework covered with canvas and painted a neutral color cuts down the plaster proscenium arch to the size that the designer plans. It is not solid, for the upper part that corresponds to the old teaser can be raised and lowered, and, like the tormentors, the side pieces can be moved on and off the stage. Although the inner proscenium is a single unit, its sides are still referred to as tormentors and the upper crosspiece as a teaser.

Tormentor and Teaser Draperies. Cloth of the same color and material as the act curtain sometimes hung at the top and sides of the inner proscenium, covering it partially. In this manner there is a definite blending of color and material from the act curtain to the neutral color of the inner proscenium.

Set Width or Opening. The distance between the sides or tormentors of the inner proscenium rather than actual proscenium width, since this width alone is considered in relation to the set and the acting areas. The set width varies in different theatres; in the little theatres it is as narrow as eighteen to twenty feet, in the larger professional ones as wide as thirty to forty feet.

Set Line. The outline of the entire set in relation to the stage floor. The front set line is the location of the downstage extremities of the set and playing areas demarcated by the tormentors of the inner proscenium. In the realistic play the actor stays within the front set line.

Teaser Height, Teaser Trim, or *Trimming Height.* The distance from the stage floor to the lower edge of the upper crosspiece, or teaser. This, too, varies from eight or nine feet in the amateur to greater heights in the professional theatre.

Return. A flat or a drapery placed between the inner proscenium or the tormentors and the downstage end of the box set in order to mask the opening made when the set is narrower than the space ordinarily allowed between the tormentors.

Special Inner or False Proscenium. A frame covered with canvas taking the place of the regular proscenium or set behind the inner proscenium opening to reduce the opening. In its special design and color it ties and blends into the set. It is not permanent equipment, being used most often in musicals and frequently in elaborate productions. It usually has its own front drop which again ties into the particular scene design. In a musical production there is a space between it and the act curtain deep enough for actors to perform before this special proscenium and its curtain.

The Floor of the Stage

Stage Floor. This is necessarily made of soft wood so that tacks and screws will go into it easily. The wood is often covered with linoleum or a floor cloth, often padded to absorb sound.

Trap. A good-sized opening, roughly six feet parallel to the foots and three feet deep, cut in the stage floor with a ladder, a ramp, or a rising and lowering platform through which an actor can ascend or be raised or descend or be lowered. Every professional theatre has provisions for a trap to be opened in practically any portion of the stage.

Elevators or Lifts. Platforms which in larger theatres make up part of the stage floor and which can be raised and lowered mechanically in sections to different levels.

Stage-floor Pocket. Sunk just below the level of the stage floor are metal receptacles that contain several outlets for electric current from the switchboard. They are usually located around the stage just outside the average set lines and are used to supply current to lights used in entrances and fixtures in the set itself. There are one or two on each side and three or four along the rear.

The Physical Equipment over the Stage and Its Use in a Production

Gridiron or Grid. The most important piece of stage machinery, used to manipulate the hanging of scenery. It is a slatted or grated frame of metal or wooden beams high up over the stage, built a few feet below the roof of the stage. In the best of the modern theatres there is just space enough between it and the roof for a man to stand erect. The gridiron should be forty to eighty feet above the stage floor if the sets are to be raised out of sight of the first rows of the auditorium. *Grid* also applies to a system of tracks above the stage area as in arena theatres allowing the movement of lighting instruments to various positions along the tracks by release of self-locking brakes.

Rope-line Rigging. Along the center of the gridiron, on a line at a right angle to the footlights, is set a row of blocks with pulleys or sheaves of a special type for stage use. Equidistant from the part of the stage within the proscenium, right and left of this center row, are other rows. Sometimes this space is divided into four rows. Ropes are passed over these block pulleys. Accordingly, there are sets of rope, three or four in a row and in rows parallel to the footlights. The number of these sets varies in theatres. A well-equipped professional theatre will have as many as twenty-five to fifty.

Lines. The ropes attached to the top of a curtain or series of flats or to the pipe, or batten, on to which electrical equipment or parts of the scenery are attached. These lines go through pulleys attached to the gridiron and are counterbalanced. By manipulating them the scenery is raised or lowered. Lines should be made of the best hemp rope, one-half-inch diameter or larger, and should be carefully examined at definite periods.

Short Line. The line attached to the side of the stage where the ropes are to be fastened.

Long Line. The rope attached to the farthest end of the gridiron. The two in the center are known as the *short-center* and the *long-center* lines. If there are only three lines in a set, the middle line is called the *center line*. In lowering a drop it is essential that its batten be perfectly horizontal. When the drop comes down from above, it is often necessary to have these different lines pulled separately. The stage manager frequently is required to call to the stagehand in charge of the lines which line needs tightening in order to make the drop hang evenly.

Set of Lines. The lines, three to five, are the short, centers, and long lines, in one horizontal row or plane, that will hang the drop or set of flats.

Snatch Line. A short line used to attach a piece of scenery to a batten for the purpose of flying it.

Trip Line. A set of lines attached to the bottom of a drop which when raised doubles the drop onto itself. Tripping is essential when the gridiron is too low to permit a full drop from being raised above the sightlines.

Pin Rail. The ends of the lines, after they have passed through the pulleys on the gridiron, are brought down at one side of the stage as a set of three to be operated as one. These are attached then to the pin rail, a long beam of wood or steel firmly built into the walls of the building and running the full depth of the playing part of the stage, with crosspieces, or pins, to which the lines may be more easily fastened. Also known as tie-off rail.

Counterweight System. The second type of rigging. Compared to the ropeline system, it is a permanent setup; steel cables are used in place of rope; these cables are attached to iron-pipe battens which run horizontal to the footlights the length of the playing area. Whatever is to be raised or lowered is attached to these pipe battens. The battens are counterweightd by steel weights placed in carriages that run along the side wall from gridiron to the stage floor. The control ropes for the carriages are locked at the pin rail. Professional houses have one or the other of these two systems of rigging. A few have both; some of the latest installations have electric control of these systems.

Fly Gallery. The pin rail was originally built on a platform at least twenty feet above the stage and known as the fly gallery. Today it is usually lowered to within about three feet of the stage floor, but the space above it is still known as the fly gallery.

Cat Walk. A narrow platform connecting the fly galleries on both sides of the stage. It is used to service equipment and to focus and control lighting instruments, which are often attached to its railings.

Counterweights. Weights attached to the end of a set of lines or weights used in carriages to balance the weight of the scenery hung so that it may be raised and lowered with ease without being hauled up as dead weight.

Sandbag. A strongly made canvas bag which, filled with sand, is used on the stage ends of the lines when not in use, so that the weight will bring down the line from the gridiron when the line is wanted for hanging a piece of scenery or drop.

Large Sandbags. Often attached to the fly-gallery end of lines to serve as a counterweight for scenery hung on those lines to facilitate raising and lowering.

Pipe Batten. A length of iron pipe about three inches in diameter attached to the steel cables. Drops, borders, scenery, or lighting equipment are attached to it to be raised and lowered onto the stage. The pipe batten is also designated according to use, such as a sky batten to light the cyclorama.

Wooden Batten. A strip of wood of almost any length, generally three inches wide and one inch thick. As border battens they are the length of the stage opening. Onto these are tacked and glued the canvas of the teaser and other borders and drop curtains; another batten is screwed to the first so that the cloth material is held between the two battens.

Flies. The space above the stage where scenery is hung by lines from the gridiron. To be of any value the flies must be high enough to hang the scenery so that it flies well above the ceiling of a standing set. *To fly* or *to raise* means to hang anything in this space.

　　a. Flyman. The stagehand who operates the rigging that controls the scenery hung in the flies.

　　　　i. To Trim. Hanging a drop so that its lower edge is in proper juxtaposition to the floor—usually parallel, though not always. Unusual scenery sometimes is not hung parallel. If a drop is lowered from the flies and is not properly hung, it is trimmed by drawing, tightening, or loosening the long, center, or short line. Drops and other parts of scenery attached to the pipe battens of the counterweight system are permanently trimmed when first attached to the batten.

　　　　ii. Make Fast. To tie a set of lines to a piece of scenery; also to tie the lines firmly to the pin rail.

　　　　iii. To Foul. Scenery "fouls" when it or its lines tangle and catch in other pieces of scenery in the flies, as when "the back wall is fouled with a drop."

　　b. Bos'un's Chair (Boatswain's chair). A suspended rope seat in which the flyman can be hoisted into flies inaccessible by ladder.

Other Parts of the Full Stage

Stage Manager's Desk or Prompt Corner. This is usually directly to the right or left of the proscenium arch, depending upon the placement of the fly gallery and the switchboard. It may or may not be on the same side of the stage with them. It holds a script, a pad of paper for notes, and cue sheets. Conveniently placed before the stage manager is the intercom system or signals that put him in communication with the various staff members and performers—direct lines to the flyman, to the electrician at the switchboard, to the soundman, to the conductor, to the curtain man, to the greenroom and dressing rooms, and to the lobby and lounge so that he may signal the audience at the beginning of the acts two minutes before curtain. For expediency, accuracy, and silence, the stage manager should always signal warnings and cues, even though he is near enough to speak them. He *rings up* and *rings down* the curtain, even though his signals are given by lights. The stage manager's desk is also frequently in communication with the front of the house or box office.

Switchboard or Control Console. The center of all the distribution of electric current to the lighting instruments on the stage and to the auditorium. Without going into the full description of the construction and mounting of the switchboard and the latest electronic devises, here are a few of the requisites. Controls for each branch circuit open and close the current for each light on the stage. Each light unit on the stage should be separately controlled from the board. It should be possible to control groups of like units, classed by location or color, such as all the X-ray units or all the blue footlights as opposed to the red. The switchboard is often on the floor level, but frequently it is raised from the floor level, like the fly gallery. Present theatre construction is placing the lighting control system at the rear of the auditorium along with sound and motion picture control. Front-of-house control makes for easier cueing and communication.

Portable Switchboard. A board mounted in a box that is equipped with casters so it can be moved from place to place. Most productions use their own portable switchboards and attach them to the company switch for current. The house switchboard usually handles the auditorium or house lights and sometimes the foots and overhead lights.

Dimmer. The mechanical object or electronic resistor that regulates the flow of current and thereby varies the intensity of light coming from a lighting instrument. Dimmer systems may be operated directly or through remote control. Various types are in use including the plate, slide reactor, variable transformer, and the electronic. Theoretically there should be a dimmer for each switch on the board, but usually there is only a limited number. In this case the electrician can connect those lights which require dimming and leave others constant.

Master Control. The handle or button that controls the series of individual light switches or dimmers which have been interlocked mechanically or electrically to act as one unit.

Grand Master. The dimmer control handle or switch that controls the entire set of lights in the switchboard.

    a. Terminology.

        i. Dim down. Take light down on dimmer, usually to a determined intensity.

        ii. Dim up. Take lights up on dimmer.

        iii. Fade-outs. The gradual elimination of all light on the stage by means of dimmers; differs from black-outs in that it is gradual.

        iv. Black-out. An immediate switching off of all lights. Used mostly in revues, it may also be used in plays when all the lights in a room are switched out by an actor.

House Lights. All lights in the auditorium except the exit lights. House lights should always be in control from the switchboard and not from anywhere else. They should be on dimmers.

Work Lights. Lights used solely for illuminating the stage when it is not being watched by an audience, as at rehearsals and when scenery is being shifted. They are also lights behind the setting for the stagehands, who otherwise would have to work in the dark. Work lights should be special lighting equipment; if the stage it not equipped with them, border lights are used for work lights.

Emergency Lights. All lights used to light the stage and auditorium as well as at exits in case of an emergency such as fire or failure of the regular service. Usually they have their own generating power, separate from the general source. They should not be all attached to the switchboard but should be near it to be controlled by the electrician. The stage manager should see that the electrician tests them before every performance.

Sound Control. The center for control of sound amplification and music and sound effects recorded on tape and records. Amplified sound is effective for many performances, particularly musicals, depending on the size and acoustics of the auditorium.

Property Table. Property tables are placed right and left stage or at a position advantageous for distribution of "props" to the actors as they need them. Actors must return all props to the prop table within reason of performance demands. Properties are distinguished according to their use:

    a. Personal—articles of personal use particular to the character.

    b. Hand—articles which the actor handles.

    c. Set—articles and objects on the stage floor such as furniture, tree stumps, and so on.

    d. Trim—articles which add to the decor of the set—curtains, pictures on walls, and so on.

Dock. The place where old scenery is stored and often painted, frequently a far corner of the stage. In winter and summer stock and repertory theatres it is usually in a separate shed or addition to the main stage.

Paint Frame. A frame into which scenery is fastened for painting. It may be stationary and require ladders for the scene painter to mount in order to reach the various heights, or it may itself be movable up and down through a slot in the floor, thus allowing the painter to remain on the floor. Its placement is similar to the scene dock.

Loading Door. The large double door through which scenery is brought onto the stage from the outside. It always opens directly from the stage onto an alley that should be large enough to admit large trucks or vans.

Stage Exit. There will always be a door leading from the stage to the outside corridor and to the stairs leading up to the dressing rooms and to the back outside door of the theatre known as the stage door. It is used by the actors and the crew and all people dealing with these two groups. By this door there should always be an emergency light which is lit during performances.

Call Board. A bulletin board located backstage and near the stage door, on which are posted important notices for actors, including rehearsal calls, rules of the company, the next booking date, time and place of departure, hotels and rates, and so forth.

Stage Dressing Room. Many stage fire laws prohibit the opening of the dressing rooms onto the stage, because in case of fire the actors would be trapped and unable to escape. Accordingly, actors must go out into the corridor to get to dressing rooms. However, there is likely to be one dressing room (especially if there is a second door for escape and if it can have a fire door) leading directly from the stage. If these two conditions are not possible, there is certain to be one dressing room at the entrance to the corridor. In either case this is the stage dressing room, and it is not used regularly by any one member of the cast, but by whoever during the course of the action of the play has to change his costume quickly. It is fully equipped. If nobody has a quick change, it may be used by the star, although often the star's dressing room is equally convenient.

Quick-change Room. If there is not a stage dressing room leading offstage where an actor may change his costume in less time than it takes for him to go to his own, the crew will erect a small one with flats. Props will place chair, table, mirror, and clothes hangers in it.

Green Room. The resting and reception area for actors, usually immediatley accessible from backstage.

The Interior Set

Plot. A layout and schedule of sequence of particular objects, occurrences, or specifications in connection with a performance—for example, scene plot, property plot, light plot, and sound plot. The stage manager prepares these plots for the different heads of departments.

Floor Cloth. A canvas cloth is used to cover the wooden surface of the stage floor to deaden the sound of leather heels on wood between the places where rugs are placed, and in exterior scenes. Traveling companies carry their own cloth, and the first thing done in erecting the stage is to put it in place. It is tacked down and should be stretched very tight. It is usually light tan but for special productions it is painted to represent grass, cobblestones, etc.

Sometimes such a cloth is not used in one- and two-set living room productions, but in its place a soft carpeting covers the entire floor space within the set and a few feet beyond it offstage.

The floor cloth or carpet should not be so large as to cover the floor pockets offstage. The floor cloth is often called the ground cloth or stage cloth.

Set. The complete arrangement of the scenery with its accompanying properties and lights. *To set* is to place the scenery, properties, and lighting equipment in position on the stage; one says "the stage is to be set up" or "the stage is set."

Set Height. The average living-room set has a height of twelve to fourteen feet.

R1, R2, and R3. The lettering in chalk on the back of flats for those which are being set up on the right side of the stage. R1 is the one set farthest downstage and next to the tormentor.

L1, L2, and L3. The lettering on flats on stage left.

C1, C2, and C3. The markings on the flats to be set up along the rear forming the rear wall. C1 is the first flat on the stage right. The lettering of flats varies somewhat according to the specifications particular designers or stage carpentry shops may prefer.

Flat. The basic unit of scene construction; a wooden frame, reinforced and covered with canvas or muslin. The canvas is glued and tacked to the width of the frame, not over the edges. The height varies from nine feet in small theatres to fourteen or sixteen feet in regular professional theatres to twenty or twenty-two feet for special productions. The average width is five feet nine inches, because this just allows a flat to be loaded into a box car for road travel. Flats may also be made of aluminum or pipe framing covered with plastic sheeting. A flat is made of: *stiles*, the vertical members; *rails*, the bottom and top crosspieces; and the *togglebar*, any supporting crosspiece of a flat other than the top and bottom rails.

Two-fold. Two flats hinged together so as to stand alone.

Door Flat. A flat containing an opening into which the door frame with the door is inserted; a sill or saddle iron spans the opening to keep the legs of the flat from bowing.

Fireplace Flat. A flat containing a low opening for the recess of a fireplace.

Plug. A piece of scenery that is inserted into an opening of a unit such as an arch, window, or door to effect a change in function.

Fireproofing. A chemical-compound component that makes scenery, curtains, drops, and the like uninflammable. Materials fireproofed will burn when brought into direct contact with flame, but the flame will not travel along the fireproofed surfaces by itself. Fireproofing is required by law of all scenery, curtains, etc.

Corner Block. A triangle of three layers of wood, glued together with the grains placed alternately at right angles to each other. They are used to reinforce the corners and joints of flats: a *keystone*-shaped block is used to reinforce a butt joint. The nails used, called *clout nails,* are made of soft iron that can be easily clinched.

Loose-pin Hinge. A hinge from which the pin may be removed to separate the two parts. It is used almost exclusively on the stage, not only for doors but when flats are hinged together.

Lash Lines. The sash cord attached near the top on the right-hand side on the back of the flats which allows them to be lashed together. The *lash-line cleat* is an iron attached to the flat about three feet from the floor on both the right and the left sides. There is also a third cleat on each flat on the left side, just below where the sash cord is attached on the right. The cord of one flat is hooked over this upper cleat of another flat and laced tightly to the lower one alternately so that when tied the two flats will be held firmly together.

Battening Flats. Nearly always the flats along the rear wall are not only lashed tightly together, supported by stage braces, but also battened together. They are laid face down side by side on the stage floor, and one batten is laid across the top and one along the bottom and nailed. Each flat is then fixed firmly to the batten, making the rear wall steady and lessening the possibility of cracks between the flats. Then the whole rear wall may be flown as a single unit.

Stiffeners. The wooden battens that steady a section of flats. They are nailed as previously mentioned or are held in place by hooks designed for the purpose.

Dutchman. A strip of canvas tacked and glued across the crack between two flats on their front surface and painted the color of the set. This makes the rear wall look solid and prevents the outline of the flats from being evident to the audience. It is also a strip of black or dark cloth tacked across the crack between two flats in the back or behind the crack of an opened door so light will not "spill" through; also called a *stripper.*

Jigger. A wooden dutchman inserted between two hinged flats of a three-fold, which makes it possible to fold the three flats together so that they can be moved and stacked easily.

Stage-brace Cleat. A metal cleat having an eye in one end in which the hook of a stage brace can be caught. It is attached to the frame of the back side of the flat just above the middle.

Stage Brace. A hardwood brace of adjustable length with a hook on one end for fastening to the eye in the stage-brace cleat on the back of a flat, and an iron with a hole in it at the other. Through this a stage screw is put and screwed into the stage floor. Thus door frames are steadied so as not to shake when the door is closed. High flats which are joined by lash lines are also supported by stage braces.

Stage Screw. A sharp screw fitted with a handle, used as a means of fastening the stage brace into the stage floor.

Jack. A triangular brace hinged or nailed to a piece of scenery to support it.

Thickness Piece. That portion of a window, door, or arch frame which recedes in or back and thereby becomes the thickness of the wall; also a one-foot-wide flat used to project on stage.

Jog. A term also used for the above one-foot flat. Also it is used as a verb to denote such a treatment of setting up scenery as when one flat of any size juts out at approximately a right angle to the perpendicular flat going upstage. Jogging the set includes a series of such setting up.

Flipper. A small scenery flat hinged to another flat.

Rake. A convention of long standing, now frequently discarded, allows the side walls of a set to slant slightly in toward the center of the stage. This enables the upstage entrances to be in better view from the sides of the auditorium. The rake is the angle at which the side walls come on the stage from the tormentor, or proscenium arch.

Backing. A drop or flat used behind an opening in the set as in a door, an arch, or a window; also called a window backing, door backing, sky backing, or hall backing. Sometimes it is very elaborate, as in the case of a full drop when seen through French windows. More often it consists of two small flats, hinged together and painted a neutral color, which are placed for backing behind a door.

Masking and "To Mask Off." A backing or other piece of scenery set in such a way as to prevent the audience's seeing backstage through an opening. Its meaning is made clear in this statement: "The backing doesn't mask." It is used in connection with door backings as well as drops.

Backwall. Rear wall of stage proper or of setting.

Drop. A piece of scenery made of canvas or muslin fastened to battens at top and bottom, hung in the flies to be lowered or "dropped" into position for a scene. It is painted with perspective or a plain sky color. In the older theatres scenes were played before a drop. Today drops are used almost solely as back-drops, hung far upstage usually on the last set of line, and have the distant landscape painted on them. They are the backing seen through French windows, over a wall or balcony in an exterior set, and so on.

Ceiling. The scenery unit of wooden frame and painted canvas that rests upon the side and rear flats of a box set to represent the ceiling of the room. This unit should be painted light neutral gray or tan. The ceiling is hung on two sets of lines, one back and one forward. It must be hung so that the downstage edge is close to the teaser and so that the people in the front row in the audience do not see up into the flies. When a ceiling is hung in the flies, the front row of lines is detached. The ceiling is usually the first piece of scenery rigged; in a setup, however, it is the last piece of scenery to be lowered into position.

Ceiling Plate. A metal plate with a ring screwed to the battens of a ceiling for flying.

Sightlines. The line of sight from the sides of the auditorium and from the top of the balcony will determine the size and playing area of the stage visible from all parts of the auditorium.

Fourth Wall. The imaginary side of the room toward the audience. It has theoretically been removed so that the spectators may look in.

Lighting

We have already placed the footlights. In addition, the most important lighting equipment and terminology are:

Layout. The distribution of the various pieces of electrical equipment for a particular production laid out in working drawings and specifications.

Light Area. Generally speaking, the spot on the stage that will be covered by two spotlights hitting from right and left. The imaginary interior set that we have been discussing will have approximately six light areas—three downstage and three up. They are usually numbered as follows: 1 is DL; 2 is DC; 3 is DR; 4 is UL; 5 is UC; 6 is UR. On a large full set, especially an exterior, there will be nine areas. Each of these should have two spotlights covering it.

Spotlight. The general terminology for all single lights that direct a ray of light to a designated spot or area. They contain high-powered incandescent or quartz lamps of 500, 1000, and 1500 watts and in a hood that can be tilted at any angle. The more efficient instruments are equipped with ellipsoidal reflectors that throw light up to 150 feet.

Baby Spot. A small spotlight containing a 250-watt bulb and having the other equipment of a spotlight. Baby spots are ordinarily used to cover special small areas on the stage from a distance of some 20 feet.

Hood. The large metal receptacle of the light instrument housing the lamp.

Lamp. A general term used for a single electric light bulb. Lamps vary from 50 watts for the footlights to 5000 watts in the larger spotlights. The brightest source for projection instruments is the Xenon bulb.

C-clamp. A clamp used to attach a lighting instrument to a pipe batten.

Gator and Gaffer Grips. Sawtooth clamps for attaching lighting units to doors, shelves, and so on.

Lens. An optical glass that is used to gather or disperse by refraction rays of light that pass through it; an essential element of a spotlight. Spotlights with stepped lens throwing a soft-edged beam of light are called *fresnels.*

Gelatin. The color medium placed in frames for lighting equipment such as flood and spotlights. It is a thin sheet of glutinous substance colored with aniline dye.

Cinemoid. A more durable fire-resistant plastic material used as a color medium to filter light; colored glass can also be used, but it is not obtainable in a wide range of colors, and there is danger of breakage.

Shutter. Shutters are metal flippers, mats, irises, or any other means of cutting off entirely or in part the light from an electrical instrument. They are mounted on the outside of the instrument in front of the lens. The stage areas covered from a spotlight will be approximately a sixth of the average playing space. By means of shutters it can be narrowed from a full spread down to an area the size of a face. The latest ellipsoidal lighting instruments incorporate the shutter system and are designed to frame areas, project patterns, and help create special effects.

    a. *Barn Door.* A shutter unit placed immediately in front of the lens to shape the beam of a spotlight.

    b. *High Hat or Stove Pipe.* A cylindrical unit used with spotlights to minimize spill light and make the beam more defined.

    c. *Snoot.* A cone-shaped unit attached to the front of a lens, used to restrict the area of coverage for highlights, "pools of light," or eye sparkle.

Gobo. An assembly used for masking flares or spills from the lighting instrument.

Cable. Rubber- or fiber-insulated wires carrying electric current from the switchboard or from the floor pockets to the fixtures to a given source. Actors should be careful to avoid tripping on them both off and on the stage. Stage managers should see to it that the cable to a lamp onstage is not exposed by having a small rug put over it.

Pin Connector. A two- or three-prong fiber connector used to join cables and lighting instruments. The improved *lock connectors* are now preferred over the pin connectors. For safety precautions the ends of cables using pin connectors should be tied in a knot when joining the pieces. *Floor plugs* are the connectors to floor pockets.

Tormentor Lights. The electrical equipment, either a stand with a spotlight or a strip of lights, placed directly behind the tormentors. Usually the flats of a set are lashed to the tormentor, which obviously eliminates the use of these lights. Frequently, however, they are not, but the downstage end is placed directly back of the tormentors to allow for these lights. In exterior scenes such lights are almost always used.

X-ray Border. A row of lamps in reflector sections usually suspended from a border batten on the first lines downstage to light the acting areas. There are usually six to twelve units in a section, and each section is wired for two, three, or four colors. The metal hood in which the reflector units are mounted is equipped with color-frame slides for each compartment.

Fluorescent Lighting. A cool, high-efficiency light source adaptable for general lighting primarily. It disperses an even intensity of low-brightness light over a wide area with a minimum of shadow.

Balcony, Booth Spotlight, or Front Lighting. Several large spotlights covering the stage areas and placed in front of the balcony or in the projection booth in the auditorium. Together with spots place in the box-tester light bridge or near the X-ray border they cover all stage areas. X-rays and foots blend and tone these area lights into an evenly lighted stage. Sometimes there are openings in the ceilings of auditoriums that allow for additional front lighting. These are called *beam lights* or *ceiling lights.*

Back Lighting. Lighting from rear and above an element to give it highlights and a sculptured quality.

Backing Strip. A small portable strip of light equipment hung by doors or in front of all backings. It contains low-wattage lamps and furnishes a diffused light for the backing. Actors should be careful not to stand in front of these, thereby casting a shadow while they are waiting to enter.

Floodlight or Flood. A lighting instrument composed ·of a metal hood that contains several low-wattage lamps or one large one without lens. It is shaped to throw a strong flood of light on broad surfaces like backdrops or entrances from close range. It is sometimes hung and sometimes used on a stand.

Scoop. A floodlight with variable focus from medium beam to wide for a 10-foot to 20-foot throw using 1500-watt to 2000-watt quartz lamps.

Olivette. The old-fashioned inefficient floodlight.

Special. A spotlight focused so that it covers a special person or an area in which important or emphatic action takes place. It may be referred to as *door special, chair special, throne special,* and so forth. It gives special and added illumination to the important and much-used area.

Ultraviolet Lights. Special equipment used in conjunction with special fluorescent paints, make-up, or materials to produce the familiar black-light effects.

Strobelight. A special lighting instrument producing intense pulsating light used for slow-motion effects and psychedelic lighting. The rate of flashes can be controlled.

Color Wheel. A rotating disc with different colored gels attached to a spotlight. It can be operated manually or by remote control at varying speeds.

Polarized Light. Light that passes through a filter that allows only the light rays traveling along the same path to pass through. Some effect machines use polarized light to project kaleidoscopic colored images.

Light Bridge. A long, narrow platform suspended by adjustable lines directly over the inner proscenium opening or any other portion of the stage. On this are placed the spotlights for the upstage areas, special spots, and so on. One or two operators adjust the focus of the spots and change gelatins for the different acts. Because of the steady rise in salaries of union labor, it is common practice to use more lamps previously set and angled for successive scenes; also known as a *catwalk.*

Boom, Boomerang, or Tower. A mounting for spots and floods allowing instruments to be set one above the other; used for side lighting and back drops.

Pantograph. A suspension system for the counterbalanced raising and lowering of lighting units.

Follow Spot. A carbon arc or electric spotlight giving a high-intensity beam mounted with special equipment so that an operator can direct the beam of light in narrow or wide flood focus in any direction and thereby accompany an actor in his various movements over the stage; used in musical comedy mostly but also in productions of certain plays for highlighting effect.

Remote Control Color Changers and Spotlights. Control devices allowing use of various colors to be placed in spotlight beam by remote control and allowing positioning and varying spotlight distribution with dimming and irising all by remote control.

Revolving Batten. A lighting batten supporting a four-sided magazine compartment containing color media, frosts, reflectors, and so forth, and wired in circuits to allow for changes of lighting by revolving unit according to plot. Units can be operated electrically or mechanically.

Cross-Connect Unit. A distribution unit which carries power, signals, or both from the controls to the lighting equipment. They permit one or more lighting instruments to be connected to any control circuit.

Preset Panel. A system of calibrated devices allowing the storage of complete lighting cues for one scene or more. These preset devices are hand-set to match the desired circuit reading across the board for each total lighting cue. Electronic dimmer control works through the control console.

Backstage Terminology

We now come to terminology used for cues, rehearsals, calls, and the removal of one set and setting up of another.

Cue. Any word, speech, move, sound, or light that is a predetermined signal to an actor or stagehand to perform a subsequent function in connection with the performance.

Cue Sheet. A tabulation of all the stage manager's responsibilities for sound, entrances of actor, change in lights, and so on. Often this is not a separate sheet but is simply represented by blue-penciling in the prompt copy. Every actual cue should have a warning cue.

Sides. Bound half-pages containing all of an actor's lines with short lead-in cues.

Stand-by. A term meaning to be ready to perform an act as soon as the cue comes. A stage crew stands by to strike a set. An actor stands by to take a curtain call. The term is also used for an actor who, though not performing, covers an important role and is ready to perform the part in the event of an emergency. An *understudy* differs from a standby in that he is performing in a minor role while understudying one or more other roles.

Tag Line. An actor's line of speech at the close of a particular climax or situation that succinctly points up or comments on the preceding speech or situation.

Curtain Line. The last line of a scene or act spoken by an actor before the curtain comes down.

Take five or *Take a Break.* Permission from the stage manager to stop a rehearsal and relax for a few minutes.

Take a Call. This term is used when an actor comes before the audience and bows.

Act Call or *"Places."* The signal given by the stage manager to summon the actors to the stage to begin an act. It is the signal in the foyers, lobbies, lounges, and so forth, of the theatre announcing that an act is about to begin. It is rung by the stage manager, generally two minutes before the rise of the curtain.

Dry up. To forget lines.

Dress the Set. To add decor to a setting.

Clear Stage. A command given by stage managers to all stagehands and actors, not including those who begin or open the scene, to leave the stage and to take with them all tools and appurtenances that do not belong onstage at opening of scene.

Heads Up. A warning phrase that an object is falling or being lowered from above. When called, each person on the stage should stop and look up to see whether or not he is in danger. The lowering of a drop or any object or piece of scenery from the flies demands this call.

Spike. To mark the position of a piece of scenery or property. Temporary markings are made with chalk or masking tape. Different color spike marks are used to distinguish one scene setup from another. Usually fluorescent tape is used when shifts are made during blackouts.

Strike. The call the stage manager gives for the stage crew to clear the set already standing. If it is between acts, it includes the setting up of the next set. If it is the end of the play, it means to strike and clear the stage. It includes the striking of all scenery, properties, and lights. The call "Strike" is also used for the removal of a single object; for example, "Strike that chair."

Shift. The process of striking and setting up the scenery, properties, and lighting equipment. The procedure for the shift is given in full later. Also used for changing position of a single object; for example, "shift the sofa."

Snatch Basket. Any kind of hand basket used by a prop man to gather small props during a shift.

Run. A synonym for sliding, as running a flat across the floor to its setup place or its pack; also to run a piano off the stage.

Kill. To eliminate a piece of scenery or property from a set; sometimes in dress rehearsals to take it permanently from the set, other times to remove it only from the immediate setting. In reference to light instruments, it means to turn the light off, either permanently or temporarily.

Breakaway. A property or part of a setting constructed in such a way as to break apart on cue.

Pack or Scene Pack. Flats stacked face to face or back to back against the wall of the stage. The tilt of a flat should be as slight as possible to keep it from falling back, because stacking it at a decided angle with the weight of others on it warps and bends it permanently. Great care should be taken in stacking the scenery of the second and third acts before the performance begins so that the center flat of the rear wall is at the bottom of the stack nearest the wall. Next to these are flats on the right and left of the center, then the flats on the upstage right and left, until the top flats, or the first ones that the carriers come to, are those which are to be lashed to the left and right tormentors.

Live Pack. A set which is yet to be used even though it has already been used once in the performance.

Dead. Scenery and properties that are of no further use in a performance. Those appurtenances which are not to be used after an act that is over are said to be dead. The pile of scenery that is stacked and not used again is known as the *dead pack* or *stack*.

The Exterior Set

We shall now define those parts of stage equipment which occur more often in an exterior set.

Wing. A flat set at either side of the stage parallel to footlights at intervals approximately seven feet back of each other so that backstage is not disclosed to the audience. For interiors wings are no longer used, but for exteriors they still remain the most satisfactory way to mask off the sides of the stage. Wings are marked R1, R2, etc., and L1, L2, etc., with 1 being the downstage, or first, wing. Most stages do not require more than three wings to mask the sides.

They formerly were set in grooves. Today they have a return on the offstage end that allows them to stand by themselves. This helps to mask the open spaces between them from the front seats of the auditorium.

Spot- and floodlights are usually placed behind the wings.

Wood wings have an irregular outer edge of profile board to simulate tree trunks. Occasionally there will be an opening in them to represent further the realism of the space between the trees or its branches.

Border. A painted stretch of canvas attached to the batten lowered from the flies, usually about three to four feet deep and running the entire width of the stage. Today no first-class theatre uses such a thing for a ceiling, although originally this was the accepted convention. In exteriors, however, borders are necessarily used to mask the flies from the first rows. The sky border is painted blue. Borders are placed directly in front of the wings and spaced at about seven-foot intervals to mask. First border, second border, and so on refer to positions from front of stage with first border being closest to act curtain.

Foliage Border or Cut Border. A border made of canvas or similar materials, the lower parts of which are cut following an irregular design, generally to represent tree branches or foliage. Theatrical net is attached to the cut edges to keep the irregular cut parts in position.

Border Light or Strip. A long trough of low-wattage lights almost as long as the acting stage is wide. It is suspended by lines from the gridiron. Placed usually behind each border, it lights the upstage areas. The average number for a stage is four.

Strip Lights. A general term applied to a row of low-wattage bulbs mounted in a long metal hood. They are used in many places, as for border or tormentor and sometimes ground row. They produce a generally shadowless illumination in a range of color and serve as a supplementary role to spotlights for toning and blending.

Spotlight Strip. A row of baby spotlights mounted on a frame and hung on a batten. Some productions use it instead of X-rays. It also takes the place in exterior scenes of the strip light in the borders.

Set Piece. Door frames, arch frames, mantelpieces, stairs, platforms, windows, and other heavy architecturally built objects are known as set pieces. They fit into scenery and are often used with draperies or a cycorama for a set.

Exterior sets use the exterior cyc and wings and then add fences, walls, pumps, mounds, trees, ramps, steps, and so forth, for their set pieces.

Leg Drop. Made of one or more vertical strips of canvas, with battens at top and bottom, it is used for cutouts and tree trunks.

Grass Mats. A canvas or burlap backing to which is sewed or glued artificial material that fairly resembles grass and is painted green. Grass mats are often used just offstage by the exterior door of an interior set and almost always in exterior sets, especially around the foot of trees to cover the break between the tree and the stage floor.

Ramp. The sloping part of a platform that gradually rises from the stage floor to a level. A mound or walk up a cliff is technically referred to as a ramp rather than by the name of the object it represents.

Levels. Platforms designed by one, two, or three steps, constructed of a hinged framework that closes up flat and has a flat, detachable top.

Parallel. A platform support that folds up for easy storage and transportation.

Practical. Anything used for its true functional purpose—as opposed to ornament —for example, scenery built solidly so that is can stand the weight of the actors and be used by them to sit or stand on. *Nonpractical* is the reverse of this insofar as a flight of steps or rocks or tree stump or mound may look solid but is constructed so that it may not hold average weights. Sometimes a set piece will be partially practical and partially nonpractical; for instance, a hillside ramp will have parts on which an actor can walk or sit and some parts that must be avoided. The same is true of rocks on a stage. Practical also refers to windows that work, light switches that operate lights, and so on.

Ground Row. A piece of scenery, usually long and low, representing the distant perspective of mountains, hills, and so forth, placed in front of the backdrop or cyclorama in order to complete the exterior set and to mask the horizon cyc lights—practically another name for cutout.

Cutout. A piece of flat scenery having an irregular outside edge, usually made of profile board, representing distant objects. Cutouts are usually larger than ground rows since they often represent nearer objects such as houses, wharves, and trees. They serve the same purpose in exterior scenes and are often used as backings for windows in interior sets.

Ground-row Strips. These strips of lighting equipment are placed in front of the ground row to help give a greater sense of distance and perspective. Accordingly, low-wattage lights are used.

Cyclorama or Cyc. A smooth curved surface of canvas or other material, generally used as a sky backing for the scenery. In the best theatres in recent years it has taken the place of the original backdrop. Cyclorama may also mean any set of curtains or draperies enclosing the scene on three sides.

Cyclorama Screen. A sky backing of translucent material that allows for rear projection of images as visual effects or projected scenery.

Cyclorama (or Cyc) Lights. Strips or row or lights that illumine the cyclorama. Those at the bottom are designated as horizon lights, those at the top as cyc overheads.

Linnebach Projector. A large lantern for projecting the image from a slide onto a large drop, cyc, or set. This image becomes part of the setting.

Effect Machine. An electrical instrument, with a clock or motor mechanism, which projects images in movement on the backdrop or gauze drop. Snow, rain, clouds, rippling water, and fire can be represented.

All offstage or onstage sound machines, and so on, are also called effect machines. Common ones include:

a. Thunder Sheet. A three-foot-wide and from six- to twelve-foot-long sheet of common or galvanized iron from sixteen to twenty-four gauge or a sheet of laminated profile board of the same size. The depth of tone depends on the size of the sheet. It is hung up and either shaken by hand or beaten with a padded hammer.

b. Wind Machine. A wooden drum or cylinder revolved by a crank under a tightened layer of canvas.

c. Glass Crash. A wooden box or a bag filled with odds and ends of broken glass and bottles, shaken to represent the offstage noise of broken glass; a *crash box.*

d. Snow Machine or Cradle. A cloth canopy with holes hung behind a border. Confetti or similar material filters through the holes when the cradle is shaken or swayed slowly; also used for falling leaves and blossoms.

e. Rain Machine. A revolving drum or barrel covered with screening and turned by a crank. Dried peas or beans falling inside produce the effect of rain.

f. Smoke Pot. A unit enclosed in a metal box complete with leads and connector. When used with smoke powder it produces a chemical smoke. A similar unit may also be used with flash powder to produce a flash of light and puff of smoke for theatrical effects.

Tower. A high stand or platform of wood or steel with one or more levels on which to place powerful spotlights. It is upstage right or up left or behind the tormentors, according to its use, and it will contain instruments to simulate sunrise, sunset, moonlight, and so on.

Gauze or Scrim. A large, seamless transparent mesh curtain, generally stretched tight between top and bottom battens. It is used for special effects such as "visions" when lit from behind; lit from front it has an illusion of solidity. It can be plain or painted; sometimes it is used in back of stage and in front of cutouts and painted drops in order to make them seem more distant, more blended, and more real.

Old Terms

Now and then one will hear in the theatre a few terms and descriptions of former days.

Tab. The tab curtain was far downstage next to the act drop. It was used as a background in burlesque and vaudeville houses for a single or duo act performed on the apron while the next setting was being prepared. Today it is made of the same material as the act curtain and furnishes a backing when the latter is drawn aside for the actors to take a bow. It allows for a change of scenery the moment the act curtain is lowered.

Prompter's Chalk. A warning line painted or chalked on stage floor offstage to mark limit of sightlines before coming in view of the audience.

"In One," "In Two," "In Three." Phrases used to design the hanging of a drop. They refer to the distance back from the act drop and coincide with the placement of the wings. "In one" would mean a drop on lines directly in front of the first wing; "in two," the second wing; etc. The terms also specify that a scene is played below the set of wings and drops indicated.

Olio. Except in vaudeville houses this term is seldom used. It is the backing, flown halfway between "in one and in two," giving a greater space for the actor to perform than "in one" and yet not enough to prevent the setting of the next scene.

Rolled Curtain. A canvas drop usually covered with advertisements with a cylinder fastened along the bottom edge. A rope system rolls the cylinder, thus raising or lowering the curtain.

Front Scene. In the old drama a front scene was played before a painted drop; a full stage set was followed by a front scene with the drop as background. This was called "played as a front scene" or "played in one." Today this refers to a small box set in front of a full stage set, to which a later set returns.

Forms of Scenery

Different treatments of scenery and productions are ever appearing. The structural arrangement and handling of scenery and acting spaces are constantly widening in scope and possibilities. The more common ones should be recognized and known by the beginning director and actor.

Architectural Stage. The playing space with a permanent architectural composition, normally made up of steps, ramps, and platforms, that remains unchanged for different plays and scenes in plays. The description can also apply to the stages of the Greek, Roman, and Elizabethan theatres with their formal permanent constructions.

Box Set. The walls on three sides are filled with flats of one kind or another, with framed ceiling. Originally borders were used for the ceiling, but today a framed ceiling is in common practice.

Drapery Set. The entire acting area is surrounded with drapery used as borders, legs, traverse and diagonal curtains; the latter permit the stage to be sectioned off. This set is also used in conjunction with set pieces.

Permanent, Skeletal, or Multiple Set. Used in plays requiring settings in many different places. It consists of the main, practically constant, arrangement of flats and the insertion of various additional pieces, such as different-colored and architecturally constructed door frames, fireplaces, windows, and furniture, to change the locale of the setting.

Portal Set. The original portal entrances were two permanent side doors or arches, one on each side of the downstage areas. They were used in early theatres until the nineteenth century. In the modern theatre the portal set is one that has the same downstage flats throughout all settings of a production. By a change of the rear wall flats and the two upstage side-wall flats, the set takes on a wholly new aspect for the new scene.

Projected Scenery. Usually projected from the rear and used as a substitute for painted backdrops; background decor particularly in space staging.

Raked Stage Set. The raked stage, common in earlier theatres, is a permanent stage floor that slopes upward from the front edge of stage to the backwall. However, as an integral part of a set design, a raked stage may be built on top of the level stage floor or portions of it. As an element of design, raked stages vary in angle of pitch and direction according to the demands of stage action.

Revolving Stage Set. A large circular part of the stage floor which in its initial construction is equipped with machinery and propelled by a windlass below so that it may be revolved. Three and sometimes four sets can be erected on a revolving stage, which can revolve from one setting to another in a few seconds. The settings must be erected on it, before the play begins, in rotation, like the segments of a pie.

Recently, revolving stages have been set up in a regular stage floor, thereby slightly raising the floor of the revolving stage and becoming a circular platform on rollers. In this and in the sliding stage, the proscenium opening must have a slightly raised ramp to the floor of the platform to mask the rollers.

Sometimes the act curtain is lowered for the changes; at other times the change is made in darkness with music or stage noises to fill in the thirty-odd seconds that it takes to make the shift.

Sculptural Stage. Close in purpose to the architectural stage except that the playing areas are shaped and arranged in relation to the demands of the dramatic action of the play and for flexibility in lighting. The surrounding is usually neutral (cyc, bare walls, drapes) or in tune with the overall mood of the play.

Simultaneous Set. An arrangement of different settings in full view of audience simultaneously where actions of the play take place from one setting to another, not necessarily in sequence. It is a carryover from the mansions of the medieval era.

Sliding or Wagon Stage Set. A low platform mounted on rollers, running on tracks, as wide as the proscenium opening and large enough to contain a set. It rolls to either side of the scene so that with two sliding stages one may be used while the other is being set up, a quick change of scene will follow. Sometimes three wagons are used, the third coming in from the rear. The wagons may also scissor in—two platforms of length equal to the proscenium opening and of varying depths are pivoted at the downstage corners to affect change of scenery.

Space Stage. A completely open stage, bare or sculptural, where the primary feature is lighting controlled to pick out the significant actions staged in a void.

Unit Set. The unit set is very similar to the permanent set in that many of the flats stand throughout an entire performance. The change in place is made by rearranging the flats and set pieces and by adding new pieces and killing others.

Winged Set. As the term implies, the winged set is composed of wings, borders, and backdrop or cyc. It is the oldest form of scenery, developing as the stage did from the classical, formal, or permanent structure.

Design and Production Staff

Scene Designer. The person responsible for designing the physical setting, including the set and hand props, and for supervising their execution. Working with the director, costume designer, lighting designer, and technical director, he strives for unity in the production concept. With the director he discusses basic concepts, theatrical images, theme and viewpoint, style of production, scheme of production, mood and atmosphere, period, locale, space relationships, acting areas, entrances, levels, color and texture, and everything else involved with ground planning. Costume and lighting designers along with the technical director should be part of these preliminary discussions to resolve problems related to their areas. Budgets and working schedules should also be made firm then.

Costume Designer. The person responsible for designing all costumes and costume props and supervising all phases of acquisition and execution. He works in collaboration with the director and other designers. Particularly he discusses style of production, period, locale, seasons, mood, characterizations and character relationships, size and location of entrances, size and shape of furniture, levels, and steps. He considers the physical needs of actors. In preparing sketches and color plots he confers with the scene designer regarding set, drapery, upholstery colors and textures; with the lighting designer regarding gelatin colors; and with the director and stage manager regarding rehearsal costumes and costume props (purses, glasses, gloves, swords, canes, parasols, and so on).

Lighting Designer. The person responsible for the visual aspects of production. He works in collaboration with the other designers and the director. He is concerned with information relating to his area of responsibility: style of play and production, mood of play and of each scene, color schemes, atmospheres, motivated light sources, specifics of area lighting and effects, and technical considerations such as heights, trims, and masking.

Technical Director. The person responsible for planning, organizing, and supervising the production work. In consultation with the director and designers he develops a budget and work schedule. He supervises the implementation of the schedule by overseeing the construction, rigging, painting, and assembly of the set. He expedites drafting, orders materials, controls inventory of equipment and materials, keeps time records, and in general coordinates all aspects of production.

Shop Carpenter. A person directly responsible to the technical director, charged with constructing the production based on the draftings and construction drawings. He makes trial assemblies for all articulating units before forwarding the units to the painters.

Stage Carpenter. A person directly responsible to the technical director, charged with the preparation of the stage, including hanging, rigging, and final assembly of the set and fixed prop units. He supervises the running of the performances, which involves setting up, shifting, flying, and striking scenery, and operating other functioning parts including the act curtain.

Property Master. A person directly responsible to the technical director. His work is divided into two periods: planning and running the show. In the planning period he is in charge of procuring or constructing all set and hand properties, curtains, hangings, break-aways, lighting fixtures, and so on. When the show is running, he is in charge of the storage, placement for use by the actors, maintenance, striking, and setup of the props.

Other Staff Members. People involved in backstage operation and production include heads of drafting, costume construction, wardrobe, makeup, fly gallery, and special projects, along with the chief electrician and sound technician. The complexity of the physical production naturally determines the number of assistants and crew members for each department.

Company Crew. Each production that goes on the road travels with a crew that includes a stage carpenter, a *props,* an electrician, and sometimes a *sound man.* These must be union members. The carpenter is in charge of the whole production. He has the layout of the set and work with the house carpenter in the rigging and setting up of the production. The props attends to the hand props (objects used by the actors during the course of the play) and also organizes the grips who are to handle the furniture, all set pieces, rugs, floor cloth, levels, ramps, curtains, and so on. The electrician or *lights* attends to all lighting setup and electrical machines. The sound man takes care of the sound amplification and all sound and music effects. The props also attends to the trunks of the company, both personal (those collected and delivered to the hotels) and theatre (those collected and delivered to the dressing rooms). A commercial production may have a company crew to supplement the house crew.

House Crew. Theatres have a staff, or crew, of workers that consists of a stage carpenter, a property man, and an electrician. In addition to these chiefs there are a varying number of *grips,* or stagehands, who handle the scenery and the properties. Their number depends upon the stage union's decree as to how many *hands* it will take to "work" the show. Each of these chiefs has assistants.

Stage Management

Stage Manager. As his title implies, the stage manager is the person who is in complete charge of backstage, including the actors and the crews. He is at all times associated with the crews in the setting up of the production and in the running of a performance. He knows the entire production and possesses all layouts, plots, and cue sheets.

Since he has such responsibilities, it is difficult to enumerate completely his duties, especially as in all emergencies he is the one empowered to act.

Before rehearsals he assists the director in casting; he helps get the manuscript into condition; he obtains all records of the cast (telephone numbers, addresses, etc.); he checks with the Equity representative to see that all members of the cast are or will become Equity members; with the business manager he arranges for rehearsal halls, getting permits to use them and so on.

The stage manager should be present at all rehearsals. His duty is to lay out the floor plan of the set on the floor of the rehearsal hall; to arrange the rehearsal furniture and props for the directors; to attend to the posting of all notices, calls for rehearsals, and similar details; to keep the record of rehearsal time and cost of heat, light, doorman, and all such expenses of the rehearsal hall; to arrange for costume fittings with costume designer; to check actors who are to underdress for quick changes; to assign dressing rooms; to help the director plot rehearsals so that no time is lost during costume fittings; to make out these plots as rehearsal progresses; to spot properties, to keep a complete list of appointments, rehearsals, etc., for the cast, director, technicians, etc.; to follow closely all the business and instructions given by the director and to be able to take charge of rehearsals if he is called away; to keep the prompt script up to date in duplicate (this requires a lot of night work). If there are children in the cast, he obtains their permits; if fire or guns are used, he obtains permits. He arranges scenes that may be used for television, radio, and other publicity appearances. Larger productions may divide these many responsibilities between a production stage manager and a stage manager.

Assistant Stage Manager. The stage manager may have an assistant even though the production is a simple one. If it is elaborate scenically, he should have two. The duties of these assistants vary as the division of work varies with each particular production. Each accordingly should know all the duties of the stage manager, as he can never be certain what particular responsibility is going to be his. During rehearsals he instead of the stage manager may "hold the book." He may arrange the furniture. He may even work out sounds that are required during the course of the play. He must be ready to take care of the hundred and one details and to run the errands that are always necessary during rehearsals. He should be alert and quick to anticipate the opportunities of being useful to the stage manager and to the director.

Holding the Book. With a new play in rehearsal this is a highly responsible duty. During the early stages it consists of following carefully the script of the play; crossing out all lines that are cut; adding any new ones; writing in all business and positions onstage that the director gives the actors. For these directions the abbreviations that have been given and used in the exercises under Stage Positions should be used. In addition to the directions the stage manager will also draw, on the right-hand margin of the script, small ground plans, signifying the positions of the characters on the stage. Further involved crosses and movements will be diagrammed. The book holder should check in some way the pauses in or between speeches so that he will not prompt when the actor is pausing deliberately. The sign "—" is suggested for this.

When the business has been set and the actors know their lines, prompting begins. A good prompter is quick to give the cue, often sensing the hestitation even before the actor actually "goes up" in his lines. This is especially demanded of the prompter during a performance. At rehearsals actors vary as to whether or not they wish to have a moment to think. Usually at the first rehearsals, during which they go without their parts, they do; but in the later rehearsals they will want the cue quickly. A prompter will do well to find out the actor's desires in this matter.

A prompter should never leave the book while the actors are rehearsing but take his rest while the actors and director are taking theirs.

The book holder will, during the first rehearsals, sit at a table downstage on the apron beside the director. As the play progessses in the rehearsal period and the business is set and the director is back in the house getting his "perspective" on the performance, the prompter will sit on stage right just above the tormentor. During the performance his position will vary as the set varies. He is usually at any downstage opening, behind the fireplace, a window, or a doorway. If possible, he should be downstage so that in prompting his voice will go upstage and not out into the audience.

The position from which the assistant stage manager is to prompt is known as the prompt side. It will vary between the acts of the same play, usually being placed on the side of the stage on which the longest scenes are to be played and in which there is the best opening. An actor should always know which the prompt side is, as it is not always coincident with the placing of the stage manager's box. The assistant stage manager usually prompts in a regular production during the first week of playing. If changes of script are being made, of course the prompting is continued until the play is set. Then it is unnecessary to hold the book except for noise and light cues. Occasionally a company will have an old actor who never is certain of his lines and who is likely to "go up" or "blow up" at a different place at any performance. When such is the case, the assistant stage manager should always stand with the script ready to prompt every scene in which that actor appears. The prompt book should be marked in such a way that scenes can be found quickly.

Technical Rehearsal. Before technical rehearsal the stage manager should arrange with the business manager the number of grips needed. Depending on arrangements made with the house, part of the technical staff may be furnished by the house, the remainder by the production. The stage manager must keep a record of the number of hours each man works.

Before technical rehearsal the stage manager should, with the assistance of the prop man, mark the positions of furniture on the ground cloth. These positions, of course, will already have been established by the director and scene designer. A different color or mark should be used for each new setup of furniture.

The stage manager supervises the technical rehearsal held exclusively for the crews to work out the routine of shifts, to work out sound effects, to set cues, and to perform other technical features of the production. He should be able to rely on the stage carpenter for working out the routine, but he must be able to suggest tactfully short cuts, time-saving moves, better routines, and so on. This also holds true for the property man and electrician.

Shift Routine. The following is a suggested routine for shifting from one interior to another:

The stage manager calls "Strike," claps hands, or makes some other pre-determined signal for the shift to begin. At his signal the flyman should raise the ceiling and then the backdrop. The stage crew should come onstage and remove the rear backing. Next, they should begin to strike the scenery, beginning at the center of the rear wall of the set, unlashing it and taking it over to a part of the stage that has been cleared for the purpose of stacking it. If it is battened, after the grips have unlashed each end the flyman will raise it into the flies. Then the grips will strike the sides of the set. At the call to strike, two of the props should begin to take the furniture away from the rear wall and draw it to the middle of the stage. Then they go to the side walls and draw furniture offstage only when the grips have removed the rear wall. They should be sure to have a place backstage cleared for receiving this furniture, and it is best to have it on the opposite side of the stage from where the scenery is being stacked.

An important factor in the quick changing of properties is to have second-act furniture placed near the space where the first act furniture is to be stored, so that when the props carry the furniture from the stage to the clear space ready to receive it they can quickly take a piece from the place allotted for the second act and bring it downstage center with them as they return. They continue this process until all the furniture is cleared from the first set and all the furniture for the second set is onstage.

The props who is handling the small props, or "trim," as soon as the call of strike is given, goes to the rear wall and removes anything on it that is to come off. He takes out, often in a basket specially provided for the purpose, the small, breakable knickknacks. When he has finished with the rear wall, he goes to the side walls for the same purpose, being careful to keep ahead of the grips in the shift. He carries these properties offstage and brings on the small properties for the second act. The props also shifts the rugs, set pieces, and levels. The light crew should remove cables in the way of shifts, lamps, and fire logs as well as changing gelatins and refocusing lights. The sound crew should remove their equipment of wires, speakers, and mikes immediately if they interfere with a shift. The stage manager should always remain downstage center through the entire shift.

When the crews have finished striking the side walls, they begin building up the second act set. They start at the tormentors and work toward the center of the rear wall. They can begin to build up the side walls almost immediately after they have struck the first act, but they must not put in the back wall until they make sure that all the large properties are onstage. From experience, however, we learn that they will seldom have to wait, because if the property people are taking off the old furniture and bringing on the new at the same time, they will have it all placed before the stage crew gets to the rear wall.

The grips, after they have completed the rear walls, put into place the backings for the doors and windows of the second act.

The props, as soon as the grips have put in the side walls, begins placing the furniture along those walls and dresses them with trim while other props set the mantels, doors, or windows.

As soon as the lights are set, the electrician reports to the stage manager; same with the sound man.

As soon as the walls of the set, ceiling, and backings are in place, the stage carpenter reports to the stage manager.

As soon as the properties are in place, the props makes his report to the stage manager. When the rear wall is finished, the props can put into place the properties that go on near it. The furniture in the middle of the room can be arranged at any convenient time during the shift. The flyman lowers the ceiling and then the backdrop.

Then the assistant stage manager checks up on all the hand props on stage and the exact placement of furniture on their markings. To save time, the assistant should check on these as they are being put in place.

When the set is an exterior, either to be set up or to be struck, the routine is similar although usually much simpler. The exterior set is usually made up of a cyclorama or backdrop.

The prop crew removes the furniture and set pieces through the back. They bring on through the rear the properties for the next act.

The grips remove the side wings.

The reversal of this process is used if the shift goes into another exterior. If the next scene is an interior, the process of setting it up as given above applies.

Dress Rehearsal. Before dress rehearsal and after he has consulted the producer or the company manager, the stage manager should post a list of the actors and the dressing rooms they are to use. The assignments he makes will depend on the importance of the actors and on their sex and age as well as on the position of the dressing rooms.

The stage manager should advise actors when they may bring their costumes and make-up to the theatre. He should advise the company manager which actors want trunks sent to the theatre.

The successful running of a dress rehearsal depends to a large degree on the stage manager. Careful organization, control, and a thorough knowledge of the production will do much in smoothing over the numberless problems that will arise.

The number of dress rehearsals will depend on the size of the production. The final dress rehearsal should function as a performance.

Performance Routine. The opening night is naturally filled with excitement and tension. It the backstage routine has been well organized during technical and dress rehearsals, much will have been done toward achieving a smoothly running technical production for the performance. This is conducive to a good performance by the actors. A carefully organized and smoothly running stage not only saves long waits between acts and unfortunate mishaps during the course of the play but also has an excellent effect on the actors. It puts confidence and stability into them, whereas confusion behind the scenes makes them more nervous, excitable, and uncertain.

The routine onstage during a performance is highly involved. Let us suppose that the performance begins at eight-thirty.

a. At seven-thirty, or at a time specified by the stage manager depending on the complexity of make-up, all the actors in the first act should be in their dressing rooms. Equity rule requires that all actors be checked in a half hour before curtain time. The stage manager will also check the stage and crew heads; see that the curtain operates; have a report from the electrician that all lights are in order and the same from the sound man.

b. The crews are setting the scenery for the first act. This may be true even if the production has only one set, since the fire laws of some states require the scenery to be struck between performances. No lights should be on except the work lights. The stage manager or his assistant should see that all people are kept off the stage.

c. At eight o'clock the assistant stage manager calls, "Half hour." At eight fifteen, he calls "Fifteen minutes." Then he should check up on all the properties on the stage. At eight twenty-five, he calls, "Act I," at which time all the actors should come down to the stage and make a definite report to the assistant stage manager that they are there. On this trip from the dressing rooms, he should recheck that the entire cast are present, no matter how late their entrance is in the play. The stage manager should signal the lobby and lounge bells that Act I is to begin.

d. The stage manager should give the cue to the electrician to light the stage.

e. The production is ready to begin. In many theatres, however, the stage manager has to await word from the house manager as to when he is to begin, because people may be coming in in such numbers that it would be unwise to ring up the curtain at that moment. However, the wait here should not be long, for it is bad for the actors and establishes a bad principle for the audience. The maximum time of waiting should be seven minutes after the scheduled time.

f. Word has now come back for the play to begin.

g. The stage manager calls, "Places."

h. The actors go on stage, and the prompter to his place.

i. The stage manager signals all heads involved in cues. He signals the electrician who brings up the front lights, if any, and lowers the house lights.

j. The stage manager then signals to the flyman to raise the curtain.

k. The play begins. On his time sheet the stage manager records the actual curtain time.

The time sheet is a printed form that the stage manager keeps in his box on which he records the actual time of the raising and lowering of the curtain for each act and scene. It gives, accordingly, the playing time of each act, and he and the producers can tell whether or not the company is dragging the performance. On this sheet is also a place to note the weather, a rough estimation of the size of the audinece, its reaction to the performance, and the number of curtain calls. Also there is a space in which to make any report to the management, as, for instance, lateness of an actor or a stagehand in arriving at the theatre or for a cue, other behavior out of the normal, complaints, and other matters.

This report is sent daily to the producer's office, whether the company is playing in New York or on the road.

l. During the course of the act, the stage manager and his assistant must see that there is absolute silence backstage and that actors do not stand around talking and making noise when they are not in the scene. One or the other must then get from the cue sheet or prompt book the noises for which he is responsible and be waiting for his cue. He must further check up with the electrician any cues that he may have and see that everything is done correctly on cue. He will also check with the sound man.

m. The assistant stage manager should see that the actors are ready for each of their entrance cues.

n. The prop man must be near his prop table to see that each person has his hand properties before he goes onstage.

o. Two minutes before the act is over, the stage manager should give a signal to the stage crew to stand by.

p. About eight speeches before the end of the first act, the stage manager should give a warning cue to the curtain man, the light man, and all others concerned. He records in his time sheet the time that the curtain falls. When the cue for the curtain comes, he gives the signal for its lowering.

Every curtain takes some time to lower. The director and stage manager should have gauged this carefully so that the cue for the curtain will produce the right dramatic effect. This avoids having the actors hold a forced position for any length of time after the last word while the curtain is being lowered. If the last words of an act are vitally important and the whole meaning of a part of the play depends upon the audience's getting them, the direcor should have planned business to follow these last words so that the actors can be following through as the curtain falls. In this case the curtain has the final word for its cue.

Even though curtain calls do not come at the end of our first act, the light man should be careful not to kill applause by bringing on the house lights too soon. He should wait until it begins to die down before bringing them on and should do so on cue from the stage manager.

q. The stage manager calls "Strike" whether or not there is to be a change of scenery and goes to the down center of the stage near the act curtain. The actors, as soon as they are through with this act, even those who do not have any change of costume, must leave the stage.

r. If it is a one-set play, the intermission is comparatively simple, as the props merely checks on the new properties required for the second act, and the lights make whatever changes they have for gelatins and readjust the focus of any instruments.

If there is a change, as soon as the curtain is lowered the stage manager calls "Strike," and all workers go into the regular shift routine, striking the first act and setting up the second. If the set is an interior, the procedure of the shift will be very similar to the one outlined under Technical Rehearsal.

s. The assistant stage manager two minutes before the end of the time allotted for the intermission calls the actors, who come at once and directly to the stage. The stage manager signals the lobby and lounge.

t. The actors get their hand props.

u. When the stage manager has received reports from the three technical heads, he calls, "Clear stage." All but the actors who are to open the scene leave the set at once, taking with them all tools and working materials.

v. The stage manager goes to his position, signaling the lights to bring up the footlights and lower the house lights.

w. The stage manager records the time.

x. He gives the signal for the curtain.

y. The second act has begun.

For the shift from second to third act, the same routine is followed.

The stage manager, usually in conjunction with the director or producer, decides the number of curtain calls and who is to take them. There will usually be two lists: curtain calls for the opening night and those for the entire run. These he will post on the call board. In stock companies a new order must go up each week.

After the performance the stage manager must mail his report to the producer's office.

After the show has opened, the stage manager on a designated morning each week must rehearse the understudies, going through the entire play. His assistants are usually understudies, besides other members of the company. Understudies must be present at each performance a half hour before curtain time and should stay until at least half through the performance. Some stage managers will require them to remain during the whole performance.

On long runs, the stage manager will periodically hold company rehearsals to keep up the playing of the cast, the timing, and actions or business that members of the cast may blur during a long run. The frequency of these company rehearsals depends on how well the cast keeps up the performance.

When a show closes or moves from one location to another, the stage manager must be present to supervise the work.

On the Road. When a company travels, the stage manager should know the rigging and handling of the sets, properties, sound, and lights, although the company carpenter actually superintends the rigging with the house carpenter, the props with the house props, sound with the sound engineer, and light with the house lights. However, the stage manager will find that most of this whole first day of each stand on the road will be spent in the theatre.

The advance man will already have arranged for the orchestra, the numbers, and so on, but the stage manager will arrange with the leader of the orchestra for the cues, volume, and other details.

The stage manager checks all material that arrives at the theatre and will post dressing-room assignments.

He also holds understudy and company rehearsals when on the road.

Appendix B

Exercises for Body, Voice, and Emotion

Bodily Responsiveness (see page 72)

Exercises in Relaxation
Relaxing the entire body:

1. Hold the body erect, arms over head, reaching as high as you can. Slowly bring the arms down, then drop the head, then the shoulders, then bend at the waist, then relax the knees until the body is hanging as much like a rag or bent-over scarecrow as you can make it. Then slowly straighten the knees and pull up the body as though a string were tied to a point between the shoulders, first straightening at the waist, then the shoulders, then slowly the head, leaving the arms hanging loosely at your sides. This exercise should be used not only during a practice period but at any time during the day when the body becomes tense.

2. Folding and unfolding. Hold the body erect, alert, the arms and hands reaching as high as possible above the head. Slowly relax the arms, dropping them to the sides on the count of five. As they pass the head, let it relax and drop slowly to the neck. Then let the shoulders go, then relax at the waist, the arms always leading the body as it folds down. Then soften the knees, drop on to one knee, on to both. Then fold the entire body up into as small a ball as possible on the floor. If this process has been properly followed, the body should be completely relaxed, and the position one of utter comfort. Hold this position for five counts, and then slowly unfold, reversing the process, the mid-point of the back below the shoulders leading up. First up with one knee, then with both, then straighten at the waist, pull up the shoulders; let the head come up last. No tension whatever should be allowed to come in the unfolding process, but the relaxation attained in folding should be kept throughout. Repeat, folding on the count of ten, holding five counts, unfolding on the count of ten. This exercise relaxes the body and then brings it into position in complete poise.

Relaxing different parts of the body:

1. For the head:

This exercise will be successful only if it is practiced with complete relaxation of the head, neck, and shoulders. The arms are permitted to hang normally at the sides. Drop the head on to the chest, then roll it around in a complete circle four times to the right and four times to the left. Then enlarge the movement to include the shoulders. Enlarge it still more so that the waistline becomes the pivot point. Then return to the second movement and finally to the head movement, bringing the head back into position.

2. For the torso:

(a) Stand with the feet set firmly but slightly apart. The knees should be kept flexible throughout this exercise, ready to give with the flow of movement. Now make an entire circle with a center point at the waist as pivot starting to the left, going as low as you can, then coming up to the right; reach as high as you can (the arms are free at the sides), and then make the same circle starting to the right. When the body is making the movement with ease and a strong flowing motion, let the arms follow through, but be careful that the body continues to lead, the arms merely carrying through the movement.

(b) Take the same circle on the diagonal, first with the body slightly turned to the left and the right foot forward and then with the left foot forward and the body turned to the right.

3. For the arms and legs:

(a) Whirl first the right and then the left arm in a circle, letting the movement come from the torso and be carried through the arm. Then let both arms follow through their circles at the same time. They should be completely relaxed, and the impulse of the movement should come from the shoulder.

(b) Let the arms hang loose at the sides. Start the left arm swinging slightly. Increase the movement until the swing goes through as large an arc as you can easily make with the arm relaxed. Gradually decrease the arc until the arm hangs easily at the side again. Repeat with the right arm. All this movement should come from the shoulder.

(c) Stand with the weight on the right foot; start the left leg swinging like a pendulum, at first slightly and then increase the motion. Be careful that no strain slips into this movement and that it is kept a free and easy swing from the hip. Increase the movement as much as you can easily, and continue until the leg seems to swing of itself. Then slow down the movement, and stop it easily. Repeat with the right foot and leg.

(d) Stand with the weight on the right foot, the left leg hanging freely but not raised so that there is any strain on it. Shake the leg, then just from the knee, then just the foot itself, then the entire leg again. Drop it easily to the ground, change the weight, and repeat with the right leg, knee, foot, and leg. During this exercise the rest of the body should be relaxed, and no tension should come into the shoulders, neck, or any other part of the torso. It is best to keep the head poised and not look down at the leg.

4. For the hands:

(a) Shake the hands one at a time, letting the movement come through the arm from the shoulder so that the hands themselves are completely relaxed. Then shake them together. Then move the fingers as rapidly as you can, one after the other, as though you were touching the strings of a harp. Be sure that you bend each finger at every joint with each movement. Keep the hands relaxed throughout, then go back to the shaking movement; shake them as hard as you can, and then drop them easily at your sides.

(b) Imagine that a heavy, but very soft, velours curtain is hanging before you. Reach as high as you can, and bring the hands down the curtain, feeling the material as you come down.

Relaxation for the breaking up of a fixed inhibition during rehearsal or a performance:

1. Raise the hands high up over the head, then lower them to the sides. While you are doing this, start walking in place. Increase the speed of raising the arms as you change the walking to running in place.

2. The same, only instead of walking and running in place, walk and run around the room.

3. The same, only now add to the action the speaking aloud of the speech, over and over again. This will be difficult. Stop and say the speech.

Vocal Responsiveness (see pages 72-77)

Exercises for the Development of Breath Control

These exercises will help the actor to speak a sentence correctly so that he will have sufficient breath to give the increased emphasis that is necessary for the final words. It will also make it possible for him to give long speeches with the desired climactic effect and to phrase long sentences correctly.

In practicing the following exercises, be certain to keep the voice steady without jerks, breaks, or wavering. The actor should be in a standing position, at rest in an easy erect posture. Under no conditions should the exercises be continued after the breath is gone through straining or forcing the air by means of tightening the throat muscles or collapsing the chest. The chest should be kept firm and expanded at all times; the throat must be opened and relaxed throughout.

1. Take a deep breath, and see how far you can count under normal conditions. This exercise should be practiced until you can easily count sixty on the exhalation of one breath. Be careful never to force the count. The moment the

breath is forced by rasping or the throat grows tense, stop and begin again until you can count sixty without effort.

2. Take a deep breath and exhale slowly, issuing a constant flow of the sound *s*, while someone counts aloud. This should be practiced until the count of forty can be reached on one exhalation.

3. Inhale deeply, and exhale with a continuous *ho-o-o-o* sound as you walk. Keep the sound steady. This should be practiced until you can walk twenty-five steps on one breath.

4. Take the gymnastic position for arm circling—the two feet apart, chest high, head back, the arms extended at right angles at the sides. Make small circles with the arms, and count with each circle made. This should be practiced until you can count thirty-five, keeping the voice steady and firm.

5. Take other gymnastic exercises; and by constant practice in correlating them with breathing, develop breath control so that you can increase the number of counts possible on one exhalation.

6. See how many times you can repeat the following sentence with one breath: "Now is the time for all good men to come to the aid of their country." With each repetition be sure that the greater emphasis is on "aid of their country."

7. Repeat the foregoing exercise, and with each repetition of the sentence increase the intensity and volume with which it is spoken. Build the whole so that the final repetition is the strongest and greatest in volume.

8. Take the sentence "Now is the time for all good men to come to the aid of their country while the little gray fox jumps lazily over the broad white fence," and repeat it three times on one exhalation. Again be careful to emphasize the ends of the two clauses.

9. Draw a diagram representing the inflection of the sound from a sea wave breaking on the shore. Repeat "Now is the time for all good men to come to the aid of their country" so that its sound will have the same inflection as the diagram.

10. Take the vowel sounds *ee* and/or *eh, ah, aw, oh, oo,* and repeat them with the sea-wave diagram in mind, building with each repetition to a final climax. Be sure that your vowel sounds are full, open throated, and clear.

Exercises for Relaxing the Throat

1. Yawn, and then speak, first the syllable *moh,* then the word *more,* and the sentence "The more unconsciously that can be done the better."

2. Take the sentence "More can be done about speech than can be said," and say it:

    (*a*) Yawning before each word.

    (*b*) Yawning before each of the three phrases.

    (*c*) Yawning once and then speaking the entire sentence.

3. The test for an open and relaxed throat is as follows: Without voicing them,

speak the syllables and the words *ho, ha, hey, home, whey, what, where, whoa.* If no rasping sound results, the throat is open and relaxed. Now speak the syllables and words aloud, but before speaking each one make the test as above. This test of not voicing a word first will prevent the actor from hurting his throat in a scream; it eliminates the tension and tightening of a throat that usually comes when he must scream, and should be applied immediately before the scream.

Exercises for Resonance

In order to help improve resonance and develop an appealing voice quality, work on the following exercises. Be sure to practice them slowly at first, so that you consciously make and hear the overtone of each word that you speak. Then increase the speed until you are speaking at a natural rate; that is, let your consciousness be thinking of the sentence itself, leaving the resonance to come of itself. Note the words that are most conducive to obtaining resonance.

Be sure that the breath stream is not only well supported but directed forward, through the mouth for oral sounds and through the nose for nasal sounds. We omit here exercises for chest and head resonance.

1. *Nasal resonance:* Be sure that the soft palate is free from rigidity and sluggishness:

(*a*) Chant *nga, ng, nga, ah.* Feel the vibration of the nostrils on *ng* and the freedom from vibration on *ah.*

(*b*) Consciously throw the sound against the roof of the mouth, and say "One, up, nine, up, one, up, nine, up," and so on.

(*c*) "He said a pun in fun, and she ran with her fan in her hand."

(*d*) "He 'phoned in a low tone to ask for a loan, and I rendered a penned note sending him funds."

(*e*) "Running round the town like flying sand, singing simple sounds, I ended all my ranting noise and soon regained my long-lost poise."

2. *Oral resonance:* Be sure that the throat and back of the mouth are open and free from strain and that the lips and tip of the tongue and soft palate are flexible, light, and sure in their action. The breath should be sustained without effort and directed well forward through the mouth. Concentrate on eliminating nasality entirely. Practice on the following sentences which contain few nasal consonants:

(*a*) "And now abideth faith, hope, charity, these three; but the greatest of these is charity."

(*b*) "After life's fitful fever he sleeps well."

(*c*) "Variety is the very spice of life."

(*d*) "Be there a will, then wisdom finds a way."

Exercises for the Development of Range in Pitch

1. Say the syllable *ho-o-o-o* in your normal speaking tone. Then say it on each note of the speaking scale, going down by half notes to the lowest pitch that

you can reach and returning to a half note below normal. Continue, starting with a half note below the normal and returning to a half note below that. This will develop the lower register. Repeat the exercise, going up the scale to the highest pitch that you can reach without strain and returning to a half note above the starting point. This is for the development of the upper register. At first you can use a piano for this exercise.

2. Use the following sentence in the same manner as the *ho* of the first exercise, speaking the entire sentence on a single tone each time: "I love his avowal." Be sure to prolong the vowels to their full value.

3. Repeat the following sentence in a low, deep register, and analyze its meaning from the contents and the reading. Repeat in a high register, and see how the speaker's meaning changes just from mere change of pitch: "Father, I am paying your compliments to the lady; madam, I can conceive of nothing equal to the happiness of pleasing you, and the pleasure of being your husband is a glory which I would prefer to anything else on earth."

4. Pronounce the following sentence with as many different emotions as possible, and note the use of different pitches for the different emotions: "I shall never go away."

Exercises in Enunciation

1. To work on the loosening of the jaw, roll the head around, with the neck as a pivot, keeping the jaw loose. Then roll it saying the alphabet. This also relaxes the throat.

2. Practice opening and closing the jaw with the motion of biting, taking one large bite after another rapidly without touching teeth.

3. Speak the following syllables in succession, opening the jaw wide on the *ah* sound and closing it between syllables: *pah, fah, tah, lah, kah, dah.*

4. For the lips:

Speak the following exercises first without voicing the sound and without any whispering sound but with complete formation by the lips. Then, when the lips have become accustomed to making the shapes for the words, speak the sentences aloud, being careful to enunciate clearly and distinctly.

(*a*) "Now is the time for all good men to come to the aid of their country."

(*b*) "The little gray fox jumped lazily over the broad white fence."

(*c*) "Father, I am paying your compliments to the lady; madam, I can conceive of nothing equal to the happiness of pleasing you, and the pleasure of being your husband is a glory which I would prefer to anything else on earth."

(*d*) After practicing these three sentences many times, say them silently in a different order, and be sure that everyone in the class can tell which one of the three you are saying at the time:

i. "Around the rugged rock the ragged rascal ran."

ii. "She sells seashells by the seashore."

iii. "Peter Piper picked a peck of pickled peppers; where is the peck of pickled peppers Peter Piper picked?"

(*e*) Do the following exercise for the full value and clarity of the vowel sounds. Do it as written, then substitute an *l*, and afterward an *r*, for the *m*. Repeat all three also adding the same consonant to the end of the syllable. *May, mah, mă, moh, maw; mē, mĕ, mi, mi, miu, moy, mow, moh, muh.*

(*f*) "Singing songs, making mongs, taking tongs, baking bongs, ringing gongs, selling wrongs."

(*g*) Read aloud, without chorus repetition, the patter song of the Major-General from William S. Gilbert's *Pirates of Penzance*. Pay particular attention to the enunciation of each word. At first the reading will be slow. Repeat again and again until you can read the lyrics in two minutes. A tape recording will help immensely to evaluate your own problems.

I am the very model of a modern Major-Gineral,
I've information vegetable, animal, and mineral.
I know the kings of England, and I quote the fights historical,
From Marathon to Waterloo, in order categorical;
I'm very well acquainted too with matters mathematical.
I understand equations, both the simple and quadratical;
About binomial theorem I'm teeming with a lot of news—
With many cheerful facts about the square of the hypotenuse.
I'm very good at integral and differential calculus,
I know the scientific names of beings animalculous;
In short, in matters vegetable, animal, and mineral
I am the very model of a modern Major-Gineral!

I know our mythic history, King Arthur's and Sir Caradoc's,
I answer hard acrostics, I've a pretty taste for paradox.
I quote in elegiacs all the crimes of Heliogabalus,
In conics I can floor peculiarities parabolous.
I can tell undoubted Raphaels from Gerard Dows and Zoffanïes
I know the croaking chorus from the *Frogs* of Aristophanes,
Then I can hum a fugue of which I've heard the music's din afore,
And whistle all the airs from that infernal nonsense *Pinafore*.
Then I can write a washing bill in Babylonic cuneiform,
And tell you every detail of Caractacus's uniform;
In short, in matters vegetable, animal, and mineral
I am the very model of a modern Major-Gineral!

In fact, when I know what is meant by "mamelon" and "ravelin,"
When I can tell at sight a chassepot rifle from a javelin,
When such affairs as sorties and surprises I'm more wary at,
And when I knew precisely what is meant by "commissariat,"
When I have learnt what progress has been made in modern gunnery,
When I know more of tactics than a novice in a nunnery,
In short, when I've a smattering of elemental strategy,
You'll say a better Major-General has never *sat* a gee—
For my military knowledge, though I'm plucky and adventury,

Has only been brought down to the beginning of the century;
But still, in matters vegetable, animal, and mineral
I am the very model of a modern, Major-Gineral!

Exercises in Projection

1. Use the lyrics from a song. Speak directly into the auditorium from the stage.
    (*a*) Begin low, and think solely of projection, focusing and directing the tone at one point.
    (*b*) Increase volume gradually through several repetitions.
    (*c*) Give the first part of a lyric as a projection exercise, standing profile on stage; then with back to the audience. Use large volume in each case.
2. From the stage, practice shouting a sentence to the rest of the class sitting in the farthermost part of the auditorium. Then, in a well-modulated voice, give the same sentence over again using projection.

Emotional Responsiveness (see pages 77-78)

Exercises for the Body

1. Lie down flat on the floor; take plenty of time to relax the body and mind.
    (*a*) Hear a noise.
    (*b*) Feel a snake crawling along by your side.
    (*c*) See somebody about to step on you.
    (*d*) Your mouth is open, and a fly has flown in.
    (*e*) Smell smoke.
2. Sit in a chair. Relax. Feel and express:
    (*a*) Horror.
    (*b*) Joy.
    (*c*) Pity for yourself.
    (*d*) A tremendous religious experience.
    (*e*) Regality and stateliness.
    (*f*) Humility.
    (*g*) Yourself as the focal attraction of a crowd.
    (*h*) Yourself very much out of the group. (You know nothing about the subject of conversation.)
    (*i*) Yourself explaining something to a group of children.
3. The following differ from the previous exercises in so far as the process of feeling the emotion will be slower in arriving and will build to a greater expression.
    Sit in a chair relaxed. Drop your head down; close your eyes; drop your hands in your lap. Feel as if you were about to go to sleep. Then feel anger, keep feeling it more intensely until you cannot keep your eyes closed and then until you cannot sit still any longer.
    Do the same with the following emotions: joy, hatred, love, religious ecstasy, grief.
4. Responsiveness followed by pantomimic action.

Lie on the floor and relax; sit in a chair and relax; stand relaxed. Then feel and express:

(a) The moment before an experience in your life when you were terrified and then the moment of reacting to the fear

    i. When you are afraid of a mouse.

    ii. When you have to go to the cellar at night in the dark.

    iii. When you come back from the cellar.

    iv. When you are lost on a mountain.

    v. When your house is on fire.

    vi. When you walk by a cemetery alone at night.

    vii. When you are sure that there is nobody in the house and then you hear footsteps upstairs.

(b) An experience of joy at

    i. Receiving a Christmas present.

    ii. Winning a letter.

    iii. Receiving a promotion.

    iv. Reaching a mountaintop.

    v. Winning an athletic contest.

(c) An expression of anger

    i. When you cannot find your schoolbooks and it is late.

    ii. When your younger brother or sister tells your parents that you are in love.

    iii. When you are falsely accused of a minor crime.

Exercises for the Voice

1. Sit in a chair and relax; drop your head down; close your eyes; drop your hands in your lap. Then think of the following phrases expressive of the emotion. Keep thinking of them and feeling the emotion until the phrase is given vocally. Be sure that after each phrase you begin the following one in a highly relaxed condition. Be sure also that no self-consciousness or thought, except the one sentence, creeps into consideration; that is, do not think how you have seen it done or how a person would do it or even how it should be done. Do not be surprised or discouraged at how long it will take you to utter the phrase or that if you wait too long you will become conscious and think you cannot do it—this is a typical and natural state to show when self-consciousness or an inhibition sets in.

    (a) "I can't stand it!"

    (b) "Oh, it's marvelous!"

    (c) "I hate you!"

    (d) "My darling!"

    (e) "Oh, heaven help me!"

    (f) "Oh, why did I do it!" and then with
        "Why did she have to die!"

(Note the difference in the emotional feeling and expression in these last two phrases, the first being more introspective.)

2. Sitting in a chair and leaning on a table, relaxing each time:

(*a*) See your father drop dead, and give a vocal response.

(*b*) Hear footsteps above you; hear them descend the stairs and come to the doorway. When the door opens, give a vocal response.

(*c*) Be eating spinach, and get a mouthful of sand.

(*d*) Be tied in the chair, and be tortured. Supply your own words without thinking of what you are going to say.

(*e*) Be tied in the chair, and smell smoke which tells you that the house is on fire.

Exercises in the Feeling of an Emotion

(First internally, then through body expression, finally giving it vocal and physical reactions.)

Use a full stage for the expressive movement in the following. In each case supply your own sentences. They are to continue as long as your physical reaction does.

1. You are having a nightmare. A tiger is pursuing you. You are running on sand and can make no headway. The tiger nearly gets you, and you wake up.

2. You are lost on a mountaintop and are calling for help. You eventually collapse.

3. You are on the seventh floor of a house. The house is on fire. Discover that the door to your room is locked.

4. Enter a room, to find something on which your brother's life depends. You hunt for it all over the room, think you find it when you have not; and finally, when you are in despair, find it and run out of the room.

Exercises for Two People, Employing Body, Voice, and Action

For speeches, first whisper the alphabet; then repeat, using full vocal utterance. Repeat by whispering improvised lines—with or without sense—then repeat exercise, giving the improvised lines full vocal tones and expression. These exercises are most valuable if there is no consciousness of the sentences' correctness.

1. *A* is a professional actor. *B* is an amateur actor. *B* has not been doing his scene satisfactorily for *A*. *A* nags *B* more and more. *B* loses his temper. *B* is tired, nervous, and overwrought. *A* and *B* quarrel with each other. *B* becomes hysterical. *A* gives up in despair.

2. Stage the return of the prodigal son. *A*, the son, first makes his plea to *B*, the father, who is adamant. *B* finally relents, agrees to forgive *A*, and accepts his return.

Index

189 — Movement → L to R

R to L

Without it, precipitous tempo just for the sake of "keeping it going fast" can prove disastrous to the dynamics of farce.

Much used in farce are *gags*—bits of business or impromptu lines, not intrinsic to the action but put in merely for their ability to provoke laughter. (However, gags may be interpolations to those who work on the actions, but to the audience they must appear motivated.)

So far we have listed the specific elements of locale, character, and the like that are benefited by pantomimic detail. Now let us turn to the more general, overall contributions of pantomime.

Gives Continuity

This special contribution to the script comes from the fact that our pantomimic dramatization is, as we said, based on observation of life. This makes the action of the play recognizable as truthful and akin to life. The reason for this lies in the fact that careful observation results in a natural sequence of action, and this brings continuity to the behavior of actors throughout the playing of the various scenes. Continuity is often referred to as *follow-through*. Good pantomimic business is never without this element which is dependent upon several factors:

MOTIVATED MOVEMENT   As studied in a previous chapter, stage movement should be filled with the sense of "reason why." In other words, the movement must be executed with a purpose. A cross is made to look out of a window, to pick up a book, or to get away from something unpleasant. A reason for moving, whatever it may be, relates the movement directly to the playing of the scene, thereby giving it conviction and truthfulness.

PSYCHOLOGICAL MOTIVATION   These are the relationships between the various characters which are responsible for movement and business. Perhaps an easy exercise will demonstrate the possibilities of follow-through: Let us send four people up on the stage, three to remain onstage and one to go off with the following instructions: Make three entrances, the first to greet one whom you like and trust wholeheartedly; a second to greet one whom you despise; a third to greet one whom you fear and dread. After each greeting make an appropriate farewell and leave the stage. During these exercises, we in the audience must test the amount of feeling that the actor carries with him before and after he relates himself to each person. In other words he is expected to keep the psychological relationship throughout the little scene. If he grasps the person's hand and drops it immediately, he destroys the continuity and the truthfulness of the playing. One can concentrate on maintaining the psychological motivation by entering a "sphere of influence" that extends just offstage of the entrance and the exit. This is a magic area in which the actor dares not break the contact by lapsing into indifference or lifelessness. He must carry the audience toward, right up to, and beyond the object of motivation.

TENSION AND VITALITY IN RELAXATION   The ability to stay alert when you are not actively in a scene onstage is a delicate process but absolutely necessary to the scene's continuity. It is difficult to explain just exactly how to maintain this tension in relaxation. Most assuredly it is not a matter of "reacting all over the place." Playing with a handkerchief or a necklace, coughing, twirling mustaches, and so forth, during a scene belonging to someone else is an unforgivable breach of stage etiquette. Keeping alive during a scene that is not yours is more a matter of listening and breathing rhythmically to the flow of the scene around you. It is a matter of maintaining the timing of the scene so that what you do or say next is in the rhythm of what has gone before.

Brings Enrichment and Vitality

Along with continuity and truthfulness come also enrichment and vitality. A director can take a set of characters and a given locale and place them on stage with nothing further in mind than that they speak their lines clearly, move around a little, and then go offstage on cue. On the other hand he can treat these things with loving care. He can become deeply interested in the psychological behavior of his characters and in certain marked aspects of his locale and atmosphere. He searches first for the truthful facts about these things; then he turns these facts over to his imagination. There, they are elaborated upon, intensified, clarified, in short, made more interesting. For example, the beach scene along the harbor in O'Neill's *Ah, Wilderness!* is an instructive illustration of business that reveals a character's attitude and state of mind. O'Neill has set up a clandestine meeting between the two young lovers, Richard and Muriel. At the opening of the scene Richard is anxiously awaiting Muriel—kicking at sand restlessly, twirling his straw hat, and later rereading Muriel's letter. In the directions O'Neill has him kiss the letter and pocket it hurriedly as he looks around sheepishly. Continuing in the soliloquy Richard expresses passionate longing, shame, self-disgust, rapture, apprehension, fear, and cynicism. The atmospheric touches include moonlight and an orchestra heard faintly at intervals; the setting and props include trees, sand, a pier, and an overturned rowboat on the beach. For further illustration, Richard's moment of rapture can be motivated out of the distant music to which he dances with ecstatic release, or in his poetic reading he can leap onto the overturned rowboat and orate his feelings to the moonlit skies, or the mournful sound of distant boat horns can set off his more despairing thoughts.

In enriching the facts this way, either playwright or director can give much vitality to the script. The result is warmer, more appealing, and at the same time more significant. This point becomes especially important in the direction of a play that is generally referred to as "historical." In addition, many of the social dramas and comedies of ideas, past and present, have a talky, static quality that needs enlivening. In a later section we suggest how this may be done.

First, however, let us examine the standards whereby we judge the pantomimic dramatization in a play.

Essentials of Good Pantomimic Dramatization

In creating pantomime some easily understandable and recognizable visual statements of place, character, or situation should be given at once. The more closely characteristic pantomime is the better. Further information should be fitted in as fast as clarity permits. Above all, there should be no false leads. Once the main point is established in the minds of the audience, subsidiary details fall into place easily; but if the audience becomes confused in the beginning, it will lose subsequent details, and instead of entering into the play it will spend time trying to puzzle it out. We list below certain essentials of good pantomimic dramatization that should guide the director in his use of it.

Appropriateness

The matter of appropriateness is particularly important. The director must visualize the scene and be certain that his pantomimic details fit into it and the characters and situation. Here, again, it becomes a matter of how well the director has observed life and how imaginatively he has incorporated facts.

Suppose, for instance, that we are establishing the interior of the bunk-house where two of the scenes in *Of Mice and Men* take place. The locale is described as follows: "walls, whitewashed board, floors unpainted. There is a heavy, square table and around it up-ended boxes for chairs." In addition we have these facts about character: "Enter the boss. He is a stocky man, dressed in blue jeans, flannel shirt, black unbuttoned vest—ordinarily he puts his thumbs in his belt. . . . Slim enters, a tall, dark man, in blue jeans and short denim jacket—he smooths out his crushed hat, creases it in the middle, and puts it on. . . ."

All the details of this scene should be appropriate to the general indications of character, locale, atmosphere. For instance, we know that these men will move and sit in a manner that is hearty, rugged, and definite. Their gestures will not be in a delicate or drawing-room vein but strong and practical. They play solitaire rather than bridge and loll about the pieces of furniture. Contrasted with these details are those which would be appropriate to the pleasant, restrained atmosphere of *Candida*.

Naturalness

This essential of good business is closely related to the degree of realism in which the play is to be expressed. In the typical modern production there is, as a rule, a high degree of reality, and we expect business to be as natural as possible. Naturalism can be attained by maintaining the follow-through of which we spoke in the previous section—sustaining the psychological motivation. The importance of furniture arrangement in relation to natural-ness of business is discussed later.

Richness of Detail

The amount of imagination with which a director presents the facts of locale, atmosphere, and character contributes another essential of good busi-ness—richness. Referring to the scene in which a girl is reading beneath a tree, you will find a demonstration of the possibilities for enrichment through bringing your imagination into play. We speak later about con-trolling the imagination.

Precision and Selectivity

So often, and especially in the case of amateurs, there is a blurred and inde-cisive quality to individual performances. This is usually due to indefinite and hurried strokes in executing pieces of business. Both the director and the actor should have a clear and concise understanding of what the busi-ness is and should then polish and refine it until the result is definite and clean cut and unvarying from performance to performance.

There is much in this chapter on pantomime that is intimately bound up with the theory of acting. Taking the subjective approach, it is possible to execute a piece of business with precision by having a definite understand-ing of what is to be done. Complete understanding of what is being done, however, may result (especially in the directing of amateurs) in business that is true but, as we say, too small to "carry." Part of making business precise lies in the technique of being most selective in choosing its details. This selectivity sharpens the projection of the action. If we recall from experience the deft but precise movements of the expert bartender, seam-stress, or typist, we realize that it is because they are so proficient in their field that their actions seem unusually clear and sharper than normal activ-